THE BLUE GUIDES

Albania
Austria
Belgium and Luxembourg
China
Cyprus
Czechoslovakia
Denmark
Egypt

FRANCE
France
Paris and Versailles
Brittany
Burgundy
Loire Valley
Midi-Pyrénées
Normandy
South West France
Corsica

GERMANY
Berlin and Eastern Germany
Western Germany

GREECE
Greece
Athens and environs
Crete

HOLLAND
Holland
Amsterdam

Hungary
Ireland

ITALY
Northern Italy
Southern Italy
Florence
Rome and environs
Venice
Tuscany
Umbria
Sicily

Jerusalem
Malta and Gozo
Mexico
Morocco
Moscow and Leningrad
Portugal

SPAIN
Spain
Barcelona

Sweden
Switzerland

TURKEY
Turkey
Istanbul

UK
England
Scotland
Wales
London
Museums and Galleries
  of London
Oxford and Cambridge
Country Houses of England
Gardens of England
Literary Britain and Ireland
Victorian Architecture in
  Britain
Churches and Chapels
  of Northern England
Churches and Chapels
  of Southern England
Channel Islands

USA
New York
Boston and Cambridge

Dylan Thomas's Boathouse Study, Laugharne

BLUE GUIDE

WALES

John Tomes

A&C Black
London

WW Norton
New York

Wales and the Marches
First Edition   1922, by Findlay Muirhead
Second Edition   1926, by Findlay Muirhead
Third Edition   1936, by Findlay Muirhead
Fourth Edition   1953, by Findlay Muirhead
Fifth Edition   1969, by Stuart Rossiter and Harold Carter
Sixth Edition   1979, by John Tomes

Wales
Seventh Edition 1990; reprint with corrections 1992, by John Tomes
Eighth Edition   1995, by John Tomes

Published by A & C Black (Publishers) Limited
35 Bedford Row, London, WC1R 4JH

© John Tomes

ISBN 0 7136 4074 X

A CIP catalogue record for this book
is available from the British Library.

Published in the United States of America by
WW Norton & Company, Incorporated
500 Fifth Avenue, New York, NY 10110

Published simultaneously in Canada by
Penguin Books Canada Limited
10 Alcorn Avenue, Toronto,
Ontario M4V 3B2

ISBN 0-393-31267-4   USA

Maps and plans by Robert Smith
Photographs by Susan Benn

Educated at Oxford, where he gained his degree in Modern Languages, and after
careers in the Royal Air Force and the aero-engine industry, **John Tomes** was invited
to update the Blue Guides to Greece and Sicily. Subsequently, he became author of
Blue Guides *Scotland, Wales, Belgium and Luxembourg* and *Holland*, a group which
he saw through several editions before relinquishing the latter two. His other travel
books include the *Shell Book of Exploring Britain* (A & C Black), of which he is
co-author with the late Garry Hogg.

The publishers and the author have done their best to ensure the accuracy of all the
information in Blue Guide Wales; however, they can accept no responsibility for any
loss, injury or inconvenience sustained by any traveller as a result of information or
advice contained in the guide.

Please write in with your comments, suggestions and corrections. Writers
of the best letters will be awarded a free Blue Guide of their choice.

Printed in Great Britain by The Bath Press, Avon

PREFACE

Easily accessible, and long and confidently established as a holiday choice, the Principality of Wales—as more fully outlined in the Introduction to Wales below—invites with rich and often astonishing variety.

Previously published as 'Blue Guide Wales and the Marches', this new edition is the second to be devoted solely to Wales. For the Marches—the bordering English counties with their lush countryside and historic cities such as Chester, Shrewsbury and Hereford—see 'Blue Guide England'.

Comments and Suggestions. A continually evolving guide such as this (with this edition, in its eighth decade) profits immensely from the contributions of its users. Comments, corrections and suggestions—whether on fact, on layout and style, on content, or the result of personal discovery—will always be welcome.

Acknowledgements are due first to all who have contributed to the distinguished reputation of this Guide since the publication of its first edition in 1922. For this Eighth Edition the author and editor are grateful to the staffs of the headquarters and of many local Tourist Information centres of the Wales Tourist Board, as also to those of several other organisations, these including Cadw: Welsh Historic Monuments, the National Trust, the three National Parks of Wales, Forest Enterprise, and the Countryside Council for Wales. Counties, districts, cities, towns, museums and sites of all kinds, as also heritage, archaeological and wildlife societies and trusts, have also invariably been ready with information and advice and generous with brochures, leaflets and suchlike. On a more personal note, the author thanks Ken and Catherine Holt for climbing a mountain and exploring a remote river bank in successful search for an ancient chapel and traces of the Romans, while, as always, he once again has pleasure in recording the very real contribution made by his wife, as map reader, typist and perceptive critic.

Background sources. The author wishes to mention the following as having been particularly valuable for reference and background: 'Encyclopaedia Britannica'. 'Dictionary of National Biography'. 'The Mabinogion', translated by Gwyn Jones and Thomas Jones (Dent, Everyman's Library). 'The Shell Book of Exploring Britain', by Garry Hogg and John Tomes (A & C Black). Several publications by the various organisations and others mentioned above. 'The Penguin Guide to Prehistoric England and Wales', by James Dyce (Penguin Books). 'Ancient Monuments of Anglesey', by O. E. Craster. 'A Guide to Gower' (Gower Society). 'History of the French Invasion of Fishguard', by Pamela Horn (Preseli Printers). 'Walk Snowdonia and North Wales' and 'Walk South Wales and the Wye Valley', by David Perrott and Laurence Main (Bartholomew).

A NOTE ON BLUE GUIDES

The Blue Guide series began in 1918 when Muirhead Guide-Books Limited published 'Blue Guide London and its Environs'. Findlay and James Muirhead already had extensive experience of guide-book publishing: before the First World War they had been the editors of the English editions of the German Baedekers, and by 1915 they had acquired the copyright of most of the famous 'Red' Handbooks from John Murray.

An agreement made with the French publishing house Hachette et Cie in 1917 led to the translation of Muirhead's London Guide, which became the first 'Guide Bleu'—Hachette had previously published the blue-covered 'Guides Joanne'. Subsequently, Hachette's 'Guide Bleu Paris et ses Environs' was adapted and published in London by Muirhead. The collaboration between the two publishing houses continued until 1933.

In 1931 Ernest Benn Limited took over the Blue Guides, appointing Russell Muirhead, Findlay Muirhead's son, editor in 1934. The Muirheads' connection with Blue Guides ended in 1963 when Stuart Rossiter, who had been working on the Guides since 1954, became house editor, revising and compiling several of the books himself.

The Blue Guides are now published by A & C Black, who acquired Ernest Benn in 1984, so continuing the tradition of guide-book publishing which began in 1826 with 'Black's Economical Tourist of Scotland'. The Blue Guide series continues to grow: there are now more than 50 titles in print with revised editions appearing regularly and many new Blue Guides in preparation.

'Blue Guides' is a registered trade mark.

CONTENTS

MAPS AND PLANS

NOTES ON USING THIS GUIDE

'Blue Guide Wales' is in two parts. The first provides *Background and Practical Information*, the subjects covered being listed in the Contents. Intending visitors with no firm plans as to where to tour may be helped by the section headed Introduction to Wales, which outlines the main features of the country, as also by the section describing the three National Parks. The second part of the book comprises detailed descriptions along 46 *Routes* which criss-cross virtually all Wales (see Plan of Routes). Since Routes not infrequently cross or run close to one another, it is advisable to be aware of places lying either side of the road being travelled; use of the comprehensive *Index* will then ensure that places within easy reach, but described under other Routes, are not missed.

History, Antiquities and People. Throughout any tour of Wales prehistory and history always accompany the traveller, usually in the visible form of man's activity, ranging from ancient burial mounds and earthworks through ruined abbeys and castles to more recent and intact sites. Both for background interest, as also to avoid repetition, the first part of this book includes an outline *History of Wales*; and, for the same reasons, there are also *Biographical Notes* identifying selected people who are not covered in any detail in the History or Routes texts.

Distances. The preamble to each Route (other than those devoted to individual towns) states its total distance. Both in the preambles and texts, italicised distances are those between points along the basic Route, i.e. each italicised distance is the distance from the previous one. For obvious reasons distances can only be approximate.

Maps. The maps on the inside front and back covers show Wales as a whole, but is not of course intended to take the place of motorists' maps. Of these there is a wide choice, from which the following may be mentioned. All are on single face. *Wales Tourist Board* Tourist Map (One inch = 5 miles). Including all Wales and much of the Marches, this is an admirably clear map and ideal for overall planning. On the reverse there are several town plans; 14 tours are outlined; and there are details of all Wales Tourist Board information centres. *Michelin* Sheet 403 (1:400,000. One inch = 6.30 miles), with an index of places, covers all Wales and the English West Country and Midlands. *Estate Publications* Leisure Map Wales (1:250,000. One inch = 4 miles) includes the Marches and is usefully overprinted to show most sites of tourist interest, the principal of these being indexed. *Ordnance Survey* Travelmaster Sheet 7 (1:250,000. One inch = 4 miles) is a physical map which includes all Wales, the Marches and the English western Midlands. Additionally, for local touring and exploration, most visitors will probably choose the relevant *Ordnance Survey* Landranger sheets (1:50,000. One mile = 1.25 inches).

Opening Times are given for most sites and these were confirmed as late as possible before going to print. Nevertheless times can and do change; telephone numbers are therefore given for most sites and visitors with a special interest or perhaps travelling from some distance away are advised to telephone to check times.

Additional telephone numbers, useful for visitors planning a tour and not wishing to call several individual sites, are:

National Trust, North	01492-860123
National Trust, South	01558-822800
Cadw: Welsh Historic Monuments	01222-465511

Cadw: Welsh Historic Monuments publish Standard Opening Times applicable to most Cadw sites, these times being:

Summer (last week March–last week Oct): Daily. 09.30–18.30.

Winter (last week Oct–last week March): Mon–Sat 09.30–16.00. Sun 14.00–16.00.

The telephone number 01222-465511 is that of the Cadw central information facility in Cardiff.

Some general Opening Times points worth bearing in mind are:

In most cases dates given are inclusive, eg March–Oct means 1 March–31 Oct.

At some larger sites last entry times may be up to an hour before the formal closing time.

It can be assumed that virtually all sites will close for some or all of the period 24 Dec–1 Jan.

Although no blanket ruling can be given regarding public holidays, the trend is increasingly towards opening even if Monday is not a normal opening day.

Although a number of churches feature in this Guide, sadly, due to modern vandalism, a great many will be found to be locked. In some cases the name and whereabouts of the key holder will be found on the door or adjacent notice board; more often, initiative and perseverance will be required to achieve entry.

There remain a large number of sites, some of which do not admit visitors (no adm.), some of which allow informal entry, while many others may be viewed only from outside. The local form will usually be clear enough, but the warning must be given that some sites are ruins and the fact that access is possible does not necessarily mean that it is safe.

Tourist Information Offices are operated by various levels of the tourist industry, e.g. Wales Tourist Board, counties or districts, national parks, individual cities and towns. In the Routes text the entry *Inf.* advises that there is a manned office, which may, however, in the case of smaller places be open in summer only (roughly Easter–Oct).

Telephone Numbers given are valid as of 16 April 1995. Calls prior to this date should omit the second digit (1) from the area code.

Asterisks draw attention to places of special attraction or interest.

Abbreviations. In addition to generally accepted and self-explanatory abbreviations, the following occur:

CCW = Countryside Council for Wales
FE =Forest Enterprise
NNR =National Nature Reserve
NT = National Trust
RNLI = Royal National Lifeboat Institution
RSPB = Royal Society for the Protection of Birds
WTB = Wales Tourist Board

BACKGROUND INFORMATION

Introduction to Wales

Although an integral part of the United Kingdom, nothing could be more mistaken than to regard Wales simply as a westward extension of England. Wales has a long and colourful history of its own, large parts of the land in the past enjoying prolonged periods of independence; most of the true Welsh can claim their own ethnic origin, Brythonic Celt rather than Anglo-Saxon; and the separateness of the country's identity, the very real sense of a national homogeneity, will quickly impress itself on the visitor as soon as he crosses the border (no formalities) and encounters tongue-twisting Welsh names and signs, hears the distinctive and musical Welsh accent and appreciates the still widespread and natural use of the Welsh language.

In shape Wales is roughly a vertical rectangle (some 160 miles from north to south, and some 50 miles from west to east) from which Anglesey and the Lleyn project at the northwest and Pembroke at the southwest, between north and south curving the huge crescent of Cardigan Bay. A large part of the country is hilly or mountainous, the principal range towards the west being the Cambrian Mountains running from north to south behind the coast. This range, known better for its parts than as a whole, includes the magnificent Snowdon massif (3560 ft) before reaching southward to embrace legendary Cader Idris (2927 ft), the broad moorland dome of Plynlimon (2468 ft) with the sources of no fewer than five rivers, and finally petering out as the heights of Towy and Brechfa forests, the latter only a few miles north of Carmarthen. In the northeast the principal upland features are the often steep and wooded Clwydian Hills and the Berwyns (several heights around 2000 ft), while farther south the heights of Brecon Beacons National Park, also with several summits of over 2000 ft, stretch for some 45 miles between Llandeilo in the west and the English border. South again is the high ground broken by the series of once largely industrial valleys which slice in from the busy coast. In the east the border lands are mainly undulating, pastoral country, varied here and there by upland moor, a description which applies also to much of the southwest, to the northeast immediately behind the string of coastal resorts, and to Anglesey and much of the Lleyn. Other scenic features of Wales are the many lovely river valleys (Wye, Conwy, Teifi, Towy); lakes and reservoirs, frequently in moorland or afforested settings; and some spectacular cliff scenery, especially in the south west. Indeed, apart from the resort areas with their holiday camps and caravan sites and the industrial southeast, there are few parts of Wales which cannot claim to be scenic, and few also which do not offer almost limitless opportunities for walking.

But, leading attraction though it is, there is a lot more to Wales than its scenery, and a list of just some of the other things the country has to offer could include the wide choice of holiday resorts strung around an ever-changing coast; a wealth of remarkable prehistoric and Dark Ages sites, the former especially notable in Anglesey and scattered across Presely, the latter mainly the hillfort settlements which seem to crown just about every significant hilltop in Wales; several of the largest, most imposing and most historic castles in Europe; religious establishments, ranging from abbeys—

which, though today only skeletal ruins, still spur the imagination to conjure up both the monastic simplicity and the liturgical pomp of the Middle Ages—through historic, still active cathedrals, to a wealth of interesting churches, some solidly Victorian, many others humble, tiny and primitive; great mansions, splendidly decorated and furnished and many owned by the National Trust; the famous little railways of Wales; museums and art galleries, from Cardiff's superb National Museum of Wales to modest but invariably interesting local collections; legend, weaving and much else.

National Parks

Wales offers three fine national parks; Snowdonia in the northwest, Brecon Beacons roughly south central, and Pembrokeshire Coast in the southwest.

SNOWDONIA (*Inf.* Snowdonia National Park, Penrhyndeudraeth, LL48 6LS. Tel. 01766-770274. Information Centres at Aberdyfi, Bala, *Betws-y-Coed, Blaenau Ffestiniog, Dolgellau, Harlech and Llanberis). The largest (840 square miles) and scenically the most dramatic and varied of Wales's parks, Snowdonia stretches from Conwy in the north to Aberdyfi in the south, averages some 25 miles in breadth, and between Tremadog Bay and Aberdyfi includes a long and varied coastline. Stock-raising family farms are typical of the area which is also a stronghold of Welsh language and culture.

Snowdonia embraces several mountain ranges, with 15 peaks over 3000ft, as well as wide tracts of forest and moorland. The various areas merge into one another but can be identified (roughly from north to south) as the *Carneddau Range* (Rtes 1C, 6B, 9); *Gwydir Forest* (Rtes 6B, 6C, 7); *Snowdon* (Rtes 7, 8, 9, 10); *Moelwyns and Siabod Range* (Rte 7); *Arenig Range* (Rtes 15, 16); *Rhinog Range* (Rte 17); *Coed-y-Brenin* (Rte 16); the twin *Arans* (Rte 20); *Cader Idris* (Rte 21).

BRECON BEACONS (*Inf.* Brecon Beacons National Park, 7 Glamorgan Street, Brecon, LD3 7DP. Tel. 01874-624437. Information Centres at Abergavenny, Llandovery, the Mountain Centre and Craig-y-nos Country Park). Brecon Beacons National Park covers 519 square miles; some 45 miles long from west to east (Llandeilo to Abergavenny) and an average of some 15 miles depth from north to south. The greater part of the park is above 1000ft (with several heights over 2000ft) and the whole area, especially Brecon Beacons and the Black Mountains, is very popular with walkers and pony trekkers. Scenery apart, the park is known for its several prehistoric sites, for Roman remains at Y Gaer near Brecon (Rte 26A) and at Y Pigwn near Trecastle (Rte 27) and for the great 13C castle of Carreg Cennen (Rte 24). Although the park is named for its principal mountain group, the Brecon Beacons are in fact only a small part of the whole which conveniently divides into the following five distinct areas (from west to east): *Black Mountain* (Rtes 24, 27, 33); *Fforest Fawr* (Rtes 26B, 33); *Brecon Beacons* (Rte 26B); *Black Mountains* (Rtes 25A, 32); *Monmouthshire and Brecon Canal* (Rte 30B).

PEMBROKESHIRE COAST (*Inf.* Pembrokeshire Coast National Park, County Offices, Haverfordwest, SA61 1QZ. Tel. 01437-764591. Information Centres at Broad Haven, Haverfordwest, King's Moor Common, Newport, Pembroke, St. David's, Saundersfoot). Pembrokeshire Coast National Park embraces some 225 square miles around the coast and, in the north, spreads some ten miles inland to include the Presely Hills. Rtes 42 to 46 all traverse parts of the park, which conveniently divides into four sections. The *Coast*, most of it with grand cliff scenery, is traced by a Coastal Path of 186 miles between the estuary of the Teifi in the north and Amroth on Carmarthen Bay in the south. *Islands* include the monastic island of Caldey off Tenby, and also St. Margaret's, Skokholm, Skomer, Grassholm and Ramsey, all nature reserves. The *Presely Hills* are noted for their prehistoric remains and as the source for some of the stones of Stonehenge. *Daugleddau* is the tidal estuary of the Western and Eastern Cleddau rivers.

Aspects of Wales

Bards. The bardic tradition is purely Celtic and in some aspects seems to have been associated with the Druids. Later—as prophets, exhortators, and as the guardians and tellers of tales—the bards filled the gap left by the Roman extermination of the Druids, playing a semi-political role in encouraging local pride and enjoying positions of honour at princely courts, where, needless to say, flattery of the prince and his line was an essential skill (as early as the 6C Gildas censures Maelgwn Gwynedd for being over-influenced by bardic flattery). Hywel Dda's codified legal system (10C) shows that by this date there had developed three grades of bard. Chief bards (who won their positions through competition, were awarded a chair of honour, and received a harp as symbol of office) ranked as senior officials. A chief bard's field of poetry, however, was limited to the lord and his family, God, and the saints. The second grade provided for the household what the chief bard did for the princely family, and was given more latitude of subject, in particular being allowed to sing of love and nature. The third grade (loosely called Minstrels) embraced a whole range of popular entertainers, restricted only in that they might not trespass on the metres or subjects of the upper grades. This third grade is important not least because it was they who told the popular tales which later found written form as the 'Mabinogion'.

The above system survived into late medieval times, when the patronage of the princes began to be superseded by that of the gentry, and bards, no longer court officials, made regular circuits of patrons' halls. At the same time popular entertainers scarcely ranking as bards wandered around on unofficial begging circuits and, though at the time despised, were nonetheless important for their influence on folk poetry. At the Caerwys eisteddfodau of 1523 and 1568, in an attempt to safeguard professional standards, a system was introduced by which apprentices progressed through three grades and were licensed to make a circuit of the halls of the gentry. Anybody unlicensed yet seeking patronage was officially classified as a vagabond.

Despite the above, however, the bardic system went into decline and the 17C saw the rise of poets independent of patronage and, more important, freed from ancient conservative poetic tradition.

Today's bardic system (with the *Gorsedd;* or Assembly, or Council), in some respects based on dubious foundations, was introduced in 1792 by Edward Williams (Iolo Morganwg), a self-taught scholar whose passion was ancient manuscripts bearing on Welsh history. His lead was followed up by enthusiasts who organised local eisteddfodau. In modern Wales a bard is a poet whose qualities have been recognised at an eisteddfod, and the Gorsedd has a defined role which includes the safeguarding of bardic custom and ceremony as well as much of the responsibility for the administration of the National Eisteddfod.

Choirs. As long ago as the 12C Giraldus was writing of the Welsh love of music and of their gift for singing in harmony. However, the development of today's choirs, although of course rooted in this national gift, dates from the early 19C when the Industrial Revolution brought crowded living conditions in the valleys, a boost for nonconformity, and the spread of chapels which became the focus of social life and which, still today and with their variety of biblical names, are very much a feature of the Welsh scene. Music was needed for the services, song schools were formed and from these roots grew the choirs. Sadly many influences—television; pop music; the fact that communities are no longer isolated; the decline in religion and thus of the role of the chapels (many of which are today closed or put to other uses)—are bringing a fall in the number of choirs, the probable future being significantly fewer but more sophisticated choirs. Local Tourist Information will advise on choirs welcoming visitors to their rehearsals.

Coracles, made of intertwined laths of willow and hazel to a design which has changed little since the Iron Age, may occasionally be seen on the rivers Teifi, especially between Cenarth and Cilgerran, and Towy near Carmarthen. Those on the latter, the waters of which are calm, are light and oval in shape; those on the Teifi, however, with its turbulent eddies, narrow at the waist and lie deeper in the water. National Coracle Centre at Cenarth.

Crafts. There does not appear to be any significant craft which is peculiar to Wales. Nevertheless many skills are traditional (for example the carving of love-spoons, the traditional Welsh courting gift up to about the 17C), and craft studios, workshops and retail outlets will be found in most parts of the country, among the products being textiles and fabrics; woodwork; slate and stonework, slate sculpture being a particularly attractive souvenir of a craft which reached its peak in association with the huge quarries of the 19C; jewellery, with craftsmen using local stones, and designs which reflect Celtic tradition; pottery, Portmeirion (not in fact made in Wales, though it can certainly be bought there) being perhaps the best known; and wrought-ironwork, a tradition dating back to the firedog of the 1C BC found at Capel Garmon and which reached a peak with the 18C work of the Davies brothers.

An **Eisteddfod** (plural, eisteddfodau) originally meant simply a meeting of bards, whether in poetic competition or simply to discuss professional problems. Although bards had for centuries won their positions through competition, the first recorded bardic contest is that of 1176 convened at Cardigan by Rhys ap Gruffydd. This, though the word eisteddfod was not used, had many eisteddfodic features, notably the fact that the festival was proclaimed a year and a day in advance, this being considered, as it still is today, essential to the achievement of high standards. The prizes, for both poetry and music, were miniature silver chairs, symbols of the chairs of honour of the chief bards. In 1450 the term eisteddfod was used for a festival at Carmarthen, important for having been the occasion when metrical rules were codified which even today apply to the principal or Chair Poem of the Royal National Eisteddfod. Later important eisteddfodau were those of 1523 and 1568 at Caerwys when the licensing of bards was introduced.

During the 16 to 18C both bards and eisteddfodau sank to a local and largely impromptu level.

The conception of an eisteddfod as a major public occasion dates from the Corwen eisteddfod of 1789, an occasion which (under the patronage of the Gwyneddigion, a society of London Welshmen) marked both the start of a series of successful eisteddfodau and also a return to the custom of proclaiming the festival a year and a day in advance. Similar eisteddfodau flourished in the 19C, one noteworthy development being the inclusion of choral competitions as a result of the development of the chapel choirs.

The *Royal National Eisteddfod of Wales* was established between 1861–80 as a means of achieving worthy national standards, of safeguarding the Welsh language, and of promoting Welsh culture. The governing body is the Court of the National Eisteddfod of Wales, and the festival is held alternately in North and South Wales annually during the first week of August. The National Eisteddfod (with details of the now wide-ranging competitions) is proclaimed by the Gorsedd at least a year and a day in advance, normally at a traditional ceremony within a Gorsedd Circle of Stones (itself laid out to a ritual pattern), the rites being to the accompaniment of harp music. These circles of stones will be found in many places at which the National Eisteddfod has been proclaimed. For the *International Eisteddfod*, see Rte 13, Llangollen.

The Flag (Red Dragon). The origin of Wales's flag, a red dragon on a green and white field, is lost in legend but may derive from Roman custom, a dragon having been the emblem of the cohort. In post-Roman times and legend warriors sometimes became known as 'dragons'. Arthur's father was Uther Pendragon, the 'chief dragon', and legend tells that he had a vision of a fiery dragon, interpreted by his seers as a sign that he would mount the throne. Legend (see below) tells too of the struggle between the red dragon of Wales and the white dragon of England, foretelling the victory of the former, a tradition that was fostered by the bards and made true by Henry Tudor whose standard was a red dragon. As Henry VII he incorporated the Welsh dragon in the Royal arms, where it remained until James I displaced it in favour of the Scottish unicorn. In 1901, however, the red dragon was officially recognised as the Royal badge of Wales, and in 1959 the Queen commanded that the red dragon on its green and white field should be the Welsh flag. The *Leek*, the national emblem, may well have been introduced into Britain by the Romans. Of many theories as to why it became the Welsh emblem the most popular is that in some ancient battle the Welsh wore leeks in their caps as an identification; the battle was won and thus the leek remained in favour.

Industrial Archaeology (see also Mining). The industrial proliferation of the past included the huge slateworks of Snowdonia; the copper, gold, silver and lead mines of northern and central Wales; the iron-making of Bersham near Wrexham; the many mills, and the ubiquitous woollen and textiles industry; and, above all perhaps, the explosive developments in coal, iron, tinplate and steel, with the accompanying network of railways and canals, which during the 18C and 19C transformed the southern valleys.

Many causes—new processes and materials; foreign competition; a move to the ports; the exhaustion or flooding of mines; the replacement of coal by oil—led to an often rapid decline which left in its wake a desert of abandoned sites ranging from individual kilns to entire mines and factories. Today, though, and increasingly, the best of these sites are being identified, recorded, and in many cases restored, converted to museums or otherwise opened as tourist attractions.

Legend. Most of the legends of Wales live on in the 'Mabinogion', the creation of the bards of the Dark Ages, freely using material from their own imaginations, from romanticised historical or quasi-historical figures (e.g. Arthur and Macsen Wledig, the latter the Roman Magnus Maximus), and from folk tales and characters coeval perhaps with the earliest Celts. The earliest known written forms of the stories are in the 'White Book of Rhydderch' (1300–25; National Library of Wales) and the 'Red Book of Hergest' (1375–1425; Jesus College, Oxford). The 'Mabinogion' was translated by Lady Charlotte Guest, wife of a Merthyr Tydfil ironmaster, in 1838, but the engaging stories, with their improbable heroes but many easily identified place names, are now available in modern and very readable form in the translation (1948; with an admirable interpretive introduction) by Gwyn Jones and Thomas Jones (Everyman's Library).

The hero Arthur figures prominently in the 'Mabinogion' and thus in Welsh legend. He slew a giant and was mortally wounded on Snowdon, and a number of burial chambers, older than Arthur by around 2000 years, bear his name. On the Presely Hills standing stones commemorate two of Arthur's sons, killed by a great boar.

Vortigern and Merlin are two other characters associated in legend with Wales, and since the legend refers to much visited places (Carmarthen and Dinas Emrys) and also relates to the Welsh Dragon flag, it is told below.

Vortigern, King of Britain during the 5C, invited the Saxons Hengist and Horsa to help him against the Picts and Scots, rewarding them with land. But Hengist and Horsa were not satisfied, and soon the British were at war with the Saxons, Vortigern having to flee both the Saxons and his own angry people. Reaching Wales, he was told by his wizards that he must build himself a strong tower, and after much searching Vortigern chose Dinas Emrys. However, every time his masons started to build, the foundations were swallowed by the earth, whereupon the wizards said that Vortigern must find a youth born of no earthly father, kill him, and sprinkle his blood on the mortar. Messengers were sent far and wide, until one, reaching Carmarthen, overheard a dispute between two youths, Dinabutius and Merlin, in which the former mocked Merlin for never having had a father. Brought to Vortigern and questioned, the mother (a king's daughter) admitted that a spirit in the shape of a man had lain with her, thereafter disappearing and leaving her pregnant. Merlin however mocked the wizards, telling Vortigern that his tower kept falling down because there was a pool below, the home of two sleeping dragons, one red and one white. Digging proved Merlin right, and when the awoken dragons started to fight and the red dragon killed the white dragon, Merlin interpreted this as the eventual victory of Wales over England. This theme became a favourite with the bards, leading to the adoption of the Red Dragon as the emblem of Wales and the realisation of the prophecy through the accession of Henry VII.

Little Trains, narrow gauge, frequently steam-drawn and in most cases tracing their (often horse-drawn) origins to the industrial needs of the 19C, have well repaid their rescuers' enthusiasm by today ranking among Wales's most popular tourist attractions. Industrial Railway museum at Penrhyn Castle.

Mining in Wales, once a vigorous national feature, has since the early years of this century experienced a steady and even dramatic decline, the reasons including exhaustion, alternative materials, foreign competition and lack of demand. *Gold* was known in Wales in prehistoric times, but is was the Romans who started serious mining. Between then and the present day frequent ventures have been launched, but although gold is extracted the return has never justified continuing operations and Welsh gold is now very rare. There are a number of places where old workings can be explored, by far the best being the Roman and later Dolaucothi mines near Pumsaint. *Copper* was mined in Anglesey from Roman times until the late 19C, the opencast scars on bleak Parys Mountain remaining as reminders of this prosperous past. The copper mines around Snowdon carried on until about 1916, the remains of some of their buildings today being a feature of the Miners' Trail up the mountain, while on Great Orme today's visitor can view and squeeze through Bronze Age workings. *Lead* was mined in several places, notably on the plateau between Trefriw and Betws-y-Coed where between 1838 and the First World War there were as many as 19 mines, some producing over 2000 tons a year until defeated by competition from richer American deposits. Among other disused lead mines are those which rise beside the mountain road between Devil's Bridge and Rhayader. *Slate* has been quarried and mined since the time of the Romans, but operations are now on a much diminished scale compared to the peak period of the late 19C. Slate quarrying and mining has left scars which, though ugly, can at the same time because of their sheer size be awe-inspiring. Today some of these huge gashes into the mountains have been converted into imaginative tourist attractions (notably above Blaenau Ffestiniog), while the great disused quarries at Llanberis are the site of one of the world's largest pumped-storage power stations. *Coal* is still mined, but on a very small scale compared to the past.

Principality. Wales is frequently referred to as the Principality of Wales, and it is certainly true that from early times until the accession in 1485 of the Welshman Henry Tudor to the English throne as Henry VII Wales was in whole or in part ruled by princes. These included Llewelyn the Great and Llewelyn the Last, both of whom effectively if briefly held all Wales, and Owen Glendower who declared himself Prince of Wales. But the most lasting and perhaps most formal princely declaration was that of 1284 at Caernarfon when the English conqueror Edward I conferred the title of Prince of Wales on his infant son just born in the castle. Today the title is still normally conferred on the heir to the throne, but the term Principality has no administrative significance and Wales is constitutionally an integral part of the United Kingdom.

Welsh Mountain Sheep, the native breed of the Welsh uplands, are one of the hardiest and most productive breeds in Britain. The sheep are small and normally white, though black and brown fleeces occur. The fleece is light in weight but of good quality, and Welsh lamb is renowned. Variants of the breed are Black Welsh Mountain and Badger-faced Welsh Mountain, the latter being rare and thought to be descendants of the original breed before the introduction of improvements. Among other Welsh sheep, all named after their place of origin, are Beulah Speckle Face; Lleyn; Llanwenog, with brown hornless heads; and Kerry Hills, also hornless and with black spots on faces and legs.

Welsh Black Cattle will be seen in many parts of Wales, and since 1966 have been increasingly exported, especially to countries where their hardiness is much valued. The breed has existed in Wales since pre-Roman times, but in its modern form derives from two strains, the compact Anglesey and the larger Pembrokeshire (Castlemartin). Though good milk providers and sucklers, Welsh Black are primarily beef cattle.

Woollen Industry. The Welsh woollen industry, known to have been well established before the Normans arrived, is perhaps the oldest such in Europe. By the 15C, if not considerably earlier, cloth fairs were a familiar feature of Wales and the Marches, and the 15–18C saw a steady climb to prosperity until by the end of the 18C production of cloth had reached such a level as to be largely dependent on exports. Knitting was an important allied activity, particularly in Merioneth where, according to Pennant, the women had learnt to knit as soon as they could talk. Stockings, gloves, and woollen caps (known as Welsh wigs) were among the popular articles offered to coach travellers and bought also by middlemen for resale in London and elsewhere in England.

In Wales spinning and weaving were essentially home crafts, side activities to farming and other occupations. However, because of the difference in cost between a spinning wheel and a loom, a separation developed between cottagers spinning yarn and the more prosperous owners of looms to whom they sold it. These latter were frequently farmers, who insisted that their employees be as skilled at the loom as in the fields and in many cases found their cloth to be more profitable than farming. All this ended with the Industrial Revolution, Wales showing herself loath to give up the traditional ways and slow to adopt machinery. The decline which then set in lasted through to the late 1960s when an upsurge in tourism brought with it a demand for traditional Welsh work, a demand which is now being met by a reborn and increasingly prosperous industry which is successfully adapting traditional designs to modern requirements.

History of Wales

Prehistory (BC)

Much of Wales was under ice during the Ice Ages (until approximately 20–25,000 years ago) and man first made his way here as the glaciers retreated. The earliest trace is a skeleton found in Paviland Caves (Gower), radio-carbon dating placing this in the 19th millennium BC. Other evidence of man's early presence is provided by remains found in the limestone caves of the northeast, and perhaps also by shell heaps, though these are of unknown age.

The ice was replaced by swampy valleys and pine forests, these features and the local lack of flint confining man to open upland or to the coast. During the third millennium (Neolithic, or New Stone Age) there was a general drift of peoples northwards following the European coast, this drift embracing Wales and bringing primitive agriculture, domesticated animals, and, later on, the first visible structures made by man. Around 1800 BC, at the dawn of the Bronze Age, these early people seem to have been joined in both the south and north by others who crossed the North Sea and drifted westwards; these are sometimes called the Beaker People, known for their round barrows and pottery and probably also responsible for many standing stones.

Other than hillforts the **Prehistoric Monuments** of Wales belong to the New Stone and Bronze Ages. There is a great deal of overlapping in both time and place, but roughly the monuments divide as below.

Burial Chambers or *Long Cairns* (2500 BC or earlier). Used for communal burials, these were megalithic structures, i.e. made of massive stones covered by a mound. Few signs of mounds survive, what remains now usually being the chamber capstone, frequently still resting on its uprights. In this Guide the term 'burial chamber' is normally used. Some maps and local names, however, may refer to these sites either as 'cromlechs' (curved stones), a term first used in the 16C, or as 'dolmens' (Breton for 'table stone'), a term invented by an 18C French archaeologist.

Standing Stones (c 1800 BC) may have served a variety of purposes, including deity symbols, memorials, and boundary or route markers. They are sometimes called 'menhirs' (long stones).

Round Barrows (c 1800 BC) are associated with the Beaker People who gave their dead individual burial.

Stone Circles and *Alignments* (1800–500 BC) probably marked places at which the people met for both ritual and secular purposes.

In the Dark Ages (roughly the period between the Roman departure and the Norman arrival) prehistoric sites were frequently associated with Arthur and other heroes, and were also protected under ancient law.

During the later Bronze Age (say 400–100 BC) there was continuing westward drift from the continent, now of men armed with metal weapons, by some authorities considered to be the first Celts.

Celts is the generic name for the ancient peoples who inhabited central Europe. During the last five centuries BC these people embarked on an expansion which took them into France, Spain, and Italy, down the Danube into the Balkans, and (by 300 BC) into Greece and Asia Minor, where later those who held on became the Galatians. Two sets of Celts, the Goidels and the Brythons (Britons), reached the British Isles. The Goidels crossed in the 4C BC directly to Ireland, and may also have been the metal-weaponed people who came to Wales; if these latter were Goidels, then their speech, later to become the Gaelic of Ireland and Scotland, took no permanent root in Wales either now or as the result of their invasions after the Roman withdrawal (see below). Rather later the Brythons crossed the Channel and spread through England and Wales. **Druidism** was the Celtic religion up to the time of the Romans, the Druids themselves being not only priests but, more importantly, teachers, administrators, and judges exercising an authority which, backed by religion, crossed the many tribal boundaries. Druidism accepted many gods, preached immortality through rebirth, and sometimes practised human sacrifice. In Wales, Druidism was strongest in Anglesey.

It was thus the Brythonic Celts who in the Bronze–Iron Age centuries immediately preceding the Roman invasion provided the main influx into Wales (as also Cornwall and Cumbria) and whose language became Welsh. These were the people who penetrated the valleys, made a start with land clearance, developed farming, and began to live in villages. And it was these people who, now and later, built the drystone, wood, and earthwork hillforts (often referred to as British Camps), the remains of which are such a feature of the Marches and Welsh landscapes. At the same time, up on the moors, the earlier people and their ways lingered on.

Roman Period (AD 61 to early 5C)

Suetonius Paulinus attacked northern Wales and Anglesey in 61, and between 74 and 78 Frontinus crushed much of the south (the Silures and the Demetae). In 78 Agricola arrived in Britain (he stayed some seven years), at once subduing the Ordovices in central Wales and also completing the conquest of the northwest and Anglesey where the Druids were exterminated. Wales was held throughout the centuries of the Roman occupation of Britain, but, except to a limited extent along the south coast, always as a military zone controlled by legions based on Deva (Chester) in the north and on Isca (Caerleon) in the south. From these places roads penetrated westwards to stations such as Segontium (Caernarfon) and Maridunum (Carmarthen), with smaller forts even farther west. In the east the linking road ran through Viroconium (Wroxeter) and Castra Magna (Kentchester), both in the Marches. In the west the north to south link was

Sarn Helen (perhaps from the Welsh 'sarn heolen', a paved causeway) which ran from Caerhun through Tomen-y-Mur and Llania, beyond the latter bearing west for Maridunum and east and south for Y Gaer (Brecon) and Nidum (Neath).

Thus Wales was never fully romanised, its inhabitants continuing to follow a more or less independent existence in and around their hillforts. The Silures, transferred from their hillfort capital to Venta Silurum (Caerwent), were the exception. In the Marches Roman remains include walls and an amphitheatre at Chester, and the fine site of Vironconium. In Wales the outstanding sites are the amphitheatre at Caerleon, the extensive walls of Caerwent, and clearly defined forts such as Y Gaer near Brecon and Castell Collen near Llandrindod Wells.

Irish, Anglo-Saxons, and Norsemen (Dark Ages. Early 5C to 1066)

The Romans were withdrawing early in the 5C and as their grip loosened the Welsh coast became open to the attacks of Irish (Goidelic) pirates, on their heels coming settlers in large numbers who established themselves particularly in the northwest (in what would become the principality of Gwynedd, today Anglesey, Caernarfon, Meirionnydd (Merioneth), Aberconwy and Colwyn), and in the Pembroke peninsula. It is generally accepted that Goidelic became the language in these areas until the 7C, and it is known that there was an Irish dynasty of kings in the southwest from the late 3C to the early 10C. Thus Wales became divided between the native Brythons and the Goidel invaders, the struggle between the two and the more or less simultaneous introduction and spread of Christianity now becoming the two main features of Welsh history.

The struggle between the Brythons and the Goidels, though obscure in its details, eventually resulted in complete victory for the former who, under the leadership of the northerner *Cunedda*, probably a romanised Northumbrian, forced the Goidels out of northern Wales, Cunedda's descendants becoming the rulers and establishing their headquarters at Deganwy on the Conwy estuary. The most notable of these descendants was *Maelgwn Gwynedd* (Maglocunus, died 547), known from the writings of his contemporary, the monk and chronicler Gildas, who while describing Maelgwn's court as licentious at the same time suggests that he was a Christian, at one time even eager to exchange his position as prince for that of a monk. Despite their defeat and absorption it was the Irish who brought Christianity to Wales, actively spreading the Faith and thus leaving their permanent legacy. These missionaries, named 'sancti' by Gildas (a word which soon became 'saint'), generally led the lives of hermits and often became known for their healing powers; hence the Holy Wells found throughout Wales, many of which date back to this time. One saint was Dewi, or David, later adopted as patron of Wales. Such was the influence of these saints that they before long achieved a status equal to that of the local lord, and it became the custom that the latter should grant the holy man a piece of land as a sacred enclosure ('llan'). In 546 St. Dubricius (or Dyfrig), Bishop of all Wales, divided his see into three, appointing Deiniol to Gwynedd, Padarn to central Wales and Teilo to the south.

Wales is rich in Early Christian monuments, such as inscribed stones, graveslabs, and crosses, dating from the 5C onwards. Many bear interesting Latin inscriptions; others bear Ogham characters, the oldest written form of Goidelic and thus of Gaelic (the writing takes the form of strokes or notches along a base line). The oldest known example of written Brythonic is a stone of c 650 in Tywyn church.

Towards the end of the 6C the Brythons had to face the onslaught of new invaders, the pagan Anglo-Saxon tribes who had swept across southern Britain, and there now started a struggle which would continue with little respite until Henry Tudor ascended the English throne as Henry VII some nine hundred years later.

The hero Arthur, if he ever existed at all, appears to date from about this time. Traditionally he was born at Tintagel in Cornwall, the son of Uther Pendragon and Ygrayne, and would have been a Christian chieftain (but not a king) who, as a military leader, perhaps serving Ambrosius, a chief with Roman blood seeking to restore Roman law and order, led the Brythons against the Saxons. He is credited with victory at Mount Badon (?Liddingstone, near Swindon) and may have died in battle, reputedly being buried at Glastonbury. Arthur's association with Wales, as opposed to with the Brythons generally, is largely a matter of bardic legend.

In 577, after a victory at Deorham near Bath, the invaders reached the Bristol Channel, and in 613 Ethelfrid, the Anglian king of Northumbria, defeated an army of Brythons near Chester. It was these two battles which geographically determined the Wales of today. The first cut off the Brythonic people of what is now known as the English West Country, and the second those of today's Cumbria. For the first time contained within their own frontiers, the still free Brythons of the mountainous west now began to call themselves 'Cymry' (fellow-countrymen) and the land 'Cymru' (whence Cambria). The name Wales derives from the Anglo-Saxon 'wealas' meaning 'foreigners'. The Brythons' hopes of reunion were finally shattered in 634 when Cadwaladr ap Cadfan, who had penetrated far to the east, was defeated south of the Tyne, this enabling the Angles (or English as they would be called) to consolidate up to the foothills of the Welsh mountains. Only eight years later the Christian Oswald of Northumbria was killed by the pagan Penda of Mercia at Oswestry, this opening the way for the rise of that warlike people who inhabited England's Midlands and had their capital at Tamworth. In c 784 Offa, the greatest of all the Mercian kings, constructed the long dyke which bears his name.

Offa's Dyke, built more as a line of demarcation than as a fortification, runs from the coast near Prestatyn southwards across the neck of Wales to Chepstow. Thus substantially the dyke still marks the border, the place names to the east being English and those to the west largely Welsh. Many sections of the dyke are still clearly visible and a waymarked path follows its 167 miles length. **Wats Dyke**, possibly the work of the earlier Mercian king Aethelbald (716–57), is a shorter dyke (38 miles) running east of Offa's Dyke between the Dee estuary and Oswestry.

By the middle of the 8C the Mercians became Christian, and it was also at about this time that the Welsh first submitted to the practices and ritual which later resulted in the absorption of the Celtic Church by the Roman; an important date was 768 when the Welsh accepted the Roman Easter, the date of which had long been a major cause of dispute between Augustinian and Welsh authorities.

Throughout the 9 and 10C Wales suffered under the savage raids of the Norse pirates (Vikings), who made their way round the north of Scotland, settling there, in Ireland, and on the Isle of Man. That they did not to any lasting extent colonise Wales was due in large part to *Rhodri Mawr* (Roderick the Great of Gwynedd, died 879), who became ruler of all Wales except the extreme southeast and southwest, and also to the activities of

Alfred the Great on whom the Welsh had to rely after Rhodri's death. The Norse presence survives in place names, particularly in Pembroke, and in the intricately carved designs on stone monuments of the time. Rhodri Mawr's line continued as two branches, in the north and in the south, his best known descendant being his grandson *Hywel Dda* (Hywell the Good, died 950), a member of the southern branch. Through marriage Hywel added Dyfed—today's Pembroke, Carmarthen and Ceredigion (Cardigan)—to his lands, and through force Gwynedd, but he is best remembered for the great assembly he convened at Whitland which succeeded in codifying the tribal customs of the various parts of Wales into a single legal system which remained in force until the arrival of Edward I. Meanwhile the Norse raids continued, St. David's being sacked as late as 1088.

Although Hywel Dda's legal code survived, the political unity he had given to much of the country did not, and until just before the Norman invasion Wales became four distinct principalities, with borders more or less definitely fixed. Gwynedd was the dominant power in the north. To the south of Gwynedd was Powys, corresponding roughly to the modern Powys but including also parts of Meirionnydd and England's Salop. This principality's ruling families, though often disunited, frequently sided with the English and continued to exert a powerful influence in the Marches until well into the Middle Ages. In the south and southwest ruled the princes of Deheubarth, comprising the earlier principalities of Dyfed, Ceredigion (Cardigan), Ystrad Tywi (Vale of Towy, Carmarthen) and Brycheiniog (Brecon). Occupying the southeast was the principality of Morgannwg (Glamorgan), which by now included the former principalities of Glwysing and Gwent (eastern Glamorgan and Monmouth). These Welsh princes continued to divide the country and quarrel for supremacy until just before the Norman Conquest when *Gruffydd ap Llewelyn* (1039–63), an adventurer not of any royal house, succeeded in uniting the Welsh people and threatening the border. He was finally defeated and killed by Earl Harold Godwinson who, as King Harold, was to lose his own life three years later when defeated by the Norman William the Conqueror at Hastings.

Despite the splintering into principalities, the internal strife and the fighting with the English, it would be wrong to picture the Welsh scene of the time simply as one of disorder. Wales still enjoyed Hywel Dda's legal code, with a defined system of administration. Each principality was divided into a number of cantrefs, roughly synonymous with the Anglo-Saxon hundred, and each cantref comprised several cymydau (commotes), each of these subdividing into trefs. There were no towns and scarcely any villages in Wales at this time, these trefs being no more than groups of farmsteads, each the property of a particular family. Each cantref was ruled by a lord, answerable to the prince. Status within the cantref depended upon birth, and certain distinct classes were recognised: royalty, noblemen, freemen, unfree persons, and slaves. The relations of these classes were legally defined, and courts existed for the redress of wrongs. Descendants of a common ancestor to the ninth degree, known as cenedl (kindred), were automatically bound together in a common, self-governing unit, and the law of gavelkind was observed, i.e. at the death of a father his land was divided equally among his sons, the division being made by the eldest and the choice starting from the youngest. This arrangement held good until the time of Henry VIII.

From the Normans to Edward I (1066 to 1272)

Welsh Lords	**English Kings**
Rhys ap Tedwr (Tudor) died 1093	William I (the Conqueror) 1066–87
Gruffydd ap Cynan died 1137	William II (Rufus) 1087–1100
Gruffydd ap Rhys died 1137	Henry I 1100–35
Madoc ap Maredydd died 1160	Stephen 1135–54
Owain Gwynedd died 1170	Henry II 1154–89
Rhys ap Gruffydd	Richard I 1189–99
(Lord Rhys) died 1197	John 1199–1216
Llewelyn ap Iorwerth	Henry III 1216–72
(the Great) died 1240	Edward I 1272–1307
Llewelyn ap Gruffydd	
(the Last) died 1282	

One of the results of the activities of Gruffydd ap Llewelyn was that the Normans, after William the Conqueror's victory at Hastings in 1066, regarded Wales as a danger. William, whose commitments elsewhere prevented him from giving Wales his personal attention, established three Marcher Lordships under earls of Chester, Shrewsbury, and Hereford. He encouraged these earls to extend their territories westwards at the expense of the Welsh, and to bring the Welsh leaders under Norman vassalage. The earls pursued the policy with vigour, but though some definite results were achieved (by 1098 Hugo d'Avranches, or Hugh Lupus, Earl of Chester, had virtually conquered Anglesey), the main objective of subjugating the entire peninsula was not realised.

Motte-and-bailey Castles were a Norman introduction, first appearing on the English side of the border c 1055 when Edward the Confessor invited Norman knights to help him resist the inroads of the Welsh under Gruffydd ap Llewelyn. Old Radnor is one which dates from this time. After 1066 and the establishment of the Marcher Lordships such castles proliferated. The standard castle was a ditch (moat), usually dry, surrounding an earth mound (motte), the rim of which bore a palisade protecting an inner tower, or keep. (The basic word 'moat', or 'mote', or 'motte', came to be used loosely both for the ditch and for what had been heaped out of it.) Annexed to the tower (sometimes within the main defence, sometimes extending outwards and with some defence of its own) was a flat area known as the bailey, used for all those activities which could not be contained within the tower, e.g. stabling. Remains of large numbers of these castles are found in Wales, although in many cases only the motte and ditches are obvious, the bailey not being readily recognised. Only in the 12C were these primitive castles succeeded by stone keeps (later becoming full castles), often, when strength and space allowed, standing on the early mottes.

About 1081 *Gruffydd ap Cynan* (died 1137) came over from Ireland, whither his father had fled, to claim his patrimony in Gwynedd which he succeeded in freeing from Hugh Lupus. At about the same time *Rhys ap Tewdwr* (died 1093), a descendant of Hywel Dda, returned from exile in Brittany to claim his lands in Deheubarth. Supported by Gruffydd ap Cynan he defeated his rivals, his rights were recognised by William I, and there followed twelve years of peace. At his death, however, his son *Gruffydd ap Rhys* (died 1137) had to face the full weight of the Normans who now swept into the south. Gwent was overrun by William FitzOsbern, Earl of Hereford; Glwysing by Robert FitzHamon of Gloucester; Brycheiniog fell to Bernard of Newmarch, and Dyfed and Ceredigion to the house of Montgomery. Farther north, however, Roger de Montgomery, Earl of Shrewsbury, made little progress, and thus Powys and Gwynedd, still independent, became separated from the rest of Wales.

William II made expeditions into Wales in 1095 and 1097, penetrating as far as Meirionnydd, but by the time of his death in 1100 the Normans, especially in the south, were tending to contract marriages with the leading Welsh families, some of these Welsh-Norman lords even playing with ideas of independence. One such was Robert of Belesme, son of Roger de Montgomery, who tried to establish a western kingdom with Shrewsbury as his capital. But his plans were frustrated by the accession of Henry I, who was successful not only in checking both his own rebel barons and the Welsh but also in consolidating Norman gains. He also planted Flemish colonies in the Pembroke and Gower peninsulas, where their descendants still remain, speaking English.

The accession of Stephen (1135) and the consequent civil war in England gave the Welsh an opportunity from which they profited, everywhere taking up arms and recovering much of their territory. *Owain Gwynedd* (died 1170) and his brother Cadwaladr, the sons of Gruffydd ap Cynan, had obtained control in Gwynedd and now harried the northern Marches, seizing the border fortress of Mold; Powys was united under *Madoc ap Maredydd* (died 1160), who took the castle of Oswestry. But Henry II acceded in 1154, soon turning his attention to Wales where he defeated Owain Gwynedd in 1157 and, in 1163, *Rhys ap Gruffydd* (Lord Rhys; died 1197), the able and energetic son of Gruffydd ap Rhys. However, these two princes rallied their armies, and, supported by Owain Cyfeiliog, prince of Powys, and other leaders, in 1165 forced Henry to withdraw. After this his troubles with Becket occupied Henry's attention, and Rhys ap Gruffydd was able to extend his sway over southern Wales so effectively that Henry, while on his way to Ireland in 1171, met and acknowledged him.

With varying fortune Rhys ap Gruffydd remained in power in the south until his death in 1197, and the Wales of this time has been vividly recorded by Giraldus Cambrensis (Gerald of Barry; died c 1223), the son of a Norman settler in Dyfed, who became a noted scholar and churchman. In 1188 he made a tour in the train of Archbishop Baldwin who was seeking recruits for the crusades (died 1190 in the Holy Land, professing himself appalled at the excesses of the crusaders he had recruited), and he recorded his reflections in two works 'Itinerary through Wales' and 'Description of Wales'. His picture is of a frugal and poor people living in simple huts, yet bred to arms and having a bold individuality and courage. They seem to have been a pastoral people, with little inclination to trade. Of particular interest, and of course still true today, is the report that the Welsh had a love of poetry and music, including a natural gift for singing in harmony.

Castles. It was Henry II who introduced stone keeps into England, as successors to the motte-and-bailey castles, and during the later 12C these began to appear also in Wales. One of the first, and still surviving, was that at Dolwyddelan.

Religious Houses. The 12C also saw the development in Wales of the Norman monastic system. The monastery in pre-Norman Wales had been of the usual Celtic type, with an abbot and a community of monks occupying individual cells. Such monasteries had however already begun to decline as far back as the 8C, and the Normans dissolved the surviving houses in favour of their own type. The Benedictine Order was the first to be introduced into Wales, houses being established at Brecon (late 11C), St. Dogmaels (1118), and Ewenny (1141). The Savigniac Order founded abbeys at Neath (1130) and Basingwerk (1131), but in 1141 this Order was merged with the Cistercian, because of its charity and simplicity by far the most popular in Wales. The first Cistercian houses were on the border at Tintern (1131) and in the heart of the country at Whitland (1140). From these, others were colonised (some under the patronage of native princes) at Cwmhir (1143), Margam (1147), Strata Florida (1164), Strata Marcella (c 1170), Aberconwy (1186), Cymmer (1199), and Valle Crucis (1199). The Cistercians, of whom Rhys ap Gruffydd was a liberal patron, came to own large tracts of land and their farming methods had a marked influence on the native agriculture; indeed their successful sheep rearing set a pattern which persists today. The Premonstratensians established themselves at Talley (before 1197), and the Augustinians later at Penmon.

After the death of Owain Gwynedd in 1170, the power of Gwynedd was weakened by a struggle for supremacy among his sons. In the south, though the agreement between Rhys ap Gruffydd and Henry II stood until the latter's death in 1189, the absence of Richard I on crusades was the signal for disorder. Rhys ap Gruffydd reduced many of the Norman castles, but his desperate struggle to keep his independence was cut short by his death in 1197.

In 1194 *Llewelyn ap Iorwerth* (died 1240), grandson of Owain Gwynedd and later styled Llewelyn the Great, became prince of Gwynedd. He was to become the most powerful ruler in Wales since the Norman invasion. First he had to overcome the rivalry of Gruffydd ap Gwenwynwyn (died 1216), a prince of southern Powys who, departing from the normal pro-English policy of his house, attempted to lead a national revival. Llewelyn succeeded in taking over the whole of Powys, the result being that under his rule all northern Wales enjoyed almost complete independence. In 1204 he married Joan, a natural daughter of King John, but despite this in 1211 he had to face an attack by his father-in-law, who himself held lands in the Marches and feared Llewelyn's growing power. After this experience Llewelyn sided with the English barons and obtained rights for Wales under Magna Carta. In the same year he invaded southern Wales, making himself overlord of the feeble successors of Rhys ap Gruffydd and forcing the Normans to surrender many castles. It was not only militarily and territorially that Wales prospered under Llewelyn; he was also a patron of the bards, he encouraged the study of the Welsh laws, and he gave generously to the monastic orders. In 1238 he entered the monastery of Aberconwy, where he died two years later.

Despite all he had achieved, and although he had his son Dafydd (died 1246) recognised as ruler in Wales by the lesser princes, Llewelyn the Great had given Wales only a superficial unity. There was no central government; province was divided from province, commote from commote; and the system of gavelkind, with its continual division of property, was a constant weakness. Such unity as there was died with Dafydd. But only for ten years, for in 1255 *Llewelyn ap Gruffydd* (Llewelyn the Last), grandson of Llewelyn the Great, overcame his brothers and began a campaign designed to clear the English out of Gwynedd and to establish his own authority throughout Wales. His opportunity was that of his grandfather, the strife between the English king and the barons, and Llewelyn was soon close to his objectives; the English were thrown back from Gwynedd, and Llewelyn, demanding the homage of the other chieftains, proclaimed himself Prince of Wales, a title which was recognised by Henry III in 1267 under the Treaty of Montgomery.

Edward I. The Conquest of Wales (1272 to 1307)

Only five years after the Treaty of Montgomery Edward I became king; his declared intention was to control his barons and to deal with unruly Wales and Scotland. Llewelyn the Last, seemingly unaware of the changed spirit in England, refused to pay homage and in 1277 Edward launched his attack and, by establishing a series of fortresses backed by the new weapon of sea-power, forced Llewelyn (Treaty of Conwy) to pay homage in London and to give up virtually everything except a part of Gwynedd reaching from the Conwy to the Dyfi and his now empty title. In 1282 Llewelyn's brother Dafydd rose against Edward, and Llewelyn, eager for revenge, joined him. Edward's response was shattering. He pushed through Gwynedd, extending his line of fortresses; took Anglesey, the granary of Wales; forced Llewelyn back into the fastnesses of Snowdon, whence he retreated southwards to be killed in a skirmish at Cilmeri; and finally disposed of the Welsh 'dynasty' by executing Dafydd. With these events—until the arrival of Owen Glendower on the scene a hundred years later—all serious hopes of establishing an independent Wales were ended.

Edward remained in Wales for about three years to secure his position and establish the direct rule of the English Crown. He issued the Statute of Rhuddlan (1284; sometimes called the Statute of Wales), which provided for the government of the conquered principality; he divided Llewelyn's small remaining patrimony of western Gwynedd into the shires (counties) of Anglesey, Caernarfon, and Merioneth; he created the county of Flint as a buffer for that of Chester; he reorganised the administration of the provinces of Cardigan and Ystrad Tywi (Carmarthen); he suppressed the Welsh code of laws stemming from that of Hywel Dda, imposing instead the English system; finally, he embarked on a massive programme of castle construction, in the shadow of some of their walls creating 'English boroughs'.

Castles. The motte-and-bailey castle had been followed in the 12C by the stone keep. Now, a hundred years later, Edward built in Wales huge concentric fortresses of a type previously developed on the Continent and in the Near East, much of the work being in the hands of James of St. George, an engineer whom Edward had brought back from France on his return from the last crusade. Detail depended on the site, but ideally the concentric castle consisted of two baileys or wards, square in shape and enclosed by strong buttressed walls. The inner ward, which contained the domestic buildings, was normally placed well within the outer, the whole being reinforced whenever possible by a moat. The castle was entered across a drawbridge and through an immensely strong gatehouse, which often also served as keep; if there could be a seaward protection, and perhaps a dock, so much the better. Edward completed castles at Flint, Rhuddlan, Builth, and Aberystwyth; he also built large new fortresses at Conwy, Caernarfon, Beaumaris, and Harlech, below these establishing 'English boroughs'; finally he took over and strengthened castles already built by the Welsh at Criccieth, Bere, Dolbadarn, Ewloe and elsewhere. Other castles built by the Lords Marcher (Denbigh, Caerphilly etc.) were to a similar pattern to the king's, although that at Caerphilly actually preceded the royal castles in date.

English Boroughs, the nearest approach to anything like a town hitherto seen in Wales, were founded below the walls of the castles mentioned above and also of some of the castles taken over from the Welsh. They were granted charters, often before the castles themselves were complete, and English traders, who were expected also to form part of the garrison, were encouraged to settle, to the exclusion of the native Welsh, usually compensated with land in other districts. Each town, protected by walls, was laid out on a regular plan, with wide streets at right angles and a central market place. As the Welsh were forbidden to trade in places other than these markets, the boroughs inevitably became the administrative centres for the regions surrounding them.

Efficient and orderly though Edward's measures may seem, it was no part of his plan to knit Wales into a unified nation. The largely self-governing lordships of Denbigh and Montgomery and those in southern Wales were left undisturbed, partly as a reward for their help in overcoming Llewelyn and partly no doubt because by this time the border lords had become so powerful that interference would have been both impolitic and difficult. Indeed the system of lordships was extended, so that others of Edward's helpers could have their share of the spoils. These included many Welsh lords who had had no wish to support Llewelyn; Powys and Deheubarth were amongst those who sided with Edward, and several leading families willingly provided him with administrators. The result was that much of Wales remained, as before, under the rule of numerous petty barons and outside the jurisdiction of the central courts in London.

Edward's measures inevitably led to rebellions, though none was effective and the last (by Madog ap Llewelyn) petered out in 1294. However he remained well aware that he had to continue to guard against revolt as much by his own barons as by the Welsh, the two by now not always distinguishable, and in 1301, in a move designed both to gain Welsh sympathy and to confront the barons with a royal Welsh authority, he revived the title of Prince of Wales, conferring this on his son, born at Caernarfon in 1284. Edward I died in 1307.

Edward II to Henry Tudor (Henry VII) (1307 to 1485)

Welsh Lords	English Kings	
	Edward II 1307–27	
	Edward III 1327–77	*Plantagenets*
	Richard II 1377–99	
Owain Glyndwr (Owen Glendower) died c 1416		
	Henry IV 1399–1413	
	Henry V 1413–22	*Lancastrians*
	Henry VI 1422–61	
	Edward IV 1461–83	
	Edward V 1483	*Yorkists*
	Richard III	
Harri Tewdwr (Henry Tudor)	Henry VII (Harri Tewdwr) 1485–1509	

Note: Henry VI, deposed in 1461, was murdered in 1471. Edward V, with his brother one of the boy 'princes in the tower', was declared illegitimate by Richard III and murdered; he was never crowned.

Wales appeared to settle down and apart from minor rebellions during the reign of Edward II the 14C was a peaceful one, the country becoming more prosperous and ports such as Rhuddlan, Beaumaris and Haverfordwest developing into trading centres. It was also the century in which Welsh poetry rose to perhaps its greatest heights with the work of Dafydd ap Gwilym, described by Borrow, who translated some of his poems, as the Horace of Wales. With the death of the strong Edward III, however, the Lords Marcher again began to stir and the royal officials became increasingly rapacious. Revolt was in the air and came to a head in the person of *Owen Glendower* (Owain Glyndwr; died 1416), an enigmatic figure who has been both lauded as a popular national hero and condemned as a bloodthirsty tyrant seeking his own aggrandisement.

As a descendant of the princes of northern Powys, and also, through his mother, as a representative of the royal line of Deheubarth, Glendower had claims to be regarded as a rightful Prince of Wales. Nevertheless he had been a courtier in London, had fought under the banner of Richard II, and had made no protest on the accession of Henry IV, so his revolt in 1400, sparked off by Henry's refusal of redress when Lord Grey of Ruthin seized some Glendower land, came as a surprise. Raising his standard on the Dee, Glendower soon laid waste the English settlements in northeast Wales, and what started as perhaps an act of personal pique became an excuse for Wales to unleash its resentment against the English and initiated a bitter struggle that lasted for nearly fourteen years and devastated much of Wales and the Marches.

At first Glendower had the advantage of facing a king who was insecure in his position (Henry was holding prisoner the young Earl of March, nephew of the powerful Marcher landowner Sir Edmund Mortimer and, as direct descendant of Edward III, a threat to the throne). Furthermore Henry underestimated the Welshman's personal qualities and the strength of the national sentiment to which, as a member of two princely houses, he could appeal. An early and important success was the battle at Pilleth; not only did Glendower for the first time decisively defeat a royal army and thus establish himself as a national leader, but here he also captured Sir Edmund Mortimer. Mortimer's position was of course equivocal, and it was not therefore surprising that he sided with Glendower, sealing the alliance by marrying one of Glendower's daughters.

Glendower was declared Prince of Wales and he held parliaments at Machynlleth, Dolgellau and Harlech. He sought alliances with the Scots and Irish, and to secure French support he concluded a treaty with Charles VI for the provision of troops; he even entered into negotiations with the Pope at Avignon. He appointed bishops, issued pardons under his Great Seal, and mapped out a statesmanlike policy, demanding the independence of the Welsh Church from Canterbury and proposing the establishment of two Welsh universities. He also formed an alliance with the powerful Duke of Northumberland and his son Hotspur, at the start disastrous as, while Glendower was engaged in the south, Hotspur, coming to his aid, was intercepted by the royal forces near Shrewsbury and killed (1403). Later, in 1405, Glendower, Northumberland and Mortimer signed the Tripartite Indenture by which England and Wales were to be divided among the three.

Glendower exercised great military skill, and, though Henry made at least five expeditions against him, not one of them came within sight of crushing the revolt. Despite this, in the end Glendower failed. The French support proved weak, Henry's position strengthened, especially with the defeat of Northumberland in 1408, enabling him to concentrate his attention on Wales, and although Glendower pressed into England as far as Worcester, he was thrown back by Prince Henry (later Henry V) who in 1408 seized Aberystwyth and, soon afterwards, Harlech. Glendower, now forced into outlawry, by 1412 had disappeared from the scene, dying four years later in an unknown hiding-place. (In 1413 and again in 1415 Henry V offered a pardon, but Glendower never responded.)

Wales was exhausted. Politically the country finished the long revolt virtually where it had started; still partly under English law, still partly ruled by barons. Economically the consequences were disastrous. The lords of the manor lost their rents and services, their houses and farm buildings had been destroyed and their lands neglected; Welshmen generally suffered heavy penalties, were barred from public life, and had every possible disadvantage heaped upon them. Nevertheless the people had experienced a new upsurge of national feeling, and the old idea preached by the bards, that a prince of Brythonic blood should rule in Britain, was still kept alive. Despite repression and a huge burden of fines and debts, the national spirit remained uncrushed, expressing itself by a flourishing of the arts, particularly in the field of literature; poets and prose writers abounded, old manuscripts were transcribed for the first time, and the intricate canons of Welsh verse were reduced to their final form.

The Wars of the Roses—a series of English dynastic civil wars fought over 1455–85 between the houses of York and Lancaster and spanning the reigns of Henry VI, Edward IV and Richard III—spilt over into Wales, bringing years of strife which would, however, have a triumphant conclusion. In Wales, Lancaster held sway, not only by virtue of Henry VI's royal castles and Welsh estates, but also because of the backing of the Tewdwrs (Tudors), an old-established family whose prestige was on the ascendant. Owen ap Maredydd ap Tewdwr, an Anglesey landowner (executed by the Yorkists), had married Catherine of Valois, widow of Henry V, and his sons Edmund and Jasper had been created earls of Richmond and Pembroke. Edmund, who had married Margaret Beaufort, a descendant of John of Gaunt, died before the birth of their son Henry Tudor (Earl of Richmond). Between the ages of five and twelve this boy survived the seven-year-long siege of Harlech, but when in 1471 the death in battle of Henry VI's son made him the main claimant to the English throne he had to flee into exile in Brittany. But his uncle Jasper proved a loyal and valuable supporter, and it was to a great extent due to his efforts that in 1485 Henry Tudor returned from exile, landing near Milford Haven on 7 August. On 21 August he won the Battle of Bosworth Field, Richard III was killed, and Henry became Henry VII. If for England Bosworth Field marked the final triumph of Lancaster over York, for the Welsh it meant the fulfilment of an ancient prophecy, and the fact that a Welshman (a Briton) now occupied the English throne.

The Tudors

(Henry VII, 1485–1509, Henry VIII, 1509–47, Edward VI, 1547–53. Mary I, 1553–58. Elizabeth I, 1558–1603)

Two important acts were passed during the reign of Henry VIII. The Act of Union (1535) removed the privileges of the Lords Marcher, converting their lands into shires, and decreed that Welsh shires and boroughs should return members to the English parliament. The Act for Certain Ordinances (1542) reconstituted the Council of Wales and the Marches, first established by Edward IV, and enacted that courts of justice should sit twice a year in every county; at the same time all Welsh laws which were at variance with the laws of England were declared void, this including the damaging system of gavelkind which now gave way to primogeniture. Thus Wales now officially enjoyed the same liberties as across the border, and the ruling classes found new careers open to them in England. Welshmen entered the army and navy and the learned professions, making names for themselves in Church and State. Indeed in many ways the Tudor years, and especially the reign of Elizabeth I, were, outside the country, the most brilliant in Welsh history, one noteworthy example of Welsh initiative in England being the foundation in 1571 of Jesus College, Oxford, by Hugh Price, treasurer of St. David's.

Within Wales though the picture was greyer. For the upper class of country squires the Tudor succession might mean a break with the past and the abandonment of native traditions in favour of English custom. But the peasantry remained poor and Wales predominantly pastoral. The two principal exports remained cattle and cloth, and scarcely any effort was made to exploit the great mineral wealth of the country. The Dissolution of the Monasteries, though in Wales none of these was very wealthy, also brought the disruption of a cultural tradition, learning having been very largely under the care of the monks. Tithes and Church lands too passed into the hands of laymen, usually the local gentry, the country clergy thus being reduced to an unbefitting state of poverty.

The Dissolution apart, the Reformation created remarkably little disturbance in Wales. Some of the finest scholars fled to the Continent, but others equally brilliant were content to accept the new religion, and the main stream of native Welsh history now began to assume a largely religious and educational character. In the years 1567 to 1588 three works, as remarkable for what they were as for what they achieved both for religion and for establishing a classical written Welsh, were written in Wales, though published in London. Richard Davies, Bishop of St. David's and a leading spirit behind the moves for a national Church policy, worked together with his friend William Salesbury of Llanrwst, generally credited with being author of the first book printed in Welsh in c 1545, the result of their joint labours at Abergwili being the publication in 1567 of Welsh versions of the Book of Common Prayer and of the New Testament. The translation of the Book of Common Prayer was mainly the work of Davies, while that of the New Testament (except for some epistles translated by Davies, and the Book of Revelation, contributed by Thomas Huet, precentor of St. David's) was by Salesbury. Then in 1588, after eight years of work, William Morgan, vicar of Llanrhaeadr-ym-Mochnant and later Bishop of Llandaff and St. Asaph, saw his translation of the entire Bible issued by the royal press and distributed throughout the parishes of Wales; it would later be replaced in the reign of James I by the Authorised Version, translated by Bishop Parry of St. Asaph, helped by Dr John Davies of Mallwyd, the first real Welsh lexicographer.

The Stuarts and the Commonwealth

(James I, 1603–25. Charles I, 1625–49. Commonwealth, 1649–60. Charles II, 1660–85. James II, 1685–88. William III and Mary II, 1688–94. William III, 1694–1702. Anne, 1702–14)

With the accession of the Stuarts the special favour enjoyed in England by Welshmen came to an end. In addition the Council of Wales and the Marches, for long a guardian of Welsh interests and an anchor for law and order, now declined in importance until it became little more than an intermediary between the local courts and the King's Council in London. It was abolished in 1689. Nevertheless the tradition of loyalty to the Crown continued under the early Stuarts, and the development of Puritanism in England at the start of the 17C was little felt in Wales.

During the Civil War (1642–48) Wales tended to be Royalist, though attempts by the King after his defeat at Naseby to recruit infantry in south Wales met with little success. Later, in the north, Denbigh (which had temporarily sheltered the King after defeat at Rowton Moor) held out for 11 months until August 1646 while Harlech did not fall to Parliament until

March 1647. In the south, Wales was overrun by Parliament by the end of 1645, only Raglan Castle surviving as a Royalist island until August 1646. What is sometimes called the Second Civil War (1648) started in Wales in March 1648 when Colonel Poyer, Parliamentarian governor of Pembroke, openly declared for the King with most of South Wales rising in support. But the rising was defeated in May at St. Fagans, near Cardiff, and by 11 July Pembroke Castle had been battered into submission.

As has been noted, Puritanism had been slow to develop in Wales. Nevertheless the roots were there. In 1588 John Penry of Brecon sent two appeals to parliament urging a Puritan policy for Wales, while later Rhys Pritchard (1579–1644) of Llandovery became celebrated for his Puritan preaching and writing. William Wroth (died 1642), another Puritan, in 1639 founded a community at Llanfaches, this now generally being accepted as the first dissenting chapel in Wales. The Civil War intervened, but with its close Cromwell, doubtless mindful of Welsh Royalist loyalties, was not slow to act. Within a month of the King's execution in 1649 he passed an Act for the Better Propagation and Preaching of the Gospel in Wales, which gave his 70 commissioners almost unlimited control over Welsh Church affairs. As a result huge numbers of incumbents were dismissed (330 out of 520 in St. David's and Llandaff alone), their place being taken by carefully selected itinerant preachers. Not until the Restoration and the Act of Uniformity (1662) were the ejected clergy restored, several Puritans in their turn losing their positions.

The Eighteenth Century. Methodism and Education

(George I, 1714–27. George II, 1727–60. George III, 1760–1820)

Daniel Defoe, passing through Wales in 1722, described a scene of calm and apparent content. He found the Welsh gentry 'civil, hospitable, and kind' and that 'they valued themselves much upon their antiquity' and 'had preserved their families entire for many ages'; rural life, and the trade in cloth and cattle, was still carried on in the old way. But this calm was to a great extent illusory; beneath the surface was gathering the storm that broke over Wales in the shape of the Methodist Revival, a movement which, together with the closely allied educational movement, was to alter the life and thought of the Welsh people, which created new organisations, evolved new habits, and brought about a wholly changed social atmosphere.

It was the continued disregard of the problems of Wales both by the Welsh gentry and the English parliament that led inevitably to the great rupture in the Established Church, conservative, pro-English, and indifferent or even opposed to the particular needs of Wales. Directed from England, it was becoming increasingly out of touch with the people; all the bishops were English (no Welshman was elected to a Welsh see between the reign of Anne and 1870), and the majority were also non-resident, regarding the Welsh sees, without exception poor, merely as stepping stones to more remunerative positions; plurality was rampant, and such country clergy as did attend to their parishes were hampered by poverty and unfitted by education to administer to the spiritual needs of the people.

In such fertile ground the seeds of dissent were sown, at first unwittingly by men whose real concern was the education of a people the mass of whom at the opening of the century was illiterate. An early example was Stephen Hughes (1623–88), an ejected Puritan minister who published religious literature in Welsh. Later came Sir John Philipps of Picton (died 1736), a wealthy Pembrokeshire landowner and one of the founders of the Society for the Promotion of Christian Knowledge, who issued devotional books and founded schools in which children were encouraged to read in their own language. Most influential of all perhaps was Griffith Jones (1683–1761), rector of Llanddowror, who, helped both by Sir John Philipps and Mrs Bridget Bevan of Laugharne, organised a system of itinerant teachers; so successful was Jones that by the date of his death nearly a third of the entire population of Wales could read the Bible.

Thus a basis of popular education was provided upon which the Nonconformist movement could at last develop. The first Nonconformist chapel had been founded (by William Wroth) as long before as 1639, and the Quakers (Society of Friends), Baptists, and Independents had all opened chapels in the 17C, but teaching, falling on illiterate and ignorant ground, had made little impression. Now all was changed, and for the first time since the Reformation an appeal could be made to the people themselves. There were a number of able and eloquent Methodists ready to seize this opportunity. One was Hywel Harris (1713–73) who at Trefecca in 1752 founded an institution for dissenters on a communal system. Others were Daniel Rowlands (1713–90), curate of Llangeitho, who soon became one of the most popular preachers in Wales; William Williams (1717–91) of Pantycelyn, whose hymns have become part of Welsh literature; and Peter Williams (1722–96), who made a name as a Welsh Bible commentator. Towards the close of the century Methodism began to spread through northern Wales, a leading influence here being Thomas Charles (1755–1814) of Bala, one of the founders of the British and Foreign Bible Society.

At first the Methodists attempted to work within the framework of the Established Church—they had no intention of forming a separate denomination—but their departures from conventional discipline and the opposition this aroused among the bishops (all, it should be remembered, English) finally led to schism in 1811 when an independent, dissenting communion, known as the Calvinistic Methodists, was founded. The communion's adherents were mainly drawn from the farming and labouring classes, while the gentry remained faithful to the Established Church. After the death of John Wesley (1703–91), who generally had kept aloof from Wales, the Wesleyan Methodists began to infiltrate, and at the same time the Baptists and Independents increased their influence. But the Calvinistic Methodist Church remained independent, and is today usually known as the Presbyterian Church of Wales.

The 18C was also not without its cultural advances. The Morris brothers of Anglesey became widely known as men of letters and patrons of the arts. Lewis (1701–65) was a poet and scholar; Richard (1703–79) was also a patron of the arts, while William (1705–63) was founder in 1751 of the Cymmrodorion Society to encourage Welsh literature, science, and art. Goronwy Owen (1723–69), son of a tinker and also born in Anglesey, was inspired by Lewis Morris and became leader of a group of poets writing in a classical style still alive today. Other important events of the century were the eisteddfod at Corwen in 1789 which marked the rebirth of such festivals, and the introduction by Edward Williams, in 1792, of what has become today's bardic tradition. At the same time, and given impetus by the growth in coach travel, cultivated Englishmen began to take a discerning interest in Welsh scenery and antiquities.

The Nineteenth and Twentieth Centuries

(George IV, 1820–30. William IV, 1830–37. Victoria, 1837–1901. Edward VII, 1901–10. George V, 1910–36. Edward VIII, 1936. George VI, 1836–52. Elizabeth II.)

The developments of the 19 and 20C can conveniently be recorded under headings.

Industry (see also the opening paragraphs of Rte 37). The Industrial Revolution had already exploded in south Wales by the later years of the 18C, its stimulus being the combination of iron ore and coal, the attendant metal industries, and the convenient ports. Over only a few years small market towns such as Merthyr Tydfil, Newport, and Cardiff became centres of industry, quiet valleys were torn apart for iron and coal, and a network of railways began to spread across the country, including I.K. Brunel's Great Western which by 1845 had reached Treffgarne, only ten miles short of Fishguard. Such a change in a short time, while bringing prosperity to some, brought grinding hardship to the majority and with this came social unrest, the two best known occasions being the Chartist Riots of 1839 and the Rebecca Riots of 1843.

Chartist Riots. Largely as a result of the inadequate Reform Bill of 1832, a 'People's Charter' was drawn up in 1837 by the London Workingmen's Association, the charter's six points being equal electoral areas; universal suffrage; payment of Members of Parliament; no property qualification for voters; vote by ballot; and annual parliaments. This movement for social equality spread rapidly over much of Britain, the Welsh miners being among the most militant groups. A petition signed by over $1\frac{1}{4}$ million people was rejected by parliament in July 1839, and in November rioting broke out in Lancashire, Yorkshire, and Wales, where an attack on Newport was led by the ex-mayor John Frost. The operation was poorly planned, the Chartists walked into a trap, and Frost and other leaders were sentenced to death, this sentence later being reduced to transportation. In 1842 another petition, this time with nearly $3\frac{1}{2}$ million signatures, was rejected. Chartism then went into decline, this being accelerated when the repeal of the Corn Laws in 1846 much bettered the lot of the working classes.

The **Rebecca Riots** were confined to south Wales. Though caused by the same economic circumstances as the Chartist troubles, the riots were in the first instance directed against tollgate charges (which hampered the small itinerant traders) and took their name from Genesis XXIV 60 'And they blessed Rebekah and said unto her, thou art our sister, be thou the mother of thousands of millions, and let thy seed possess the gate of those which hate them'. The rioters, often disguised as women and led by group leaders called 'Rebeccas', destroyed tollgates and their houses, and then, encouraged by success, demanded redress of other grievances. The disorders were quelled, but in south Wales tollgates disappeared.

In Wales, and especially in the south, the industrial upsurge did not last long into the following century. The demand for better quality ore for improved and more specialised steel manufacturing, two world wars linked by the depression of the 1930s, cheap imported coal and development of other sources of power, all these brought a steady decline. But by the early 1980s the lessons of over-dependence on confined sectors of industry were already fast being learnt and diversification, lighter industries and business parks were increasingly becoming the pattern. Fired by the encouragement of foreign investment, the momentum gathered and the decade saw explosive change both in attitudes and in industrial scope. The scars of lost industries may long persist—and many of these are being put to good tourist industrial archaeology use—but in the 1990s Wales is in many respects seen as a model for the future, a judgement underlined by the decision to build a second Severn Estuary road bridge (open 1996).

Politics. The conservative attitude of the Methodists, who felt interference with the supposed Divine Will to be sinful, and also of the older Dissenters who although maintaining a tradition of liberty were disinclined to bring about reform through force, did not at first favour the rise of a representative political party. But the Industrial Revolution meant that the reign of the landowning classes, who had long monopolised parliamentary representation, was at an end, and at length a new party arose, the Liberal Party, which expressed the aspirations of a rising middle class whose wealth was based on industry. In the General Election of 1868 Wales returned 22 Liberal members out of a total of 30, and less than half a century later it would be a Welsh Liberal, David Lloyd George, who would lead the British in the First World War. Not long after the birth of the Liberals, the working classes too began slowly to find political expression, and the first Labour Member of Parliament in Britain was returned for Merthyr Tydfil in 1900.

In recent years many factors, not the least being the hardships caused by the reorientation of industry, led to increased pressure for more control of local affairs. Plaid Cymru, the Welsh National Party, won seats in parliament; Cardiff was granted capital status in 1955; the Welsh flag was given royal approval in 1959; the post of Secretary of State for Wales was raised to cabinet rank in 1964; efforts to spread the use of the Welsh language will everywhere be evident to the returning visitor; and devolution in some form or other remains a live issue.

Culture and Education. The cultural advances of the 18C, with the rebirth of eisteddfodau after the Corwen festival of 1789, have already been noted. The 19C saw the founding of the annual National Eisteddfod. The desire for national expression also entered the field of education. The first institution of university rank was established at Aberystwyth in 1872, this being followed by university colleges at Bangor and Cardiff (1883). In 1893 these were combined to form the University of Wales, to which a fourth college, at Swansea, was added in 1920, while in 1971 St. David's College, Lampeter, became constituent.

Charters for the establishment of a National Museum and a National Library were granted in 1907, and these institutions—at, respectively, Cardiff (but now with branches throughout Wales) and Aberystwyth—rank among the culturally most valued and influential in Wales.

Religion. In the sphere of orthodox religion there had been from the mid 19C a movement to break away from the domination of the Church of England, but it was not until 1920 that an Act for the Disestablishment of the Church in Wales was passed, and the four Welsh dioceses of St. Asaph, Bangor, Llandaff and St. David's were combined into an independent and self-governing body, though still in communion with the Church of England. Its archbishop has no fixed see. A new diocese of Newport and Monmouth was formed in 1921 (St. Woolos Church at Newport became a full cathedral in 1949), and another of Swansea and Brecon in 1923.

Conservation and the Countryside have become increasingly important themes during the present century, and especially so since the last war. Snowdonia, Brecon Beacons and Pembrokeshire Coast National Parks were all designated during the 1950s, Country Parks now abound, and there is impressive and continuing evidence of the rehabilitation of The Valleys.

Biographical Notes

These notes identify and elaborate on selected personalities about whom users may like to know more. Well known names are not generally included, nor are people who are sufficiently identified in the History or Routes texts.

Agricola, Gnaeus Julius (37–93). Roman general and governor of Britain, where he spent some seven years, conquering north Wales and Anglesey and southern Scotland. His daughter married the historian Tacitus. May have died of poisoning.

Baldwin (died 1190). Archbishop of Canterbury. His visit to Wales in 1187 was the first ever by an archbishop. In 1188 he toured Wales with Giraldus (then archdeacon of St. David's) preaching the Third Crusade. Professing himself appalled by the excesses of the crusaders, he died on reaching the Holy Land.

Bolingbroke, Henry (1367–1413) = Henry IV (1399). Son of John of Gaunt by Blanche of Lancaster. For several years he travelled and fought as an adventurer, but when on John of Gaunt's death in 1399 Richard II confiscated the estates of Lancaster Bolingbroke landed in Yorkshire and was joined by the Percys and other barons. Richard II, absent in Ireland and unpopular because of his arbitrary taxation, lost all support and soon surrendered at Flint. Richard died the following year, probably as the result of hardships of winter imprisonment rather than by murder as told by Shakespeare.

Borrow, George (1803–81). Philologist and linguist (he even translated the New Testament into Manchu). Travelled widely, acting as agent for the British and Foreign Bible Society. He became something of a tramp, wandering the roads of England and Wales, in the latter context being known for his 'Wild Wales' (1862), a description of a tour he made with his step-daughter. The book is on sale at many site shops.

Bradshaw, John (1602–59). Born at Presteigne. Lord President of the Parliamentary Commission which brought Charles I to trial, Bradshaw's signature headed the list of those who signed the death warrant. He refused to let the King speak in his own defence. Later he pronounced sentence of death on many Royalists.

Brunel, Isambard Kingdom (1806–59). Engineer, mainly of docks, railways and steamships. His associations with Wales include the south coast railway (Great Western) and initial work on the docks at Milford Haven.

Burges, William (1827–81). Architect and decorator. His monuments in Wales are Cardiff Castle and Castell Coch. He is also associated with Salisbury chapter house, Brisbane and Cork cathedrals, and the College of Hartford, Conn.

Burne-Jones, Sir Edward (1833–98). Painter and designer. In 1862 Burne-Jones, William Morris, and D.G. Rossetti started a successful applied arts business. Burne-Jones most made his mark as a designer, and stained glass windows made from his designs are widespread, with several examples in Wales.

Bute, 3rd Marquess. John Patrick Crichton Stuart (1847–1900). Inherited from his father the 2nd Marquess (first builder of Cardiff docks) huge estates in Scotland and in and around Cardiff. In 1868 he became a Roman Catholic, an incident which may have suggested to Disraeli the plot for his novel 'Lothair'. The 3rd Marquess published several erudite works, largely on religious topics. In Wales he is best known for commissioning the work by Burges on Cardiff Castle and Castell Coch.

Caractacus, or Caradog or Caratacus, was the British chief of the Catuvellauni tribe, and son of Cunobelinus, chief of the Trinobantes. He led the resistance against the Romans in 43–47, and after defeat at Wallingford on the Thames retreated into Wales, where a number of hillforts bear his name. He was finally defeated in 51 by Ostorious Scapula, most probably at the Caer Caradog near Cerrigydrudion, after which he and his family were taken to Rome, where the emperor Claudius allowed them to live.

Caröe, William Douglas (1857–1938). Architect. Son of the Danish consul in Liverpool. Caröe's work was largely ecclesiastical, and in Wales he is known for his fine work at Brecon.

Clive, Robert (1725–74). Founder of the British empire in India. Went to Madras as a clerk in the East India Company, but soon made a name in the fighting which marked the Anglo-French struggle for India. His defence of Arcot prompted Pitt to call him a 'heaven-sent general', and there followed his campaign against Suraj-ud-Dowlah (notorious for the Black Hole of Calcutta) which ended with Clive's victory at Plassey. In 1760 Clive returned to England, was made Baron Clive (Irish peerage) and became Member of Parliament for Shrewsbury. Back in India in 1765–67 he pushed through many reforms and left Britain supreme. On his return to England attempts by jealous enemies to impeach him largely misfired, but nevertheless, in ill health and depressed at being treated 'like a sheep-stealer', he took his own life. His son Edward, Governor of Madras, acquired Powis Castle (now home of an important Clive of India Museum) by marriage and became Earl of Powis.

Cobbe, Frances Power (1822–1904). Social writer and worker, and suffragist. Contributed to newspapers and reviews on such topics as vivisection (of which she was a strong opponent), destitution, women's rights, and divorce. Of her many works may be mentioned 'The Duties of Women' (1881) and her autobiography (1894). Buried at Llanelltyd.

Dafydd ap Gwilym (c 1340–c 1400). Poet and chief bard, described by Borrow, who translated some of his verses, as the Horace of Wales. Wrote nature poems, usually in the 'cywydd' form, a short ode with each line having the same number of syllables. Probably born at Broginin near Aberystwyth, he is said to have eloped with a princess of Anglesey. He may be buried at Talley or Strata Florida.

Davies, John (c 1570–1644). Welsh lexicographer. Rector of Mallwyd (1604). Assisted Parry, bishop of St. Asaph, with his Welsh bible of 1620. His own major work was 'Antiquae Linguae Britannicae Dictionarium Duplex' (1632), in Welsh-Latin and Latin-Welsh parts.

Dyer, John (1700–58). Welsh poet born at Aberglasney, which district he describes in his 'Grongar Hill'. His longest work is 'The Fleece', an epic in blank verse covering the subject of wool from the sheep through to the cloth trade.

Edward II (1284–1327). Irresponsible son of Edward I. Born at Caernarfon Castle and made Prince of Wales in 1301. Acceded in 1307. Probably homosexual. Notorious for his favourites and their influence over him, the first being Piers Gaveston murdered by the barons in 1312, followed in 1318 by the Despensers (father and son, both Hugh) who, effectively, ruled England until 1326 in which year Isabella (of France, whom Edward had married in 1308) led a revolt against Edward who found himself deserted. In Glamorgan he took refuge in the Despensers' Caerphilly Castle, but

Isabella followed and, after an attempt to escape by sea from Chepstow, Edward was forced back into Cardiff. He and the younger Despenser were taken at Llantrisant Castle, both Despensers then being put to death while Edward was murdered the following year.

Evans, Christmas (1766–1838). Orphan son of a cobbler he became a Baptist minister because the Presbyterians demanded an academic standard he did not have. After a period in the Lleyn, he was in Anglesey for over 30 years, becoming the centre of the Baptist movement and attracting huge crowds to his oratorical and emotional sermons.

Geoffrey of Monmouth (died 1154). 'Historian' and churchman. Nephew of a bishop of Llandaff. Born at Monmouth, where he may also have been a monk. His best known work is his 'Historia Britonum' (c 1139), claiming to be a translation from a Celtic source but today generally accepted as Geoffrey's own work and to be a mixture of ancient tradition, pure fiction, and only to a very small extent fact. Whatever it was, it gained for its author a name for erudition and the appointments of Archdeacon of Llandaff (c 1140) and Bishop of St. Asaph (1151). He may also be the author of a 'Vita Merlini' (a life of Merlin) in Latin verse. The 'Historia Britonum' laid the written foundations of the Arthurian legend, and was widely accepted as history until as late as the 17C. It provided Shakespeare with the story of King Lear.

Germanus, Saint (?378–448). Bishop of Auxerre (418), of which he was a native. In 429 the British bishops asked the help of their colleagues in Gaul in their struggle against the Pelagian heresy. Germanus and Lupus of Troyes were sent to Britain, one event during their visit being the Alleluia Victory near Mold. In 447 he again came to Britain, this time with Severus of Treves; a combination of miracles and vigorous preaching soon led to the decline of Pelagianism. Germanus was for some time in Wales, becoming the subject of several legends, amongst these that he cursed Vortigern for incest. He lives on in several place-names.

Gibson, John (1790–1866). Sculptor, born at Conwy. First made his name in Rome, where he was befriended by Canova. Best known for his bas-reliefs, and as the first British sculptor to use colour.

Gildas (c 516–570). Probably a monk, the earliest British historian. His main work was 'Gildae Sapientis de excidio et conquestu Britanniae', comprising a preface, a history, and an epistle. The history, which is cursory, reviews the history of Britain from the arrival of the Romans until the author's own time; the epistle is largely a condemnation of the vices of his countrymen.

Giraldus Cambrensis (c 1146–1223). Nobleman, churchman, scholar, and historian. Born at Manorbier of mixed Welsh-Norman parentage, then studied in Paris until 1172. Archdeacon of Brecon (1175) and of St. David's (1180). Accompanied Prince John to Ireland and wrote a history of the conquest. In 1188 he accompanied Archbishop Baldwin through Wales preaching the Third Crusade, as a result of this writing his 'Itinerarium Cambrense' which gives a picture of Wales of the time. In 1198 he was proposed for the bishopric of St. Davids, but Rome did not approve. His friendship with such men as Innocent III, Richard I, John, Stephen Langton and others provided valuable background for his writings.

Gower, Bishop Henry (died 1347). Member of a noble English-speaking Gower family. Best known for his benefactions and as an architect, in the latter capacity being the originator of an attractive and unusual local form of Decorated Gothic. In 1322–23 he was chancellor of Oxford University.

Henry IV. See Bolingbroke.

Herbert of Cherbury, Lord Edward (1583–1648). Diplomat, soldier, and writer. Brother of the poet George Herbert. 1610: fought in the Netherlands for the Prince of Orange. 1617–24: ambassador in Paris. 1624; created Baron Cherbury. 1644; surrendered Montgomery Castle to Parliament. His written works include religious philosophy, poems, and an autobiography.

Herbert, George (1593–1633). Poet. Brother of above. His poems, in Latin and English, are largely of a metaphysical religious nature, and he also wrote hymns. Ordained priest in 1630.

Hopper, Thomas (1776–1856). Architect. First made his name through alterations for the Prince Regent to London's Carlton House, after this becoming fashionable with the nobility and gentry. In Wales his monument is Penrhyn Castle.

Horton, Thomas (died 1649). Parliament's commander who (with Philip Jones) defeated Poyer and Laugharne at St. Fagans. Signed the King's death warrant. Died in Ireland, where he was accompanying Cromwell.

Hubert de Burgh (died 1243). Served Richard I, John, and Henry III, under the latter two being Chief Justiciar, the king's closest adviser. He reached the height of his power when in 1227 he declared Henry III to be of age, and when, as the result of four marriages, he had acquired extensive lands, including White, Skenfrith, and Grosmont castles.

Isabella, Queen. See under Edward II.

Johnson, Dr Samuel (1709–94). Writer, lexicographer, and conversationalist. See also Thrale, Hester Lynch.

Jones, Inigo (1573–1651). Architect. His patron was the Earl of Arundel who sent him to Italy where he studied the style of Palladio. He was so successful in Venice that he was invited by Christian IV to Denmark where he designed the palaces of Rosenborg and Frediksborg. Through the influence of Anne of Denmark, wife of James I, he became architect to the English court (1604) and Surveyor of Royal Buildings (1612). He held the same posts under Charles I but was heavily fined after the Civil War and died in penury. In Wales, his name is associated with a variety of buildings, though seemingly never with any proof.

Jones, Philip (c 1618–74). Born in Swansea, of which, as a Parliamentary supporter, he was made governor in 1645. In 1648, with Horton, he defeated Laugharne and Poyer at St. Fagans, afterwards being made governor of Cardiff Castle. Throughout the Commonwealth he was a trusted adviser to Cromwell, but somehow he survived the Restoration, keeping his estates and in 1664 even acquiring Penmarc and Fonmon castles.

Landor, Walter Savage (1775–1864). Poet, prose writer, and idealist with republican sympathies. In 1808 he went to Spain and at his own expense raised a troop to fight Napoleon, a venture which failed and cost Landor a lot of money but provided the material for one of his finest poems, 'Count Julian'. There followed the Llanthony Priory affair, after which Landor lived on and off in Italy.

Laugharne, Rowland (died after 1660). Home was at Laugharne. Successful Parliamentary commander in south Wales, taking Haverfordwest, Tenby, Carew, Cardigan, Picton, and Carmarthen. But Laugharne was dissatisfied with his rewards, complaining also that he had had no refund for personal moneys paid on Parliament's behalf and that for two years he had had to pay his soldiers out of his own pocket. He then joined Poyer's revolt, being defeated with him by Horton and Jones at St. Fagans. Laugharne, Poyer, and a Colonel Powell were sentenced to death, but

Cromwell decided that only one should be executed, the choice being made by lot. Poyer was the loser.

Luxmoore, Charles (1794–1854). Helped by his father John Luxmoore, who was successively Bishop of Bristol, Hereford, and St. Asaph, Charles held at the same time the deanery of St. Asaph, the chancellorship of St. Asaph, the position of prebend of Hereford, and three rectories.

Magnus Maximus (died 387). Roman commander. While in Britain he was proclaimed emperor by disaffected local troops. After denuding Britain of troops he crossed to Gaul where he killed Gratian, co-emperor with Theodosius I. Theodosius then recognised Magnus as emperor in Gaul, Spain, and Britain. In 387 the ambitious Magnus crossed the Alps, but was defeated and beheaded. He passed into Welsh legend ('Mabinogion') under the name of Macsen Wledig.

Margaret of Beaufort (1443–1509). Countess of Richmond and Derby and mother of Henry VII. After the death of her husband, Edmund Tudor, she married in succession the son (died 1482) of the Duke of Buckingham, and Thomas Stanley, later Earl of Derby. Throughout his exile in Brittany she and Stanley were in constant communication with her son, Stanley doing much to help his cause. Margaret became known for her many foundations, these including Christ's and St. John's colleges at Cambridge, and chairs of Divinity at Oxford and Cambridge. In Wales she is associated with the chapel at Holywell.

Marten, Henry (1602–80). As a Member of Parliament Marten was always outspoken against Charles I. Although he played no significant part in the Civil War, he was one of the King's judges and signed the death warrant. At the Restoration he was imprisoned in Chepstow Castle where he died ten years later. Although a Puritan he kept a mistress, and while in Chepstow he published 'Henry Marten's Familiar Letters to his Lady of Delight'.

Merlin. Wizard of Arthurian romance who may possibly derive from an early bard. Traditionally he had a spirit father and a human mother (for this, as also for Merlin and Vortigern, see under Legend). An ancient 'Vita Merlini', which associates Merlin with Scottish legend, may be the work of Geoffrey of Monmouth. Geoffrey also collects the legends of Merlin and Arthur in his 'Historia Britonum'.

Morris, William (1834–96). Poet and artist. In 1862 Morris, Burne-Jones, Rossetti and others started an applied arts business. Stained glass windows and other decoration from his designs are often met in England and Wales, and in later years he became interested in printing, acquiring a private press. He founded the Society for the Protection of Ancient Buildings, largely because of his disapproval of the restoration work of Sir George Gilbert Scott.

Myddelton, Sir Hugh (died 1631). Engineer. Born near Denbigh. He is known for London's New River (1609–13), a 40-miles-long aqueduct bringing water from springs near Ware in Hertfordshire to a reservoir at Clerk's Well (Clerkenwell).

Mytton, Thomas (c 1597–1656). Parliamentary leader and commander. Native of Halston, Salop. His many Civil War successes included the taking of Ellesmere, Oswestry, and Shrewsbury. In 1645 he was appointed commander for north Wales, further successes including Ruthin, Caernarfon, Beaumaris, Conwy, Denbigh and Harlech.

Owen, Sir Hugh (1804–81). Born in Anglesey. Promotor of Welsh education, his main achievement being the establishment of the University

College of Wales at Aberystwyth. He also played a large part in the reforms of the National Eisteddfod, and was concerned in the revival (1873) of the Society of Cymmrodorion which had died in 1843. Also did much philanthropic work (London-Welsh Charitable Aid Society. London Fever Hospital. National Temperance League). Knighted in 1881 for services to Welsh education.

Owen, Sir John (1600–66). Royalist commander. Born in Caernarfonshire. Knighted in 1644 by Charles I, at which time he was governor of Harlech. In 1648, at Caernarfon, he attemped a last uprising for Charles I but was defeated at Llandegai. He retired to Anglesey, where in 1659 he headed another uprising.

Owen, Robert (1771–1858). Social reformer born at Newtown (museum). He early made his name as an efficient yet humane cotton mill manager, and is most associated with the New Lanark mills in Scotland of which he became manager and part owner. Here, for a labour force of 2000 including 500 children, he built improved housing, opened a cost price store, and started the first infant school in Britain. Later (1825), impatient over government lack of support for his plans for industrial reform and for self-contained communities, he founded New Harmony in Indiana USA, but this failed and Owen lost most of his money. On his return to England he was accepted as the workers' leader and became much involved in the growth of trade unionism, as also in such fields as education and marriage law reform. His four sons all settled in America, the eldest sitting in Congress and achieving many social reforms. Buried at Newtown.

Patti, Adelina Juana Marina (1843–1919). American singer. She made her first appearance in 1859 in New York as Lucia in 'Lucia di Lammermoor'. Sang at Covent Garden in 1861, soon becoming world famous. Her marriage at Brecon in 1898, her third, was to the Swedish Baron Cederström. She bought her home at Craig-y-Nos in 1878.

Pelagius (c 360–c 420). British theologian who may have spent his early years at the monastery at Bangor-is-y-Coed. For the rest of his life he was in Rome, Africa, and Palestine. The main plank of his philosophy was the freedom of the human will, as opposed to the current official doctrine of original sin. His views were spread largely through the enthusiasm of his younger and bolder Italian friend Coelestius. In 429 St. Germanus, Bishop of Auxerre, was sent to Britain to combat the heresy, which later was also a source of worry to St. David.

Pennant, Thomas (1726–98). Traveller, naturalist, and prolific writer. Native of Downing, near Holywell, his first publication (1750) was an account of an earthquake felt here. He made tours of Scotland in 1769 and 1772, and, as a result, published 'Tour in Scotland' and 'Flora Scotica'. His 'Tour in Wales', written as the result of several journeys, was published in 1778.

Philips, Katharine (1631–64), Poetess. She made her home (The Priory, Cardigan) a centre of a Society of Friendship, the members of which addressed one another by romantic names, she being Orinda, to which her admirers prefixed 'matchless'. It was she who pressed Jeremy Taylor to write his discourse on friendship.

Poyer, John (died 1649). In 1642, as mayor of Pembroke, he sided with Parliament. In 1648, alleging that Parliament had not repaid moneys he had disbursed on its behalf and that he had had to pay his soldiers out of his own pocket, he declared for the King and was joined by Laugharne who had similar grievances. The pair were defeated at St. Fagans and Cromwell battered Pembroke into surrender. In 1649 Poyer, Laugharne and a Colonel Powell were sentenced to death, but Cromwell decided that only one of the trio, to be chosen by lot, should die. Poyer lost, and was shot in London's Covent Garden.

Rees, Abraham (1743–1825). Encyclopaedist. Between 1778–88 he published a revised and expanded edition of Ephraim Chambers's 'Cyclopaedia' (shortened title), claiming to have added over 4400 new articles.

Repton, Humphry (1752–1818). Landscape gardener, in Wales responsible for Plas Newydd. Although a follower of 'Capability' Brown, he was far less rigid in his attitude, maintaining that the house must always be the principal factor in a design and that the gardens should be subordinate.

Richard II. See under Bolingbroke.

Richard, Henry (1812–88). Native of Tregaron. His lifelong theme was the need for arbitration in international disputes, these principles first being made public in a speech in London in 1845. From 1845–88 he was secretary of the Peace Society, as such attending a series of international conferences. He also did much for Wales, serving as representative for Merthyr and becoming known as the 'Member for Wales'.

Roberts, Samuel (1800–85). Social and political reformer, and leader of Nonconformist opinion. Advocate of free trade, franchise extension, Catholic emancipation, and temperance. He was also active in fighting for special railway routes through Wales. In 1827 he advocated a system of inland penny post, and in 1883 his efforts at general postal reform were recognised by an official testimonial and award. Between 1857–67 he was in America, with his brother Richard, preaching racial equality.

Rowlands, John. See Stanley, HM.

Scott, George Gilbert (1811–78). Controversial architect, widely associated with cathedral and church restoration, his work in Wales including St. Asaph's, Bangor, Brecon and St. David's cathedrals. The criticism was made that he remodelled rather than restored, and it is ironic that it was his work that to a great extent led to the founding (by William Morris) of the Society for the Protection of Ancient Buildings (1877). His sons George (1839–1907) and J. Oldrid (1842–1913) and his grandson Giles (1880–1960) were all distinguished architects.

Scott, Robert Falcon (1868–1912). Leader of Antarctic expeditions in 1900–04 and 1909–12, on the latter occasion reaching the South Pole, only to find that he had been forestalled by Amundsen. He and his companions all died during the return sledge journey. His companions included Petty Officer Evans, whose home was Rhossili on Gower.

Shelley, Percy Bysshe (1792–1822), Poet. Shelley was in Wales on and off between 1811–13. The first occasion was a visit to his cousin Thomas Grove at Cwm Elan near Rhayader, after his expulsion from Oxford because of his pamphlet 'The Necessity of Atheism'. Soon after, he eloped with the schoolgirl Harriet Westbrook, marrying her in Scotland, and then moving to Wales, staying (April–June 1812) near Cwm Elan at Nant Gwyllt where Shelley hoped to establish an aesthetic community. Both places are now submerged below the Elan reservoirs. Later Shelley and Harriet moved to Tan-yr-Allt, scene of the Tremadog incident. After this they were briefly at Gwynfryn near Criccieth. In 1814 Shelley virtually deserted Harriet when he fell in love with Mary Godwin, and in 1817 Harriet drowned herself in London's Serpentine. Shelley then married Mary Godwin (as Mary Shelley, author of 'Frankenstein'), but in 1822 he too died by drowning in a storm at sea off Italy.

Simon de Montfort (c 1200–65). Born in France, youngest son of Simon IV de Montfort, leader of the Albigensian Crusade. Came to England in 1230, becoming a powerful figure during the reign of Henry III, with whom however he had constant quarrels, culminating in his rebellion of 1263 in which he defeated and captured the king and his son, the future Edward I, and then set up an early form of parliamentary system. However Edward escaped and in 1265 defeated and killed de Montfort in battle at Evesham.

Stanhope, Lady Hester (1776–1839). Niece of William Pitt, she from time to time acted as the statesman's private secretary. In 1810 she suddenly left England and settled on Mount Lebanon, where through a combination of sheer personality and careful fostering of the local belief that she had the gift of divination, she achieved a position of almost absolute authority over the Druse tribe.

Stanley, Sir Henry Morton (1841–1904). African explorer. Born John Rowlands at Denbigh, he was placed in St. Asaph workhouse at the age of six. Nine years later he ran away and sailed as a cabin boy to America where he was adopted by Henry Morton Stanley. During the American Civil War he served in the Confederate army, later travelling across America and becoming a recognised descriptive writer. After travels in Asia Minor and Tibet, and after being first with the news of the fall of Magdala in Abyssinia, he was commissioned by Gordon Bennet of the New York Herald to go to Africa to find David Livingstone. In this he succeeded in 1871. Later, he traced the course of the Congo and discovered the Mountains of the Moon. Knighted in 1899.

Stephenson, Robert (1803–59). Engineer. Surveyed the Stockton and Darlington railways. His monument in Wales is the Conwy tubular railway bridge. His similar bridge across Menai Strait was burnt in 1970.

Street, George Edmund (1824–81). Architect and architectural writer. His preference was the Gothic style and he specialised in ecclesiastical buildings.

Taylor, Jeremy (1613–67). Divine, writer, and Royalist. As a Royalist he lost his rectorship of Uppingham and was later captured at Cardigan. After this he found refuge as private chaplain to Richard Vaughan, 2nd Earl of Carbery, at the latter's mansion of Golden Grove near Llandeilo. Taylor's perhaps best known work is 'Golden Grove; or a Manuall of daily prayers and letanies' (1655). His 'Discours of the Nature, Offices, and Measures of Friendship' (1657) was written on the prompting of Katharine Philips ('matchless Orinda') of Cardigan. Taylor was imprisoned in 1654–55, a second time in 1655 at Chepstow, and in the Tower in 1657–58, on all occasions apparently because of his episcopal views rather than simply as a Royalist. At the Restoration he was made Bishop of Down, Connor and Dromore (in Ireland) and also Vice Chancellor of the University of Dublin. His second wife, Joanna Bridges, born at Mandinam, was said to have been a natural child of Charles I.

Telford, Thomas (1757–1834). Scottish civil engineer, specially known for his canals (Caledonian in Scotland), roads, and many still surviving bridges. In Wales his main achievements were what is now the A5 road, the Menai and Conwy bridges, and the Pontcysyllte aqueduct.

Thrale, Hester Lynch (1741–1821). Writer and social figure. Born near Pwllheli. Best known as the friend of Dr Johnson, a frequent resident of her house at Streatham, London, which became a regular meeting place for many distinguished people of the time. After her husband's death (he was a Southwark brewer) she married Gabriele Piozzi, an Italian musician, living at Brynbella near St. Asaph where Piozzi died. His widow then retired to Bath where she died soon after celebrating her 80th birthday with a ball for over 600 people. She wrote poems, essays, letters etc., and also much about Johnson, including 'Anecdotes of the late Samuel Johnson'.

Trevithick, Richard (1771–1833). Engineer and inventor. In 1801 his road locomotive became the first ever to pull a load of passengers by steam, and in 1804 he was active in Wales with tramroad steam locomotives.

Vaughan, Henry (1622–95). Poet and mystic. Self-styled 'The Silurist' because the tribe of the Silures had inhabited the part of Wales in which he lived (Brecon area). A Royalist, he fought at Rowton Moor. As a poet he is known for his mystical view of nature and his works are thought to have influenced Wordsworth. Henry Vaughan's twin brother was Thomas, who gained some repute as an alchemist and poisoned himself with fumes of mercury.

Whistler, Rex (1905–44). Painter, decorator, and stage designer. Killed in action in Normandy while serving in the Welsh Guards. Among his works are the decorations in the restaurant of London's Tate Gallery (1926–27) and those at Plas Newydd (1937). He did stage designs for Covent Garden, Sadler's Wells, and C.B. Cochran revues.

Williams, John (1582–1650). Archbishop of York. Native of Conwy. During the Civil War he held Conwy for the King whom he afterwards joined at Oxford. Later, on discoverng that Sir John Owen, now at Conwy, had on the King's orders seized some property which had been entrusted to his care, Williams went over to Parliament and helped Mytton to take Conwy in 1646.

Williams, William Charles (died 1915). Able Seaman, Victoria Cross. Native of Chepstow (memorial). In the Dardanelles, while helping to move lighters to the shore, he stood firm under continuous fire holding on to a vital line until he was killed. Described by his commander as 'the bravest sailor I have ever met'.

Williams-Ellis, Sir Clough (1883–1978). Welsh architect and landscape designer, best known for his creation of Portmeirion. Won Military Cross during First World War. Chairman of Stevenage New Town Corporation. Knighted in 1972. His style is generally Classical and Georgian. A vigorous conservationist, he wrote several books.

Wilson, Richard (1714–82). Welsh-born landscape painter. An original member of the Royal Academy where he exhibited until 1780. His work was not appreciated until after his death and he lived in London in some poverty until his brother's death brought him a small property near Mold (Plas Colomendy).

Yale, Elihu (1649–1721). Born near Boston, Mass. In 1672 he went to India, becoming governor of Madras. On his return to England he became known for the generosity with which he gave away the books, etc, he had collected. After being invited to help a struggling college in America, Yale sent off a cargo of books, pictures, etc., the sale of which raised so much that it was decided to give his name to the new college building at Newhaven. In 1745 the whole institution became Yale University. Buried at Wrexham, the family home.

PRACTICAL INFORMATION

Wales is an integral part of the United Kingdom (there is no formal border) and so far as day-to-day practical matters are concerned—postal, currency, health, bank and shop hours, public holidays and suchlike—practice in Wales is essentially the same as in England (see 'Blue Guide England') which for virtually all overseas visitors will be the United Kingdom port of entry and in which they are likely to spend some time before moving on to Wales. The Practical Information text below therefore covers only matters specific to Wales.

Before Departure

Weather and Touring Season. In general the weather in Wales is much as in England; changeable, with only rare occasions of extreme heat or cold. The main touring season spans from Easter into October. July and August can be crowded months; nevertheless even during these months it is perfectly possible to enjoy many out-of-the-way roads and districts. From most points of view May, June and September are best for comfortable touring.

Advance Information. Outside Wales, the Wales Tourist Board (WTB; see below) is represented by the *British Tourist Authority* with offices world-wide and including Australia (Sydney); Belgium (Brussels); Brazil (Rio); Canada (Toronto); Denmark (Copenhagen); France (Paris); Germany (Frankfurt); Ireland (Dublin); Italy (Rome); Japan (Tokyo); Mexico (Mexico City); Holland (Amsterdam); New Zealand (Auckland); Norway (Oslo); Singapore; Spain (Madrid); Switzerland (Zurich); USA (Atlanta, Chicago, Los Angeles, New York).

In London there is the convenient *British Travel Centre* (12 Regent Street, London, SW1Y 4PQ. Tel. 0171-409-0969). Here there is a section devoted to Wales and offering a generous choice of literature as also travel and accommodation booking facilities.

Disabled Visitors. Wales Tourist Board in conjunction with Wales Council for the Disabled publish 'Accessible Wales. A Guide for Visitors with Disabilities'.

Getting to Wales. As noted above, virtually all overseas visitors will reach Wales by way of England. Notes on road and rail approaches from England are included below under the headings Road Travel and Rail Travel.

Organisations

Local Government. Counties. The counties of Wales, originally a historic 13, were in 1974 merged to become eight. Now (1995)—with April 1995 to April 1996 serving as a transition period—the eight counties are to increase to some 20 unitary or all-purpose authorities, designated as either rural counties or urban county boroughs. Counties are primarily concerned with the provision of local services; Wales's tourist services infrastructure, how ever, remains based on the Wales Tourist Board and other organisations described below.

Wales Tourist Board (WTB). Among its several responsibilities the Board operates information centres throughout Wales, several of which are open all year and all of which are open from about Easter to September or October. All centres are well provided with both general and local publications, and the great majority will book both local accommodation as also accommodation throughout Wales (Book-a-bed-ahead).

Wales Tourist Board publishes both directly and indirectly a wide range of literature, some of it free, some priced. Titles and scope vary to reflect public demand and a list of current titles can be requested from Wales Tourist Board, Department WB, Davis Street, Cardiff, CF1 2FU.

Head Office. Wales Tourist Board, Brunel House, 2 Fitzalan Road, Cardiff, CF2 1UY. Tel. 01222-499909.

North Wales Tourism Ltd, 77 Conway Road, Colwyn Bay, LL29 7LN. Tel. 01492-531731.

Mid Wales Tourism Ltd, Canolfan Owain Glyndwr, Machynlleth, SY20 8EE. Tel. 01654-702653.

Tourism South Wales Ltd, Pembroke House, Phoenix Way Enterprise Park, Swansea, SA7 9DB. Tel. 01792-781212.

London. Wales Information Bureau, British Travel Centre, 12 Regent Street, London, SW1Y 4PQ. Tel. 0171-409-0969.

Outside the United Kingdom the Board is represented by the British Tourist Authority (see Advance Information above).

Cadw: Welsh Historic Monuments, Brunel House, 2 Fitzalan Road, Cardiff, CF2 1UY. Tel. 01222-465511. Cadw—the word meaning to conserve—protects and presents the built heritage of Wales and carries out the Secretary of State's responsibilities for ancient monuments, for grant-aiding archaeological rescue and for grants to owners of historic buildings. A membership scheme, 'Heritage in Wales', allows free access to all Cadw sites and also reduced price access to sites in the care of similar English and Scottish organisations. Membership cards (with a 'Heritage in Wales' membership pack), valid for one calendar year, can be bought from Cadw or from most Cadw sites. Illustrated guide books are available for most sites (catalogue, with order form, from above address or telephone), and throughout the summer there are programmes of events.

Forest Enterprise (FE; Victoria House, Victoria Terrace, Aberystwyth, SY23 2DQ. Tel. 01970-612367). is one of the two divisions of the Forestry Commission, the other being Forest Authority, concerned with departmental matters. Forest Enterprise is in evidence throughout much of Wales, important parts of its work being the provision of information and also recreational facilities such as visitor centres, picnic sites, forest drives, forest trails and camping and caravan sites. Trails, of varying length (two miles is about average), usually start from parking and picnic sites and make a round. For many trails leaflets are available, but not necessarily at the site itself (although 'honesty boxes' are increasingly being installed) and visitors planning to enjoy FE facilities are advised to start by going to the nearest information centre. Two leaflets (free)—Forests of North Wales; Forests of South Wales—can be requested by post from the above address; these leaflets, with small maps, locate forests and summarise walks and facilities. Also free, Camping and Caravan Sites; Cabins and Holiday Houses; Conservation; Recreation in your Forests.

Forest Enterprise also issues a wide range of priced publications, a free catalogue of which can be obtained from the above address. These publications are available through leading booksellers and most FE information centres. The Forest Guides, containing a wealth of information and written in readable non-technical style, can be recommended.

FE Visitor Centres at Betws-y-Coed (Rte 6C); Coed-y-Brenin (Rte 16); Bwlch Nant-yr-Arian (Rte 23A); Gwarnant (Rte 26B); Afon Countryside Centre (Rte 35); Cwmcarn (Rte 37E).

The **National Trust** (NT) was founded in 1895 by a group of people who foresaw the threats arising from increasing population, spreading industry, and inadequate planning. The group's aim was to set up a body of private citizens willing to act as trustees for the nation in the acquisition and ownership of land and buildings worthy of permanent preservation. Only 12 years later, under the National Trust Act of 1907, Parliament gave the Trust the right to declare its land inalienable, this meaning that today the majority of the Trust's properties cannot be sold or compulsorily acquired. The Trust is in no way a government department, but a charity supported mainly by the subscriptions of its members and by the contributions of visitors to Trust properties. Members have free access to all properties including those of the National Trust for Scotland. In Wales the Trust owns or protects many, often extensive, areas of countryside and coast, to most of which there is free public access. It also owns several small and large buildings, including a number of great houses, complete with their original decoration, furniture, and pictures.

The Trust may be joined at most of its properties, or by application to the Membership Department, National Trust, PO Box 39, Bromley, BR1 1NH. Tel. 0181-464-1111. Other addresses:

Headquarters: 36 Queen Anne's Gate, London, SW1H 9AS. Tel. 0171-222-9251.

North Wales: Trinity Square, Llandudno, LL30 2DE. Tel. 01492-860123.

South Wales: The King's Head, Bridge Street, Llandeilo, SA19 6BB. Tel. 01558-822800.

The **Countryside Council for Wales** (CCW), absorbing the functions of the former Nature Conservancy Council and the Countryside Commission, is accountable to the Secretary of State for Wales. In general terms the Council is charged with conserving the natural features and wildlife of Wales at the same time providing opportunities for public access and enjoyment. The Council also has specific responsibilities for National Parks, Areas of Outstanding Natural Beauty, Country Parks, Heritage Coasts, and Long Distance Routes (such responsibilities including designation; advice on planning and management; the development of paths, bridleways, picnic sites, car parks and suchlike) while also providing specialist advice to government departments, local authorities, voluntary organisations and interested individuals pursuing countryside management projects with or without grant aid.

One of the Council's statutory functions is the establishment, maintenance and management of Nature Reserves. Although generally responsible for such reserves, the Council does not necessarily own them, and in some cases leases them to, for example, local naturalists' trusts. A number of the more important reserves are mentioned in this Guide. For several such there is open or partially open access, but in other cases access is only by permit. For many reserves there are interpretive booklets and nature trail leaflets. These will sometimes be available at reserves or local information centres, but anyone wishing to visit reserves is advised to write first to the appropriate CCW regional office, i.e. *North Wales*: Hafod Elfyn, Ffordd Penrhos, Bangor, LL57 2LQ. *Mid Wales*: Plas Gogerddan, Aberystwyth, SY23 3EE. *South Wales*: 44 The Parade, Roath, Cardiff, CF2 3UH. General information (including leaflets, posters, maps) from Countryside Council for Wales, Headquarters Offices, Plas Penrhos, Ffordd Penrhos, Bangor, LL57 2LQ.

The **Welsh Development Agency**, set up in 1976, undertakes the inter-related functions of land reclamation, environmental improvements, the provision of industrial estates, and encouragement and financial backing for industry. To the visitor the Agency's work will be most apparent in the measures designed to treat the industrial scars of the past, especially in The Valleys (see beginning of Rte 37).

The **National Gardens Scheme** publishes annually a guide to gardens open to visitors on certain days throughout the year, the entry fees going principally to charities supporting nursing. The guide can be bought from March onwards from leading booksellers.

Travel, Accommodation, Food and Drink

Road Travel. Within Wales there is only one trunk motorway, this (M4) running roughly with the south coast. Other roads, the main ones increasingly trunk dual carriageway, are of general British Isles standard, but smaller roads in some areas are hilly and twisting. Main road passes such as Llanberis (1169ft. Rte 8A) or Bwlch Oerddrws (1178ft. Rte 20A) should present no problems, but the road across Bwlch-y-Groes (1790ft. Rte 20B) is in large part narrow and steep. Some of the remoter places mentioned in this book are accessible only by narrow lanes, not always suitable for large cars.

The principal road approaches to Wales are, in the *North*, A55 from Chester, running the breadth of the north of the country through Conwy to Bangor on the Menai Strait. Known as the North Wales Expressway, this largely dual-carriageway road bypasses many towns and is making increasing use of tunnels, the latest being below the Conwy estuary. In the *Centre*, Telford's A5 from Shrewsbury serves Llangollen and Betws-y-Coed before crossing the Menai Strait for Anglesey and Holyhead; or, farther south, M50 from Tewkesbury becomes A40 just short of the Welsh border, thence continuing through Monmouth, Brecon and Carmarthen into the Pembroke peninsula. In the *South*, M4 from London crosses the Severn and then roughly parallels the south coast. (Note: A second and wider Severn estuary bridge, some three miles downstream of the original, will when opened in 1996 become the M4 while the original bridge will become M48, the two roads merging west of Chepstow). Between all the above principal road approaches, there is a big choice of smaller roads.

Express Coach Services to Wales from most major centres in England and Scotland are operated by National Express Ltd, Ensign Court, 4 Vicarage Road, Edgbaston, Birmingham, B15 3ES. Telephone enquiries to London (0171-730-0202); or Bristol (01177-954-1022); or Cardiff (01222-344751 or 371331); or Swansea (01792-470820). Within Wales, coach services are operated by local companies. Crossville (helplines at Aberystwyth, Tel. 01970-617951. Bangor, Tel. 01248-370295. Swansea, Tel. 01792-

475511) operates the useful Traws Cambria service, with daily south–north and return links between Cardiff and (northwest) Bangor and (northeast) Chester.

Rail Travel. The main line for *North Wales* is from London (Euston), via Crewe and Chester, the line then following the north coast to cross the Menai Strait for Holyhead. Off this line there are branch services from Hawarden to Wrexham, and from Llandudno Junction to Betws-y-Coed and Blaenau Ffestiniog. The main lines for *Central Wales* are from Shrewsbury, one heading more or less due west for Aberystwyth or Aberdyfi, linking to the scenic coastal line (Cambrian Coast Railway) which makes its leisurely way northwards around Cardigan Bay to Barmouth, Harlech, Porthmadog and Pwllheli; while the other line (from Craven Arms) meanders southwest across the Heart of Wales (the name of the line) to Llanelli and Swansea. The main line for *South Wales* is from London (Paddington) through the Severn Tunnel to Cardiff, Swansea and Fishguard. Off this line branch services include from Newport to Abergavenny and Hereford; from Newport and Cardiff up The Valleys; from Whitland to Pembroke Dock; and from Clarbeston Road to Haverfordwest and Milford Haven.

Proposed privatisation—if, when, and however implemented—is likely to bring significant change.

Accommodation. Hotel and other accommodation is of the range of standards to be found elsewhere throughout the British Isles, and establishments are listed, described and graded in the usual choice of general and specialised publications, these including those directly or indirectly published by Wales Tourist Board and usually covering, as individual volumes, Hotels, Guesthouses and Farmhouses; Bed and Breakfast; Self Catering.

Accommodation of all kinds can be much in demand during the main holiday season. Reservations can be made in several ways, these including direct; through Holidays Wales Ltd, 149 St. Helen's Road, Swansea, SA1 4DF. Tel. 01792-645555; or, at a late stage, by using the Book-a-bed-ahead facility available at most Tourist Information centres.

Food and Drink *Food*. Welsh lamb is famous, and many visitors will also enjoy local salmon, trout (including sewin, a sea trout found only in Welsh waters) and seafood, as also local cheeses of which Wales boasts some 40 varieties. As to Welsh specialities, mention may be made of Laver Bread (bara lawr), misleadingly named since laver, or lawr, is a form of seaweed; traditional flat welshcakes; a fruit loaf known as bara brith (speckled bread); a shallow fruit cake called teisen lap; of cawl, a thick soup which includes meat, root vegetables and leeks; and of the cockles from Penclawdd, on the north shore of Gower. Recently, too, there has been increasing interest in traditional Welsh recipes, several of which feature in the Taste of Wales publication 'Wales—Good Eating Guide'. The aim of the Taste of Wales scheme is to promote Welsh foods; members of the scheme are listed in the above guide and their establishments display the Taste of Wales sign (red dragon on a green background).

As regards *Drink*, there are Welsh whiskies and beers, and also, perhaps surprisingly, Welsh wines, while visitors travelling Rte 6B can sample the water of Trefriw Wells.

Outdoor Pursuits

Wales is well known for the scope of outdoor activities it offers and a choice of Wales Tourist Board, local authority, Forest Enterprise and other publications cover such activities both broadly and specifically. For Wales Tourist Board publications, apply Wales Tourist Board, Department WB, Davis Street, Cardiff, CF1 2FU. For Forest Enterprise publications, apply Victoria House, Victoria Terrace, Aberystwyth, SY23 2DQ. Walking and climbing, riding (pony trekking) and beach activities are the most popular.

Walks and Climbs. Virtually all Wales is walking or climbing country, the choice extending from short and simple strolls along a river or canal bank to the ascent of mountains such as Snowdon and Cader Idris. And within this span there is also a wide variety, many walks being in one way or another specialist, e.g. nature trails; forest trails; archaeological trails, including industrial archaeology; walks or climbs tackling high, lonely or difficult terrain demanding a prudent approach and the use of special clothing and equipment; walks or climbs with, for the unwary or foolhardy, hazards such as hidden mine shafts, rusting machinery or even discarded explosive. There is even an Owen Glendower walk.

This Guide, while indicating the better-known areas, and even some individual walks within them, can only touch the fringe of an activity which in its own right is the subject of a library of specialised maps and literature. As noted above, Wales Tourist Board and Forest Enterprise, as also, and often more fully, local authorities, publish walking and climbing information, while two guides by David Perrott and Laurence Main (John Bartholomew and Son. 'Walk Snowdon and North Wales' and 'Walk South Wales and the Wye Valley') each detail some 40 walks with accompanying maps and notes on, for instance, rights of way, history, legend, natural history and useful addresses.

Riding (Pony Trekking). Much of Wales is ideal for pony trekking, a holiday activity which is becoming increasingly popular, whether simply for a half-day or for a week or longer. The Wales Trekking and Riding Association (Standby House, 9 Nevill Street, Abergavenny, NP7 5AA. Tel. 01873-858717) approves the standards of the many centres listed in their 'Discovering Wales on Horseback', and WTB's brochure 'Wales—Britain's Activity Country' includes a section on Riding and Trekking Holidays.

Beaches. With some 750 miles of varied coastline facing north, west and south, Wales can offer virtually every kind of beach and beach background, ranging from the sands of the popular resorts to remote open sweeps, hidden coves, and beaches below towering cliffs. Wales Tourist Board's three regional guides (North, Mid and South Wales) include special sections on beaches, with notes on their characteristics (sand, shingle, safety, facilities etc.).

Other Pursuits. WTB free brochure 'Wales—Britain's Activity Country' provides information on specialised activity holidays under such headings as Adventure, Educational, Rambling, Riding and Trekking, Shooting and Water Sports. The brochure includes a useful Quick Reference Guide and accompanying map.

The Welsh Language

By *V. Eirwen Davies* BA and *Gwerfyl Moss* BA

The Welsh Language belongs to the Celtic branch of the Indo-European family. Goidelic developments of Celtic are Scottish Gaelic, Irish or Erse, and Manx; Brythonic developments are Welsh, Cornish and Breton. It seems probable that Welsh was already spoken in the 6C, at the time of the emigration to Brittany, and the earlier verse material found in Welsh may contain 6C elements, afterwards modified. A few glosses of the 9–11C are known, as also some poems which probably belong to the same period. The tales usually called 'Mabinogion' are known in 12C and 13C redactions, but there were certainly much earlier forms. The works of many of the bards of the 12C, with a few compositions even going back to perhaps the 9C, have been preserved, and from those times to this a vast amount of literature has been produced.

Welsh is phonetically written, each letter having one sound, except for *Y* which has two.

Consonants. Generally consonants are pronounced as in English, but *c* and *g* are always hard as in *cat* and *gun*, *ch* is pronounced as in the Scottish *loch*, *f* as *v*, *th* as in *sympathy*, *dd* as the *th* in *though*, *ff* as in *four*, and *ph* as in *phrase*. There is no real equivalent to the Welsh *ll* though the tl as in *Bentley* or *Pentland* is close; the true sound can be produced by placing the tip of the tongue against the front teeth and emitting the breath sharply without voice.

The consonants *j*, *k*, *v*, *x* and *z* are absent from Welsh. *W* and *i* can be both vowels and consonants, in the latter case corresponding to the *w* in *well* and the *y* in *yes*. Examples are *wedi* (after) and *iar* (hen).

Vowels. The vowels *a*, *e*, *i*, *o*, *w*, when long, are pronounced as the vowel sounds in *far*, *glare*, *meet*, *more* and *fool*; and when short as in *cat*, *get*, *pin*, *hot* and *took*. The vowel *u* is sounded as the Welsh long i in South Wales, but in North Wales it is more akin to the French u or German ü, both produced with rounded lips. In monosyllables (except as noted below) and final syllables y has the same sound as the Welsh *u* (known as clear sound), but the y heard in non-final syllables is pronounced as in English *sun* (known as obscure sound). Thus the Welsh word *Cymry* (the Welsh) embraces the two sounds and is pronounced as in English Kum-ree. Although monosyllables, the following y words are all pronounced as the *u* in the English *sun* …y and yr (the), *fy* (my), *dy* (thy, your), *myn* (by), and some borrowings such as *syr* (sir) and *ffrynt* (front).

Diphthongs. *Ae, ai, aw, ew, iw, yw, wy, oe, oi*, and *ou* are pronounced by giving the two letters their individual proper sounds in fairly rapid succession, but tending to stress the first sound more than the second. *Ei, eu* and *ey* are pronounced as in the English *eye*, and *ow* as in the English *cowl*. Generally, in monosyllables (e.g. *pwy* = who, *mwy* = more), *wy* is produced by imitating the English *oo* with *ee*, but with some stress on the w. Sometimes the sounds of wy are distinguished by a circumflex. For instance, in gwyr (knows) it is the w sound that is stressed, whereas in gwyr (men) it is the clear-sound y.

Accent. The accent falls regularly on the penultimate syllable except in the case of contractions when it falls on the ultimate and is sometimes indicated by an acute accent (caniatáu = to permit) or by a circumflex (caniatâd = permission).

Mutations ('In the Celtic languages, a change of an initial consonant, depending on the character of the preceding word'—Shorter Oxford English Dictionary). Mutations occur, medially and radically, in many grammatical constructions. Depending, usually, on the preceding word, the initial consonants of the word that follows will sometimes change, and knowledge of these sound changes, or mutations, is essential to a proper understanding of Welsh (recommended grammar: 'Teach Yourself Living Welsh' by T.J. Rhys Jones, Hodder and Stoughton). Mutations often make it difficult for the layman even to derive a meaning from a dictionary since the Welsh word must be sought under its (to the uninitiated probably unknown) radical form rather than under the mutated form in which it is likely to be met. In the Glossary below, mutated forms are given for several words often forming part of place names.

Articles. There is no indefinite article in Welsh. The article is y, yr (before a vowel), 'r (after a vowel). For example, y *cartref* (the home), yr *afal* (the apple), o'r *ty* (from the house).

Genders. Welsh recognises only masculine and feminine; there is no neuter. There are no rules, other than that the names of trees are usually feminine.

Plurals. No rules. Plural terminations are *au, on, ion, i, ydd, oedd, edd, ed, od, ant, aint, er* and yr. Plurals may also be formed by internal vowel changes; for example, *bardd* (poet), plural *beirdd*, or *ffon* (stick), plural *ffyn*. Or by both internal vowel change and addition; for example *brawd* (brother), plural *brodyr*, or *cwch* (boat), plural *cychod*, or *gardd* (garden), plural *gerddi*. There are also occasions when endings are dropped in order to form plurals; for example *plentyn* (child), plural *plant*, or *mochyn* (pig), plural *moch*.

Adjectival Termination. The chief adjectival terminations are aid, aidd, ain, ig, as, inol, us, adwy, ys, llyd or lyd, gar.

Glossary

This Glossary is largely, though by no means exclusively, of words associated with place names.

pl = plural. sg. = singular. masc. = masculine. fem. = feminine. dim. = diminutive.
OE = Old English. adj. = adjective. obs. = obsolete.

Aber, Mouth (of a river)
Adar. sg. *aderyn, ederyn*. Birds
Aden, Wing
Adwy, Gap. Pass
Ael, Brow. Headland
Aeron, Fruits
Afanc, Beaver. Monster
Afon, River
Alaw, Water lily (obs.). Tune
Allt, Wooded hill or cliff
Am, Around. About (in compounds)
Amlwg, Visible. Open. Obvious
Ap, Son of
Ar, Bordering on. Upon. High place
Aran, High place. Mountain
Arddu, Very black
Arian, Silver
Aur, Gold
Awst, August (month)

Mutations of B are F and M

Bach, Corner. Retreat. Small
Bala, Efflux of a river from a lake
Ban. pl *bannau*, Height. Mountain. Lofty
Banc, Bank. Hill
Banw, A sow
Bara, Bread
Barclod, Apron
Barwn, Baron
Bedd, Grave
Beddrod, Graveyard
Bedw, Birch tree
Bedwas, Birch grove. Place of birches
Benglog, Mutation of *Penglog* = Head
Berr (fem.), Short
Berw, Building
Betws, Bede-house; probably from
  Anglo-Saxon *bed* (prayer) and house
Blaen, Source. Point. Head of a valley
Boch, Cheek (part of the body)
Bod, Abode. Dwelling
Bon, Stem. Lower end
Bont, Bridge
Braich, Arm
Braith (fem.), Speckled
Bran. pl *brain*, Crow
Bras, Fat. Productive. Great
Bre, Hill
Brig, Summit
Brith (masc.), Speckled
Bro, Vale. Plain
Broch, Badger
Bron, Slope of a hill
Brwyn. sg. *brwynen*, Rushes
Brych, Speckled. Variegated
Bryn, Hill
Bu, Ox

Buarth, Cattle enclosure. Farmyard
Buwch. pl *buchod*, Cow
Bwch. pl *bychod*, Buck
Bwlch. pl *bylchau*, Pass. Defile
Bychan, Small
Byrr (masc.), Short

Mutations of C are G and Ch

Caban, Cabin
Cad, Host. Battle
Cadair. Cader, Chair. Seat. Stronghold
Cadarn. pl *cedyrn*, Mighty
Cadno. Cadnaw, Fox
Cadw, Conserve
Cae, Field
Caer, Fort. Thence, part of town name
Cafn. pl *cafnau*, Trough
Cail, Sheepfold or pen
Cain, Bright. Beautiful
Calan, New Year
Calch, Lime
Cam, Crooked or bent. Footstep or stride.
  Injury or wrong
Camlas, Canal
Canol, Middle. Centre
Cant, One hundred. Rim. Circle
Cantref, A Hundred (medieval division of
  land)
Capel, Chapel
Car, Kinsman. Friend
Carn, Cairn. Stone outcrop
Carnedd. pl *Carneddau, carneddi*, Cairn or
  stone outcrop. Mountain
Carreg. pl *cerrig*, Stone
Carrog, Stream. Brook
Cas, Castle
Caseg. pl *cesig*, Mare
Castell. pl *cestyll*, Castle
Cau, A hollow
Cawl, Soup
Cawr, Giant
Ceann, Head. Top
Ced, Gift
Cefn, Back. Ridge
Cegid, Hemlock
Cegin, Kitchen
Cei, Quay
Celli, Grove
Celyn or *Cellyn* (on some maps), Holly
Cemaes or *Cemais*, Bend (of coast or river)
Ceredigion, Cardigan
Cerrig. sg. *carreg*, Stones
Cesail, Nook
Ceunant, Ravine
Chwech. Chwe, Six
Chwefror, February
Chwith, Left (directional)

Ci. pl *cwn*, Dog
Cil. pl. *ciliau*, Retreat. Nook.QL
Church
Claf, Sick
Clafdy, Hospital
Clawdd. pl *cloddiau*, Ditch. Hedge
Cleddau. Cleddyf, Sword
Clegyr, Rocks. Stones
Cloch. pl *clychau*, Bell
Cloddfa, Pit
Clogwyn, Cliff. Crag
Clos, Close. Small field
Clun, Meadow
Clwyd, Gate. Perch
Clyd, Cosy
Clyder, Sheltered valley
Clywed, To hear (*Clywedog*, a common river
 name meaning the water that can be heard)
Cnicht (OE), Knight
Cob, Dyke
Coch, Red
Coed. sg. *coeden*, Trees. Forest. Woodland
Coes, Leg. Limb
Coetan, Quoit (often used for burial chambers)
Coll. pl *cyll*, Hazel
Coll. Colled, Loss. Slaughter
Cop. Copa, Summit
Cor, Choir. Cowhouse
Corn, Horn
Cornel, Corner
Cors. pl *corsydd*, Bog
Craig. pl *cregiau, creigiau, creigydd*, Rock
Crib. pl *cribau*, Ridge
Croen. pl *crwyn*, Skin
Croes, Cross. Crosswise
Croesffordd, Crossroads
Crog, Cross. Hanging or overhanging
Crom (fem.), Crooked. Bent
Cron (fem.), Round
Crud, Cradle
Crug. pl *crugiau*, Mound
Crwm (masc.), Crooked. Bent
Crwn (masc.), Round
Crwth, Type of musical instrument. Concave
 vessel
Crwyn. sg. *croen*, Skins
Crythor, Minstrel (player on the crwth)
Cul, Narrow
Cut. pl *cutiau, cwt, cytiau*, Hut
Cwm. pl *cymoedd, cymau*, Valley. Cirque
Cwn. sg. *ci*, Dogs
Cwrt, Court
Cwymp, Fall. Slope
Cwys, Furrow
Cyff, Stem. Trunk
Cyfyng, Narrow
Cymer. Cymmer, Confluence
Cymraeg, The Welsh Language
Cymru, Wales
Cymry, The Welsh
Cyngor. pl *cynghorion*, Advice
Cyngor. pl *cynghorau*, Council
Cyrn. sg. *corn*, Peaks
Cytiau. sg. *Cut*, Huts

Mutations of D are Dd and N

Dafad. pl *defaid*, Sheep

Dan, Under. Below
Dar. pl *deri*, Oak
Dau (masc.). *Deu* (in composition), Two
Deg, Ten. Also Mutation of *Teg* = Fair
Deheu. De, South. Right (directional)
Deheubarth, The southern part
Derw. sg. *derwen*, Oaks
Dewi, David
Diffwys, Precipice
Din. Dinas, Fortification. Thence, part of town
 name
Dir, Mutation of *Tir* = Land
Dol. pl *dolydd, dolau*, Meadow
Dor. pl *dorau*, Door
Dre, Mutation of *Tre* = Homestead
Drem, Mutation of *Trem* = Sight. View
Drud. pl *drudion*, Brave. Mighty
Drum, Ridge
Drwg, Bad. Evil
Drws. pl *drysau*, Pass. Door
Drys, Bramble
Du. Ddu. pl *duon*, Black
Dulas, Black-blue
Duw, God
Dwfr. Dwr. pl *dyfroedd*, Water
Dwy (fem), Two
Dwyf. Dwy, God
Dwyrain, East
Dwyran, Two parts
Dydd Llun, Monday
Dyyd Mawrth, Tuesday
Dydd Mercher, Wednesday
Dydd Iau, Thursday
Dydd Gwener, Friday
Dydd Sadwrn, Saturday
Dydd Sul, Sunday
Dyffryn. pl *dyffrynnoedd*, Valley
Dyfrydog, Unpleasant. Bad
Dyfyrm, To shorten. Curtail
Dyserth. Diserth, A retreat. A place apart
Dysgl, Dish
Dywarch, Mutation of *Tywarch* = Sod. Turf

Ebrill, April
Edwi, To fade. Wither
Efwr, Cow parsnip. Hogweed
Eglwys. pl *eglwysi, eglwysau, eglwysydd*,
 Church
Eifl, Two-pronged. Fork
Einion, Anvil
Eligug, Guillemot
Epynt, Horse-track. Bridleway
Erch, Pale colour. Terrible
Erw, Acre
Esgair, Long ridge. Escarpment
Ewenny. Ewenni, From Aventia, a
 Franco-Celtic goddess

Mutations of F are B and M

Fach, Mutation of *Bach* = Small
Faen, Mutation of *Maen* = Stone. Boulder
Faes, Mutation of *Maes* = Field
Fair, Mutation of *Mair* = Mary
Fal. Fali, Valley
Fan, Mutation of *Ban* = Height. Mountain
Fawn, Mutation of *Mawn* = Peat

Fawr, Mutation of *Mawr* = Large. Great. Extensive
Fechan (fem), Small
Fedw, Mutation of *Bedw* = Birch tree
Felindre, Mutation of *Melin* = Mill
Ferched, Mutation of *Merched* = Women
Ffair, Fair
Ffin, Border. Limit
Fflur, Flowers. Blossom
Ffordd. pl *ffyrdd*, Road
Ffos. pl *ffosydd*, Ditch. Embankment
Ffraw, Rapid. Violent
Ffridd. *Ffrith*, Moorland. Meadows
Ffrwd. pl *ffrydiau*, Stream
Ffynnon, Well. Spring
Fihangel, Mutation of *Mihangel* = Michael
Foel, Mutation of *Moel* = Bare or rounded mountain
Forwyn, Mutation of *Morwyn* = Maiden
Fychan, Mutation of *Bychan* = Small
Fyrddin, Mutation of *Myrddin* = Merlin

Mutated forms of G are C, Ng, or (dropped)

Gadair, Mutation of *Cadair* = Chair. Stronghold
Gaer, Mutation of *Caer* = Fort
Gafr. pl *geifr*, Goat
Gallt, Wooded hill or cliff
Gam, Mutation of *Cam* = Crooked. Footstep. Injury
Ganol, Mutation of *Canol* = Middle. Centre
Gardd, Garden
Garn, Mutation of *Carn* = Cairn. Outcrop
Garreg, Mutation of *Carreg* = Stone
Garth, Hill. Promontory
Gast, Bitch
Gau, False
Gawres, Mutation of *Cawres* = Giantess
Gefail. pl *gefeiliau*, Smithy
Gelli, Mutation of *Celli* = Grove
Gelyn, Enemy
Ger, Near. By
Gerig. *Gerrig*, Mutations of *Cerrig* = Stones
Glan, Edge. Brink. Shore
Glân, Clean
Glas, Blue. Also, in some uses, Green
Gleisiad, Young salmon
Glo, Coal
Gloddfa, Mutation of *Cloddfa* = Pit
Glyder, Mutation of *Clyder* = Sheltered valley
Glyn, Valley. Glen
Gobaith, Hope
Goch, Mutation of *Coch* = Red
Godre, Foot of a hill. Edge
Gogledd, North
Gogof, Cavern
Golau. *Goleu*, Light (illumination)
Gorffennaf, July
Gorllewin, West
Gors, Mutation of *Cors* = Bog
Gorsad, Station
Gris. pl *grisiau*, Step
Gro, Gravel
Groes, Mutation of *Croes* = Cross
Grug, Heather
Gwaelod, Bottom
Gwair, Hay

Gwastad, Level area
Gwaun. pl *gweunydd*, Moorland. Downland
Gwen (fem.), White
Gwern, Alder. Damp meadow
Gwernog, Marshy
Gwig, Haven. Woodland
Gwr, Man. Husband
Gwrach, Witch
Gwrych, Shrubs. Hedge. Bristles
Gwryd, Fathom
Gwy, Water. River Wye
Gwydd, Trees
Gwydd, Goose. Wild
Gwyddelod, The Irish
Gwyddfa, A wild place
Gwyllt, Wild. Savage
Gwyn, White
Gwynt, Wind
Gwyr, Oblique. Slanting
Gwyr, Men
Gwyrdd, Green
Gwyryddon. *Gwyryfon*, Maidens

Haf, Summer
Hafod, Summer residence
Hafren, The river Severn
Hebog, Hawk. Falcon
Heli, Brine
Helyg. *Helig*, Willows
Hen, Old
Hendre, Winter residence
Hengwm, Old valley
Henrhyd, Old ford
Heol, Paved road
Hir, Long. Tall. Tedious
Hiraeth, Longing
Hwylfa, Path. Entry
Hydd, Stag
Hydref, October
Hyll, Ugly

Ifan, Evan. John
Ionawr, January
Isel, is, isaf, Low, lower, lowest

Kil (Gaelic), Retreat. Church

L at the beginning of a word always signifies a mutation
Las, Mutation of *Glas* = Blue. Green
Llaeth, Milk
Llain, Blade. A stretch
Llaith, Damp. Wet. Disease
Llam, Leap
Llan, Enclosed place. Church. Hence a part of many place names
Llanerch, Clearing
Llanfair, Church of Mary
Llaw, Hand
Llawnt, Lawn
Llawr, Floor
Llech, Slate. Flagstone
Llechwedd, Slate slope
Lled, Width
Lleng, Legion
Llethr, Slope
Llew, Lion
Llidiart, Gate
Llif, Flood

Llith, Bait. Lesson
Llithrig, Slippery
Lliw, Colour
Lliwedd (obs.), Troop. Crowd. Nation
Llog, Interest payment. Part of a monastery
Llong, Ship. Damp (fem.)
Llwng, Damp (masc.)
Llwyd, Grey. Brown
Llwyn, Grove. Woodland
Llwynog, Fox
Llychau. sg. *llwch*, Lakes. Muddy marsh
Llydan, Wide
Llygad, Eye
Llyn. pl *llynnoedd, llynnau*, Lake
Llys, Place. Court. Enclosure
Llyw, Rudder. Ruler (a chief)
Llywarn. pl *llewyrn*, Fox

Mutation of M is F

Ma. In compounds *Fa*, Place. Plain
Mab. pl *meibion*, Son
Maen. pl *meini, main*, Stone. Boulder
Maes. pl *meysydd*, Field
Mai, May (month)
Mair, Mary
Mall, Rotten. Evil
Mam, Mother
Man, High place
March. pl *meirch*, Steed
Marian, Beach
Mawn, Peat
Mawr, Great. Big. Extensive
Mawrth, March (month)
Medi, September
Mehefin, June
Mei, Halfway. Centre
Meibion. sg. *mab*, Sons
Meirion. *Meirionydd*, Merioneth
Melin, Mill
Melyn, Yellow
Merch. pl *merched*, Woman. Daughter
Merthyr, Burial place of a saint
Mign, Bog
Mihangel, Michael
Mil, Thousand. Beast
Milwr. pl *milwyr*, Soldier
Min, Edge. Border
Moch. sg. *mochyn*, Pigs. Rapid (adj.)
Moel, Bare or rounded mountain
Môr, Sea
Morfa, Coastal marsh
Morwynion. sg. *morwyn*, Maidens
Mur, Wall
Murddyn, Ruin
Mwd, Mud
Mynach, Monk
Mynydd, Mountain
Myrddin, Merlin
Nadolig, Christmas

Nant. pl *naint, nentydd, nannau*, Valley. Stream
Naw, Nine
Neuadd, Hall
Newydd, New
Nos, Night

Ochr, Side. Slope

Od, Snow
Oer, Cold
Og, Harrow (agricultural)
Ogo. Ogof, Caves
Olau. Oleu, Mutation of *Goleu* = Light
Onn. pl *ynn*, Ash
Or, Border. Rim. Edge

Mutations of P are B, Mh, Ph

Pair, Cauldron
Pant, Hollow ground
Parc, Field. Park
Pasg, Easter
Pedwar, Four
Pell, Far
Pellaf, Farthest
Pen, Head. Top
Penglog, Head, Skull
Penmaen, Rocky headland
Pennant, Upper reaches or head of a valley
Pentre. Pentref, Village. Hamlet
Pig. dim *pigyn*, Point. Summit
Pili-pala, Butterfly
Pinc, Pink
Pistyll, Waterfall. Rapids
Plas, Hall. Mansion. Place
Plynlimon, Five chimneys
Poeth, Hot. Burnt
Pont. pl *pontydd*, Bridge
Porffor, Purple
Porth. pl *pyrth*, Landing place. Port
Pren, Tree. Timber
Pridd, Soil. Earth
Prys. Prysg, Shrubs
Pump, Five
Pwll, Pool

'r (after a vowel), The
Rhaeadr. Rhaiadr. Rhayader (English spelling), Waterfall
Rhagfyr, December
Rhan, Share. Part
Rhewyn, Pool. Gutter. Drain
Rhian. Rhiain, Maiden
Rhiniog. Rhinog (on some maps), Buttress
Rhiw. pl *rhiwiau*, Hill
Rhod, Circle. Wheel
Rhodwydd, Embankment. Earthwork
Rhos, Moorland. Rose
Rhudd, Red. Ruddy
Rhwth, Open. Glaring
Rhyd, Ford
Rhydd, Free
Rhyn, Headland

Saeth, Arrow
Saith, Seven
Sarn, Causeway
Sarthes (obs.), Reptile. Serpent
Sior, George
Skirrid, Anglicisation of *Ysgyryd* = Rugged
Stryt, Street
Sulgwyn, Whitsun
Sych, Dry

Mutations of T are D, Nh, Th

Tachwedd, November
Taf, Dark. Black

Tafarn, Tavern
Tal, Front. Forehead. End. Tall
Tan, Under. Beneath. Fire
Tarw. pl *teirw*, Bull
Teg, Fair. Comely
Teisen, Cake
Teledu, Television
Telyn, Harp
Telynor, Harpist
Teyrn, Monarch. King
Tir. pl *tiroedd*, Land
Tomen, Mound
Ton, Wave. Surface. Green
Torr, Flank
Traeth, Shore
Traffordd, Motorway
Trallwng, Muddy hollow (Welshpool)
Traws, Across
Tre. *Tref*, Habitation. Village
Trem, Sight. View
Tri, Three
Tro, Turn. Bend
Troed. pl *traed*, Foot
Tros, Over
Trothwy, Threshold
Trum, Ridge
Trwyn, Nose. Headland
Try, Very
Tryfan, Very high peak
Tryweryn, Very wet
Tud, People. Country
Twle. *Twlch*, Knoll
Twll, Hollow
Twm, Tom
Twmp, Tump
Twr. pl *tyrau, tyroedd*, Tower
Twrch, Pig. Boar
Twrch daear, Mole
Twt, Tidy. Neat
Ty. pl *tai*, House
Tyddyn, Farmstead
Tylwyth Teg, Fairies

Tyn, Small Farm
Tyrau. sg. *twr*, Towers
Tywarch. pl *tyweirch*, Sod. Turf
Tywyll, Dark
Tywyn, Shore

Uchel, uch, uchaf, High, higher, highest
Uchtryd, Upper ford
Udd, Lord
Un, One
Undeb, Union
Urdd, League. Society

Velindre (frequent but incorrect spelling of
Felindre), Mill

Wastad, Mutation of *Gwastad* = Level area
Wen (fem.), White
Wern, Mutation of *Gwern* = Alder. Damp
    meadow
Wrach, Mutation of *Gwrach* = Witch
Wrth, Near. By
Wyn (masc.), White
Wyth, Eight

Y (before consonants), The
Ych. pl *ychen*, Ox
Yd, Corn
Ym (before m), In
Ymenyn, Butter
Yn, In
Yng (before C), In
Ynys, Island
yr (before vowels), The
Ysbyty. *Yspytty* (on some maps), Hospice
Ysgall. sg. *ysgallen*, Thistles
Ysgol, School
Ysgor, Rampart. Defence
Ysgubor, Barn
Ysgyryd, Rugged
Ystrad, Valley. Strath
Ystryd. pl *ystrydoedd*, Street
Ystum, Shape. Curve
Ystwyth, Pliable. Agile. Winding

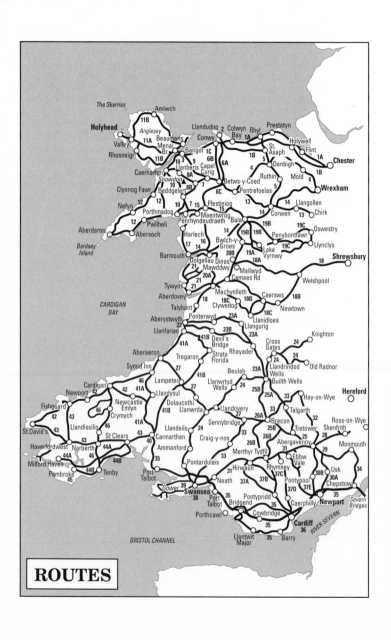

ROUTES

1

Chester to Bangor

As far as Llandudno Junction, a short way east of Conwy, there is a choice of roads, one fringing the coast (Rte 1A), the other running a short way inland (Rte 1B). There are plenty of connecting roads, and in parts both Routes use A55, a fast road (North Wales Expressway) bypassing many places and, after Colwyn Bay, increasingly making use of tunnels to overcome the problems of the hill-backed coast.

As far as Conwy, the coast offers little that is scenic and indeed between Mostyn and Colwyn Bay the stretch is essentially one of popular resorts, caravan parks, holiday camps and, here and there, shoddy building. The inland road is both pleasanter scenically and more interesting; places lying between the two roads are included under this latter Route.

Conwy to Bangor—scenically more interesting along cliffs and with views across to Great Orme and Anglesey—is described as Rte 1C, while Llandudno and its environs are covered as a separate Route (Rte 2). The total distance from Chester to Bangor is some 60 miles.

A. Coastal road to Conwy

A548 to Abergele. A55 to Conwy. Total distance 43m.—*13m*. **Flint**.—*7m*. **Mostyn**.—*6m*. **Prestatyn**.—*3m*. **Rhyl**.—*4m*. **Abergele**.—*6m*. **Colwyn Bay**.— *4m*. **Conwy**.

Chester (see 'Blue Guide England') is left by A548 which, running to the north of the Dee and soon entering Wales, traverses land reclaimed by the embanking of the river in 1752 and in three miles beyond the border turns south to cross the here canalised river at *Queensferry* where the royal ferry of the past has today been replaced by bridges. *Connah's Quay*, just beyond, no longer a port of significance, is said to derive its name from a local publican.

13m. **Flint**, although now a modest enough small town, can boast two historical firsts; it was chosen as the site of the first of Edward I's Welsh fortresses, and the associated borough was the first in Wales to receive a charter (8 September 1284).

The remains of the once formidable *Castle* sprawl over a low rock platform beside the shore (Cadw; see p.11).

History. Begun in 1277, and completed by James of St. George in about 1281, the castle was in 1312 the scene of the meeting between Edward II and his raffish favourite Piers Gaveston on the latter's return from exile in Flanders. Later, in 1399, it may have been here that Richard II met Bolingbroke (soon to be Henry IV), Richard then effectively becoming a prisoner. In Shakespeare's 'Richard II' the cringing king pleads 'What you will have, I'll give, and willing too; For do we must what force will have us do', whereupon, according to the chronicler Froissart, even Richard's favourite hound deserted him to fawn on the upstart. Two and a half centuries later, during the Civil War, Flint was held for Charles I by Sir Roger Mostyn until taken by General Mytton in 1647 and then slighted.

That the castle was once considerably larger than is immediately apparent today may be judged from the remains, on the south side, of an extensive outer ward, separated from the inner castle, as also from the borough, by moats. The main plan is roughly a square with a three-quarter drum-tower at each of three angles. At the southeast angle, outside the main enclosure and separated from it by a moat, is a large circular tower which, with its own well, both served as a keep and commanded the entrance to the inner ward, the link to which was a rampart walk along a wall across the moat.

Beyond Flint the road continues parallel with the railway beside the *Sands of Dee*, at low tide a dreary expanse of sand and mud. Giraldus records that in 1188 he crossed the quicksands near Bagillt 'not without some degree of apprehension'; and in 1637 Edward King, Milton's Cambridge friend, was shipwrecked and drowned here, 'Lycidas' being the poet's contribution to a book of memorial verses. *4m. Greenfield*, at the foot of Greenfield Valley Heritage Park, for which, as also for Basingwerk Abbey and Holywell, both just inland, see Rte 1B (park either here off A548 or, for Basingwerk, off B5121). *3m.* **Mostyn**, though today little more than an industrial strip, can nevertheless claim touches of history. The manor of Mostyn was granted in 1295 to Edward I's architect James of St. George and he probably died there in 1308; it was from Mostyn Hall that the Earl of Richmond (the future Henry VII) escaped from the soldiers of Richard III by leaping from a window; and during the Civil War it was Sir Roger Mostyn who held Flint for Charles I.

6m. **Prestatyn** (*Inf.*) and, *3m* farther, **Rhyl** (*Inf.*) are virtually linked very popular holiday resorts with splendid beaches and plenty of varied, lavish and extrovert entertainment. Prestatyn, geographically and historically at the north end of Offa's Dyke, is cut by the railway, much of the town proper being to the south while the Promenade with the Central Beach entertainment complex and more modest amusement areas to either side is to the north. The principal feature at Central Beach is the *Nova Centre* (open all year. Tel. 01745-888021) which includes pool, fitness facilities, restaurants, Starlight Room and even an Offa's Dyke Interpretative Centre. Rhyl, on the east side of the mouth of the river Clwyd and also cut by the railway, boasts a combined Parade and Marine Drive over two miles long. Among the several attractions along here are the slim *Sky Tower* (Easter–Oct: daily 10.00–17.00 or 20.00. Tel. 01745–331071); the *Sea Life Centre* (daily from 10.00. Tel. 01745-344660); and the *Sun Centre* (Easter–Sept: daily 10.00 or 11.00–22.00. Tel. 01745-344433) for all manner of water-based family entertainment.

Rhyl is left by Foryd Bridge spanning the river Clwyd (for Rhuddlan, St. Asaph and Bodelwyddan, all a short way south, see Rte 1B), to the south now being *Morfa Rhuddlan*, the marsh where in 795 the Welsh under Caradoc were routed by Offa of Mercia. Today the flanking road threads a succession of huge caravan sites and holiday camps.

4m. **Abergele** forms, with *Pensarn* on the coast, a joint resort, modest by comparison to such as Rhyl, Prestatyn and Colwyn Bay but popular with quieter and less demanding families content with a pebble beach which, however, reveals sand as the tide falls.

A55 is now joined, this road running below *Gwrych Castle*, a flamboyant castellated folly of 1815, to reach (*2m*) *Llandulas*, at the mouth of the Dulas, with a church designed by G.E. Street, and traditionally the place at which in 1399 the Earl of Northumberland betrayed Richard II into the hands of Bolingbroke. But it seems more likely that it was on Anglesey that, to quote

David Hume, 'that nobleman, by treachery and false oath, made himself master of the King's person'.

4m. **Colwyn Bay** (*Inf.*) is a straggling resort which has inexorably filled the gap between, on the east, what was once the village of Old Colwyn and, to the west, Llandrillo-yn-Rhos. The beach is served by a length of Promenade with many attractions including, principally, *Eirias Park* with a Leisure Centre, Dinosaur World (Easter–Oct: daily 10.00–18.00. Tel. 01492-518111), picnic and adventure play areas. The very popular *Welsh Mountain Zoo* (daily 09.30–16.00 or 17.00. Tel. 01492-532938), spread through attractive grounds on a wooded hill a mile southwest of the town, is best known for its birds of prey and, weather permitting, their free-flying displays. Colwyn Bay merges with **Rhos-on-Sea**, site of an abbey during the 12C and still preserving St. Trillo's Chapel, a humble little place of venerable if undetermined age built over an ancient holy well (below the foreshore wall in the west of the town; not visible from a car but indicated by a plaque). Here, too, on the seafront, is the Harlequin Puppet Theatre (tel. 01492-548166), Britain's only purpose-built puppet theatre.

For (*2m*) **Llandudno Junction** and, *2m* farther, **Conwy**, as also for the Conwy estuary, see Rte 1B. For **Llandudno**, see Rte 2.

B.   Inland road to Conwy

A483, A55 and B5125 to Hawarden and Northop. A55 for Holywell. A5151 to Rhuddlan. A525 to St. Asaph. B5381 to Llandudno Junction for Conwy. Total distance 48m.—*7m.* **Hawarden.**—*11m.* **Holywell.**—*9m.* **Dyserth.**— *2m.* **Rhuddlan.**—*2m.* **St. Asaph.**—*15m.* **Llandudno Junction.**—*2m.* **Conwy.**

Chester (see 'Blue Guide England') is left by Grosvenor Bridge, A483 and A55 for (*7m*) **Hawarden**, a small place which was for some 60 years the home of W.E. Gladstone (1809–98), the statesman, who in 1839 married the daughter of Sir Stephen Glynne whose family had acquired the Hawarden estate after the Civil War. *Hawarden Castle* (no adm.), Gladstone's home, was started in 1750 and enlarged and castellated by Sir Stephen Glynne in 1809. Although there is no admission to this new castle, there is limited access to the ruins in the park of the historically interesting *Old Castle* (tel. 01244-531547). First a British fort, then in 1264 the scene of a meeting between Simon de Montfort and Llewelyn the Last, the earliest stone structure dates from about 1280 and was briefly held in 1282 by Llewelyn's brother, Dafydd. There was considerable extension some 200 years later, but, after two Civil War sieges, the castle was slighted in 1646. Today, the chief remains are the circular keep and the hall, the whole within a double earthwork. In the town the parish *Church* has a window by Burne-Jones and also a Gladstone Memorial Chapel with marble effigies by W.B. Richmond of Gladstone and his wife, both of whom, however, are buried in Westminster Abbey. Adjacent to the church, *St. Deiniol's Residential Library* provides another link with Gladstone; founded here by him in 1895 for the encouragement of scriptural learning, the library houses large theological collections (tel. 01244-532350).

2m. *Ewloe Castle*, the extensive ruins of a stronghold of Llewelyn the Great and Llewelyn the Last, has as its most interesting feature a well-preserved D-shaped tower of about 1210 in the centre of the upper ward; the rest of the building, including the circular west tower, dates from about 1257, two years after Llewelyn the Last began his campaign to drive out the English and establish his own authority throughout Wales. At (*3m*) *Northop* the church, with an early 16C tower, is said to have been a foundation by Lady Margaret Beaufort. *2m. Halkyn* with, to the west and roughly paralleling the road, the long ridge of Halkyn Mountain (943ft), much scarred by quarries and lead mines, the latter originally worked by the Romans whose Via Antonina from Deva (Chester) to Kanovium (Caerhun) is believed to have used this ridge.

4m. **Holywell** (Trefynnon) owes its name to its well which over perhaps 1000 years up to the Reformation—and continuing later—was a renowned objective of pilgrimage. The well is still here and, together with the adjacent St. Winefride's (or Beaufort) Chapel and the parish church, forms a part of a pleasant compact grouping below the main town on B5121, the road dropping down to the coast.

Legend and History. In the 7C St. Beuno built a chapel (probably on the site of today's parish church), and legend tells that, soon afterwards, Caradoc, a prince of Hawarden, visited here and attempted to rape Winefride, Beuno's niece. She fled towards the chapel, but failed to reach this sanctuary before the thwarted Caradoc slashed off her head. Where the head fell, there at once gushed a spring. Beuno, coming out of the chapel, replaced Winefride's head, the spring nevertheless continuing to flow and the lady living on to become an abbess and a saint whose remains were in 1138 entrusted to the abbey at Shrewsbury. Caradoc, however, was swallowed by the ground.

The well soon became a place of pilgrimage, healing (to quote from a 'Life of St. Winefride' published in 1485) 'al langours and sekenesses as well in men as in bestes'. Among royal pilgrims were Richard I in 1189; Henry V both before and after Agincourt, on the latter occasion reputedly travelling on foot from Shrewsbury; and James II in 1686, the Old Pretender being the result of his prayers for a son. From 1240 to 1537 the well was in the care of the Cistercians of nearby Basingwerk, and when in about 1490 it was decided to build a new chapel (perhaps the first one actually over the well) a principal benefactor was Margaret Beaufort. With the Reformation the well survived destruction, apparently because it was regarded as medicinal, but pilgrimages became dangerous (though not for the Catholic James II) until the advent of the more tolerant 18C. Today the well remains an important Catholic shrine.

St. Winefride's Well (summer: daily 09.00–17.30. Winter: daily 09.30–16.00. Tel. 01352-713054) was long an unfailing spring, but by 1917 mining in the hills above stopped the flow and water has since been chanelled from a reservoir. The spring is within a polygonal basin in what now forms the crypt of the chapel, adjacent being a medieval bath in which St. Beuno's Stone is supposed to be the stone on which Beuno sat while instructing Winefride. Custom is that pilgrims pass three times through the inner well (perhaps because of a prayer written by a 12C prior of Shrewsbury that pilgrims might have their wishes granted at least at the third time, but more likely deriving from the Celtic practice of triple immersion) and then kneel on St. Beuno's Stone to complete their devotions. The figure of St. Winefride dates from 1888.

St. Winefride's (Beaufort) Chapel (key from Well ticket office) is a notable example of Perpendicular architecture with a wealth of stone and wood carving, this including an external frieze of beasts, both real and mythical. The nearby *Church of St. James*, built in 1770, is last in a long succession on this site, starting perhaps with St. Beuno's original chapel and including possibly two medieval churches from the last of which a 15C tower survives.

Greenfield Valley Heritage Park (parking off B5121), the wooded valley linking Holywell with the ruins of Basingwerk Abbey, was in the 18 and

19C busy with newly-established industry, and today the course of the old railway provides a pleasant trail passing some modest industrial monuments and also Abbey Farm Museum and Visitor Centre (Easter–Oct: daily 10.00–17.00. Tel. 01352-714172). The rather scanty ruins of *Basingwerk Abbey* sprawl over a pre-Norman fortified site. Founded in 1131 by Ranulph, Earl of Chester, as a house of the Savigniac Order, the abbey became Cistercian only a few years later (in 1147). At the Reformation the buildings were largely demolished and sold, the timber roof of the choir going to St. Mary-on-the-Hill at Chester, that of the refectory possibly to Cilcain, and stained glass to Llanasa and, possibly, Dyserth. Of the church, the few remains, effectively only some lower courses, are limited to the west and south walls, some pier bases and something of the transepts. Of the domestic buildings, there is rather more, the open space immediately to the south of the church representing the cloister, with (along the east side, from north to south) the sacristy, the chapter house with traces of the bench around the walls, the parlour, and the novices' lodging and warming house extending south. The large room to the west of the warming house was the refectory, with internal arcading on its west wall and traces of the hatch to the kitchen, though of this last, against the southwest corner of the cloister, little remains other than the base of the fireplace against the south wall.

3m (from Holywell) *Gorsedd* where there is a choice of roads, the direct road to St. Asaph being A55 while this Route bears northwest along A5151. Thomas Pennant (1726–98), whose 'Tours in Wales' was published in 1778, is buried at Whitford, a mile north of the road fork. From a crossroads reached a mile and a half after the Gorsedd fork a diversion may be made a mile northward to see the *Maen Achwynfan*, a cross of the 10 or 11C, nearly 11ft high and one of the tallest of its type in Britain. The somewhat crude carving has not been interpreted and whether the cross commemorates a person or an event is not known.

For a short distance A5151 runs with the course of Offa's Dyke. *4m.* *Trelawnyd*, sometimes called Newmarket, is known for a huge prehistoric cairn on Gop Hill (just north), while at *Llanasa* (a mile and a half northeast of Trelawnd) the church has stained glass from Basingwerk. *2m.* **Dyserth**, a small place at the foot of a limestone hill, offers a picturesque cascade and a church with a 15C Jesse window possibly from Basingwerk. On the hill, earthworks mark the site of a castle built by Henry III in 1241 but soon taken and destroyed (in 1263) by Llewelyn the Last, and, above, *Craig Fawr* is a National Trust property of geological and other interest. A main feature is a small disused quarry where the limestone bedrock is exposed, revealing shell and small marine animal fossils deposited some 300 million years ago when this place was a reef lapped by a shallow sea. *Bodrhyddan Hall* (June–Sept: Tues and Thur 14.00–17.30. Tel. 01745-590414), on A5151 just west of Dyserth, is a 17C manor house showing armour, furniture and portraits.

2m. **Rhuddlan** is a name notorious in Welsh history since it was from here in 1284 that Edward I issued his statute providing for the government of the conquered principality. Traditionally, the statute was enacted on the site now occupied by *Parliament House* in the main street (corner of Parliament Street) of today's small town, the wording of today's tablet misleadingly implying that the statute assured the rights and independence of Wales rather than that it laid down the terms of the country's subjugation. For some seven centuries, from the 10C up to the Civil War, Rhuddlan's story was that of its *Castle* (Cadw; see p.11).

History. A primitive native fort of perhaps the 10C was succeeded by a motte-and-bailey of 1073, the builder being Robert of Rhuddlan, a kinsman of the Norman Hugh Lupus. Giraldus enjoyed hospitality here in 1188, apparently being impressed by the 'noble castle' traces of which survive today as Twt Hill (see below). In 1277 the victorious Edward I started work on today's castle, the architect being James of St. George and the castle Edward's second in Wales (Flint was the first). By 1282 Rhuddlan had been completed, as had also the task of diverting and canalising the river Clwyd, the mouth of which was previously two miles away. Edward was thus able to supply himself by sea and Rhuddlan continued to enjoy the status of port until about a century ago. In 1282 Edward's queen gave birth here to her daughter Elizabeth (later, wife of John I, Count of Holland); the year 1284 was that of the Statute of Rhuddlan and in 1292 the Dominican priory (see below) was founded.

Prior to the building of the castle Rhuddlan would have been no more than a settlement around the motte-and-bailey; now Edward created one of his boroughs, and it was from this that modern Rhuddlan developed. In 1399 Richard II was here, virtually the Earl of Northumberland's prisoner and on his way to meet Bolingbroke at Flint. The castle continued in use until the Civil War when it fell to General Mytton (July 1646); two years later it was slighted, thereafter for centuries serving as a ready source of building material.

The rectangular castle was designed on a concentric plan, a walled inner ward standing within and above an outer curtain of walls and towers, a design which enabled both outer and inner bowmen to shoot at the same time. The whole was guarded on the southwest by the river, and on the other sides by a moat filled by tidal and river water. There were diagonal east and west gates, each protected by flanking towers, four levels high and with seven-sided rooms above a circular base. Around the outer ward perhaps the most interesting surviving feature is the dockgate and moat inlet at the angle nearest to the river. *Twt Hill*, Robert of Rhuddlan's Norman motte, is 300 yards southeast by a footpath which continues for about the same distance to *Abbey Farm*, incorporating some remains (south cloister) of the late 13C Dominican priory.

In the town the twin-nave church dates in part from the 13C; Edward I's daughter was christened here and some ancient graveslabs are probably from the priory.

The river Clwyd is crossed, this Route then bearing south along A525 for (*2m*) **St. Asaph** (Llanelwy), astride a ridge between the Clwyd and the Elwy, a small place which by virtue of its cathedral ranks as a city. The *Cathedral* is small, too, in fact the smallest medieval one in Britain.

History. There is some evidence that St. Asaph may have been the site of the Roman station of Varae. More certain is that the town grew as the result of the founding of the cathedral in the 6C by St. Kentigern (also known as St. Mungo), his successor in 570 being Asaph, holder of an administrative post at the local monastery. At this time the place was known only by its Welsh name of Llanelwy (the holy enclosure beside the Elwy), the English name of St. Asaph not being recorded before 1100. There is no sure record of any bishops between Asaph and 1143, though the succession may well have been continuous. Among later bishops were Dr Morgan (1601–04), translator of the Bible into Welsh; William Lloyd (1680–92), one of the 'seven bishops' tried for refusing to have the Declaration of Indulgence read; and Samuel Horsley (1802–06), the opponent of Priestley in the Trinitarian controversy. John Luxmoore, father of the notorious pluralist Charles Luxmoore, held the see from 1815–30.

Giraldus thought little of the cathedral, describing it in 1188 as 'paupercula sedis Laneluensis ecclesia', and a century later, in 1282, it was destroyed by the English. Edward I then wished to rebuild at Rhuddlan, but Bishop Anian II (1268–93) insisted that the new cathedral be at St. Asaph and got his way, such was the power of the Church even against a conqueror such as Edward I. Today's building was therefore started by Bishop Anian II, and completed by his two successors. The woodwork was burnt in 1402, but the church was reroofed and restored by Bishop Redman (1471–96); the tower was rebuilt in 1715, after its destruction in a storm, and the choir was remodelled in c 1780. There was major restoration by Gilbert Scott in 1869–75, and further restoration in 1929–32. In 1920 Dr A.G. Edwards, bishop since 1889, was enthroned as the first archbishop of the newly constituted Church of Wales.

Outside stands a monument to Bishop Morgan, buried in the cathedral, and to his fellow translators of the Bible into Welsh.

Inside the cathedral the refurbished roof painting and gilding (1967) celebrate the investiture of Prince Charles as Prince of Wales. The Decorated Nave, begun in the 13C by Anian II, has 14C arcades with continuous mouldings and a 15C clerestory. In the South Aisle, the more interesting of the two, are a recumbent effigy of a bishop, almost certainly Anian II; the curious Greyhound Stone, bearing unexplained heraldic decoration; and tablets to Mrs Hemans (died 1835), the poetess (her best known lines are: 'The boy stood on the burning deck, whence all but he had fled'), who lived for several years near St. Asaph, and to H.M. Stanley (died 1904) of African fame, who, as the youth John Rowlands, was an inmate of the St. Asaph workhouse. The transepts are contemporary with the nave and something of Bishop Redman's 15C roof has survived. The South Transept now serves as a chantry chapel, the gift in 1957 of the Guild of All Souls; here there is an exquisite little 16C Spanish ivory Madonna, said to have come from an Armada galleon. The aisleless Choir was mostly rebuilt by Gilbert Scott in the style of the 13C but also incorporates some genuine work of that period which escaped the English destruction of 1282. The stalls here date from the restoration by Bishop Redman, but the sedilia and the east window, with glass of 1968, are 14C (restored). The 18C bishop's throne stands over Bishop Morgan's tomb.

The cathedral's Chapter Treasury (shown on request, though normally not Sun) is known for its collection of early bibles and prayer books. The collection includes copies of the first prayer book of Edward VI (1549), one of which belonged to Roger Ascham, the 16C scholar, and shows notes in his own hand; the first Welsh New Testament (1567); Bishop Morgan's Bible (1558), used at the investiture in 1969 of Prince Charles; the second and third editions of the Welsh Prayer Book (1586, 1599); and Middleton's and Prys's Metrical Psalms in Welsh (1603, 1621). Other curiosities here include the Triglot Dictionary (Welsh, Greek, Hebrew) of Dic Aberdaron (1780–1843; see also Rte 12, Aberdaron), who is buried here; prehistoric and Roman material; a copy of the newspaper 'Commonwealth Mercury' announcing the death of Oliver Cromwell; and a collection of Victorian autographs.

For St. Asaph to *Denbigh*, *Ruthin* and *Corwen*, see Rte 5.

This Route continues west along B5381, but a short diversion (two miles northwest) may be made along A55 to **Bodelwyddan**, with a 'marble' church and a castle, the latter the focus of a major leisure, heritage and cultural complex. The *Church* was built in 1856–60 by Lady Willoughby de Broke as a memorial to her husband. The design of John Gibson, the arcades are of marble but the exterior is white limestone while, inside, the font is by Hollings of Birmingham, the curious lectern by Kendal of Warwick, and the bust of Lady Willoughby by M. Noble. To the south of the choir are the graves of Canadian soldiers who died during the First World War at nearby Kinmel Park camp.

`*`* `*`Bodelwyddan Castle (Easter–Oct: daily except Fri but open Fri in July and Aug 10.00–17.00, last adm. 16.00. Tel. 01745-584060), essentially of the 19C but with roots reaching back to the 15C, was by 1982 in sorry condition after over 60 years' service as a girls' school. Imaginatively taken in hand by Clwyd County Council, determined to create a distinguished cultural focus in this area of Wales, the main part of Bodelwyddan (Williams Hall) was in July 1988 reborn as a sumptuous Victorian country mansion and splendid setting for important Victorian collections of fine and decorative art from the National Portrait Gallery, the Victoria and Albert Museum and the Royal Academy of Art.

History. The original 15C house here was owned by the Humphreys family (formerly of Anglesey), their successors during the later 17C being the Williams family, the 18 and 19C members of which from time to time extended and remodelled what soon became a mansion. Of Georgian aspect by the 18C, Bodelwyddan was in the early 19C not only further extended but also castellated, the principal architect being J.A. Hansom. The estate remained in the ownership of the family (which became Hay Williams) until 1920 when it became the girls' school (Lowther College) which, as noted above, closed in 1982. Rescued in 1983 by Clwyd County Council, the interior was redesigned and decorated for its new role by Roderick Gradidge. Much of the furnishing and decoration belongs to the 19C house, while much else, but always compatible, is new design or furnishing brought in from elswhere, notably, of course, the Victoria and Albert Museum as also the Clwyd County Council collection.

The permanent collections are on two floors, linked by a Jacobean-style staircase which, with the staircase hall, represents the architectural core of Bodelwyddan. The ground floor rooms, together with the first floor Bedroom, are the historically decorated and furnished rooms and the home of the loans from the National Portrait Gallery, the Victoria and Albert Museum and the Royal Academy of Art. The remainder of the first floor is devoted more to museum-style displays and special exhibitions.

Whenever possible the portraits are matched to the rooms in which they hang. Thus portraits of savants hang in the Library; those of women of the early 19C will be found in the Ladies' Drawing Room decorated in late-Regency style; and the theme of the Billiard Room is sporting. Among the artists whose work may be seen here at Bodelwyddan are J.F. Watts (with a corridor specially designed for his important series of late 19C portraits), Ford Madox Brown, Margaret Carpenter, Hubert von Herkamer, W. Holman Hunt, Edwin Landseer, Thomas Lawrence, Edward Novello, John S. Sargent, David Wilkie and A.J.S. Wortley. In the Drawing Room and Sculpture Gallery the emphasis is on John Gibson, others represented here being Thomas Woolner and Princess Louise.

On the first floor the Bedroom, mid Victorian in character, shows portraits of Queen Victoria's family. Elsewhere on this floor the exhibition themes are the Victorian Art World, Victorian Portraiture, Victorian Photography and the History of the National Portrait Gallery.

Other attractions at Bodelwyddan include, on the second floor, a hands-on exhibition (Victorian Extravaganza) of Victorian amusements and inventions, and, outside, extensive gardens with a maze, woodland walks, an aviary and play areas.

From Bodelwyddan A55 in five miles reaches Abergele on Rte 1A, on the way passing the village of *St. George* (Llan Sain Sior), by local repute the place where St. George slew the dragon.

B5381, the continuation of this Rte 1B, can be joined by a minor road leading south to Glascoed.

6m (from St. Asaph along B5381, here a Roman road) A548 is crossed, two miles south down which is *Llanfair Talhaiarn*, the burial place of John Jones ('Talhaiarn', 1810–69), a poet sometimes acclaimed as the Welsh Burns. *3m. Dolwen*, two miles northwest of which, in the church of *Llanelian-yn-Rhos*, is preserved the graveslab of Ednyfed Fechan, minister of Llewelyn the Great. *6m.* **Llandudno Junction** where the Conwy Estuary is reached and this Route merges with Rte 1A. For the Vale of Conwy to the south, see Rte 6.

The **Conwy Estuary** (A55 tunnel bypassing Conwy) has long been known for its mussels, mentioned by Tacitus, praised in verse by Drayton and Spenser, and, together with other fishing, still supporting an industry. *Deganwy* (Dinas Conwy, the fort on the Conwy), today a straggling resort on the coastal road to Llandudno, once guarded the north shore and slight remains of the castle survive. Frequently mentioned in Welsh history, the castle is said to have been a favourite seat of Maelgwn Gwynedd as early as the 6C and it may have been here that he received Gildas who later wrote so maliciously about him and his licentious court. The first medieval castle was probably built soon after the Norman conquest, perhaps by Hugh Lupus, Earl of Chester, but today's ruins are those of a castle built by a successor Earl of Chester in 1211. Henry III was besieged here by the Welsh, and Deganwy was finally destroyed by Llewelyn the Last in 1263.

2m. ****Conwy** (*Inf.*) lies beyond the Conwy river, here crossed by three adjacent bridges. The modern road bridge, opened in 1958, superseded Telford's graceful suspension bridge of 1826, still, however, open to pedestrians and cyclists and its toll house now a *Telford Exhibition* (NT. Tel. 01492-592246). The third bridge, carrying the railway, is a tubular one built in 1846–48 by Robert Stephenson.

With its splendid castle and contoured enceinte of high town walls complete with 21 towers, Conwy is the most dramatic and historic place along this northern Welsh coast.

Early History. There would probably have been a primitive settlement around the Norman motte-and-bailey which stood on the site of today's castle, but Conwy's early history is more that of the Cistercian abbey of Aberconwy, founded in 1172 and completed 15 years later. In 1198 Llewelyn the Great granted a charter to the abbey, which later became renowned for its library; he became a monk here in 1238 and died here in 1240. In 1245 Henry III plundered the abbey, and in 1283 Edward I, requiring the site for his castle and borough, removed it to Maenan, the only traces surviving being parts of St. Mary's Church. From now on the history of Conwy becomes that of its castle.

After crossing the bridge from Llandudno Junction, the castle towers on the left while ahead, across from the castle entrance, are *Tourist Information* and the *Castle Visitor Centre* with an exhibition on Edward I and the castles he built in Wales.

**Conwy Castle (Cadw; see p. 11), though smaller than some, is theatrically set and one of the most picturesque of Welsh fortresses. The ground plan is an irregular rectangle along an east–west axis, the curtain walls being 15ft thick and enfiladed externally by eight cylindrical towers of which the four on the east are crowned by smaller, circular turrets. A rampart walk is carried round the flattened inner face of the towers by corbelled-out galleries. Of the two wards the western is the larger and the castle proper, while the smaller ward beyond served essentially as a royal palace.

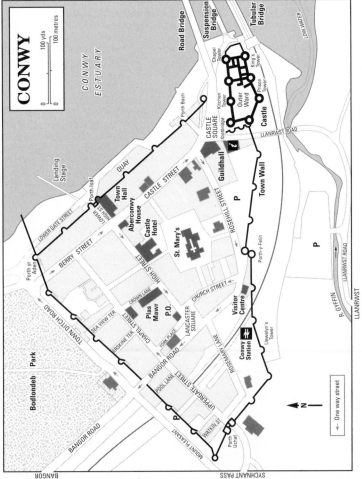

History. On the site of a Norman motte-and-bailey, the castle was begun by Edward I in 1283, the work being largely that of James of St. George, and completed a little over four years later, together with the associated borough which received a charter as early as 1284. In 1294 Edward was besieged here (nearly having to surrender through famine) during a Welsh uprising, the castle being in part garrisoned, in accordance with the terms of the charter, by the Anglo-Norman settlers who were the borough's first citizens. A century later, in 1399, Richard II sought refuge here on his return from his ill-timed visit to Ireland and just before his surrender to Bolingbroke (Henry IV) at Flint, and then, only two years later in 1401, Owen Glendower's supporters success-fully seized both town and castle. During the Civil War the castle was first held for Charles I by Archbishop Williams of York, who was a native of Conwy, then later by Sir John Owen, but in 1646 it was taken for Parliament by General Mytton. It was finally dismantled in 1665.

The modern entrance is into a projecting barbican, formerly reached by a steep ramp and drawbridge, remains of the former and of its portcullis still being visible. Immediately south of this projecting barbican was a small fortified terrace and inner barbican from which the main gateway leads into the outer ward. The absence of a definite gatehouse is unusual in a castle of this date, some defensive compensation however being provided here by the exceptionally strong barbican and the abrupt right-angle turn immediately beneath the two towers.

The OUTER WARD encloses along its south side the Great Hall, its irregular shape dictated by that of the outer curtain wall. Rather unusually the wooden roof was supported by stone arches, one of which (restored) remains. The kitchens were, inconveniently, on the opposite side of the ward, below the Kitchen Tower, while on the east side, sunk in the solid rock, is the massive cistern, vital because the castle had no well. Here the INNER WARD or PALACE is entered, on the south side (first floor) being the King's Banqueting Hall, with his withdrawing room to the east and what was probably his bedchamber at the southeast (King's Tower). The Queen's Hall occupied the first floor on the east side of the ward, with, on the north, Chapel Tower (today with a castle chapels exhibition and a model of Conwy as it probably was in about 1312); opening out of this tower a small oratory provides a welcome delicate touch. A gateway below the Queen's Hall leads to the EAST BARBICAN flanking the whole east end of the castle and possibly once doubling as garden for the queen; at the northeast corner are the remains of the original watergate stairs. Other TOWERS are, along the south side from east to west, Bakehouse Tower, with a large oven, Prison Tower, with dungeon, and South-West Tower. Along the north wall, also from east to west, are the Stockhouse Tower where criminals suffered in the stocks, the Kitchen Tower and the North-West Tower.

The *Town Walls*, some 1400 yards in circumference and contemporary with the castle, form with the castle one integral defence scheme, the walls being remarkable for their height (around 30ft), their 21 towers and the hilly area enclosed. From the castle an anticlockwise circuit follows the Quay of 1831 (along which will be found what claims to be the smallest house in Britain) to Porth Isaf (Lower Gate) at the foot of High Street, thence continuing to Porth-yr-Aden at the north corner; from here a spur, once ending in a tower, runs out to the water to protect the entrance to the harbour. Continuing southwest from Porth-yr-Aden the walls climb to their highest point to reach Porth Uchaf (Upper Gate), with its outer and inner barbicans the most elaborate of the three main gateways, and then descend generally east passing Llewelyn's Tower on their way to Porth-y-Felin (Mill Gate), set in an odd angle. This eastern entrance to the town would probably have been associated with a ferry across the river Gyffin. Beyond, the top of the wall carries no fewer than 12 conspicuous garderobes, some of them still roofed, said to have been reserved for the royal clerks.

Despite the importance of the castle, the borough's growth seems to have been slow. A mere 60 houses are recorded in Elizabethan times, and Pennant, writing in the 18C, remarks on the few inhabitants. Modern Conwy dates largely only from the arrival of the railway during the 19C.

From Castle Square, Rosehill Street, leading generally southwest, soon reaches *Conwy Visitor Centre* (June–Sept: daily 09.30–18.30. Feb–May and Oct–Dec: daily 10.00–17.00. Tel. 01492-596288) for a film on Conwy's history, brass rubbing and a Welsh craft shop, the street at this point curving northwest for Lancaster Square at the head of High Street close to either side of which there are three places of interest. To the left, *Plas Mawr* (Cadw; see p. 11), the Great Mansion built in 1577–80 by Robert Wynne of Gwydir, is one of the finest examples in Britain of an Elizabethan town house, notable in particular for its elaborate plaster ceilings, copied from Gwydir Castle. The house came to the Mostyn family in the 18C and was in 1991 given by Lord Mostyn to the nation.

St. Mary's Church, off the opposite side of High Street, occupies part of the site of the 12C Cistercian Abbey which was removed to Maenan by Edward I. When this happened the abbey church became the parish church of the new Edwardian borough and some interesting survivals are to be seen, the east and west buttresses and parts of the walls, particularly on the north side, all representing the original church while the striking if muti-lated west doorway was probably that of the chapter house. But the bulk of the church grew over later centuries. To the 14C belong the lower stages of the tower, the south transept and the porches; to the 15C the upper tower, the rood screen (now without its loft though something of the stair can be seen), and the font at which John Williams, later Archbishop of York and defender of Conwy for Charles I, was christened (in the south aisle there is an effigy of Mary, his mother, who died in 1585). In the 16C the aisle roofs were raised, and in 1872 that of the nave as part of a restoration by Gilbert Scott. Connoisseurs of the curious will find on the choir floor the worn graveslab of one Nicholas Hookes (died 1637), the forty-first child of his father and himself father of twenty-one.

Aberconwy House (NT. April–Oct: daily except Tues 11.00–17.30. Tel. 01492-592246), beyond, and within the angle of High and Castle streets, has stood here since its building by a medieval merchant in the 14C. Rooms reflect periods during the house's long span and there is an audio-visual presentation.

Just beyond the northern tip of the walls, in Bodlondeb Park and in colourful contrast to the stones of Conwy's past, the *Butterfly Jungle* (April–Oct: daily 12.00–17.30 or 16.00 in Oct. Tel. 01492–593149) shows tropical butterflies, birds, insects and exotic plants.

ENVIRONS OF CONWY. In summer, launches cruise the estuary and ascend the wooded and pastoral Vale of Conwy. *Conwy Mountain* (808ft), imme-diately west, is crossed by paths and offers traces of a hillfort as an objective. *Sychnant Pass* (550ft) marks the summit of the old, but still comfortably motorable road linking Conwy with Penmaenmawr.

For Conwy to *Betws-y-Coed* and *Ffestiniog*, see Rte 6.

C.   Conwy to Bangor

A55 to Junction with A5 and A5122. A5122 into Bangor. Total distance 16m.—*5m.* **Penmaenmawr.**—*2m.* **Llanfairfechan.**—*2m.* **Aber (Abergwyn-gregyn)**.—*4m.* **Junction with A5 and A5122.**—*3m.* **Bangor.**

Along this stretch, and despite tunnels, Rte 1 becomes scenically more striking, with views across Conwy Bay to Great Orme's Head and Anglesey, and, inland, high ground crossed by many paths.

Leaving Conwy the road rounds Conwy Mountain and there is a view across to Great Orme's Head before the curved tunnel below Penmaenbach

Point (Little Stone Point) is reached. After the tunnel Puffin Island and Anglesey come into view. *5m.* **Penmaenmawr**, spread up the hillside between Penmaenbach and Penmaenmawr (Large Stone Point), is a modest resort with a long sandy beach. For those with other interests there are many walks, one of which (the History Trail, four miles. Leaflet from local shops) visits Craig Lwyd, close to a prehistoric 'axe factory' (Mynydd Rhiw) discovered in 1919, and continues to the so-called Druids' Circle at about 1200ft on the northeast slope of Moelfre (1922ft). The stones here are the remains of two prehistoric circles, long associated with the worship of two sinister goddesses, Andras and Ceridwen.

As today's motorist speeds past the quarry-scarred height of *Penmaen-mawr*, a thought may be spared for earlier travellers, many of whom preferred to use the sands at low tide. In 1685 Lord Clarendon found the path here impassable except on foot, and in 1774 Dr Johnson recorded his apprehension, even though in 1772 the bridlepath had been replaced by a road. Public houses then stood at either end of the 'pass' to encourage travellers at the start and calm them on safe arrival.

2m. **Llanfairfechan** is another modest resort, as popular for its beach as for the choice of walks exploring the high ground immediately above. For these walks there is a special local map, one walk (the History Trail, five miles) including the Aber to Kanovium Roman road, hut circles and, on the Bwlch-y-Ddeufaen (Pass of the Two Stones, 1403ft), two standing stones. *2m.* **Aber** (short for Abergwyngregyn, Mouth of the river of white shells), set back from the sea and never a coast resort, is instead known as a centre from which to explore the upland behind, including, close to Aber, the beautiful *Coedydd Aber Glen* (nature reserve). Here a trail, about three miles long, ascends the valley to the Aber Falls (Rhaeadr Fawr), on the way passing a farmstead now serving as a Countryside Council for Wales information centre. Aber also has its place in history, the Mwd (motte) being the site of a motte-and-bailey built by Llewelyn the Great; it was here that Llewelyn the Last received and rejected Edward I's demand that he should acknowledge his sovereignty, a rejection which quickly led to Edward's subjection of Wales. Off the coast are the *Lavan Sands* (Traeth Lafan), across which, before the building of the Menai Bridge in 1819–26, travellers rode to find the ferry for Beaumaris, a bell in Aber church tolling to guide them in foggy weather. Welsh legend associates these sands, and indeed much of this coast, with drowned towns, splendid palaces and once lush meadows.

4m. Junction with A5 (bringing Rte 9 from the south) and A5122 which is followed for (*1m.*) **Llandegai**, the modern development from the model village built in the 19C for Lord Penrhyn's estate workers. The name derives from St. Tegai, said to have had a cell here in the 5C. The church (16C), perhaps on the site of the saint's cell, is approached by an avenue of yews perhaps twice as old as the church itself; inside are monuments to Archbishop Williams of York (died 1650), defender of Conwy for Charles I, with his helmet and spurs hanging above, and (by Westmacott) to the first Baron and Lady Penrhyn. It was in this area, in 1648, that the Royalist Sir John Owen was defeated by a Parliamentary force under Colonel Thistleton.

*Penrhyn Castle (NT. April–Oct: daily except Tues. Castle 12.00, or 11.00 in July and Aug, to 17.00. Grounds 11.00–18.00. Tel. 01248-353084), built by Thomas Hopper in 1820–40, is, both outside and inside, a huge complex of ostentatious Neo-Norman, well worth visiting both as such and for the splendid slate craftsmanship of the interior.

History. The estate, dating at least back to the time of Llewelyn the Great, in the 17C passed into the ownership of John Williams, Archbishop of York. Later, by marriage, it came in 1765 to Richard Pennant, who developed the Penrhyn slate quarries above Bethesda and was in 1783 created Baron Penrhyn of Penrhyn in the peerage of Ireland. His successor, through the female line, was George Dawkins, who assumed the name of Pennant and commissioned Thomas Hopper to rebuild on the site of the Neo-Gothic mansion he had inherited, the result being this astonishing castle. For all its medieval Norman exterior, the interior was thoroughly modern, boasting features such as hot air heating and water closets. Dawkins's successor, again through the female line and taking the name of Pennant (George Douglas Pennant), entertained Queen Victoria and the Prince Consort in 1859 and in 1866 was created Baron Penrhyn of Llandegai. In 1949, on the death of the 4th Baron, the estate passed to his niece, Lady Janet Douglas Pennant, who in 1951 conveyed the castle and immediately surrounding grounds through the Treasury to the National Trust.

In the *Great Hall*, where the grilles in the floor are part of the original heating system, two features of particular note are the octagonal 'Norman' centre table and the Zodiac windows by Thomas Willement. The *Library*, with a billiard table mostly of slate, particularly well illustrates Hopper's richness of design in the carving on the walls, the plaster decoration in the arches, and the ribbed and bossed ceiling, while the *Drawing Room* emphasises the interior 'Norman' motif by the huge pillars of the window surrounds and the two large candelabra. By the door to the next room the spiral staircase is a survival from the 15C mansion. The sombre *Ebony Room* contains both genuine ebony furniture and, in the case of the arched surrounds of the fireplace and the doorways, plaster painted to match. It was in this appropriately gloomy setting that the coffin always rested before family funerals in the *Chapel*, the scene of daily compulsory services for the whole household, the family and guests occupying the balcony, and the staff, segregated by sexes, the pews.

The tour next moves to the keep in which the *King's Bed*, elaborately worked in brass and topped by a crown, was made for the visit of the Prince and Princess of Wales in 1894. The hangings of the bed, as also the wallpaper, were designed by William Morris, as is also the case with the *Slate Bed*, weighing nearly one ton. The *Dressing Room*, with wallpaper by Morris, contains a splendid wardrobe. From the keep the route returns along the gallery overlooking the Great Hall, passes the Chapel and reaches the *State Bedroom* where in 1859 Queen Victoria slept in the huge carved-oak bed designed by Hopper. The *Grand Staircase* has a plaster ceiling in the form of a fan vault with Norman motifs; in riotously carved stone the staircase absorbed ten years of work after the completion of the rest of the castle. In the *Dining Room*, with a fireplace, three sideboards and a curtain pole, all in polished slate, the original hand-painted decoration of the walls (c 1838) was only revealed in 1974 after the removal of the five coats of distemper which had covered it for perhaps 70 years. The *Breakfast Room* is notable for showing some of the Old Masters assembled by the 1st Baron Penrhyn, these include Rembrandt's portrait (1657) of Catrina Hoogstraet. Beyond is the *Domestic Area* where a tea room occupies the former Housekeeper's Room and the National Trust shop is in the kitchen.

The *Industrial Railway Museum* occupies the stable yard, here being models; railway equipment; tickets; several vintage engines, including the Fire Queen (1848) and Haydock (1879); a smart saloon coach (1896); and the original Llanfair PG platform sign. Also of outstanding interest are the collections of industrial prints and of examples of slate craftsmanship. In the stalls to the right of the stable yard entrance there is a *Doll Collection*, which has no connection with the castle but started with the presentation to the National Trust of a doll in Welsh costume. Spanning from the early 19C to the present day, the 1000 or so dolls are of worldwide provenance.

The *Grounds* include, near the car park, a Californian Big Tree planted by Queen Victoria in 1859, and a Turkey Oak planted by the Prince of Wales in 1894. The Walled Garden is terraced as three areas—the upper with formal beds; the middle with trees and shrubs, where something is in flower all year; the lower with a wild garden.

2m. **Bangor**, see Rte 3.

2

Llandudno and Environs

A. Llandudno

LLANDUDNO (20,000 inhab., resident) is a large and distinguished resort which combines all the facilities (including, increasingly, those required by business conferences), cheerful attractions and high-grade entertainment (a highlight is the summer visit by the Welsh National Opera) which the modern visitor demands yet at the same time attracts older visitors and families by shunning the more strident forms which would detract from the town's underlying dignity and confident elegance. Straddling the neck of the Great Orme, a tourist attraction in its own right, the main town is on the northeast side, its broad promenade (two miles long) embracing the sweeping curve of Orme's (or Llandudno) Bay with its splendid sands.

Town Centre. Mostyn Street—Prince Edward Square—Gloddaeth Street.

Tourist Information. 1 Chapel Street (Tel. 01492-876413).

Town and Local Tours. Regular coach departures (Llandudno and Great Orme) from Prince Edward Square. Town Trail booklet. Local boats from the jetty opposite Prince Edward Square.

History. Llandudno finds its distant roots on Great Orme, home of Bronze Age copper miners, then of Romans, and later, in the 6C, chosen by St. Tudno as the site of the cell from which he preached; hence the town's name, meaning the Holy Enclosure of St. Tudno. In probably the 12C a church was built here, this later becoming the parish church. Until 1854 Llandudno remained no more than a village on the slope of Great Orme, but after this date, and due in considerable part to the initiative of the Mostyn family, a purpose-built resort rapidly took over the sand and marsh that backed the bay.

The heart of the town is a gently curving rectangle bounded on the north and the south by respectively the Promenade and St. Mary's Road, and on the east and west by Vaughan Street and the park of Happy Valley. Rather farther to the east (off the Promenade, adjacent to the Arcadia Theatre) stands the modern (1981) block of the *Canolfan Aberconwy Centre* (tel. 01492-879771), a combined conference, exhibition and leisure complex.

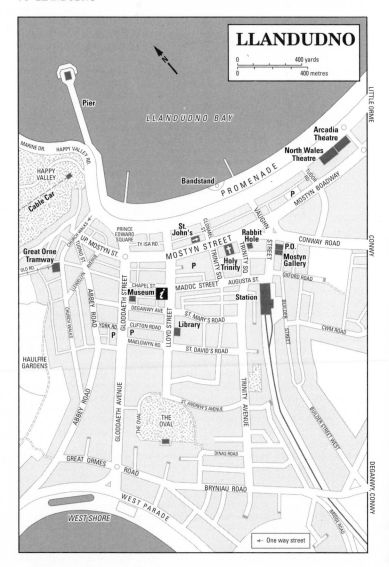

Within this central area will be found two distinguished cultural objectives—the Mostyn Art Gallery and Llandudno Museum—and also an Alice in Wonderland Visitor Centre.

The **Mostyn Art Gallery** (Mon–Sat 10.30–17.00. Tel. 01492-879201), at 12 Vaughan Street, is recognised as one of the leading public art galleries of North Wales. Opened in 1979 in a building of 1901 designed for Lady Mostyn as an art gallery (which however closed in 1914), today's gallery mounts monthly exhibitions of past and contemporary fine and applied art, both British (especially Welsh) and foreign. Additionally there are arts films, lectures and workshop activities, while craft and book shops look after tourist needs.

Farther to the west, at 17 Gloddaeth Street, **Llandudno Museum** (seasonal opening times. Tel. 01492-876517) has grown out of a fine collection of paintings, porcelain and sculpture bequeathed by the late Francis Chardon (born 1865). Exhibits today also include furniture, silver, glass, a rural Welsh kitchen and Roman material, notably from their forts at Caerhun and Prestatyn. A very different theme is offered at the **Alice in Wonderland Visitor Centre (Rabbit Hole)** at 3 Trinity Square (Easter–Oct: daily; Nov–Easter: Mon–Sat 10.00–17.00. Tel. 01492-860082), opened in Llandudno because the book's author, Charles Dodgson (Lewis Carroll), was frequently the guest here of Dean Liddell whose daughter was the inspiration for Alice.

At the west end of the Promenade and at the foot of Great Orme, the **Pier** stretches 2296ft seaward, as popular with today's visitors who enjoy the bracing views and many traditional attractions as it was with the Victorians who built it. **Happy Valley**, immediately west of the base of the Pier, is a park with gardens, a dry ski and toboggan run, a children's playground and summer entertainment, here too being the station of the Great Orme cable car (see below). The wooded hill here is *Pen-y-Dinas*, with traces of a hillfort and hut circles and also a stone known as St. Tudno's Cradle which must once have rocked and may have been associated with prehistoric ritual.

Church Walks, the road running roughly southwest from the base of the Pier, passes the station of the Great Orme Tramway (see below) and, beyond, the beautiful terraces of *Haulfre Gardens* with sweeping views. Continuing southwest, Church Walks merges with Abbey Road to reach Llandudno's WEST SHORE (also approached by Gloddaeth Avenue, the extension of the street of the same name) which, with dunes and a beach, offers a quieter alternative to the main bay and also commands a view towards Snowdonia.

Below the West Parade there is a model yacht pond, to the north of this being *Gogarth Abbey Hotel*, successor to a home of Dean Liddell, often (as mentioned earlier) visited by Charles Dodgson (Lewis Carroll), whose walks here with the dean's small daughter inspired 'Alice in Wonderland'. A memorial by F.W. Forrester, portraying the White Rabbit, was unveiled in 1933 by Lloyd George.

B.   Environs of Llandudno

•GREAT ORME, much of which is a Country Park, is a limestone mass rising sharply immediately northwest of Llandudno. As noted in the town's history, this headland—with echoes of prehistoric and early Christian occupation—provides Llandudno with its early roots. Among several publications, a local booklet, 'Discovering the Great Orme', explains the natural history; a leaflet guides around the summit nature trail; and a pictorial map, 'Secrets of the Great Orme', attractively fills in on much detail.

Great Orme may be visited by boat (the best way to see the cliffs and caves), by tramway, by cable car, by coach tour, by bus, on foot or by car. The *Great Orme Tramway* (from Victoria Station, Church Walks. Tel. 01492-

870870), in operation since 1902, enjoys all the popularity of a long tradition, while a rather different ride is provided by the *Cable Car* (from Happy Valley. Tel. 01492-877205).

For motorists there are two approaches. One is the steep direct road leading off Church Walks beside the Empire Hotel and more or less following the course of the tramway. The other is the Marine Drive circuit (see below) with the option of diverting for the summit by the road passing St. Tudno's Church.

Either of the above motor approaches; or bus or tour coach from Prince Edward Square; or the Tramway (Halfway Station); or courtesey bus from the summit car park can be used to visit the Orme's perhaps most interesting site, the *Bronze Age Copper Mines* (March–Oct: daily 10.00–17.30. For winter opening tel. 01492-870447), dating from some 4000 years ago and described by archaeologists as perhaps the world's most extensive discovery of its kind. The visit includes an introductory film followed by a guided tour of the surface and underground workings.

At the **Summit** (679ft)—barren, open, as likely as not windswept but affording long views—are a Country Park Visitor Centre (Easter–Oct: daily 09.30–17.00. Tel. 01492-874151); the starting and finishing point of a nature trail circuit of rather over three miles; and a café and shop.

Marine Drive (toll), opened in 1878 and some five miles long, makes an anticlockwise circuit. The start is near Happy Valley, from where the road gradually ascends, skirting the cliffs to reach Pen Trwyn, at Orme's northeast angle, thence bearing west to reach the diversion up to the summit along which is St. Tudno's Church. As noted earlier, it was here in the 6C that Tudno built the cell from which he preached. Today's church is a humble, small place, the oldest part of which (north wall, east of the porch) dates from the 12 or 13C, the remainder being largely 15C. In 1839 the roof was destroyed in a storm, the church then being abandoned until restored in 1855. Of note inside are 13C graveslabs, a 12 or 13C font, and, over the west door, a part of the medieval rood screen. Services, in the open weather permitting, Whitsun–mid Sept: Sun 11.00. Bus from opposite the town hall.

Marine drive continues west to Great Orme's Head lighthouse at the north tip of the headland, then bears southwest, passing above Llech Cave, said to have been used as a summer retreat by a 16C member of the Mostyn family, and then Hornsby Cave, named after a ship wrecked here in 1824. The old road (followed by the nature trail) comes in from the east, here, within the farther angle of the junction with Marine Drive, being traces of ancient hut circles and of a long hut, today mere depressions in the ground. A short way beyond, as Marine Drive rounds Great Orme's western point, there opens a fine view across Conwy Bay to Conwy Castle below its backdrop of mountains, while, more to the west, are Puffin Island and Anglesey. Now descending (through an area in which feral goats may be seen, descendants of a pair from the Windsor Royal Herd, released here in about 1900), Marine Drive runs above the ruins (no access) of a Bishop's Palace, probably built by Anian, Bishop of Bangor, in the late 13C on land given to him by Edward I as reward for baptising the royal son, later proclaimed Prince of Wales; the palace was destroyed by Owen Glendower. Marine Drive ends close to Gogarth Abbey Hotel (see last paragraph of Rte 2A).

EASTERN ENVIRONS OF LLANDUDNO. **Little Orme's Head**, the limestone headland at the east end of Llandudno's bay, boasts even finer and steeper cliffs (400ft in places) than Great Orme, and its summit (463ft; path) commands a wide view. A walk is also possible round the foot where there are several caves, in one of which, in 1587, there was found a secret Roman Catholic printing press, possibly the first press in Wales.

For *Deganwy*, on the south side of the peninsula, see Rte 1B. The castle here is said to have been a favourite of Maelgwn Gwynedd, said also to have died of plague in 547 in the church at *Llanrhos* (or Eglwys Rhos), a mile northeast of Deganwy. Today's small church, in part 13C, contains an Early Christian inscribed stone (?6C) as also monuments to the Mostyn family, and, perhaps confirming the tradition about Maelgwn, the hill above the church bears his name. *Bodysgallen Hall*, just southeast of Llanrhos and now a distinguished hotel, also has ancient associations, the name meaning Abode of Gallen and the site thought to have been the 5C home of a prince of that name. Although the hall is essentially 17C, the tower is in part 13C and may once have been an outpost of the castle at Deganwy.

3

Bangor

BANGOR (12,000 inhab.), the central part of which lies either side of a valley just south of and parallel to the Menai Strait, is of interest to the tourist largely for its cathedral, while the University College of North Wales, prominent along the north slope of the valley, gives Bangor academic distinction.

City Centre. South side of the valley; Cathedral and High Street.

Tourist Information. Theatr Gwynedd, Deiniol Road. Tel. 01248-352786.

History. Bangor owes its birth to St. Deiniol, a nobleman who founded a monastic community here in 525; the word Bangor derives from the wattle fence which surrounded St. Deiniol's primitive enclosure, 'bangori' still being used in parts of Wales to describe the plaiting of twigs in a hedge. Later, in 546, St. Dubricius (or Dyfrig), Bishop of All Wales, divided his large see into three, consecrating St. Deiniol as the bishop responsible for Gwynedd (St. Padarn got central Wales, and St. Teilo the south). Thenceforward for nearly 13 centuries Bangor's story is that of its bishopric (see below), significant change only coming with the commercial activities of the early 19C: in succession the opening of the Penrhyn quarries; the development of a port (Penrhyn); the construction of Telford's road (today's A5) in 1815–30 and of his Menai Strait suspension bridge in 1819–26; and the arrival in 1848 of the railway, with the building of Stephenson's tubular bridge two years later. Bangor was given formal municipal status in 1883, and the establishment in the following year of the University College of North Wales ensured that the city would be an educational as well as a commercial and ecclesiastical centre.

Deiniol Road runs roughly east to west along the floor of the valley, a car park below the cathedral and within the southeast angle of the junction of Deiniol Road and Glanrafon being convenient both for the cathedral and for *Tourist Information* which is at nearby Theatr Gwynedd on the north side of Deiniol Road. The *Town Hall*, across the road from Theatr Gwynedd, dates from the 16–17C but with later additions and was until 1899 the residence of the bishops. Glanrafon crosses Deiniol Road to become

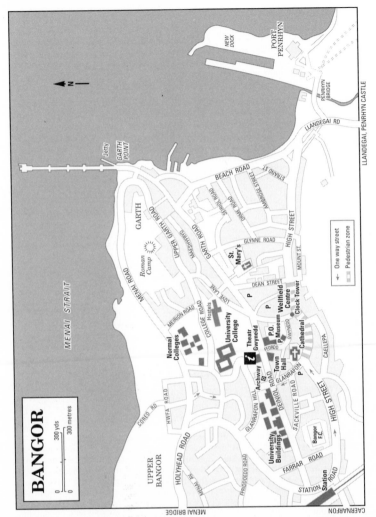

Glanrafon Hill, on this corner standing the *North Wales Heroes Archway* (1923, D.W. Thomas) which, with a number of bursaries for University College, commemorates the men of Gwynedd and Powis who fell in the 1914–18 war. The main building of the **University College of North Wales**, founded in 1884 and one of the constituent colleges of the University of Wales, spreads along the heights of the north side of the valley.

The unpretentious **Cathedral** is probably the oldest in Britain in continuous use as such.

History. The history of the see is virtually blank from St. Deiniol's time until 1071 when William II tried to force on it as bishop a Breton called Hervé; an unwelcome symbol of Norman power, he was in constant strife with his flock and soon departed. Between 1120–39 Bishop David, who is recorded as having ministered to the dying Gruffydd ap Cynan (died 1137), built the Norman cathedral, and it would have been here that Archbishop Baldwin preached the Crusade in 1188. In 1211, and again during the wars of Edward I, the cathedral was much damaged, but rebuilding was begun before 1291 by Bishop Anian I (1267–1305), who was responsible for a central tower (burnt c 1308), the Lady Chapel, and an enlarged south transept. Building continued through the Decorated period until c 1350, Bishop Anian II (1309–28) probably being responsible for the north transept and nave. Disaster came in 1402 when the cathedral was badly damaged by the followers of Owen Glendower, the ruins lying virtually untouched for nearly a century. Bishop Deane (1494–1500) largely rebuilt the choir, including the east window, and Bishop Skeffington (1509–34) added a nave clerestory and west tower. During the Civil War and the two centuries that followed, the cathedral again suffered damage and neglect. A bishop during this period was Hoadly (1715–21), whose sermon on the 'Nature of the Kingdom or Church of Christ' gave rise to a pamphleteering war known as the Bangorian Controversy (1717–21). Between 1868–84 Sir Gilbert Scott carried out a drastic restoration. His plans envisaged a lofty central tower and spire, but subsidence made this impracticable and in 1967–71 the tower was battlemented at its present height and given its small cap spire.

Four bishops of Bangor became archbishops of Canterbury: Henry Deane (1501), Thomas Herring (1747), Matthew Hutton (1757), and John Moore (1783).

Points to be noticed around the EXTERIOR are a blocked window and plain buttress (both south wall of choir), the sole surviving visible evidence of the Norman cathedral; the inscription of 1532 over the west doorway recording the building of the tower; the unusually thin buttresses of the north aisle; and the late Decorated windows (?1350) of the aisles, the side walls of which survived the damage of 1402 by Owen Glendower. The transept ends were rebuilt by Scott to what are probably, from the indications afforded by fragments discovered in the 16C walls, the original designs. The fine buttresses on the end of the south transept, including the curious dwarf example in the middle, also escaped destruction in 1402. On the east of the south transept are traces of former chapels, probably demolished in the 15–16C and their stone used in the repair of the transept walls.

INTERIOR. On the right, on entering by the northwest doorway, are various ancient stones, including the 14C slab of 'Eva, wife of Anwel'. The tiles on the floor are probably early 14C and were discovered under the floor of the choir during the 19C restoration. Here too are dog tongs, used to remove unruly dogs from the church; a 15C misericord; and some 16C Flemish wooden figures. On a nearby *Nave* pier hangs the *Mostyn Christ of 1518, thought to have been concealed by the Mostyn family at the Reformation; Christ, bound and wearing a crown of thorns, is seated on a rock. All the woodwork in the nave is modern. The nave altar frontal (1975), the main motif of which is the Celtic cross, is the design of Iris Martin and the work of Celtic Studios of Swansea. In the *South Transept* the arched tomb in the south wall was once thought to be that of Prince Owain Gwynedd (died 1170), originally buried before the high altar. However since the tomb is 13C, it is now thought that it may have been prepared for Bishop Anian I. As to where Owain Gwynedd lies, one account relates that, since he died under excommunication, his remains were secretly removed at the behest of Archbishop Baldwin and interred in the churchyard. Also in the south transept are a wallpainting (1955, Brian Thomas, two more of whose murals, depicting the six Welsh cathedrals and worthies of the Welsh Church from Dubricius to the first Archbishop of Wales, are at the cathedral's west end); a memorial to Edmond Prys (1544–1623), author of Welsh metrical psalms; and a tablet to Goronwy Owen (1723–69), the poet. In the *Choir* the stonework of the large Perpendicular windows in the east and south walls dates from 1494–1500; the glass is 19C. The stalls are 1868–79 and 1908, that of the Precentor bearing the arms of Gruffydd ap Cynan, and that of the Canon in Residence those of Owain Gwynedd; the bishop's throne is 1879; the reredos of 1881 was designed by J. Oldrid Scott.

The former close, just north of the cathedral, is now the *Bishop's Garden*, with a Biblical Garden.

The Old Canonry in Ffordd Gwynedd, a short walk eastward from the cathedral, houses the **Museum of Welsh Antiquities and Art Gallery** (Tues–Sat 10.30–16.30. Tel. 01248-353368), the Art Gallery here occupying the ground floor and mounting a programme of temporary exhibitions. The theme of the permanent collection is essentially local, but wide, the exhibits including prehistoric and Roman material as also paintings (mainly 18 and 19C), furniture, costume and much else.

Views across the Menai Strait to Anglesey can best be enjoyed from the northern tip of the city where the *Pier* of 1896, reaching half-way across the strait, has been restored to its Victorian splendour (shops, café, amusements, play area). Another fine viewpoint, inland from the pier, is *Roman Camp* (Garth Hill); in fact, despite its name and despite excavation, no proof of Roman occupation has come to light, though this area may well have included the site of a modest outpost.

For *Menai Strait* and its bridges, and *Anglesey*, see Rte 11. From Bangor to *Chester*, see Rte 1; to *Capel Curig*, see Rte 9; to *Caernarfon* and *Porthmadog*, see Rte 10.

4

Wrexham to Betws-y-Coed via Denbigh

A541 to Denbigh. A543 to Pentrefoelas. A5 to Betws-y-Coed. Total distance 46m.—*10m.* **Mold.**—*15m.* **Denbigh.**—*14m.* **Pentrefoelas.**—*7m.* **Betws-y-Coed**.

In large part high open moorland with mountain vistas.

Wrexham (*Inf.*) is best known to tourists, and especially Americans, for its *Church of St. Giles* with the grave of Elihu Yale (1648–1721), the benefactor of Yale University. The wrought-iron churchyard gates, of 1720 when they replaced a wooden lychgate, are by Robert and John Davies, and Elihu Yale's tomb (restored in 1968 by members of Yale University to mark the 250th anniversary of the benefaction) is in the churchyard west of the tower, a site chosen by Yale himself; the last two lines of the quaint rhymed epitaph are adapted from the funeral hymn to Ajax by James Shirley (1659).

Both the exterior and the interior of this church offer much else of interest, notably the richly decorated *Tower with its four graceful hexagonal turrets. Begun in 1506 the tower carries some medieval carvings, those of St. Giles, of which there are several, identifiable by his attributes of an arrow and a deer. The north porch (with, inside, a figure of St. Giles on the central ceiling boss) was restored by graduates of Yale in 1901 on the occasion of the bicentenary of their university, and—another Yale association—a stone on the tower replaces one removed and incorporated in a replica tower at the university. Inside the church, the lectern is of 1524, near it and the pulpit being the heads of the Earl of Derby and his (more celebrated) wife, Lady Margaret Beaufort, while nearby, over the choir arch, there are traces of a mural of the Last Judgement. In the north aisle there are medieval carvings on the corbels; a monument by Louis Roubiliac to Mary Myddleton (died 1747) of Chirk; and in an adjacent window the words from the famous hymn 'From Greenland's Icy Mountains', written in 1819 by Reginald Heber, later Bishop of Calcutta, on the occasion of a missionary service held here while he was staying with his father-in-law, the vicar.

In Wrexham town the *Library Arts Centre* (Mon–Sat 09.30–18.45 or 10.00–17.00 on Sat. Closed Bank Hol. Tel. 01978-261932), in Rhosddu Road, mounts a continuous programme of exhibitions, as also drama and musical events, while the *Borough (Wrexham Maelor) Heritage Centre* (Mon–Sat 10.00–17.00. Closed Bank Hol. Tel. 01978-290048), at 47–49 King Street, is an expanding museum of many aspects of regional history. *Acton Park*, in the north of the town, was the birthplace of the notorious Judge Jeffreys (1648–89), but the house was demolished in 1956.

For Wrexham to *Corwen*, via places associated with the Yale family, see Rte 14; to *Chester*, see Rte 14.

Environs of Wrexham

The **Clywedog Valley and Trail** (details from Tourism Section, Wrexham Maelor Council, LL11 11AY. Tel. 01978-292116), best for walkers, visits several features embracing industrial archaeology, a countryside centre, a working farm, a corn mill and the NT mansion of Erddig. Three of the principal sites (Erddig, King's Mill and Bersham Ironworks) are mentioned below along a motor tour starting at Bangor-is-y-Coed, four miles southeast of Wrexham and more of historical than visual interest. All sites are accessible from A525.

Bangor-is-y-Coed (Enclosure in the Wood), also known as Bangor on Dee and with a picturesque 17C bridge sometimes attributed to Inigo Jones, may occupy the site of the Roman Bovium, though Holt, six miles to the north and known to have been the site of Roman pottery works, is a stronger claimant. Bangor was also the site of a monastic foundation of c 180 at which the heretic Pelagius is said to have lived (though not as a monk) during the 4C. The monastery was destroyed in 607 by Ethelfrid of Northumbria in the last great victory of Saxon heathendom over Celtic Christianity, 1200 monks being slain as the result of Ethelfrid's assertion that praying against him was as bad as fighting against him. Some survivors are said to have made their way to Bardsey. *Hanmer*, on A539 four miles southeast of Bangor-is-y-Coed, is where Owen Glendower and Margaret, daughter of Sir David Hanmer, are believed to have been married in the church that preceded the present Tudor one.

ᐧErddig (NT. Early April–early Oct: daily except Thur and Fri 12.00–17.00. Garden 11.00–18.00. Tel. 01978-355314), two miles south of Wrexham and standing within grounds of nearly 2000 acres, is a late 17C mansion with 18C additions. One of the National Trust's more important properties, a feature of particular interest is the complete range of outbuildings and domestic offices, equipped as they once were and including a remarkable collection of portraits of the staff. The main rooms contain outstandingly good 18C furniture, and the gardens have been restored to their formal 18C plan.

History. The original house (the present central bays) was built between 1684–87 and soon turned out to be a financial disaster for the owner, Joshua Edisbury, High Sheriff of Denbighshire. Unable to meet his debts (one of those from whom he had borrowed was Elihu Yale), he fled to London before the house was even completed and died there c 1715. The following year John Meller, a London lawyer, acquired the property. To the original house Meller added two wings between 1721–24, and it was he too who collected the fine furniture which fills Erddig today. In this he was helped by his nephew Simon Yorke, to whom the property passed in 1733, remaining by direct line in the family (all called Simon or Philip) until given to the National Trust in 1973. Care for the staff was always a family tradition, one aspect of this being staff portraits, accompanied by verses by the various Philips and Simons. The first Philip completed (1774) new domestic offices to the south of the house. During the present century the house has suffered considerable damage from mining subsidence.

OUTBUILDINGS and DOMESTIC OFFICES. The *Estate Yard* is surrounded by buildings dating mainly from the early 19C and still in use today. These include joiner's workshop, sawpit, blacksmith's workshop, and wagon shed. The dovecot, just outside the yard, is early 18C. Off the *Limeyard* are the dog yard and the sawmill, the latter today containing an exhibition on the restoration of the house. In the *Outer Yard* the central enclosure was the midden where straw and dung from the stables was collected. The *Stableyard* was completed in 1774. Today it contains carriages, old cars, and bicycles. In an adjacent room is an introductory exhibition on the family and staff. The *Laundry Yard* and associated buildings was completed c 1773. Noteworthy are the stone-filled box mangle (possibly part of the original equipment) and the goffering irons used for crimping starched collars. The *Bakehouse* has scuffle ovens, from which the ashes were raked or scuffled before the dough was slid in. The *New Kitchen* with a Venetian window, is a particularly fine room, dating from 1772 when, possibly because of the danger of fire, the decision was taken to move the kitchen out of the main house. At this time it was completely detached, and the linking passage was not built until the 19C. In the basement passage hang photographs of the staff, one being a copy of a daguerrotype of 1852. The *Servants' Hall* contains Erddig's notable *Series of 18 and 19C portraits of the staff, the subjects ranging from John Meller's negro coachboy (early 18C; verses added c 1795) to portraits of 1830 of the carpenter, woodman and gardener. The principal artist of the series was John Walters of Denbigh.

FAMILY ROOMS. The Neo-Classical *Dining Room* (1826), the design of Thomas Hopper, was formerly the state bedroom and dressing room. It is hung with family portraits, among the artists being Gainsborough and Cotes. There is also a Still Life by Frans Snyders. Until 1770 the *Saloon* was two rooms, the north end being a smaller saloon and the south end a withdrawing room off the state bedroom and dressing room which now form the dining room. The early 18C furniture includes walnut chairs; a Boulle dressing table (c 1700); a plaster gilt side table; and gilt pier glasses (1723 and 1726). There is also porcelain and glass of the 16 to 18C. In the *Tapestry Room* the tapestry is early 18C Soho. The chairs, settee, and pier glass are also early 18C. In the *Chinese Room* are painted scenes, part Chinese and part English imitation, attractively illustrating ways of earning a living. The *Library* contains John Meller's legal library; also, added by

Philip (died 1804), antiquarian books and copies of his own work of 1799, 'The Royal tribes of Wales'. The pictures in the *Entrance Hall* include three works by Kneller, one being of Judge Jeffreys. The hall also contains a collection of 18 and 19C musical instruments. In the *Drawing Room* the furniture includes armchairs and a settee, possibly of 1770 and by John Cobb, cabinet maker to the royal family. Among the pictures is a small landscape by Jan van Goyen.

BEDROOMS. In the *Red Bedroom* the ingenious lifting device of the bed may have been designed for the easier nursing of Anne Yorke, who died of consumption in 1770. The *Gallery* contains mother-of-pearl models (1765–80) made by Elizabeth Ratcliffe, daughter of a Chester clockmaker and companion to the then Mrs Yorke. The pictures include portraits of the royal family of Bohemia. Amongst the furniture are gilt pier tables with mother-of-pearl tops by Elizabeth Ratcliffe. In the *North Landing* there is a clock, signed by John Ratcliffe, father of Elizabeth. The bed in the *State Bedroom* is of 1720; damaged by rain, leaking in as the result of subsidence, it was restored in 1968–70 by the Victoria and Albert Museum. The Chinese screen is thought to have been a gift (1682) from Elihu Yale. The *Blue Bedroom* has a bed dating from before 1726. The mezzotints are by Thomas Frye (1760–62).

Also to be seen are the *Chapel* (1721–4); the *Tribes' Room*, so called from Philip Yorke's book, now housing an exhibition of family documents; the *Butler's Pantry*, with 17 and 18C silver; the *Family Museum*, and the 18C walled garden, noted for old varieties of fruit trees.

King's Mill (Feb–Easter and Oct: Sat and Sun. Easter–Sept: Tues–Sun 10.00–17.00. Tel. 01978-358916), a mile short of Wrexham, although dating from 1769 stands where there has been a mill since at least 1315. Today the principal visitor feature is 'The Miller's Tale', a presentation in which the miller of 1769 tells his apprentices about life and work here.

Bersham Ironworks and Heritage Centre (Easter–Oct: daily 10.00 or 12.00 on Sun, to 17.00. Tel. 01978-261529). Bersham, two miles west of Wrexham, was the home of the Davies brothers, masters of fine ironwork. Today the 18C Ironworks and supporting Heritage Centre interpret the local industrial story, the emphasis being on John 'Iron Mad' Wilkinson who became master of the ironworks in 1762, but with material also on the Davies brothers. Facilities here include an information desk, especially for the Clywedog Valley Trail, and a shop and picnic and play area.

Wrexham is left by A541 for (*5m*) **Caergwrle**, once a Roman station occupied as an outpost of Deva (Chester) by the 20th Legion. The Castle, on a high ridge, vulnerable on one side only, this protected by a steep ditch, probably started as a Bronze Age hillfort (a particularly fine gold-decorated bowl of c 800 BC, now in the National Museum of Wales, was found here in 1820), but was built in more or less its present form—a simple polygonal enclosure with drum-towers at the angles—by Dafydd, brother of Llewelyn the Last. It was from here in 1282 that Dafydd launched the final and fatal Welsh rebellion against Edward I. Traces of *Wats Dyke*, which here generally followed the 400ft contour, can be found one and a half miles north beyond Hope, between A550 and the railway.

10m. **Mold** (*Inf.*) is a modest country town and local government centre.

History. An important battle was fought near here in c 430 (see Maes Garmon below) but it was some 700 years later that Mold took root under the protection of the early Norman motte-and-bailey, now represented by Bailey Hill within the road fork at the upper end of High Street. This was probably built by Robert Montalt (Mont Haut), the town's name almost certainly being a corruption of this. In 1167 the castle was taken by Owain Gwynedd. In more modern history Mold is known as the birthplace and home of Daniel Owen (1836–95), who, while plying his trade as a tailor, at the same time achieved renown as a Welsh novelist and story writer. Sometimes described as the Welsh Dickens, his writings rank among the more important records of the era of the arrival of the railways and of the spread of religious revivalism.

Daniel Owen's statue stands in the open pedestrian area behind the town hall, alongside being the *Library* (09.30–19.00 on Mon, Tues, Wed, Fri, or 17.30 Thur, or 12.30 Sat), in one room of which there is a replica of Owen's tailor's shop with photographs, manuscripts and other memorabilia. The large mainly 15C *Church*, with a tower of 1773 and an apsidal choir added in 1856, is internally of interest mainly for its friezes of animals. There is also some good 15 and 16C glass while another, later, window remembers the landscape painter Richard Wilson (1714–82), who died near Mold and is buried in the churchyard near the north door. Mold is also known for *Theatr Clwyd* (tel. 01352-755114), a leading entertainment complex of three theatres, a cinema and an art gallery.

Maes Garmon (the Field of Germanus; a mile northwest of Mold on the Gwernaffield road) is traditionally the site of the 'Alleluia Victory' of 430, when the native Christians under Germanus, Bishop of Auxerre, who had been sent to Britain to fight the Pelagian heresy, decisively defeated the heathen Picts and Scots who, terror-stricken by the simultaneous cry of the Christians, fled without striking a blow. The site is marked by an obelisk of 1736 beside and above the road.

MOLD TO RUTHIN (A494. 11m. A pleasant drive over the Clwydian Hills). Beyond *Gwern-y-Mynydd* the road drops into the upper valley of the Alyn (Country Park; information centre and nature trail) at the Three Logger-heads Inn, with a sign, albeit showing only two loggerheads, painted by Richard Wilson who spent his last days at nearby Colomendy. At Tafarn-y-Gelyn (four miles from Mold) the old road to Ruthin diverges to run below *Moel Fammau* (1820ft Country Park). From a car park along here a wood-land trail (three miles return) reaches the summit where there is the ruin of a tower built in 1810 to celebrate the jubilee of George III but which by 1862 had already collapsed. A494 continues to Llanferres, just beyond which B5430 leads southeast to *Llanarmon* where the church (of St. Germanus) has two unequal naves divided by an 18C wooden arcade. Inside are the effigies of one Gruffydd ap Llewelyn ap Ynyr (late 13C and unusually well preserved) and of a vested priest; also a medieval bronze chandelier with a small statue of the Virgin. For **Ruthin**, see Rte 5.

A541 out of Mold in *2m* reaches *Rhyd-y-Mwyn*, two miles southwest of which is *Cilcain* with a 14C church the chief features of which are the two unequal naves (the northern and smaller of which serves as a vestry), a Norman font, and a hammer-beam roof reputed to have come from the refectory of Basingwerk Abbey, as may also have the 15C glass in the east window. *7m.* **Caerwys** was, as its name suggests, a Roman station, later becoming a village significant enough to receive a charter from Henry III. But the village is best known for its long association with the eisteddfod, the first of which is said to have been called here in 1100 by Gruffydd ap Cynan. There was another meeting here in 1523, and in 1568 Queen Elizabeth granted permission for the bards and minstrels of Wales to be called together 'in a competitive festival', this last occasion being commemorated by a window in the church. *3m.* **Bodfari**, just beyond Offa's Dyke, is where the road leaves the hills for the Vale of Clwyd. *Tremeirchion*, two miles north, has a 13C church housing a 14C tomb-niche with the effigy of a vested priest, while in the chancel a tablet commemorates Hester Lynch Piozzi (1741–1821), Dr Johnson's Mrs Thrale, who lies here; she owned the estate of Brynbella just to the south. St. Beuno's College, just north of Tremeirchion, is a Jesuit seminary.

3m. **Denbigh** (see Rte 5) from where A543 ascends steadily through pleasant wooded country to reach open moor upland. *7m. Llyn Bran* is a small lake south of the road. Here a smaller road (B4501) branches south-east, in just over a mile reaching **Llyn Brenig*, a large reservoir (opened in 1976 by the Prince of Wales) which in conjunction with Lake Bala and Llyn Celyn regulates the flow of the river Dee. More important for the visitor, the reservoir, with its surrounds of pasture, forest and moor, provides an accessible yet unspoilt large natural environment with a nature reserve, bird sanctuary, picnic areas, fishing and sailing facilities, and walks which include nature and archaeological trails, the latter visiting sites which span from the Stone Age to a settlement of the 16C. The *Information Centre* (mid March–Oct: daily 10.00–17.00. Tel. 01490-420463) tells the story of Brenig and advises on the many recreational possibilities. *Alwen Reservoir*, a mile south of Llyn Brenig, was constructed at the beginning of the century as a water supply for Birkenhead. Attractively situated, the reservoir offers car parking, picnic site and walks.

Beyond the little Llyn Bran, A543 passes the *Sportsman's Arms*, the highest inn in Wales, to reach summit level (1523ft) on the desolate *Mynydd Hiraethog* with a sweeping mountain vista. Soon the little Alwen stream is crossed, coming from Llyn Alwen (1251ft; a mile to the west) and feeding Alwen Reservoir (see above). *7m* (from Llyn Bran) **Pentrefoelas**, see Rte 13. *7m.* **Betws-y-Coed**, see Rte 6C.

5

Rhyl to Corwen

A525 to Ruthin. A494 to Corwen. Total distance 30m.—*2m.* **Rhuddlan.**—*3m.* **St. Asaph.**—*6m.* **Denbigh.**—*7m.* **Ruthin.**—*12m.* **Corwen**.

This Route ascends the pleasant VALE OF CLWYD, over 20 miles in length and narrowing gradually from a width of eight miles at the river's mouth to four miles at Denbigh, the river being insignificant compared to the width of its valley. On the west the hills rise to the bleak high moorland of Mynydd Hiraethog crossed by the road from Denbigh to Betws-y-Coed (Rte 4). The east is marked by the more definite line of the generally fertile Clwydian Hills, ending in the south at the mass of Llantysilio and Eglwyseg mountains overlooking Llangollen and the valley of the Dee. The hills are divided into short isolated ridges and rounded summits by a series of passes, possibly ancient breaches made by the sea. The highest point is Moel Fammau (1820ft), and from Roman times the hills were a line of British resistance, many, if not most, still bearing earthwork evidence.

For **Rhyl**, see Rte 1A. For (*2m*) **Rhuddlan** and (*3m*) **St. Asaph**, see Rte 1B.

Approaching Denbigh, and just before the junction of A525 with A543 (Rte 4), the estate of *Plas Clough* off the west of A525 recalls Sir Richard Clough, associated with Sir Thomas Gresham in founding London's Royal Exchange in 1565. Just beyond, entering Denbigh and on the left, is *Denbigh Friary*, a Carmelite house founded in 1284 by Sir John Salusbury, a crusader, who was buried here in 1289. The friary was restored in 1954, the chief surviving association with the old friary being the somewhat later chapel.

6m. (from St. Asaph) **Denbigh**, with a historic castle, is an old borough on a hill overlooking the Vale of Clwyd from the west.

Natives. The town claims a number of distinguished natives, by far the best known being the explorer H.M. Stanley, born here in 1841 as John Rowlands. Others include Humphrey Lloyd (born 1568), antiquary and historian; Sir Hugh Myddelton (died 1631), the engineer, thought to have been born at Gwenynog (just southwest) and to have been brought up, with his brother Thomas, later Lord Mayor of London, at Galch Hill, a short way southwest of the castle; and Thomas Gee (born 1815), printer, publisher, Nonconformist preacher and leader of Welsh political thought.

Denbigh is mainly visited for its *Castle* (Cadw; see p. 11).

History. The first castle (on an unidentified site) was that of Dafydd, brother of Llewelyn the Last. Denbigh was a centre of resistance to Edward I, who, after his victory, entrusted the subjugation of this district to Henry de Lacy, Earl of Lincoln, who started to build the present castle in 1282, which, however, two years later in 1284, was taken and briefly held by the Welsh. De Lacy died in 1311 and the building work was continued and finished in 1322 by Thomas, Earl of Lancaster, the castle being modelled to some extent on the fortresses of Edward I, with the outer wall enclosing both castle and borough. The town was burnt in 1402 by Owen Glendower and again in 1468 by Jasper Tudor, after which the rebuilding was outside the walls. Queen Elizabeth gave the castle to Dudley, Earl of Leicester, who here entertained his sovereign in sumptuous fashion. In 1645 Charles I took refuge here after his defeat at Rowton Moor, and, after a siege of nearly 11 months, Denbigh was one of the last fortresses to surrender to Parliament, then suffering the usual fate of being slighted.

The plan of the castle is a single ward shaped as an irregular pentagon. Though much ruined it still has its impressive Gatehouse (the castle's principal feature), the archway spanning the entrance passage bearing a mutilated statue, probably Edward I but possibly Henry de Lacy. The defensive system here is ingenious; a passage between two octagonal towers leads to a large central octagonal chamber, supported at the back by a somewhat smaller octagon, and the exit into the ward involves a turn to the right. Another interesting defensive feature is the Postern (rebuilt after the Welsh occupation of 1284) on the south side of the ward; it was defended by three rectangular turns, two drawbridges and an outer barbican, of which little survives. The postern tower, and the three towers to the west, originally formed part of the town walls, a section of which still extends eastward from the postern. To the west are the remains of the Mantlet, an additional defence work on the south and west sides. Within the ward the buildings are little more than foundations. Tradition has it that De Lacy's eldest son was drowned in the well. There is an exhibition on the castle and on distinguished people associated with the town.

To the north of the castle entrance stands the tower of *St. Hilary's Church* (1334), the 'chapel within the walls', all that survives of a demolition of 1923, while just northeast of this, in the grounds of Castle House, is the shell of *Leicester's Church*, a large building begun by Leicester in 1579, perhaps intended to supersede St. Asaph, but never completed. Also to be seen is the eastern portion of the *Town Walls*, begun when Denbigh was first taken from the Welsh in, 1282 and greatly strengthened after the brief Welsh success here in 1284.

Eglwys Wen (or Whitchurch), a church rather over a mile east of the town centre, dates from the 15–16C and is of the typical local double-nave type. In the south choir is the alabaster Renaissance tomb of Sir John Salusbury (died 1578), descendant of the founder of Denbigh Friary; and in the north choir a brass remembers Richard Myddelton (died 1575), father of Sir Hugh, the engineer. There are also wall memorials to Humphrey Lloyd, the antiquary, and to Thomas Edwards ('Twm o'r Nant'; died 1810), bard and author of Welsh interludes, who is buried in the churchyard.

3m. **Llanrhaeadr**, where the *Church of St. Dyfnog* is worth a visit. Successor to one founded here in the 6C by the saint beside a holy well, the present church is mainly 15C though with a 13C tower. Grooves on the stones of the entrance archway are said to be due to arrow sharpening, recalling the days when the churchyard was used for archery practice. Inside the church there are two remarkable survivals; a Jesse Window of 1533, removed during the Civil War and buried until the Restoration, and the West Window (15C), the glass of which was reassembled in c 1845 after having been found in a shattered heap in a cottage. Also noteworthy are the hammer-beam roofs, and an ancient oak chest of two compartments (one for papers, the other for plate) and an attached alms box; keys to the three locks are held each by the vicar and two churchwardens.

4m. **Ruthin** (*Inf.*), on a hill overlooking the Clwyd, was originally Rhudd-din, meaning Red Fortress, and the town's early history is that of its castle, now a hotel. For today's visitor, though, the main appeal is likely to be the town's several attractive old buildings, notably around St. Peter's Square. Here, on the south, the *Court House*, now a bank and largely facsimile, dates in origin from 1404 when it conveniently served both as law court and prison, even having the gallows attached to the building; a short length of the gibbet still projects from below the eaves. On the west side of the square stands *Exmewe Hall*, also now a bank, with, in front, Maen Huail, a stone on which King Arthur (not always, it seems, a paragon of chivalry) is said to have executed Huail, a rival in a love affair. The hall was built in c 1500 by Thomas Exmewe, later Lord Mayor of London, and was at one time the home of Gabriel Goodman (see below). North of the square the largely 14C *Church of St. Peter* was made collegiate in 1310 by Lord Grey of Ruthin and still styles its incumbent as Warden. The choir was destroyed in 1663 and the spire is an addition of 1859. The church's two principal features are the churchyard gates by the Davies brothers and, inside, the splendid oak •Roof of the north aisle (the original nave), with over 400 carved panels, each one different, presented by Henry VII to the men of Wales who had helped him ascend the English throne. In the church, too, on the north wall of the choir, is a bust of Gabriel Goodman (died 1601), a benefactor of the town, Dean of Westminster and one of the translators of the New Testament. The Cloisters, north of the church, dating in origin from the 13–14C and once part of the original college, are now the residence of the Warden. The *Old Grammar School* (now a community centre), north of the cloisters, and *Christ's Hospital Almshouses* to the east, were both founded by Dean Goodman. In Castle Street, *Natclwyd House*, in part 14C, but mainly Elizabethan, presents a striking half-timbered frontage. *Ruthin Craft Centre* (Mon–Sat 10.00–17.00; Sun 12.00–17.00. Tel. 01824-702664), in Park

Road, embracing several individual studios as well as an applied arts gallery, also mounts programmes of specialist exhibitions.

A hotel has been grafted on to the *Castle* (no adm. except for guests), and medieval banquets are now held in the reconstructed hall (tel. 01824-702664).

History. The first castle was probably early Norman, built perhaps by Hugh Lupus soon after the Conquest. In 1277, under the Treaty of Conwy, Edward I granted the site to Dafydd, brother of Llewelyn the Last. Dafydd undoubtedly carried out some building, but when in 1282 he supported his brother's uprising Ruthin was taken for Edward I by Reginald de Grey who between 1282 and c 1296 built the rectangular fortress which survives as today's ruin. In 1400 the then Lord Grey seized some Glendower land, an act which sparked Owen Glendower's revolt, one of the first incidents of which was Glendower's unsuccessful attack on Ruthin. During the Civil War Ruthin was garrisoned for Charles I but taken by General Mytton and dismantled in 1647.

RUTHIN TO CERRIGYDRUDION (B5105, SW 13m). This road runs across the southern part of *Clocaenog Forest* (FE) reaching northwest towards Llyn Brenig. The *Bod Petrual Visitor Centre* (Easter–Sept: daily 10.00–17.00), in what was once a gamekeeper's cottage, tells all about this forest, has a lakeside picnic place and is the starting point for trails. For *Cerrigydrudion*, see Rte 13.

Leaving Ruthin A494 leads south, soon passing between (east) *Llanfair-Dyffryn-Clwyd*, with a 15C church housing a 17C Communion table and a mosaic window of 15C glass, and (west) *Efenechdyd* where the small church has an unusual tub-font dating from early Norman or possibly even Saxon times. *7m. Derwen* where, in the churchyard, there is a particularly fine Celtic cross, while the pride of the church is its 15C rood screen and loft. The road now leaves the Clwyd, just before Corwen joining A5, to the west of A494 just before the road junction being the estate of *Rug*, once a home of Owen Glendower and later the seat of the Vaughans. The ancient though much restored chapel (Cadw; see p. 11) was built by William Salesbury in 1634. *5m.* **Corwen**, see Rte 13.

6

Conwy to Betws-y-Coed and Ffestiniog

As far as Betws-y-Coed this Route travels the VALE OF CONWY, a fertile valley, below rising woodland and moor on both sides, which generally defines the eastern boundary of Snowdonia National Park. There is a choice of two scenically similar roads—Rte 6A following the river's east bank, Rte 6B the west—both with places of interest and conveniently linked by bridges at Tal-y-Cafn and Llanrwst. Boat excursions in summer from Conwy.

Rte 6C describes the road onward from Betws-y-Coed to Ffestiniog, some 30 miles distant from Conwy.

A. East Bank of the Conwy

A55 to Llandudno Junction. A470 to Betws-y-Coed. Total distance 18m.—
1m. **Llandudno Junction**.—*4m*. **Bodnant Garden**—*7m*. **Llanrwst**.—*6m*.
Betws-y-Coed.

From **Conwy**, the Conwy Estuary is crossed to **Llandudno Junction** (for all
three, see Rte 1B. For Llandudno, see Rte 2), just beyond which A470 bears
south. *2m*. *Glan Conwy* where Felin Isaf Mill (Easter–Oct: daily 10.30–18.00.
Tel. 01492-580646) is a picturesque restoration to its 19C condition
(machinery of 1730) of a 17C flour mill. *3m*. *•**Bodnant Garden** (NT. Mid
March–Oct: daily 10.00–17.00. Tel. 01492-650460), the garden of Bodnant
Hall (c 1790, but later enlarged), was laid out in 1875 by Henry Pochin, a
Lancashire industrialist with a passion for trees, and later extended by his
daughter (who married the 1st Lord Aberconwy) and grandson, the 2nd
Lord Aberconwy, who gave the greater part to the National Trust in 1949.
Later, the Trust acquired further land by purchase and by gift from the 3rd
Lord Aberconwy. Covering some 80 acres and sloping to the southwest with
splendid views towards Snowdonia, the garden, with both formal and
informal areas—an upper garden of terraces and sweeping lawns; a lower
part, the Dell, formed by a small valley and with a pinetum and wild
garden—ranks with the finest in Britain.

Just beyond, *Tal-y-Cafn Bridge* crosses the river for *Caerhun* (see Rte 6B).
4m. *Cadair Ifan Goch* (672ft)—the Seat of Red Ifan, a giant who stood with
one foot here and the other on Pen-y-Gaer across the river—approached
by a road running east from Maenan Abbey Hotel and then a path, is a NT
property commanding fine views. The hotel name, Maenan Abbey, recalls
the site to which the Cistercian monks of Conwy were moved by Edward I
in 1283 and where they remained until the Dissolution.

3m. **Llanrwst**, a place with a long and as often as not violent history, is
today a centre serving a wide district. For Gwydir Castle and Gwydir Uchaf
Chapel, both just across the river, see Rte 6B.

History. The town's name derives from St. Grwst (Restitutus), a 6C missionary active
in these parts and to whom the church has long been dedicated. The early settlement
was destroyed in a battle of 954 when the sons of Hywel Dda invaded Gwynedd but
were here defeated by the northern princes; a second time during Owen Glendower's
revolt, after which the place was as good as abandoned for several decades; and yet
again during the Wars of the Roses (1455–85) when there was continual fighting
between the Lancastrians of the Conwy valley and the Yorkists of Clwyd. With more
settled times Llanrwst became modestly prosperous, its story during the 16 and 17C
being associated with the Wynne family of Gwydir Castle across the river. By the mid
19C the town had almost twice today's population, its main activities being wool,
malting, tanning and the manufacture of harps. William Salesbury, who in 1567 first
translated the new testament into Welsh, lived here.

From the town square a short narrow road leads past *Jesus Hospital
Almshouses*, founded in 1610 by Sir John Wynne 'for 11 old men and an
old woman for their bedmaker', to the *Church of St. Grwst*, dating from 1470
(tower and north aisle 19C) and successor to a thatched building of 1170
destroyed in the fighting of 1468. The fine rood screen and loft came from
Maenan Abbey. *•*Gwydir Chapel*, adjoining the church, and not to be
confused with Gwydir Uchaf Chapel across the river, was built in 1633, it
is said to a design by Inigo Jones, by Sir Richard Wynne, who was treasurer
to Henrietta Maria, wife of Charles I. The elaborate roof, the panelling and

screens, and the various Wynne monuments are noteworthy, these last including several 17C brasses. The huge stone coffin is said to be that of Llewelyn the Great (died 1420), whose remains the monks brought with them from Conwy to Maenan, the coffin being moved here at the Dissolution. Beside this lies the effigy of Howel Coetmor, an early owner of Gwydir Castle, who fought at Poitiers in 1356 and was killed in Flanders in 1388. In the churchyard, note a stone in the wall (right, on entering), bearing a Lamb and Flag and said to have come from Yspytty Ifan, once a centre of the Knights Hospitaller of St. John.

Across the graceful, if for traffic inconvenient, Old Bridge, said to have been built in 1636 by Inigo Jones and modified in 1703 when a section was carried away, stands *Tu Hwnt i'r Bont* (The House over the Bridge), a 15C stone building once used as a courthouse but later divided into two cottages. Owned by the National Trust, the house is now let as a tea-room and shop. The nearby Gorsedd stones commemorate the National Eisteddfod held in Llanrwst in 1951.

Just south of Llanrwst, B5427 (becoming B5113) angles southeast to (8m) *Pentrefoelas* on Rte 13, on the way commanding extensive views.

Betws-y-Coed, see Rte 6C, may be reached either by A470 in *6m*, soon passing a small road climbing south to *Capel Garmon Burial Chamber* (see Rte 13); or in four miles by crossing the river to join Rte 6B.

B.   West Bank of the Conwy

B5106. Total distance 14m.—*4m*. **Tyn-y-Groes**.—*1m*. **Caerhun Church**.—*4m*. **Trefriw**.—*2m*. **Gwydir Castle**.—*3m*. **Betws-y-Coed**.

Conwy (see Rte 1B) is left through *Gyffin*, the birthplace of Richard Davies, Bishop of St. David's and translator into Welsh in 1567 of the Book of Common Prayer. *4m*. **Tyn-y-Groes**, with, just to the east, Tal-y-Cafn bridge for *Bodnant Garden*, see Rte 1A. *1m*. **Caerhun Church**, reached by a lane towards the river, dates from the 13–14C, the nave and south walls being the oldest parts. The churchyard occupies the site of the Roman Kanovium, a riverside fort along the road between Deva (Chester) and Segontium (Caernarfon) which was abandoned around the middle of the 2C but reoccupied in the 4C. Later, the Welsh named this place after Rhun, a warrior son of Maelgwn Gwynedd, but of this Roman and very early Welsh past vitually nothing visible survives though a clump of trees some 50 yards northeast below the churchyard wall marks the site of the baths. *1m*. *Tal-y-Bont*, a mile west of which *Pen-y-Gaer* (1225ft) is a hillfort associated in legend with Cadair Ifan Goch on the east bank (see Rte 6A). The hillfort sprawls over an internal area of nearly five acres, with hut circles, and on the vulnerable south and west slopes there was a massive rubble rampart, below this being four ditches and earthworks.

2m. **Trefriw Wells** (Easter–Oct: daily 10.00–17.30. Nov–Easter: Mon–Sat 10.00–17.00; Sun 12.00–17.00. Tel. 01492-640057) is a spot with a story reaching back to Roman times when, sometime between 100 and 250, the 20th Legion, perhaps prospecting for minerals, opened up a cave in which there was a chalybeate spring (rich in iron). Later covered by a landslip, the cave was reopened during the 18C by Lord Willoughby de Eresby who in 1743 built and exploited a stonework (cyclopean) bathhouse which became so popular that by 1874 there was a Victorian pumproom and bath and the bottled waters were sold worldwide. By the mid 20C, though, faced with the competition from modern drugs, Trefriw Wells had lapsed into disrepair, until rescued in 1972 and today not only on the tourist map but also, thanks to a reviving interest in natural sources, once again marketing its water. Visitors can see the original Roman cave (and sample the water direct from the rock basins) and also admire the 18C cyclopean bathhouse with its original slate bath. *1m.* **Trefriw** is a small town associated with Llewelyn the Great who had a home here and who is also said to have built a church here to please his wife who flatly refused to climb to the church at Llanrhychwyn (see below). Today the chief attraction is *Trefriw Woollen Mill* (Mon–Fri 09.00–17.00 in winter or 17.30 in summer. Shop and café open also Sat 10.00–16.00 in winter or 17.00 in summer. Sun between spring Bank Hol. and end Sept 14.00–17.00. Tel. 01492-640462), opened in c 1830 and until 1900, when hydro-electric turbines were first installed, using wheels directly driven by the river Crafnant. Visitors view all the processes in the manufacture of tapestries and tweeds from raw wool, the whole well explained by an illustrated self-guide leaflet, and there is a large shop.

SOME RESERVOIRS. There are several reservoirs in the wild country to the west of Trefriw. *Llyn Cowlyd*, the largest, is reached by a path (3m) which crosses the bleak ridge of Cefn Cyfarwydd (1407ft). *Llyn Crafnant* (603ft) is the reservoir for Trefriw whence it may be reached in two miles by a narrow lane. *Llyn Geirionnydd*, at 616ft, is the closest and most accessible, reachable by roads or lanes from Trefriw, Llanrwst or the Betws-y-Coed to Capel Curig road a short way west of Swallow Falls. All these approaches are narrow and steep, especially that from Trefriw which is a lane not suitable for larger cars. This lane passes the remote little hill church of *Llanrhychwyn*, said to have been the place of worship of Llewelyn the Great, at least until, on his wife's insistence, he built a more accessible church at Trefriw. Today's quaint and simple church has a double nave (13–16C), a 12C font and fragments of medieval glass. The reservoir, at the northwest corner of Gwydir Forest, has a picnic site from which starts a trail (¾ mile) passing lead workings (1840–1914), the levels of which are dangerous and should not be entered, the ruin of the mine's explosive store, and the old tramway. At the north end of the lake there is a monument to Taliesin, the 6C bard, who however seems to have had no known association with this district.

2m. **Gwydir Castle** (tel. 01492-641687) is a generally 16 and 19C mansion built around a 14C hall. But the castle's roots go much deeper; to a fortification of the 7C and to an early 14C tower built by that Howel Coetmor whose effigy lies just across the river in Llanrwst's Gwydir Chapel. Later the estate was acquired by Maredudd ap Ievan of Dolwyddelan (died 1525) and it was he who built the hall. John Wynne (died 1559), one of Maredudd's 26 children, enlarged the house which, though with some breaks, is still owned by the family. The family had a close association with Charles I and his queen, Henrietta Maria, to whom Sir Richard Wynne was treasurer. Some of the roof timbers have a long story, having originally been in the monastery at Conwy, later used in the construction of Maenan, and finally incorporated here after the Dissolution. The gardens, known for their peacocks, include splendid cedars planted to celebrate the wedding of Charles I.

Gwydir Uchaf Chapel (Cadw. Tel. 01222-465511. Key from adjacent Forest Enterprise office during normal working hours), to the west of the road a short distance south of Gwydir Castle and not to be confused with Gwydir Chapel in Llanrwst, was built by Sir Richard Wynne in 1673. The chapel still retains many of its original features, outstanding being the *Painted Ceiling, one of the most remarkable examples in Britain of this genre of 17C art and portraying such themes as the Creation, the Trinity and the Day of Judgement.

3m. **Betws-y-Coed**, see Rte 6C.

C.   Betws-y-Coed to Ffestiniog

A470. Total distance 13m.—*6m.* **Dolwyddelan Castle.**—*4m.* **Blaenau Ffestiniog.**—*3m.* **Ffestiniog.**

Betws-y-Coed (*Inf.*) is a sprawling and straggling overgrown village on the Llugwy just above its confluence with the Conwy and a mile and a half below the meeting of the Conwy and Lledr. With these three valleys of glen and river scenery, all parts of Snowdonia National Park and of beautiful Gwydir Forest (famed for its walks), and lying on the main A5 approach to Snowdonia proper, it is hardly surprising that Betws-y-Coed is a bustling holiday centre, liable in summer to be swamped by people, cars and coaches. The place's origins, though, are very different, the name meaning Prayer House in the Forest, this origin recalled by the *Old Church* (just east of the station), the Bede, or Prayer House, in use from the 14C or earlier until the construction of the town's new church during the 19C. This old church, with a 14C nave and choir and a 19C single transept, houses a 12C font, remains of 15 or 16C glass, a pulpit made up of 15–17C fragments, and the effigy, in unusual studded armour, of Dafydd Goch (c 1380), grandson of the Prince Dafydd who was executed by Edward I in 1283; Dafydd Goch's home was Fedw Deg, on the hill within the confluence of the Conwy and Lledr rivers.

The tourist heart of Betws-y-Coed is the complex beside the station, here being large car parks, craft and other shops, cafés, a railway museum, a motor museum, and, in the Old Stables (Y Stablau), an aquarium and three information centres. The combined *Snowdonia National Park* and *Wales Tourist Board* centre is open summer: daily 09.00–18.00. Winter: daily 10.00–13.00, 14.00–17.00. Tel. 01690-710665. *Forest Enterprise, Y Stablau* (Easter and April–Oct: daily 10.00–17.00. Tel. 01492-640578) provides an introduction to the forests of Snowdonia, with some emphasis on the local Gwydir Forest. At the *RSPB Wild Snowdonia* centre (April–Oct: daily 10.00–17.30. Tel. 01690-710768) there is a non-stop audio-visual wildlife presentation—The *Conwy Valley Railway Museum* (April–Oct: daily 10.30–17.30. Tel. 01690-710568) shows much material from the period of the old London and North Western Railway. There are also dioramas, working model railway layouts, steam and diesel locomotives and the opportunity of a short, scenic ride. The *Motor Museum* (Easter–Oct: daily 10.00–18.00. Tel. 01690-710632), housed in old farm buildings, shows a private collection of vintage and later thoroughbred cars.

Betws-y-Coed is known for its generous choice of river valley and forest walks, some of which, it should be noted, pass close to dangerous disused mine shafts. Among the many spots visited by walks are *Pont-y-Pair* (Bridge of the Cauldron), the bridge, perhaps 1470, crossing the Llugwy in the north part of the town; *Miners' Bridge*, a picturesque footbridge used by generations of miners, 50 yards above a ford where the Roman Sarn Helen crossed the river; *Artists' Wood* (walk starts and finishes at Miners' Bridge), so called because of its popularity with 19C artists such as David Cox and Turner; *Swallow Falls*, a FE *Arboretum* and *Ty Hyll*, for all of which see Rte 7; and the forest upland across to Gwydir Castle on Rte 6B, passing relics of the era of lead mining.

For Betws-y-Coed to *Bangor*, see Rtes 7 and 9; to *Llanberis*, see Rtes 7 and 8; to *Beddgelert* and *Penrhyndeudraeth*, see Rte 7; to *Corwen*, see Rte 13; to *Denbigh*, see Rtes 4 and 13.

A5 leads southeast out of Betws-y-Coed, at the town's edge crossing the Conwy by Telford's graceful iron Waterloo Bridge of 1815, the year of the battle. Immediately beyond, A470 breaks away and soon recrosses the Conwy, just before this bridge being a sign to *Fairy Glen* in which the Conwy drops through a narrow wooded gorge. A470 now ascends the lovely valley of the Lledr river, at first green and pastoral but soon becoming rocky and wilder while to the south opens the valley of the Gwibernant up which a road leads in one and a half miles to **Ty Mawr** (NT. April–Sept: Wed, Thur, Fri, Sun 12.00–17.00. Oct: Fri and Sun 12.00–16.00. Also open Bank Hol. Tel. NT, North 01492-860123), birthplace of William Morgan (c 1545–1604), first translator of the Bible into Welsh. There is a display of Welsh bibles, including William Morgan's of 1588, while a one mile nature walk explores the surrounds. *4m* (from Betws-y-Coed) *Pont-y-Pant*, crossing place of the Roman Sarn Helen from Tomen-y-Mur (Rte 16) to Kanovium (Rte 6B).

2m. **Dolwyddelan Castle** (Cadw; see p. 11) stands as a stark, square isolated keep on a ridge above the road.

History. The castle was built in c 1170, possibly by Iorwerth, father of Llewelyn the Great who may have been born here in 1173 and who later certainly used Dolwyddelan as a home. In 1281 Llewelyn the Last was here, but two years later the castle was taken by Edward I and strengthened. In 1488 the place was acquired by Maredudd ap Ievan (see Gwydir Castle), who built the village church in which his kneeling effigy in brass can be seen. After Maredudd's death the castle decayed into ruin though a modern roof and battlements were added during the 19C. An exhibition tells the story of the castles of the Welsh princes.

The ruins comprise a small ward, with a west tower and keep, this last (12C) being the oldest part with, as its most interesting feature, its curious defensive entrance. This entrance was at the first floor and was covered by a small barbican, now very ruined, reached from outside by steps along the face of the keep; inside the barbican there was a pit, covered by a drawbridge. Inside the keep the main room was originally covered by a gabled roof which was nevertheless still enclosed by the keep walls which rose above it. Traces of this can still be seen, although it was later replaced, probably by Maredudd, by a flat roof and upper room. The castle's curtain wall is early 13C, but the inner walls of the west tower date from the end of that century.

To the north of Dolwyddelan rises *Moel Siabod* (2860ft), as A470 crosses the river at Roman Bridge, which has in fact no clear Roman association, before passing over bleak hills by the *Crimea Pass* (1263ft), a name recalling a now vanished inn. On the descent which follows, two unusually interesting slate mines can be visited, the first being *Gloddfa Ganol (Easter–Oct: Mon–Fri 10.00–17.30. Also open Sun from mid July to end Aug. Tel. 01766-830664), a working mine dating from 1818 and believed to be the world's largest. At this starkly impressive site the visitor is offered instructive audio-visual presentations; machinery; a museum; the chance to watch quarrymen sawing and splitting slate blocks; huge blasted caverns; open-cast blasting; and three cottages of c 1840, furnished in the styles of the late 19C, 1914–18, and as used until the late 1960s. Additionally there are a restaurant, shops, a play area, and (extra payment) a ride in a quarrymen's train and a Land Rover guided tour into the mountain.

Although there is plenty to see and do above ground—restaurant, and a Victorian village with shops, lock-up and a pub—the most rewarding experiences at *Llechwedd Slate Caverns (daily 10.00–17.15 in March–Sept or 16.15 in Oct–Feb. Tel. 01766–830306) are below. The Underground Tramway visits parts of the mine where 19C mining conditions have been recreated, while the Deep Mine Tour using the inclined railway (claiming to be Britain's steepest passenger railway) drops to the mine's lower levels for a walk through several chambers, each with Son et Lumière.

4m. (from Dolwyddelan) **Blaenau Ffestiniog** (*Inf.*) lies darkly below hills scarred by quarrying. The principal nearby attraction is the *Ffestiniog (Pumped Storage) Power Station* (Easter–Oct: daily 10.00–16.30. Tel. 01766-830310), off A496 at Tan-y-Grisiau, which is also a request halt on the Ffestiniog Railway (see Rte 15). Opened by the Queen in 1963, this power station was the first of its kind in Britain. From the information centre (exhibition, cinema, café, shop, picnic area) visitors may book for a tour of the power station or, for the more ambitious, for the tour up the mountain to the upper reservoir's Stwlan Dam. The lower reservoir (Tan-y-Grisiau) was formed by damming the river Ystradau.

Manod, the straggling southward extension of Blaenau Ffestiniog, has huge underground quarries which, air conditioned and fitted with brick chambers, in 1940–45 sheltered many of the National Gallery's paintings. *3m.* **Ffestiniog**, see Rte 15.

7

Betws-y-Coed to Beddgelert and Penrhyndeudraeth

A5 to Capel Curig. A4086 to Pen-y-Gwryd. A498 to Beddgelert. A4085 to Penrhyndeudraeth. Total distance 23m.—*5m.* **Capel Curig.**—*4m.* **Pen-y-Gwryd.**—*7m.* **Beddgelert.**—*7m.* **Penrhyndeudraeth.**

To Capel Curig up the wooded valley of the Llugwy. From Capel Curig to Pen-y-Gwryd across high moor, then descending beautiful Nant Gwynant, a valley of lush meadows and woods with mountains lifting high on both sides.

Betws-y-Coed, see Rte 6C. *2m. Swallow Falls*, a cataract breaking its way through surroundings of rock and woodland. A short way beyond there is a Forest Enterprise picnic site and car park for the *Gwydir Forest Arboretum* (tel. 01492-640578) which, opened in 1950, now shows more than 100 tree species. Beyond, where the road crosses the river, the stone building known as *Ty Hyll* (Ugly House)—owing its name to its rough appearance, the result, it is said, of hurried construction in order to grab a freehold on what was common land—was once an overnight stop for Irish drovers bringing cattle from Holyhead to markets in England. These drovers followed what is now the old road along the river's south bank, rather less than a mile along which, between the road and the river, are the tree-covered earthworks of *Caer Llugwy*, or, on some maps, *Caer Bryn y Gefeilliau*, a Roman station occupied apparently for only some 50 years between 90 and 140. From Ty Hyll a small road climbs north to (see Rte 6B) Llyn Geirionnydd, descending beyond into the Vale of Conwy. A5 continues with the north bank of the Llugwy, soon passing on the left *Pont Cyfnyg* (Narrow Bridge) where the south bank old road rejoins. Soon there appears to the left one of the finest and most famous views of Snowdon.

3m. **Capel Curig**, encircled by mountains and at the junction of the important mountain roads to Beddgelert (this Rte) and Llyn Ogwen and Bangor (Rte 9), is a centre for walks. From here A4086 is followed along the north shore of Llynau Mymbyr and up the moorland valley of Nant-y-Gwryd. To the south Moel Siabod presents its least attractive slope while on the north the Glyders are not here impressive, but, in contrast, ahead rises the massive complex of Snowdon. *4m.* **Pen-y-Gwryd Hotel**, at 850ft, is a lonely spot at a road junction from which A4086, after a brief climb, drops down the Pass of Llanberis (see Rte 8). Popularly known as PYG, Pen-y-Gwryd has long been known to climbers and shows mementoes of the Everest team of 1953 who trained in this area. The Romans, too, knew this place and traces of a square earthwork spanning both roads just below the fork recall that this often bleak junction was once a temporary fort or marching camp.

This Route now follows A498 descending *Nant Gwynant, a lovely valley, part wooded, with two lakes and with mountains lifting on either side. Just below Pen-y-Gwryd there is a car park and view point high above *Cwm Dyli*, at this valley's foot being a power station while the great face of Snowdon towers above. *3m. Llyn Gwynant*, under a mile beyond the south end of which is the start of the Watkin Path (see Rte 8B). For the small Nantmor valley road, heading east from *Bethania* and then south and enabling Beddgelert to be bypassed, see immediately after Pont Aberglaslyn below.

The road now fringes the north shore of Llyn Dinas (176ft) to pass, north of the road and just below the lake, *Dinas Emrys*, a hill on top of which are vestiges of 12C ramparts. More interesting, though, is the legend which haunts this place, for it was here that the luckless Vortigern tried to build his tower while Merlin told of the red and white dragons (see Legend). Romantics may accept the discovery here of Iron Age relics as backing for the legend. Opposite, the southern slopes of Nant Gwynant—hills which in 1958 were used for the filming of 'The Inn of the Sixth Happiness', starring Ingrid Bergman—were in the 18 and 19C busy with copper mining, a prosperous past recalled today by *Sygun Copper Mine* (daily, hours vary. Tel. 01766-86595), off A498 approaching Beddgelert. Here guided tours, which include the large chambers hewn into the hillface, backed by a Visitor Centre with video presentation, photographs and models, combine to explain the successive steps in the mining process and also to give some idea of the working environment.

4m. (from Llyn Gwynant) **Beddgelert** is a scattered and straggling village in a wooded and pastoral setting below rocky heights at the confluence of two mountain streams, the Glaslyn and the Colwyn. It is also at the junction of three valleys (Nant Gwynant, described above; Nant Colwyn, the road to Caernarfon, Rte 10; and Aberglaslyn, see below), all carrying main roads, the result being that in summer Beddgelert can be swamped by visitors and its narrow bridge clogged by traffic.

History and Legend. A Celtic monastery was founded here in the 6C, this becoming one of the foremost houses in Wales. In the 12 or 13C the monastery was succeeded by a small Augustinian priory founded by Llewelyn the Great, but this disappeared with the Dissolution. Beddgelert was, however, more than a religious centre, in medieval times ranking also as something of a port, a role made possible by the fact that the Glaslyn was navigable at least as far as Pont Aberglaslyn and remained so until the construction of the Porthmadog embankment in the early 19C.

The village owes its name (Grave of Gelert) to a legend first made familiar by the verses of William Spenser in 1800. Gelert was the trusted hound of Prince Llewelyn, who, departing for the hunt, left Gelert in charge of his infant son. Returning, and finding the child missing, the cradle in disorder and Gelert with blood-stained muzzle, Llewelyn slew the hound—only, soon after, to find the child safely sleeping, beside him being a dead wolf killed by the faithful Gelert.

Of the Augustinian priory all that remains is the village *Church*, once the priory chapel and still showing some 13C work in the triple lancet windows at the east end and in the arcade between the nave and its north chapel. The reputed grave of Gelert—the stones apparently erected by a visitor-conscious landlord of The Goat during the 18C—is in a meadow just south of the village, reached by a path from the bridge. But it is to walkers that Beddgelert has perhaps the most to offer, the choices ranging from modest local walks along the rivers and through the woods to ascents of heights such as Moel-y-Dyniewyd (1254ft) or Moel Hebog (2566ft), or, more ambitiously, Yr Aran (2451ft) or Snowdon by either the Watkin Path or the Pitt's Head approach, for both of which see Rte 8B.

Below Beddgelert the road soon enters the **Pass of Aberglaslyn** (NT), a narrow defile in which the torrent of the Glaslyn and the road run side-by-side between steep slopes of fir. This is where the Glaslyn leaves the mountains and, as noted above, until the early 19C the river was navigable as far as *Pont Aberglaslyn*. At this bridge A498 (Rte 10) continues south to Porthmadog while this Route, now A4085, crosses the bridge.

Just beyond the bridge a small road (the old Ffestiniog road) branches east for *Nantmor* at the foot of Cwm Bychan, the head of which was during the 18 and 19C the site of an important copper mine. Beyond comes *Bwlch Gwernog*, whence another small road heads north along the wooded Nantmor valley (with forest walks) to reach Nant Gwynant between Llyn Gwynant and Llyn Dinas, for both of which see above.

From Pont Aberglaslyn A4085 skirts the reclaimed Traeth Mawr (see Rte 10). *7m.* (from Beddgelert) **Penrhyndeudraeth** is a small town with a station of the Ffestiniog Railway.

For Penrhyndeudraeth to *Ffestiniog* and *Bala*, as also for *Portmeirion* and *Porthmadog*, see Rte 15.

8

Pass of Llanberis. Snowdon

This Route describes first (Rte 8A) the Pass of Llanberis, the steep narrow
cleft which defines Snowdon's northeast flank and carries the road which
passes the starting points of three of the six principal ascent paths as also,
at Llanberis, the valley station of the Snowdon Mountain Railway. Rte 8B
describes Snowdon itself.

Snowdon Sherpa Bus. Much of northern Snowdonia is served by the Snowdon Sherpa
bus service, the network's east and southeast boundary being Llandudno to Porthmadog via Llanrwst, Betws-y-Coed, Capel Curig and Beddgelert, with links to Caernarfon, Llanberis and Bangor. Parking can be difficult around Snowdon, with
Pen-y-Pass car park often full and on-road parking prohibited between Pen-y-Gwryd
and Nant Peris. The Sherpa service not only allows the best of the scenery to be seen
but also offers flexibility for walkers. Information from local Tourist Information offices,
or Dept of Economic Development and Planning, County Offices, Caernarfon, LL55
1SH. Tel. 01286-679535.

A. Pass of Llanberis (Pen-y-Gwryd to Caernarfon)

A4086. Total distance 13m.—*1m. Pen-y-Pass.*—*3m. Nant Peris.*—*2m.* **Llanberis**.—*7m.* **Caernarfon**.

From Pen-y-Gwryd (see Rte 7) the Llanberis road, cut into this hillside in
c 1850 and affording a splendid view down Nant Gwynant, loops round
Moel Berfedd. *1m. Pen-y-Pass* (limited parking. 1169ft), at the crest of the
pass, is a youth hostel, a mountain rescue centre, and the starting place for
the Pyg and Miners' tracks to the peaks of Snowdon. From here the road
starts its descent through the *Pass of Llanberis, one of the wildest and
most desolate valleys in Wales, a narrow defile below towering black walls
of rock and in places almost blocked by boulders and debris. At *Pont-y-
Gromlech*, just over a mile below the summit, the road crosses the tumbling
Peris, by the bridge being a parking area below precipitous crags much
used by rock climbers. Soon, to the west, the arms of Crib Goch open to
give a fine view of *Cwm Glas* (approached by a footbridge half a mile
below Pont-y-Gromlech), with its two tarns (2200ft and 2700ft) overhung
by majestic precipices an awesome place and one of particular interest to
geographers and geologists for its clear evidence of glacial action.

3m (from Pen-y-Pass) *Nant Peris*, or Old Llanberis, where there is a simple
cruciform church (part 12C), with a 15C timber roof, a screen with an old
alms box, and a curious window in the west wall. The Well of Peris, in a
field just north of the road, was until comparatively recent times much
visited for both healing and wishing, a successful request being signalled
by the appearance of a sacred fish; or so Pennant reported in 1781. Skirting
Llyn Peris, the road soon kinks round *Dolbadarn Castle* (Cadw; see p. 11),
the main feature here being the circular keep thought to have been built

by Llewelyn the Great in the early 13C. Later, from 1255 for over 20 years, this was the prison of Owain Goch, older brother and defeated rival of Llewelyn the Last.

2m. **Llanberis** (*Inf.*) is a straggling and scattered community the centre of which is off the west of the bypass road at the south end of Llyn Padarn, here separated by a narrow isthmus from the smaller Llyn Peris. The natural beauty of the surroundings has long been marred by the nevertheless impressive great scars of huge slate quarries which, tier above precipitous tier, climb to a height approaching 1500ft. Quarrying finished in 1969, but in 1974 slate began again to litter the slopes as work began on excavating the deep caverns which now hide the National Grid's *Dinorwig Pumped Storage Scheme*, the largest of its kind in Europe, with its upper reservoir of Marchlyn Mawr 1600ft above Llyn Peris, the lower one. Prominent along the bypass is the large modern complex of *Power of Wales—Museum of the North* (daily 10.00–17.00 but with seasonal variations. Tel. 01286-870636. Wales Tourist Board and Snowdonia National Park information desks). Essentially this complex is a branch of the National Museum of Wales, the theme here (a joint venture with the National Grid Company) being the story and power of Wales, the themes presented by the wizard Merlin using multi-media special effects. Afterwards, visitors who wish are taken to the Dinorwig power station. Also here at Power of Wales are exhibition galleries, a shop and café.

On the far side of the isthmus separating Llyn Padarn and Llyn Peris, *Padarn Country Park* (tel. 01286-870892), opened in 1970 and one of the first of its kind in Wales, extends along the shore of Llyn Padarn and includes a network of woodland and industrial trails using the paths worn by generations of quarrymen. Within the general bounds of the park are the Welsh Slate Museum and the Llanberis Lake Railway. The *Welsh Slate Museum* (Easter Sat–Sept: daily 09.30–17.30. Other periods by arrangement. Tel. 01286-870630), a branch of the National Museum of Wales, is housed in workshops of the former Dinorwig quarry which functioned from 1809 to 1969, at its peak in 1900 employing some 3000 people. Much of the machinery has been preserved (the wheel, over 50ft in diameter, is one of the largest in Britain) and visitors can see the foundry; smithy; the pattern, woodworking and fitting shops; the sick bay and suchlike, while in summer there are demonstrations and films. The *Llanberis Lake Railway* (tel. 01286-870549) was originally the quarry railway to Port Dinorwic on the Menai Strait; at first (1840) worked by a combination of animal and gravity power, the line later became 4ft gauge and steam-operated. Saved by enthusiasts, and now narrow gauge but still steam, today's line offers a 40 minute return journey the length of the north shore of Llyn Padarn. Passengers may leave the train at the halfway station (Cei Llydan), with a picnic site, and catch a later train.

Walks from Llanberis include the waterfall of *Ceunant Mawr* (¾ mile) and the smaller Ceunant Bach, a little farther upstream. The main longer distance walk is that up Snowdon (see Rte 8B) and there are also tracks to Llyn Cwellyn (4m, Rte 10) and Beddgelert (9m, Rte 7).

Beyond Llanberis the road skirts the south shore of Llyn Padarn, soon emerging from the mountains and in rather over *2m* passing close to *Bryn Bras Castle* (tel. 01286-870210), a rambling castellated complex built in the 1830s (perhaps by Thomas Hopper) around an early 18C predecessor and known for its extensive gardens and panoramic walks. *5m*. **Caernarfon**, see Rte 10.

B. Snowdon

˙˙SNOWDON, the highest mountain in England and Wales, is despite its name generally free from snow between April and October, though drifts may linger in the gullies until early summer. The massif forms a cluster of five peaks, linked by sharp ridges, and presents fine escarpments in all directions, especially towards the east where the beautiful lakes of Glaslyn and Llyn Llydaw are overhung by sheer walls of rock. The principal heights, in their starfish formation, are *Yr Wyddfa Fawr* (3560ft), the central peak, now crowned by a cairn; *Crib-y-Ddysgl* (3493ft), half a mile north and skirted by the Llanberis Track; *Crib Goch* (3023ft; Red Ridge), a mile and a half northeast, a splendid pile of rock, rich in pinnacles and buttresses; *Lliwedd* (2497ft), the long craggy ridge running southeast, with a well-known rock wall; and *Yr Aran* (2451ft), the outlying southern peak, forming a spur towards Beddgelert. Between these mountains are six cwms or hollows, of which *Cwm Dyli* and *Cwm Glas*, separated by Crib Goch, are the most impressive. Tracks cross all the ridges; exposed and liable to high winds, these are suitable only for the experienced.

Legend and History. To the ancient Welsh the mountain was Eryri, the High Land. Its English name of Snowdon it owes to the Saxons, who spoke of the distant Snow Dun, the Snow Hill or fortress. Its present Welsh name Yr Wyddfa Fawr (Great Tomb) it owes to the legend that the summit was the tomb of the giant Rhita Fawr, slain by King Arthur. Arthur is supposed to have been mortally wounded on Bwlch-y-Saethau, and from this it is natural to accept Llyn Llydaw below as the lake into which Excalibur was thrown. Another legend is that of Vortigern and Merlin at Dinas Emrys in Nant Gwynant (see Rte 7). That prehistoric man lived on the lower slopes is known from material found near Llyn Llydaw. In medieval times Dolbadarn became a castle of the Welsh princes, and the mountain is mentioned by Giraldus. Llewelyn the Last retreated into Snowdon before his final defeat and death; Edward I created a Royal Forest of Snowdon; and Owen Glendower is thought to have found refuge here. Thomas Johnson, a naturalist, is recorded as having ascended Snowdon in 1639, and Halley is said to have made astronomical experiments on the summit in 1697. It was in the 17C, too, that the first mining began. An ascent from Llanberis is fully described by Pennant, and Wordsworth writes of leaving 'Beddgelert's huts at couching time' to witness sunrise from the peak ('Prelude'). Victorian times were prosperous for guides and their ponies (George Borrow took his step-daughter up the mountain in 1859, this being a highlight of the tour which led eight years later to the publication of his classic 'Wild Wales'), but this era ended with the building of the railway in 1896.

Ascent of Snowdon

Snowdon is ascended by the Snowdon Mountain Railway from Llanberis, or by any of the six traditional walkers' tracks, beginning at various points around the base of the mountain. Of these the finest and steepest are the *Watkin Path* from Nant Gwynant and the *Pyg Track* from Pen-y-Pass, to which the *Miners' Track*, also from Pen-y-Pass, is an interesting alternative skirting Llyn Llydaw and passing mine workings. The *Pitt's Head Track* and the *Snowdon Ranger Track*, both from the Beddgelert to Llyn Cwellyn main road, afford views of the lesser known western escarpments. The *Llanberis Track* is the easiest but least interesting ascent. It must be emphasised that Snowdon is notorious for its sudden winds and mists and that parts of the group are dangerously precipitous and craggy. The inexperienced should invariably take local advice and in any case not stray from the paths.

The **Snowdon Mountain Railway** (mid March–Oct: daily from about 09.00. Tel. 01286-870223), a narrow-gauge rack-and-pinion line, the only such in Britain, was opened in 1896 and is now operated by seven steam locomotives (some 1895–96, some 1922–23) and four diesels. The time to the summit is about one hour, the train waiting here for half an hour before the descent which takes another hour. Factors worth bearing in mind are that trains do not run to a strict timetable; that the capacity of each train is 59 passengers and that normally there has to be a minimum of 25; and that operation is dependent upon the weather. On fine days, especially in July to September, almost all trains are filled; early arrival at the station is therefore strongly recommended.

A sharp ascent begins soon after the station. A viaduct is crossed, with a good view of the Ceunant Mawr Falls, and, beyond, the Ceunant Bach Fall is also seen. After passing *Hebron* (1¼m; 930ft) the line ascends the long north spur of the mountain and crosses the Llanberis Track, Moel Eilio and Y Foel Goch being seen to the right. Beneath *Halfway* (2½m; 1600ft), to the right is the deep valley of Cwm Brwynog (Cwm of Rushes), with its amphitheatre of cliff. The foot track is again crossed just beyond *Clogwyn* (3¾m; 2550ft) and there is a glimpse left into the precipitous gorge of Cwm Glas Bach with the Pass of Llanberis beyond. Curving to the right to ascend a slope above the cliffs of Clogwyn-du'r-Arddu (Black Precipice), with a tarn at their foot, the line affords a fine view extending as far as Anglesey. It then crosses the Snowdon Ranger Track (3200ft) and reaches the saddle. *Snowdon Summit* station is just below the cairn of Yr Wyddfa.

Llanberis Track. From Llanberis (Victoria Hotel). 5m in 3 hours. The track, originally a Victorian pony trail, never diverges far from the railway and generally affords the same views. A detour on the left beyond the second railway crossing leads to the cliff edge, with a splendid view of *Cwm Glas*. Near the summit, *Bwlch Glas*, where the Pyg and Snowdon Ranger tracks join, is another viewpoint.

Pyg Track. From Pen-y-Pass. 2½ hours. This popular route was so named at the turn of the century by climbers from Pen-y-Gwyrd Hotel (PYG), who wished to distinguish it from the Miners' Track. It is also often spelt Pig Track, some justification being that one translation of *Bwlch Moch*, reached at 1850ft, could be Pigs' Pass. Llyn Llydaw and the sheer cliffs of Yr Wyddfa and Lliwedd here come into view, and the track skirts the hillside under the crags of Crib Goch. Later a shoulder is crossed, looking down 400ft into the cwm which contains Glaslyn, the Miners' Track being met above the west end of the lake. The joint path bears right up zigzags to meet the Llanberis track at *Bwlch Glas*.

Miners' Track. From Pen-y-Pass. 3 hours. The mine is Glaslyn, where copper was mined from the second half of the 18C until 1916. Its situation was so remote that the miners lived at the mine, returning on foot at weekends across the Glyders to their homes in Bethesda. From Pen-y-Pass the track passes the small *Llyn Teyrn* (1238ft), then crosses the northeast end of *Llyn Llydaw* (1416ft) by a causeway. The lake is dominated at its head by Lliwedd. The track skirts the north shore, then turns northwest, passing the abandoned copper workings near the smaller *Glaslyn* (1971ft). From Glaslyn the path zigzags up to the Pyg Track, a route up which the miners carried their sacks to Bwlch Glas, whence the ore was dragged on sledges down to Llyn Cwellyn.

Watkin Path. From Nant Gwynant. 3 hours. Sir Edward Watkin was a Victorian railway entrepreneur whose dream was a train from Manchester to Paris, and who constructed nearly two miles of Channel Tunnel before the government stopped the project. He retired to Nant Gwynant and soon built a path upwards from the South Snowdon Slate Quarries; it was opened by Gladstone in 1892. The path is perhaps the finest ascent, but it is steep and not for the inexperienced. From the road, near the Glaslyn bridge, a cart-track is followed to a fork (5 min.). Here the branch to the left is taken, climbing above waterfalls to the right. At 850ft the stream is crossed to a ruined house, a short way beyond which is *Gladstone Rock* (inscription), from which Gladstone, aged 83, opened the path, the theme of his speech being Justice to Wales. The cart-track ends at the old quarry, the point where the Watkin Path proper bears right and begins to ascend the long southwest slope of Lliwedd. The narrow saddle which the track follows between Lliwedd and Yr Wyddfa is *Bwlch-y-Saethau* (2690ft), the Pass of the Arrows, traditionally a burial place of King Arthur.

Pitt's Head Track. From *Pitt's Head Rock* ($2\frac{1}{2}$m north of Beddgelert on A4085) or from *Rhyd-Ddu*, a mile farther north. 3 hours. From the point where the two tracks meet there is a gradual climb northeast over open moor to the west extremity of the *Llechog* ridge (2400ft). Where the track is faint, there are small cairns. The precipitous north face of Llechog is followed, with views down to the tarns in Cwm Clogwyn, the ridge narrowing into the rocky razor-edge of *Bwlch-y-Maen* (3056ft), the Stone Pass. The Watkin Path is joined just below the summit.

Snowdon Ranger Track. From Snowdon Ranger hostel on Llyn Cwellyn. $2\frac{1}{2}$ hours. After nearly a mile the path to Llanberis is crossed. The slope of Moel Cynghorion is to the left, while to the right is the marshy ground of Cwm Clogwyn with its five tarns. From *Bwlch Cwm-Brwynog* (1600ft), the steep ridge of *Clogwyn-du'r-Arddu* is ascended, and the Llanberis track is met near Bwlch Glas.

9

Capel Curig to Bangor

A5. Total distance 14m.—*5m*. **Ogwen Cottage**.—*4m*. **Bethesda**.—*3m*. **Llandegai**.—*2m*. **Bangor**.

As far as Ogwen Cottage, and down Nant Ffrancon, the road is through grand mountain scenery.

For **Capel Curig**, see Rte 7. The road ascends the left bank of the Llugwy into country of increasing grandeur, the old road, now a grass-grown track, providing a pleasant alternative for walkers along the other bank. To the north are the slopes of Pen Llithrig-y-Wrach and Pen Helig, with the two Carneddau beyond in the distance, while to the south Snowdon is soon hidden behind the long eastward extremity of the Glyders, the projection nearest to the road being Gallt-yr-Ogof, the Cliff of the Caves. Soon the great rock-pyramid of Tryfan comes suddenly into view, with the mountains beyond Llyn Ogwen (Y Foel Goch, and, later, Y Garn) in the background. The road crosses the Llugwy, descending from its source of Fynnon Llugwy a mile away to the north, while to the south opens Cwm Tryfan. *Llyn Ogwen*, a lake a mile long and nowhere more than 10ft deep, is grandly set in a deep hollow between the black, rock-strewn slopes of Tryfan and the

Glyders to the south and, to the north, Pen-yr-Oleu-Wen, the precipitous southern spur of Carnedd Dafydd.

5m. **Ogwen Cottage**, at Pont Pen-y-Benglog (993ft), is a mountain school, while adjacent Idwal Cottage is a youth hostel. This area is the southern end of the National Trust's huge Carneddau Estate of over 15,000 acres, the estate including Llyn Idwal, the head of Nant Ffrancon and several mountains, amongst these being the northern slopes of the two Glyders, Tryfan, Carnedd Dafydd and the northwest slopes of Carnedd Llewelyn.

*Cwm Idwal Nature Reserve, just south, is reached by a path behind Ogwen Cottage. Established in 1954 as the first reserve to be declared in Wales, and now leased by the National Trust to the Countryside Council for Wales, this natural amphitheatre (1223ft) below volcanic rock walls piling up another 2000ft or more, is scenically awesome, botanically of a particular interest (alpines), and, as might be expected of such a place, a source of legend. Hollowed out by the same inexorable glacier which on its further descent carved Nant Ffrancon, Cwm Idwal is largely filled by *Llyn Idwal*, a sombre lake below the main precipice of Glyder Fawr, to the right of which opens a great fissure with overhanging sides known as Twll Du, or the Devil's Kitchen. In legend Prince Idwal, son of Owain Gwynedd, was drowned here by his foster-father; his spirit still haunts the lake, and that of his murderer the Devil's Kitchen. A trail makes the circuit of the lake, feral goats being among the wildlife here.

Ogwen Cottage is a focus for many demanding walks and climbs. But this is also the heart of one of the wildest districts in Wales, notorious for precipices, boulders, treacherous scree and uncertain weather, and advice should be sought before setting out for any distance or height. Walks and climbs include *The Glyders* (3279 and 3262ft); *Y Garn* (3104ft); *Elidir Fawr* (3029ft) above Marchlyn Mawr, the upper reservoir of the Dinorwig Power Station at Llanberis; the *Miners' Track*, the route from Bethesda used by the copper miners employed at Glaslyn (see Rte 8B); *Tryfan* (3010ft), with its three precipitous faces; and, to the northeast, *Carnedd Dafydd* (3426ft) and *Carnedd Llewelyn* (3484ft), named after the two brother princes who confronted Edward I, and, after Snowdon, the two highest mountains in Wales.

Immediately beyond Ogwen Cottage the road crosses the Ogwen which here spills out of its lake and, joined by the stream from Llyn Idwal, plunges down into the head of Nant Ffrancon in a series of cataracts known as the Benglog Falls (Falls of the Skull). The road, engineered by Telford in 1815–30, now enters ***Nant Ffrancon**, possibly named after Adam de Francton, traditionally the name of the man who killed Llewelyn the Last, but more probably deriving from Nant yr Afanc, meaning the Valley of the Beavers. Glacially immediate successor to Cwm Idwal, the valley is bounded by rocky mountains, those on the west side cut by tributary glacial cwms.

Just beyond (*2m*) the hamlet of *Tyn-y-Maes* a bridge crosses the Ogwen, the small road on the far side of the river being one built in the latter part of the 18C for the benefit of Irish Members of Parliament making for London. The scenery now quickly changes, the rocks giving way to the woods of Ogwen Bank on the east while to the west are the Penrhyn Slate Quarries.

2m. **Bethesda** owes its growth to the 19C development of slate quarrying, and its present name (previously it was Glanogwen), deriving from a Nonconformist chapel in the main street, to the religious fervour of the same period. The *Penrhyn Slate Quarries* were developed in c 1770 by Richard Pennant, the 1st Baron Penrhyn. The biggest opencast system in the world, the quarries form a vast amphitheatre, a mile long and some 1200ft deep, hewn in terraces out of the north end of Bron Llwyd. The mules and carts of the early days were superseded in 1801 by a special railway to Port Penrhyn, immediately east of Bangor. For (*3m*) **Llandegai** and **Penrhyn Castle**, see Rte 1C. *2m*. **Bangor**, see Rte 3.

10

Bangor to Caernarfon and Porthmadog

A487 to Caernarfon. A4085 to Beddgelert. A498 to Porthmadog. Total distance 29m.—*5m*. **Port Dinorwic**.—*4m*. **Caernarfon**.—*5m*. *Betws Garmon*.—*7m*. **Beddgelert**.—*2m*. *Pont Aberglaslyn*.—*5m*. **Tremadog**.—*1m*. **Porthmadog**.

Mountain and woodland on both sides between Betws Garmon through Beddgelert to Pont Aberglaslyn; then mountains to the west and reclaimed estuary to the east.

For **Bangor**, see Rte 3. *5m*. **Port Dinorwic**, today a yachting centre and marina, is a place which has had its touches of history, starting in the 1C when, it seems reasonably certain, both Suetonius and Agricola chose this as their crossing point for their assaults on Anglesey. Some eight centuries later the raiding Norsemen habitually sheltered here from both weather and tides, their example followed by generations of fishermen until in the 19C Dinorwic became the port at the end of the slate railway from the great quarries above Llanberis (the Llanberis Lake Railway, see Rte 8A, is all that survives). Anyone with an interest in wood may divert a mile southward to the *Greenwood Centre* (April–Sept: daily 10.00–17.30. For winter opening tel. 01248-671493) off B4366 at the Cors Bach public house between Bethel and Llanddeiniolen. Opened in 1993, this indoor and outdoor environmental attraction about the world of trees and timber offers many imaginative features of interest to both adults and children.

4m. **CAERNARFON** (*Inf.*), on the right bank of the mouth of the Seiont near the southwest end of Menai Strait, is a historic place visited for its great castle, for its rectangle of town walls protecting the 13C Edwardian borough, still the main shopping area, and for the Roman site of Segontium. The Romans were at Segontium from c 77 to c 380, and on Twt Hill, in the east of the town, evidence has been found of a Celtic settlement. Otherwise the story of Caernarfon is essentially that of its castle.

Bangor Street enters the town from the northeast, soon reaching Turf Square, once the site of the pillory and stocks. From here High Street leads west through the medieval walls while Bridge Street continues south into the large CASTLE SQUARE, also known as Y Maes, with statues of David Lloyd George (by W. Goscombe John), local Member of Parliament from

1890 to 1945, and of Sir Hugh Owen (1804–81), a pioneer of Welsh university education. The Castle, the quays along the mouth of the Seiont, and the walled town are all immediately west and northwest of Castle Square; it is well worth while to go down to the quay, often busy with fishing boats and yachts (embarkation also for Menai cruises), from where a far better impression of the great walls and their defensive strength is gained than is apparent from the somewhat cramped town side.

•**Caernarfon Castle** (Cadw; see p. 11) is a massive and commanding example of medieval fortification.

History. The first castle was a Norman motte-and-bailey of c 1100, taken by the Welsh princes not long after its construction and remaining in Welsh hands until 1283, when Edward I set James of St. George to building the castle that stands here today. The castle was completed in three main stages, the first being up till 1292, the second 1295

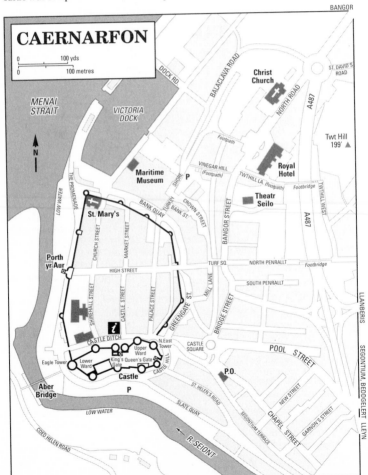

to 1308 when the master mason was Walter of Hereford, and the last 1309 to 1323. The associated English Borough was granted its charter in 1284. The use of polygonal towers has few English precedents, and that of banded masonry none. Both these are features of the walls of Constantinople, and, together with the use of the decorative eagle, suggest an intention to recall Segontium's tradition as the birthplace of Constantine the Great (what was believed to be the body of Constantine's father, Constantius I, killed at York in 305 while on an expedition against the Picts and Scots, was found in 1283 and reburied at Edward's behest). Edward II was born here in 1284, but not in the Eagle Tower as popularly supposed. The story of his presentation to the conquered Welsh as 'a Prince of Wales who could speak no English' is almost certainly apocryphal, and cannot in fact be traced earlier than 1584. In 1294 during Madog's rebellion the town was sacked by the Welsh, who breached the wall below Eagle Tower. In 1399 Richard II was here after his landing from Ireland, and in 1403 Caernarfon was unsuccessfully attacked by Owen Glendower. The Parliamentarian William Prynne was imprisoned here in 1637, and during the Civil War the castle changed hands three times, finally falling to Parliament. After 1660 it was dismantled. In 1911 the future Edward VIII was invested here as Prince of Wales, as was also Prince Charles in 1969.

Despite its externally complete appearance, the castle today is little more than a shell. It comprises two irregular wards, the upper or outer (east) of which encloses the site of the Norman motte. There are two gates, the King's Gate (north) at the join of the wards, and the Queen's Gate at the eastern extremity. The many angles of the walls are marked by polygonal towers, crowned by picturesque turrets, Eagle Tower at the castle's west end having three of these. The walls and towers along the south side, between and including Eagle Tower and North East Tower, represent the earlier building phase (up to 1292), although the upper parts of Eagle Tower were completed later. An interesting defensive feature is the almost continuous system of mural passages, carried round the inner faces of the towers and pierced with loopholes. On the south face of the castle these passages are doubled, this affording, in conjunction with the looped merlons of the rampart walk, positions for three tiers of archers.

The description below follows an anticlockwise circuit, starting with the lower ward. Visitors have a choice between using the mural passages or returning to the courtyard after each tower.

The ENTRANCE, on the north side, is through the *King's Gate*, above which is a mutilated statue of Edward II. The gate was formerly approached by a drawbridge, traces of which and of its associated defences (portcullis, arrow slits) can still be seen. The entrance passage is flanked by strong octagonal towers, and the gatehouse would have incorporated quarters for the constable, with a hall, chapel, and living rooms. Beyond the entrance a range of buildings (now destroyed, except for *Prison Tower*, an inwards extension of the west gatehouse tower) would have separated the two wards.

LOWER WARD. Along the wall between the west gatehouse and the next tower (*Well Tower*) was the site of the kitchens. From the basement of Well Tower hooded fireplaces can be seen above, and a postern here was perhaps for direct delivery of kitchen supplies. The westernmost tower is *Eagle Tower*, the largest of the castle, with walls 15ft thick and an internal diameter at ground level of 34ft. Here there are two exhibitions, one on the history of Caernarfon, the other a video about the district and the castle, while on the first floor there is a small room in which Edward II was once thought to have been born; in fact the tower would not by 1284 have reached this height. Stairs ascend to the roof with its three turrets. Stone eagles are among the weathered figures on the turret battlements, but only one (west) is recognisable. In the basement of the tower is the castle watergate. Next comes *Queen's Tower*, housing the *Museum of the Royal Welch Fusiliers*, telling the story of the regiment since its founding in 1689. Below the Queen's Tower the Hall (100ft by 34ft) filled the southeast of the ward.

UPPER WARD. *Chamberlain Tower*, with an exhibition on the Castles of Edward I, also contains a chapel (first floor); *Black Tower* has small ten-sided rooms; and at *Cistern Tower* there is a stone tank. *Queen's Gate*, at the eastern end of the castle, was originally approached by a drawbridge, evidence of which can be seen from a railed platform high above the quay. The next tower, the small *Watch Tower*, is entered through *North East Tower* beyond, which houses a Prince of Wales Exhibition. The last tower is *Granary Tower*, between which and King's Gate the wall has arrow slits, so designed that two or three archers could shoot out of a single opening.

The **Town Walls**, nearly half a mile in circumference and strengthened by towers, enclose a roughly rectangular area to the north of the castle, to which, forming a single scheme of defence, they were joined at North East and Eagle towers. The town within, with several 16–19C houses, still retains the regular pattern standard to Edward I's English Boroughs. The walls are almost complete, and had east and west gates at either end of what is today's High Street. The tower at the west gate (also known as *Porth-y-Aur* or Golden Gate) is now the headquarters of the Royal Welsh Yacht Club (founded 1847). At the east end the gate is also known as *Porth Mawr* or Great Gate. Below, in Greengate Street, the little window in the southeast corner of the arch is that of the cell which until 1835 served as town lock-up. The most interesting building around the walls is the *Chantry of St. Mary* (or Old Church), structurally incorporated within the walls at their north-west angle where the adjoining tower serves as vestry and bell-tower. The church (restored) was built in the 14C by Henry de Elierton, later master mason of the castle.

Victoria Dock is just beyond the northwest angle of the walls, here being Caernarfon's *Seiont II Maritime Museum* (Spring Bank Hol.–mid Sept: daily 11.00–16.00. Tel. 01286-675269), with a general museum section and the 'Seiont II', a steam dredger of 1937.

The Roman fort of **Segontium** (NT and Cadw; see p. 11) is half a mile southeast of Castle Square beside A4085 to Beddgelert. Probably founded in 78 by Agricola as a fort for auxiliary troops, Segontium remained occupied until c 380, one reason for its eventual abandonment possibly being the withdrawal of troops from Britain by Magnus Maximus, who came to Britain as an official of Theodosius and was then declared emperor by the disaffected legions (he would later become Macsen Wledig of the 'Mabinogion'). There is a tradition that Constantine the Great was born here, although in fact he was probably born in c 288 at Nis in the Balkans. Bar the ground plan outlined by foundations, little remains to be seen of the fort. Of considerably more interest are the *Museum*, covering not only this site but the Romans generally, and, just east, *Llanbelig Church*, dedicated to Peblig (Publicus), son of Magnus Maximus, and interesting for the continuity it provides from the days of early pagan worship; it stands close to the Roman Mithraeum (located in 1959, but now covered; plaque on house), while the modern cemetery across the road spreads over its Roman predecessor. The oldest part of the church is the south wall, which is probably 13C; the transepts and choir are mainly 14C; and the lower part of the tower (which was once whitewashed as a navigation mark for ships) is 15C.

A4085, leaving Caernarfon, passes Segontium and Llanbelig, crosses the Seiont, and ascends generally following the line of a Roman road. Ahead to the southeast rises Moel Eilio (2300ft) and to the south Mynydd Mawr (2290ft). *5m*. *Betws Garmon*, at the boundary of Snowdonia National Park, possibly derives it name from St. Germanus. Beyond, the road, beside the Gwyrfai and approaching wilder scenery, reaches *Llyn Cwellyn* (464ft), on the farther side of which the bold crag of *Castell Cidwym* (Wolf's Castle) rises sheer from the water. About halfway along the lake is the *Snowdon Ranger Hostel*, starting point of one of the recognised routes up the mountain. The house was opened as an inn early in the 19C by a mountain guide, doubtless the pioneer of the track; later the place became a monastery, and it is now a youth hostel. *4m*. *Rhyd-Ddu* (600ft) is a pleasantly situated hamlet from which a path joins the Snowdon Pitt's Head Track starting from *Pitt's Head Rock*, a mile father south. The watershed here is at 650ft, and the road now descends Nant Colwyn, with *Beddgelert Forest* (FE walks) on the west, to reach (*3m* from Rhyd-Ddu) *Beddgelert* and, *2m* farther, *Pont Aberglaslyn*, for both of which see Rte 7.

At Pont Aberglaslyn Rte 7 crosses the bridge to Penrhyndeudraeth, while this Route continues south. On the east are the wide, marshy flats of *Traeth Mawr* (7000 acres). Until the early 19C a broad estuary navigable up to Pont Aberglaslyn, this became reclaimed land between 1807–12 when the Member of Parliament W.A. Madocks (1774–1828) built his great embankment (The Cob) across the mouth of the Glaslyn. Beyond the flats rise Cnicht and the Moelwyns, while to the west of the road is Moel Ddu (1811ft). *3m* (from Pont Aberglaslyn) *Glaslyn Hotel*, beyond which the road skirts a range of steep, wooded cliffs. This is the *Coed Tremadog Nature Reserve*, a large area of oak, also botanically interesting because of the plants which have survived thanks to the absence of sheep. *Tan-yr-Allt*, beside the road just before Tremadog, was the residence of W.A. Madocks.

Tan-yr-Allt was the scene of the 'Tremadog Incident'. In September 1812 the poet Shelley, attracted by Madocks's 'generous project', came here with Harriet to offer his assistance. They occupied a house (now pulled down) at the west end of the grounds, and here much of 'Queen Mab' was written. One night the following February, according to Shelley and Harriet, the house was forcibly entered, shots were fired, and Shelley's life was attempted. Thereupon the pair departed. The incident is generally accepted to have been a successful ruse to scare Shelley away, adopted by certain shepherds who objected to the poet's habit of putting sick or injured sheep out of pain when he came across them on his walks.

2m. **Tremadog** was built by W.A. Madocks between 1805–07, and, largely unaltered, remains a good example of early 19C town planning. T.E. Lawrence (Lawrence of Arabia, 1888–1935) was born here (plaque). *1m*. **Porthmadog**, see Rte 15.

11

Anglesey

The name Anglesey is generally accepted as meaning Island of the Angles, although some authorities derive it from the Norse 'öngull' for fiord or strait. In Welsh it is Ynys Môn (the Mona of Tacitus, Ynys meaning 'island' and Môn perhaps stemming from a Celtic word for 'end'), to which is often added 'Mam Cymru' (Mother of Wales), a title arising from the island's extensive cornfields. Anglesey was occupied by man in very early times—Stone Age remains of perhaps 7000 BC have been found, while later prehistoric sites abound—and, at the close of the prehistoric period, was the chief centre of the Druids, attacked by the Roman Suetonius Paulinus in 61 and virtually exterminated by his successor Agricola in 78. Later (7–13C), Anglesey was a stronghold of the princes of Gwynedd with their capital at Aberffraw, despite which, though, the island's coasts endured some 200 years (850–1050) of Norse raids.

Scenically, Anglesey is for the most part undulating and somewhat mo-notonous, though with spectacular cliffs on Holy Island, and elsewhere some pleasant stretches of coast, especially along the north east. Through the island run the main road and railway to Holyhead, an industrial town and port with the passenger and car ferry service to Dun Laoghaire in Ireland. Otherwise, Anglesey is visited largely for its many prehistoric sites, for the mansion of Plas Newydd, for the impressive Edwardian castle at Beaumaris and for some unpretentious resorts.

The excellent *Oriel Ynys Môn visitor centre at Llangefni provides an enthralling introduction to Anglesey's story.

The direct road from the Menai bridges to Holyhead (Rte 11A) is of limited interest. Visitors in search of the best of the island should explore around the circuit described as Rte 11B.

Tourist Information. Station Site, Llanfair PG, LL61 5UJ. Tel. 01248-713177.

A. Bangor to Holyhead

A5. Total distance 23m.—*3m*. **Llanfair PG**.—*6m*. **Llangefni**.—*11m*. **Valley**.—*3m*. **Holyhead**.

The MENAI STRAIT, with for the most part green and pleasant banks, is a channel some 13 miles long and varying in width between a mile and 200 yards. The principal towns are, on the mainland, Bangor and Caernarfon, and, on the island, Beaumaris. Near Bangor the strait is crossed by two distinguished bridges—one road, the other (a mile southwest) combined rail and road—the main A5 using the latter. The *Menai Suspension Bridge* (road only) was built by Thomas Telford in 1819–26. Before this, crossing had been by ferry but the herds of cattle for sale on the mainland had had to swim. Not surprisingly perhaps, there was fierce opposition from the many interests whose livelihood depended on the ferries, as also from ship-owners determined that the passage of their tall ships should not be

Telford's Menai Suspension Bridge (1819-26)

impeded, this insistence resulting in the road being at a height of 100ft. The bridge was considerably rebuilt in 1938–41 when the structure was strengthened, the roadway widened, and the number of supporting chains reduced from 16 to four. The bridge measures 579ft between the piers and 1000ft overall. *Britannia Bridge*, a mile southwest, originally a tubular railway bridge built by Robert Stephenson between 1846–50 and similar to his bridge at Conwy, was burnt out in 1970 and the rail link was only restored with the completion (on the stonework of the original) of a new conventional bridge in 1972, this now with an extra deck which carries the A5 road. The statue to Lord Nelson, on the north shore just west of the bridge, was erected in 1873 by Admiral Lord Clarence Paget as an aid to navigation.

Motorists may choose either bridge, Telford's crossing direct to the small town of Menai Bridge while Stephenson's heads for Llanfair PG.

At **Menai Bridge**, *Pili-Palas* (mid March–Oct: daily 10.00–17.30. Nov and Dec: daily 11.00–15.30. Tel. 01248-712474), is the home of both local and exotic butterflies and insects, while on Church Island, immediately west of the town and reached by a causeway, there is a small 14C church, a foundation of 630 by St. Tysilio, perhaps later visited by Archbishop Baldwin and Giraldus, thought to have landed here in 1188.

A5, leaving Britannia Bridge, loops northward, soon passing (right) the *Anglesey Column*, 90ft high and commemorating the 1st Marquess (1768–1854) who commanded the cavalry at Waterloo where he lost a leg; the column was erected in 1817, the statue by M. Noble being added in 1860. For more about this remarkable marquess, see Plas Newydd on Rte 11B.

3m (from Bangor) **Llanfair PG** is an accepted abbreviation for *Llanfairpwllgwyngyllgogerychwyrndrobwllllantysiliogogogoch* (St. Mary's Church in a hollow by the white hazel close to the rapid whirlpool by the red cave of St. Tysilio), a name probably invented as a tourist lure, which to some extent it still is, though, with the station now closed, the longest platform ticket in the world, once the principal souvenir, now has to be bought at local shops, thus losing both authenticity and usefulness. The first Women's Institute in Britain was founded here in 1915. Today the main attraction is the *James Pringle Woollen Mill* (All year. Daily April–Oct: Mon–Sat 09.00–17.30; Sun 10.30–17.00. Nov–March: Mon–Sat 09.00–17.00; Sun 12.00–17.00. Tel. 01248-717171), a huge largely retail complex with also Tourist Information (tel. 01248-713177), a restaurant, a Welsh craft centre, gift shop and other facilities.

For *Plas Newydd*, one and a half miles southwest, see Rte 11B which starts from Llanfair PG. At *Penmynydd*, two miles northwest, the mansion (present building 1576; no adm.) was for centuries the home of the Tudors. Here was born Owen Tudor, believed to have married Catherine of Valois, widow of Henry V, their grandson being Henry VII.

4m. Pentre Berw, beyond which the road crosses the Malltraeth Marsh and the river Cefni. *2m.* **Llangefni** is the main market and administrative town of Anglesey. Here **Oriel Ynys Môn* (Tues–Sun and all Bank Hol. 10.30–17.00. Tel. 01248-724444) brilliantly presents Anglesey's spirit and story from distant prehistoric to recent times. The story is told through a series of themes—such as Stone Age Hunters, Celts, Saints, Druids, Romans, Medieval Society, Natural History, Legend—the latest in modern presentational technology being used, in some cases in conjunction with the works of island artists, notably the wildlife artist Charles Tunnicliffe. Additionally there are frequent temporary exhibitions, performances in the courtyard, a shop and picnic area. *Cefni Reservoir* to the northwest, is known for migrant wildfowl and also provides a pleasant picnic area.

4m. Gwalchmai was briefly famous as being the first village in Anglesey to have electricity (supplied by a local watermill). *7m.* **Valley**, thought to have been given its name by Telford when cutting his road through a small hill here, was, centuries earlier, a home of Iron Age man whose weapons and horse trappings found here are now in the National Museum of Wales. Today Valley is perhaps best known for its military airfield, built in 1941 and in turn fighter base, trans-Atlantic terminal, flying school and missile practice camp. Beyond Valley A5 and the railway together cross a causeway 1200 yards long to HOLY ISLAND (see also below) on which are the port of Holyhead, the conspicuous mountain of the same name with dramatic cliff scenery, and several archaeological sites. *Penrhos Country Park*, at the west end of the causeway and owned and administered by the adjacent aluminium company, is the place for woodland and coastal walks with the probability of seeing a variety of birds of both habitats.

3m. **Holyhead** or Caer Gybi (*Inf.*), in origin a Roman fort and Celtic Christian settlement, is today mainly a commercial and industrial town, but also something of a resort, owing its growth and importance to its harbour. A5 enters the town as London Road, curving across the railway by the station, just southwest of here, in Rhos-y-Gaer Avenue, being the *Maritime Museum* (May–Sept: Tues–Sun, and also Bank Hol. Tel. 01407-762816), devoted largely to the port, but also with much else of general maritime interest. On the west side of the station there is a road fork, with Victoria Road (see below) to the right and the pedestrian shopping zone of Market Street and Stanley Street to the left.

The visible evidence of Holyhead's birth, and the source of its Welsh name—the small Roman fort of *Caer Gybi*—survives in the area between Stanley Street and Victoria Road; a survival of particular interest because the Roman walls were used by St. Cybi as early as the 6C to protect the church he founded here. The fort, dating from the 3–4C and possibly built as a protection against raiding pirates, forms a rectangle with rounded towers at the corners; except on the east, the walls are largely intact but the northeast and southeast towers were much rebuilt in the 18 and 19C respectively. The church here today is mainly 15–17C, though the restored choir is 13C; the Stanley Chapel is worth a visit for the window by Burne-Jones and William Morris. The smaller church to the south, known as Egylwys Bedd (Church of the Tomb), is said to shelter the grave of a 5C pirate captain.

Victoria Road reaches Marine Square (*Tourist Information*) beyond which stretches the growing port area (car ferry terminals) in which, at the base of Admiralty Pier, Admiralty Arch marks the formal end of Telford's A5 road and commemorates also a landing here by George IV. From Marine Square, Prince of Wales Road, running westward across open green slopes, skirts the New Harbour, opened in 1873 and protected by a breakwater 1860ft long.

The remainder of HOLY ISLAND is worth visiting for its cliff scenery, its birds, and its ancient remains. From the west side of central Holyhead, near the prominent modern St. Seiriol's Church, South Stack Road heads generally southwest, rounding the south of *Holyhead Mountain* (720ft, the highest point in Anglesey), with many paths, traces of a hillfort and wide views. Approaching the coast, about two miles from Holyhead, the road bears right for *South Stack, with spectacular cliff scenery, ancient remains, an RSPB observation post and, at the foot of the cliffs, a lighthouse. A short way up this road, there is (left) a car park, across the road from here being *Holyhead Mountain Hut Circles*, named and sometimes signposted and shown on maps as 'Irishmen's Huts' (Cytiau Gwyddelod) in obedience to a tradition, without any archaeological backing, that the huts were those of the Goidelic (Irish) Celts driven out by the Brythonic Celts in the 5C. The huts represent an extensive settlement of the 2–4C. Originally the settlement may have occupied something like 20 acres, but today only 20 huts remain, of which 14 are in the main group. The huts are circular or rectangular, some of the former having traces of central hearths and slabs indicating the positions of beds and seats.

From this car park there is an easy path to *Ellin's Tower* (Easter–Sept: daily 11.00–17.00), a RSPB clifftop observation hut with powerful binoculars and a moveable video relay from among the birds. Even if Ellin's Tower is not open, this is a superb point (on the rim of sheer and unfenced cliffs) from which to view the lighthouse and the countless birds on the adjacent rocks

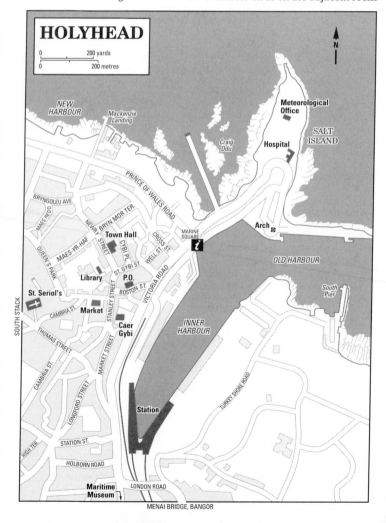

and cliffs. Farther up the road there is another parking area, from which steps lead down and across a narrow bridge to *South Stack Lighthouse* of 1808.

The drive through the southern part of Holy Island (returning to A5 at Valley) is through a compact district particularly rich in prehistoric sites. Dropping southeast from South Stack and repassing the Holyhead Mountain Hut Circles, the small road quickly reaches the T-junction, the right arm of which is signed Trearddur. In under half a mile, a short way up a road to the left, are the *Penrhos Feilw Standing Stones*, two tall stones traditionally once at the centre of a circle. The coastal road curves east, in roughly another mile reaching a minor crossroads at the head of the small bay of *Porth Dafarth*, within the northeast angle of the crossroads being traces of hut circles. In a little over a mile farther east, at Trearddur Bay, the road reaches B4545. Here, if B4545 is crossed, a minor road soon bears north and in under a mile reaches *Trefignath Burial Chamber*, consisting of a long passage once divided into several chambers; today the east chamber is the best preserved and is flanked by two upright stones. *Ty Mawr Standing Stone* is half a mile farther up this road. If, from Trearddur, B4545 is followed southeast for a mile, a side road leads south for *Rhoscolyn*. Here St. Gwenfaen founded a church in the 6C, and her well, just southeast of Rhoscolyn Head (footpath) was long supposed to cure mental afflictions. Minor roads and B4545 meet A5 at Valley.

B. Circuit of the Island

The circuit described below is a clockwise one, starting from **Llanfair PG** (for which, as also for the approaches from Bangor, see Rte 11A) and ending at Menai Bridge.

> A4080 and A5 to Valley. A5025 to Pentraeth. B5109 to Beaumaris, with minor roads to Penmon and back. A545 to Menai Bridge. Total distance 75m.—*8m.* **Newborough.**—*4m.* **Llangadwaladr.**—*2m.* **Aberffraw.**—*4m.* **Rhosneigr.**—*9m.* **Valley.**—*10m.* **Tregele.**—*6m.* **Amlwch.**—*9m.* **Benllech.**—*8m.* **Beaumaris.**—*8m.* **Penmon** and back.—*7m.* **Menai Bridge.**

A4080 bears south out of Llanfair PG, in a little over a mile reaching ****Plas Newydd** (NT. April–Sept: daily except Sat 12.00–17.00. Oct: Fri and Sun 12.00–17.00. Tel. 01248-714795), a magnificent mainly 18C mansion beside Menai Strait, seat of the marquesses of Anglesey and since 1976 belonging to the National Trust. In addition to splendid rooms, furniture, and portraits, the house contains important works by Rex Whistler, including his largest wallpainting, and a museum devoted to the militarily renowned 1st Marquess who, as Lord Uxbridge, led the British cavalry at Waterloo.

History. The original house here was built in the early 16C by the Griffith family of Penrhyn, the estate later descending by marriage to the Bagenal, Bayly, and (1737) Paget families. An early Paget, a chief adviser of Henry VIII, had acquired the large estate of Beaudesert (demolished 1935) in Staffordshire and been created Baron Paget, the creation containing the unusual provision that the title should, if necessary, continue through the female line. This happened as the result of the marriage in 1737 between Caroline Paget and Sir Nicholas Bayly, their son becoming 9th Baron Paget in 1769 when the 8th Baron died childless. In 1784 he was created 1st Earl of Uxbridge, a title which in the first creation had already been held by the 7th and 8th barons Paget. From various sources this new 1st Earl of Uxbridge acquired immense wealth, and it was he who between 1783 and 1809 refashioned Plas Newydd from a medieval manor into an 18C mansion. The first phase was 1783–86 when, to match that at the south end, another octagonal tower was built at the north end of the east front. In the second phase (1793–99) James Wyatt and Joseph Potter of Lichfield achieved a new entrance front on the west, created the Classical and Gothick interiors of the present main block, and built the stables. Potter added the north wing between 1805–09. The grounds owe much to Humphry Repton, commissioned in 1798 to advise on the layout. In 1812 the estate passed to its most illustrious owner, the 2nd Lord Uxbridge, commander of the cavalry during the retreat to Corunna and at Waterloo and after the latter battle created 1st Marquess of Anglesey. Towards the end of the battle his leg was smashed, upon which he exclaimed to Wellington, riding beside him, 'By God, sir, I've lost my leg!', Wellington replying, momentarily glancing away from the retreating French, 'By God, sir, so you have!' What must surely be a unique monument is the one in the town of Waterloo commemorating this leg. The Marquess eloped with Wellington's sister-in-law, fathered 18 children, and died aged 84 (see also Cavalry Museum below). In the 1930s the 6th Marquess removed the battlements from the parapets, shortened the pinnacles on the east front, giving them Tudor caps to match those on the entrance side, remodelled the north wing, and created a long dining room, decorated by Rex Whistler, a close friend of the Pagets, between 1936–40. In 1976 the 7th Marquess gave the house and surrounding land to the National Trust.

The car park is beside the early 19C dairy, with a National Trust shop and information centre. There is a longish walk down to the house, during which, beyond the sweep of grass on the left, can be seen the turreted and castellated stables (Joseph Potter, 1797), with, in front, the large stones of a prehistoric burial chamber.

The *Gothick Hall* (1796–98) is a lofty rectangular room rising through two storeys and having a gallery. Pictures here include a contemporary portrait of the 1st Baron Paget; a portrait by Van Dyck; and two large works by Snyders. Another portrait is of Caroline Paget. The banners, both of the Royal Horse Guards, are of the Peninsular and Waterloo campaigns. The *Music Room*, also 1796–98 and the finest room in the house, occupies the site of the hall of the original building. The carved woodwork here, as elsewhere in the house, is that of Potter's craftsmen. Among the portraits are four by Hoppner (of the 1st Marquess, his sister and his second wife, and his younger brother Sir Arthur Paget), one by Lawrence of the 1st Marquess, and one by Romney of the Earl of Uxbridge. The *Hall and Staircase*, and the remaining rooms, are generally in the Neo-Classical style (note for instance the Doric columns) associated with Wyatt. In the hall there are two portraits of early Pagets, one attributed to Leandro Bassano and the other (1578), of the wife of the 2nd Lord Paget, by Marc Gheeraedts. The eight canvases of scenes of the Duke of Marlborough's campaigns are by Laguerre, and the full-length portrait of Wellington is by John Lucas.

On the top landing there are Elizabethan portraits of the 1st Lord Paget (1549), of a young man (1585), and of Henry VIII and Queen Elizabeth. The *Landing and Gallery* and passages have more pictures, notably a portrait of Lady Caroline Paget by Rex Whistler; a group of the 1st Marquess's children, painted by Wilkin; early 19C watercolours of Beaudesert and Anglesey, the latter part of a set by John 'Warwick' Smith; and one, in the passage leading to Lady Anglesey's bedroom, of Florence Paget (the 'Pocket Venus') as a child (Henry Graves, 1850). She was the central figure of a Victorian scandal; courted by the Marquess of Hastings and by Henry Chaplin, both wealthy gamblers and rivals also of the turf, Florence accepted Chaplin but promptly eloped with and married Hastings, who however soon died of dissipation leaving Florence a widow at 26. *Lady Anglesey's Bedroom*, occupying the octagonal southeast tower, affords views along Menai Strait, including the family's private harbour (the 1st Marquess and his father always kept three yachts at Plas Newydd). The plaster frieze and chimneypiece date from the redecoration of 1793–99, but the present colour scheme was introduced in the 1930s by Lady Marjorie Manners, wife of the 6th Marquess, with the advice of Sibyl Colefax, a leading decorator of that period. *Lord Anglesey's Bedroom* also has a frieze and chimneypiece of the 1790s. The late 17 or early 18C state bed came from Beaudesert and the marine pictures are 19C English and Dutch.

The tour of the house returns down a spiral staircase of 1795 to the Gothick Hall, beyond which is the *Ante Room*, of Neo-Classical design by Wyatt. The portrait of the 1st Earl of Uxbridge as a young man is by an unidentified artist, but the one opposite, of one of his sons, is by Lawrence. Among the furnishings are Louis XV chairs; a pair of Napoleonic Sèvres vases, with campaign scenes; gilt console tables in the style of Robert Gumley and James Moore, two leading craftsmen of the early 18C; and two gilt gesso pier glasses, bearing the Paget crest in medallions. The *Octagon Room* has an identical frieze to that in the Ante Room. Furnishings include early 19C Rococo games tables, one with a chessboard bearing the lions and eagles of the Paget arms; Louis XV chairs upholstered in a pattern of naval scenes; an 18C pier glass in the style of William Kent. The picture of the Menai Bridge was painted two years after its opening. The *Saloon* represents various periods. The bay window forms the base of a round tower added in 1751; the general form of the room may date to the alterations of 1783–86; the frieze, window mouldings, and double doors are Wyatt's of 1795. The marble chimneypiece was probably bought in 1796 from the elder Richard Westmacott. The room contains some interesting pictures, among these being four large pastoral scenes by B.P. Ommeganck; Queen Victoria and her suite riding at Windsor by R.B. Davis (1837); and the 1st Marquess, by an unknown artist. The two busts, both by Reid Dick (1921 and 1925), are of Lady Caroline Paget and her mother, the 6th Marchioness. Outstanding among the furniture are the gilt pier tables and glasses (early 18C). In the *Breakfast Room* the frieze and pairs of double doors are all of c 1795–98, and the chimneypiece is almost certainly by Westmacott. Most of the pictures are seascapes.

The *Rex Whistler Exhibition*, in the octagonal tower added in 1783–86, comprises a number of portraits of the family and also examples of Whistler's skills as book illustrator, stage designer, and decorative artist. Beyond, the long dining room created by the 6th Marquess is now the *Rex Whistler Room*, containing the artist's last and largest mural, in trompe l'oeil. The basic theme is an estuary with Renaissance cities, their buildings of every style and period, some genuine, others inventions. Throughout there are frequent references to the family, and Whistler includes himself as a young man sweeping leaves. In the small room beyond can be seen architectural drawings for the house, including Wyatt's and Potter's designs. The *Cavalry Museum* is in two parts. One room is devoted to the 1st Marquess and includes a portrait by Winterhalter, while in the second room there is a vast picture of Waterloo (Denis Dighton), of particular interest for the accuracy of the uniforms. Here too is an Anglesey Leg, an artificial limb invented and patented by James Potts of Chelsea and used by the Marquess. Beyond the Cavalry Museum is the *Ryan Collection of Militaria*, the emphasis here being on uniforms and helmets.

2m (from Llanfair P.G.) *Cefn Bach* is a hamlet at a crossroads. The road north soon reaches the path to *Bryn Celli Ddu*, a well-preserved burial chamber of 2000–1500 BC. The mound is modern protection and covers only a small part of the area of the prehistoric mound, which was 160ft in diameter. The polygonal chamber, roofed by two stones and approached through an open outer passage (6ft long) and an inner passage (20ft long), was within but not in the centre of a circular area. It was surrounded by four concentric stone circles, three of which were within the cairn while the fourth marked the base. An incised stone found here, now in the National Museum of Wales, has been replaced by a replica. The road south from the crossroads reaches Menai Strait at *Moel-y-Don*, one of two claimants (the other is Abermenai Point) to be the place at which Suetonius and, later, Agricola crossed to meet and defeat the Druid-led Celts massed on Anglesey's shore.

2m. **Brynsiencyn** from where a small road runs down to Menai Strait, along here being a sea zoo and a farm park, both with fine views across to Caernarfon. *Anglesey Sea Zoo* (daily 10.00–17.00, but 11.00–15.00 in Nov–Feb. Tel. 01248-430411) offers close and informative viewing (open and from above; not as in an aquarium) of marine life, among the highlights being conger eels, a big fish forest, sea bass, crowds of lobsters, shoals of herring, a tank of flat fish and, of unusual interest, lobster breeding. Children are particularly welcome, and there is also a seafood retail shop. *Foel Farm Park* (Easter–Oct: daily 10.30–17.30. Tel. 01248-430646), a short way farther, is a working farm at which visiting families can enjoy close contact with domestic animals (in spring or early summer children can even bottle feed the lambs); tractor and trailer rides; an adventure play area, a café and farm shop.

Along A4080, just beyond Brynsiencyn, a road bears northwest almost at once reaching *Caer Leb*, an Iron Age pentagonal enclosure defended by a double rampart, at which excavation during the 19C found remains of a rectangular building and a circular hut. Beyond Caer Leb this minor road crosses another similar road to reach *Bodowyr Burial Chamber*, with a capstone balanced on three uprights. Along A4080, in another mile, a track leads north for about 300 yards to reach *Castell Bryn-Gwyn*, a site—essentially a rampart and ditch enclosing a circular area of some 180ft diameter—archaeologically traced to activity spanning from New Stone Age times until the Roman invasion. *2m* (from Brynsiencyn) *Dwyran*, with, beside the main road, *Anglesey Bird World* (March–Dec: daily 10.00–18.00. Tel. 01248-440627) with walk-in aviaries and some small animals.

2m. **Newborough**, formerly Rhosyr, is a small town which received its charter and English name from Edward I in 1303 when he transferred there people displaced by the construction of Beaumaris. From the 17C until the 1920s the weaving of marram grass ropes, baskets and mats was a thriving local cottage industry. Around the town, except to the northeast, spreads the **Newborough Warren-Ynys Llanddwyn Nature Reserve**, where the main interests are forest, marsh and dunes. The reserve comprises five sections (see below) and can be seen by using a choice of approved paths. There are also two motor roads. One, from a roundabout just southeast of Newborough, soon reaches a car park on the edge of the warren and at the start of the path across the warren to, in two miles, Abermenai Point. The other road, through the main reserve, runs from Newborough through the forest to a car park and picnic area (in summer, information and leaflets) near the shore.

Malltraeth Pool, at the north tip of the reserve, is beside A4080, two miles northwest of Newborough; protected by an embarkment built by Telford as a sea defence, the pool is mainly a bird sanctuary. South from here is

Cefni Saltmarsh, sandwiched between Malltraeth Sands and Newborough Forest and known for its sea plants and grasses. To the east and south of the marsh stretches *Newborough Forest*, planted in 1948 at which time sand frequently blocked roads and covered crops; now, thanks to the trees (mostly Corsican pine) and other anti-erosion measures, this drifting is a thing of the past. *Ynys Llanddwyn*, a promontory nearly a mile long at the south of the reserve, is geologically known for its pre-Cambrian rocks, among the oldest in Britain (more than 600 million years). In the 5C this promontory was the retreat of St. Dwynwen, patron of lovers, but the ruined church seen today dates only to the 16C. The lighthouse was built in 1873, before which the nearby tower (1800) was all that marked this hazard.

Newborough Warren, the large southeast section of the reserve, was, until the ravages of myxomatosis, the home of so many rabbits that as many as 80,000 were trapped annually. In the 13C this was agricultural land, and Abermenai, at the southeast tip and at the west end of the Menai Strait, was an important anchorage. Abermenai—a rival claimant to Moel-y-Don as the crossing point of the Romans—also has a place in legend, as the port from which Bronwen, daughter of Llyr and 'fairest maiden in the world', and her new lord, Matholwch, King of Ireland, set sail with 13 ships after their nuptial feast and bedding at Aberffraw. Storms during the 14C caused sand to cover the fields and block the anchorage, the warren ever since remaining a wilderness of dunes. The decrease in rabbits has brought an increasing spread of vegetation, marram grass being the principal plant.

Within the two miles beyond Newborough, A4080 crosses a finger of the forest, skirts Malltraeth Pool, and crosses the Cefni at the head of its estuary. *4m.* **Llangadwaladr** has a 13–14C church, interesting for a stone (nave wall, north) commemorating Cadfan (Catamanus), a king or prince of Gwynedd who died c 625. Translated, the Latin inscription reads 'Cadfan the King, wisest and most renowned of all kings'. The village's name is that of Cadfan's grandson Cadwaladr, defeated by the Northumbrians near the Tyne in 634. *2m.* **Aberffraw** was the capital of Gwynedd from about the 7–13C, but of this past there is now no trace, although in the 1970s archaeologists found evidence of a rectangular enclosure around today's village; probably Roman in origin, this later would have become the site of the palace of the princes. Today, Llys Llywelyn here (tel. 01407-840845) is a modest information centre with exhibitions, tearoom and shop. *2m.* *Barclodiad-y-Gawres Burial Chamber*, on the north side of the small Trecastell Bay, is interesting for sharing with Bryn Celli Ddu the distinction of being a burial chamber with mural art, five of the stones here being incised with designs. The chamber, re-arranged to protect the stones, comprises a 20ft long passage, a central chamber, and side chambers. The original mound, remains of which can be seen, would have been some 90ft in diameter. *2m* **Rhosneigr** is a small seaside resort, in the 18C notorious for the ship wreckers who hid in the Crigyll estuary to the north. Hanged in 1741 they are the subject of a ballad by Lewis Morris. The loop of A4080 serving Rhosneigr is completed north of the railway at *Llanfaelog*, half a mile northeast of which (just east of the minor road northward to Capel Gwyn) is *Ty Newydd Burial Chamber.*

4m. (from Rhosneigr), Junction with A5, Rte 11A now being followed west for *5m.* to **Valley** (Dyffryn) from where A5025 is taken northward. *2m. Llanynghenedl*, two miles east of which, near the south end of Llyn Llywenan (well signed; reached by B5109 and a small road north beyond

Bodedern) are *Presaddfed Burial Chambers*, one collapsed, the other still with capstone and upright. *4m. Llanfaethlu.*

DIVERSION TO LLYN ALAW (5m. E). At *Llanddeusant*, reached in about two miles, *Llynnon Mill* (tel. 01407-730797) is a stone tower working windmill of 1775, the only example on Anglesey. A minor road northeast out of Llanddeusant in two miles reaches the hamlet of *Llanbabo* with, in the 12C church, a figure of St. Pabo, thought to have been a 6C Celtic mainland chief forced to seek safety in Anglesey. *Llyn Alaw*, a reservoir of 1966, lies immediately east of Llanbabo, at the lake's southwest corner (minor road from Llanbabo) being a small information centre, a pleasant picnic site and a bird-watching hide.

4m. **Tregele**, a hamlet to the north of which is *Wylfa Power Station* (daily 09.30–16.30. Tel. 01407-711400) with an information centre, guided tours, nature trails and picnic and play area. *Cemlyn Bay*, a shingle beach rather over a mile west of Tregele, is part of a National Trust coastal property which includes a bird sanctuary, chiefly for winter migrant wildfowl, and *Carmel Head*, two and a half miles farther west (no road), marks the northwest extremity of Anglesey. The *Skerries*, a group of islets two miles northwest, have carried a lighthouse since the 18C (it was then a coal fire in a grate) and until the 19C all passing ships had to pay a toll.

1m. **Cemmaes**, on the bay of the same name, is a modest resort. The church at *Llanbadrig*, half a mile northeast and said to have been founded by St. Patrick on a journey to Ireland, possibly as thanks for being saved in a shipwreck on Middle Mouse Rock, was restored in 1884 by Lord Stanley, the local landowner; a Muslim, he insisted on Islamic style in, for example, the tiles. Beyond, *Llanlleiana*, the northernmost point in Wales, is thought to be named after a female recluse who founded a chapel here in the 5 or 6C. The headland, which is National Trust property, includes the hillfort of Dinas Gynfor.

5m. **Amlwch** is a port and resort whose fortunes have fluctuated with those of the copper mines of *Parys Mountain* to the south. Intermittently worked since Roman times, the mines were at their most prosperous in the late 18 and early 19C, at which time Amlwch was the most populated part of Anglesey. Abandoned in the later 19C, due to exhaustion, unstable prices, and foreign competition, there are now plans to re-open. Meanwhile the mountain is a bleak, deserted place with many dangerous shafts. The church of St. Eilian, a mile east of Amlwch, is 15C, with a 12C tower. It contains a 15C rood screen and loft; 15C seats and book desks; wooden dog tongs; and an ancient painting of St. Eilian (?), whose chapel adjoins the choir. In this chapel there is a curious semicircular piece of furniture, once believed to bring good luck to those who could turn round within it without touching the sides. St. Eilian's Well, near the sea, was thought to have healing powers.

2m. **Penysarn**, two miles southeast of which is Traeth Dulas, the now almost land-locked estuary of the small river Dulas. The village of Dulas was the home of the Morris brothers (monument), men of letters and patrons of the arts, and on Ynys Dulas, beyond the estuary, there is a 19C tower which once served as a marker for ships. Beyond Penysarn, A5025 in *2m* crosses the river at *City Dulas*, two miles southwest of here being *Llandyfrydog*, the church of which is mentioned by Giraldus as the scene of a sacrilege in 1098 when Hugh Lupus locked his dogs in the church; however, he paid a high price, for the dogs went mad and their owner was killed within the month. *1m. Rhos Lligwy* where this Route briefly leaves A5025 to continue east towards the small resort of *Moelfre*, off which in 1859 the 'Royal Charter', returning to Liverpool from Australia, was wrecked with the loss of 452 lives. Charles Dickens came here soon afterwards and used the tragedy as the basis of a story in 'The Uncommercial Traveller'.

About half-way between Rhos Lligwy and Moelfre there is a crossroads the south arm of which quickly reaches a group of three ancient sites—a fortified settlement, a ruined chapel and a burial chamber—which between them span perhaps 3000 or more years of human occupation. The fortified settlement, ***Din Lligwy** (half mile walk), Iron Age to late Roman and at about the centre of the time-span, is by far the most interesting of the three and, indeed, the most exciting ancient site on Anglesey, if only because this survives as a place in which ordinary people lived, as distinct from the many burial chambers marking their deaths. Probably built (or rebuilt) by local people during the closing years of the Roman occupation, the site covers about half an acre and much can still be seen of the stonework of circular and rectangular buildings inside an irregular defensive wall. Some of these buildings, or rooms, still have substantial walls, some show doorway posts, others traces of drainage systems across the floors and through the walls. *Capel Lligwy*, the chapel to the northeast, built by whatever people lived here some 800 years after Din Lligwy flourished, is now a sad, roofless place (12C; upper walls rebuilt 14C) with a simple Norman-arched doorway, a crude hollow stone which was presumably a font, and a chapel with a crypt added during the 16C. Just south of these two sites, on the right beside the road, is *Lligwy Burial Chamber*, a monument preceding Din Lligwy by perhaps 2000 years and one, also, with a long continuity of use, excavation in 1908 revealing the remains of some 30 people thought to have been buried in both Stone and Bronze Age times. The huge capstone is, not surprisingly perhaps, supported by low uprights over a natural fissure, the greater part of the chamber thus being below ground.

One of the several circular houses of Anglesey's fortified settlement of Din Lligwy; possibly Iron Age in origin, but rebuilt at the time of the Roman withdrawal in the fourth century

Beyond the burial chamber, the road soon rejoins A5025 just southwest along which, at *Llanallgo*, the church contains a memorial to the victims of the 'Royal Charter' (see above), buried in nine different churchyards. *Traeth Bychan*, the bay to the southeast, was in 1939 the scene of another sea disaster when the submarine 'Thetis', on trials, failed to surface and 99 men lost their lives.

4m. (from Rhos Lligwy) **Benllech**, a family resort with a good beach, was the birthplace of the poet Goronwy Owen. The sands merge with those of the great arc of Red Wharf Bay where care should be taken and local advice sought regarding tides and treacherous sands. Castell Mawr, traces of a hillfort on the west side of the bay, may, on the evidence of coins found here, once have been occupied by Romans. *2m. Pentraeth* was on the coast until stranded inland by land reclamation. Here B5109 is taken eastward, passing *Llansadwrn*, where, set in the chancel wall, the church contains a memorial of 520, unusual for being both to a holy man (Beatus Saturninus, Blessed Sadwen) and also to his saintly wife.

6m. **Beaumaris** is a resort and important yachting centre, pleasantly situated on Menai Strait with a view across Lavan Sands (see Rte 1C) to the mainland mountains. The town's earlier history is that of its great castle, today a major tourist attraction, and it was not until the growth of tourism, starting in the 19C, that Beaumaris began to develop into what it has become today. Although bathing is poor, with shingle, there are some interesting cruises (Starida Sea Services. Easter–Oct: daily and frequent. Tel. 01248-810251 or 810379), notably to Penmon lighthouse for a view of Puffin Island and along the Menai Strait past Bangor to the Menai Bridge; each of these cruises takes about one hour.

The *Castle (Cadw; see p. 11), now an extensive ruin, occupies an open site on level ground close to the shore. It is a concentric castle of almost perfect symmetry, encircled by a once tidal moat, and is particularly interesting for its sophisticated defences, which were, however, virtually never used. The outer curtain is superficially square, but since each of the four sides has a slight salient the form in practice is a flattened octagon, this allowing attack from any direction to be met. This outer wall is strengthened by towers. The more massive square inner defence is higher, permitting simultaneous firing from both outer and inner walls. The inner wall, also with towers, is noteworthy for its almost continuous internal passage. Another defensive trick is that the outer gateways are out of alignment with their gatehouses, this forcing an attacker to make an oblique approach.

History. Prince Madog had sacked Caernarfon in 1294, and it may have been this that prompted Edward I to start building Beaumaris, the last of his Welsh castles, the following year. At the same time the associated English Borough was granted its charter, taking the name Beau Marais (Beautiful Marsh) from an area soon to be drained by the castle moat system. The architect was James of St. George and, although the castle was never completed, it was declared to be in a state of defence by 1298. Architecturally, the inner part of the south gatehouse remained unfinished, the hall in the inner ward was scarcely started, and the towers were never properly roofed. In 1403 the castle was taken by Owen Glendower, but it was retaken in 1405. During the Civil War it was held (by a Bulkeley, the leading local family) for Charles I, but capitulated to General Mytton in 1646. At the Restoration Lord Bulkeley was reinstated as Constable, but the castle was abandoned in 1705. It nevertheless remained a Bulkeley possession until 1925 when it was made over to public ownership.

The moat, much wider than it is now, communicated with the sea by a short dock; an iron ring to which boats were tied can still be seen. This dock was defended on its east side by a projecting wing known as Gunner's Walk, in a bastion of which was the castle mill, the sluice and spillway of which remain. A wooden bridge, replacing the former drawbridge, crosses the moat to the Outer Ward, which also had another gate at its northeast, a triple doorway which was never completed and is little more than a postern. Note the out-of-alignment arrangement, referred to above, of the gates and their gatehouses. The outer rampart walk, including 12 towers, affords fine views. The Inner Ward is entered by the south gatehouse, guarded by a small rectangular barbican. The large gatehouses seem to have provided most of the living accommodation, that on the north containing on its first floor what was intended to be the hall. The basement of the northeast tower may have served as a prison. The tower on the east face of the inner ward contains the beautiful Chapel, apsidal and vaulted and with a trefoiled arcade and doorway (exhibition on the castles of Edward I).

The *Bull's Head Hotel*, close to the castle, dates in part from 1472. During the Civil War it was commandeered by General Mytton, and later both Dr Johnson and Charles Dickens are said to have stayed here. The *Courthouse* (visited in association with Beaumaris Gaol), on the corner of Castle Street opposite the castle, was built in 1614, but renovated during the 19C so that its interest today is as a Victorian survival. Also opposite the castle is the *Museum of Childhood* (Easter–Oct: daily 10.00–17.30 but 12.00–17.00 on Sun. Tel. 01248-712498), a treasure of toys and childhood nostalgia spread around several rooms and spanning roughly the last 150 years. Farther along Castle Street, Steeple Lane leads to *Beaumaris Gaol* (Easter and weekends in May June–Sept: daily 10.00–18.00. Tel. 01248-750262), built in 1829 to a design by Joseph Hansom. Cells, including punishment and condemned cells, a treadmill and a collection of documents combine to provide a grim reminder of Victorian prison conditions. On the other side of Castle Street, in the basement of the Bulkeley Hotel, the *Time-Tunnel* (Easter–Oct: daily 12.00–17.00. Tel. 01248-810415) uses static displays and audio-visual presentation to take the visitor back into Beaumaris's past.

The *Church of St. Mary* dates from the early 14C, the nave having curious window-tracery and circular clerestory windows enclosing quatrefoils. The choir was rebuilt in 1500, but some original glass fragments have been set in the south window. Among the monuments are the 16C altar-tomb of Sir Richard Bulkeley and his wife; a monumental stone to the father of Sir Philip Sidney; and, brought here from Llanfaes (see below), the carved stone coffin of Joan, wife of Llewelyn the Great and daughter of King John.

On rising ground northwest of Beaumaris the *Bulkeley Monument* (1875) commemorates the family who were for generations Anglesey's leading landowners; their seat was *Baron's Hill*, between the monument and the town.

From Beaumaris this Route runs north to Penmon Priory (c *4m* by B5109 and then minor roads) before returning through Beaumaris to Menai Bridge.

Llanfaes, now a village, was until the 13C a commercial centre and port of some importance. In 1237 Llewelyn the Great founded a priory here over the tomb of his wife Joan; in 1295 Edward I removed all the inhabitants of Llanfaes to what is now Newborough and used the town's stonework as material for Beaumaris castle; and at the Dissolution the contents of the priory, including Joan's coffin, were removed to St. Mary's in Beaumaris.

Castell Llieniog (east of B5109, about a mile from Llanfaes) is a motte, perhaps erected by Hugh Lupus when he overran Anglesey in 1098, with fragments of a small square tower which withstood a Royalist siege in the Civil War.

Penmon Priory was founded by St. Seiriol in the 6C. The church was rebuilt between 1120–70, and in 1237 Llewelyn the Great granted the monastery and its property to the prior and canons of Priestholm (Puffin Island), who then apparently moved to Penmon, reorganising the community as Austin Canons. The church and domestic buildings are now separate, the former serving as parish church and the latter in the care of Cadw.

The *Church of St. Seiriol*, successor to an earlier wooden church burnt by the Danes in 971, dates, as noted above, mainly from 1120–70, the nave being the oldest part (c 1140), while the choir, longer than the nave, is a rebuilding of c 1220–40. There is a fine Norman (c 1150) pillar piscina in the nave, used as a font until the present one (also in the nave), originally the base of a pre-Norman cross (south transept), was adapted during the 19C. Another cross, of c 1000 and with intricate though mutilated carving including a Temptation of St. Anthony, previously stood above the church on a hill to the northwest. The remains of St. Seiriol, originally on Puffin Island, were probably placed under the altar in this church. The outside area immediately south of the choir represents the site of a small cloister, the west side of which was the prior's house, now much altered and privately occupied. The *Domestic Buildings*, on the south of this cloister and with a mounting block beside the road, are a once three-storey 13C wing containing the refectory on the ground floor, a cellar below and a dormitory above. In the refectory, near the southeast corner, can be seen traces of the seat used by the monk who read aloud during meals.

The square *Dovecot* of c 1600, with a domed roof and open cupola and containing around 1000 nests, was probably built by Sir Richard Bulkeley of Baron's Hill. From across the road from the dovecot, a path leads to *St. Seiriol's Well*, probably at the site of the 6C priory. The upper part of the small building covering the well seems to be 18C, but the much older lower part may well incorporate something of the original chapel, while the adjacent foundations of an oval hut could well be those of the saint's cell.

A small road (fee for cars) continues for rather less than a mile to the headland of *Trwyn Du*, or *Trwyn Penmon*, this road providing interesting continuity with the past for it is still used by the same quarries from which James of St. George extracted the stone for Beaumaris and which, centuries later, provided footings and piers for Telford's and Stephenson's Menai bridges. Trwyn Du is a modest enough headland—with some cottages, a disused lifeboat station, an automatic lighthouse of 1837 and a mournful bell—but it provides a good view across to *Puffin Island*, once known as Priestholm and today also called Ynys Seiriol after the saint who established his settlement here in the 6C. The once large puffin population declined seriously when in the early 19C the pickled young birds were a popular delicacy. On the island there are fragments of monastic settlement.

Small roads west from Penmon lead in three miles to *Bedd Arthur* (500ft), a bluff with a rampart enclosing traces of hut circles.

This Route returns from Penmon to (*4m*) Beaumaris, from where A545 skirts the wooded shore for *7m* to Menai Bridge, see Rte 11A.

12

The Lleyn

The **LLEYN** (the Peninsula), some 25 miles long and from five to ten miles broad and dropping southwest towards the Irish Sea, provides the southern arm for Caernarfon Bay and the northern for Cardigan Bay. Scenically this is mainly mixed agricultural and wooded country, broken by groups of hills or mountains, those in the southwest affording some sweeping coastal views. The highest ground is towards the northeast where Yr Eifl lifts dramatically to 1850ft. Along the Cardigan Bay coast there are popular resorts such as Abersoch, Pwllheli and Criccieth, but elsewhere, and particularly inland, the Lleyn is generally quiet, with something of a character of its own and a stronghold of the Welsh language. Among places of specific interest are, along the north coast, the church at Clynnog Fawr and, for those willing to climb, the Iron Age hillfort-village of Tr'er Ceiri; and, along the Cardigan Bay coast, the medieval hall house of Penarth Fawr, Llanystumdwy and its associations with Lloyd George, and the native Welsh castle at Criccieth. During the Dark Ages and throughout the medieval centuries, all roads through the Lleyn were trodden by the pilgrims making their way to Bardsey (the island off the peninsula's tip), some 20,000, if tradition is to be believed, dying on the island.

The Lleyn is described below as an anticlockwise circuit from Caernarfon.

A487 to Glanrhyd (Llanwnda). A499 to Llanaelhaearn. B4417 and B4413 to Aberdaron. Unclassified to Abersoch. A499 to Pwllheli. A497 to Criccieth. B4411 and A487 to Caernarfon. Total distance 74m.—*3m. Glanrhyd (Llanwnda).—7m.* **Clynnog Fawr.—4m. Llanaelhaearn** (*Tre'r Ceiri*).—*6m.* **Nefyn.—13m. Aberdaron.—9m. Abersoch.—7m. Pwllheli.—7m. Llanystumdwy.—2m. Criccieth.—**13m. *Glanrhyd* (Llanwnda).—*3m.* **Caernarfon.**

For **Caernarfon**, see Rte 10. *3m. Glanrhyd* is a road fork at which this Route bears right on A499. The other road (A487) is described as the return leg of this Route. *2m. Llandwrog* is just west of A499.

DIVERSION TO CAERNARFON AIRPORT AND BEYOND (9m. return). The road westward out of Llandwrog soon reaches the shore at *Dinas Dinlle*, an isolated grass hill on top of which is a roughly oval fort formed by two ramparts and a ditch. Probably used by both British and Romans, the fort, together with the islets of Arianrhod and Maen Dylan to the south, also features in legend as the place where the heroic youth Lleu Llaw Gyffer, destined to become Lord of Gwynedd, 'was reared till he could ride every horse, and till he was perfected in feature, growth and stature'. Beyond, the road follows the shore across alluvial flats to reach **Caernarfon Airport**, with *Air World* (tel. 01286-830800) for a choice of sightseeing flights, notably over Snowdonia. Here, too, there is a museum (March–Nov: daily 09.30–17.30 or 16.30 in Oct and Nov), popular for its several hands-on features and also with a variety of exhibitions, restaurant, picnic area and an adventure playground built around a helicopter. *Fort Belan* (no adm.), a mile father north, is on the promontory which, with Abermenai to the north, forms the narrow entrance to Menai Strait. The fort was built by Thomas Wynne (of Glynllifon, southeast of Llandwrog), 1st Baron Newborough, in

1775 as a garrison for his Royal Caernarvonshire Grenadiers, a force of 400 men raised and equipped at his own expense; a patriotic gesture which, by the time of his death in 1807, had cost him a quarter of his fortune.

5m. **Clynnog Fawr**, a typical Lleyn village, in which the *Church of St. Beuno* is of outstanding interest. Founded by Beuno in c 616, and soon one of the first and most important stages along the pilgrimage path to Bardsey, the church seems at first to have been monastic, but by 1291 it had become collegiate, remaining such until the Dissolution. The present building dates from the early 16C, interesting external features being the north porch with its outside stair and, at the southwest angle of the chapel, a stone sundial. Noteworthy inside are, in the choir, the contemporary stalls and the book-desks with linen-pattern panelling; a rather plain rood screen of 1531, with the base of its former loft curiously prolonged into the south transept, where it is entered by a door communicating with a turret stair; dog tongs of 1815 and a dugout chest known as St. Beuno's Chest.

From the tower, a 17C passage (long used as the village lock-up) leads to *St. Beuno's Chapel*, which sheltered the tomb or shrine of the saint, destroyed by fire in 1856 but until then worshipped as miraculous. Restored in 1913, this chapel is of later date than the church, but the line of the foundations of an earlier building discovered during the restoration is marked by grey floor-slabs. The stone with a cross is traditionally the original stone set up on the ground given to Beuno by Gwyddaint, Prince of Gwynedd, but seems more likely to have been a medieval boundary marker or perhaps a pilgrim prayer-stone. *St. Beuno's Well*, beside the road on the left just south of the village, was a healing spring (Pennant described seeing a paralytic treated here). There are stone benches, steps down to the water, and niches probably intended for clothes. A diversion may be made eastward (roughly two miles return) to visit, near Ta'in Lôn, a *Museum of Welsh Country Life* (Easter–Sept: daily except Sat 10.00–17.00. Tel. 01286-660311), housed in a 17C water-mill and featuring a variety of bygone themes.

Soon the road begins to leave the coast, ascending gradually, with the steep slopes of Gurn Goch (1607ft) and Gurn Ddu (1712ft) to the east and a view seaward across to Holyhead. *4m.* **Llanaelhaearn**, a village at the foot of Yr Eifl, has a church entirely furnished with box-pews, and an ancient stone in the north transept inscribed 'Aliortus Elmatiacos hic jacet'. From the village, A499 cuts across south to Pwllheli while this Route follows B4417 along the south slopes of *Yr Eifl* (The Forks; 1849ft), so called because of the triple peaks. The central peak, Yr Eifl proper, is flanked on the northwest by a precipitous and much quarried summit (1458ft) falling to the sea. To the southwest below this, *Nant Gwrtheyrn* is also known as Vortigern's Valley, one of a number claiming to be the final refuge sought by that ill-starred royal bungler. Not that he had much luck here, for, legend relates, his palace was destroyed by fire cast from the sky while its owner drowned when, as a result, forced to leap into a wild sea.

Just south of Llanaelhaearn a path off B4417 climbs what seems a long mile to the hillfort-village of *Tre'r Ceiri* (1591ft). Dating from the 2C, but perhaps earlier, this well-preserved site covers some five acres, enclosed by a rampart with an internal parapet. Inside there are the remains of some 50 huts of varying shape, size and, probably, period, while the enclosures to be seen outside the rampart were probably for cattle. The cairn, on the summit to the northwest, is Bronze Age in origin.

6m. **Nefyn**, on the cliff, and *Morfa Nefyn* just west, with the adjacent sandy bays of *Porth Nefyn* and *Porth Dinllaen*, together form a quiet summer resort area. Porth Dinllaen, a fine natural harbour, might have become the port for the packets to Ireland, but in 1839, as the result of a single vote in the House of Commons, the choice fell on Holyhead. *5m. Tudweiliog*, rather over a mile beyond which a road (signed Sarn) bears southeast and passes, on the right in about 500 yards, a sizeable burial chamber.

8m. **Aberdaron**, two miles short of the tip of the Lleyn and today a quaint holiday and fishing village, was long a gathering place for pilgrims on their way to Bardsey, an era recalled by a 14C building which, as a café and souvenir shop, today still caters for travellers, if perhaps of a less single-mindedly pious breed. The church, the yard wall of which is washed by the sea at high tide, consists of a 12C nave and choir, and a wide south aisle added in the early 16C. Gruffydd ap Rhys is said to have sought sanctuary here when the Normans swept into southern Wales.

Aberdaron's perhaps best-known native is Richard Roberts Jones (1780–1843), a son of a local carpenter. Known as Dic Aberdaron, he was a strange vagabond and natural self-educated linguist, said to have spoken 35 languages and renowned for having compiled a dictionary in Welsh, Greek and Hebrew; it can be seen at St. Asaph cathedral where its author is buried.

Roads run southwest to within a short distance of *Braich-y-Pwll* and *Pen-y-Cil*, the two extremities of the Lleyn and both belonging to the National Trust. The former was the spot from which pilgrims once embarked for Bardsey, a holy well (the pwll) and the ruins of a chapel today recalling how piously active this place must once have been.

Bardsey Island, 450 acres rising to 500ft, is two miles off the tip of the Lleyn. The name is of Norse origin, and the Welsh name Ynys Enlii, meaning Island of the Currents, reminds that the narrow strait is treacherous. Known also as the Island of 20,000 Saints, Bardsey was an important pilgrimage objective from the 5 or 6C onwards, three pilgrimages here being reckoned as the equivalent of one to Rome. St. Cadfan, from Britanny, is said to have founded the first monastery here in 429; in c 545 St. Dyfrig is thought to have died and been buried here, though Llandaff cathedral also claims his relics; and after the destruction in 607 by Ethelfrid of Northumbria of the great monastery of Bangor-is-y-Coed, the surviving monks may have found refuge here. In the north part of the island are the 13C remains of the Augustinian St. Mary's Abbey, in the churchyard of which lie some of the 20,000 'saints' reputedly buried on the island. Owned since 1979 by Bardsey Island Trust, the island is still used for religious retreat, but there is also emphasis on nature, Bardsey being an official Site of Special Scientific Interest and the home of a Bird and Field Observatory. Limited self-catering accommodation (Trust Officer, Stabal Hen, Tyddyn Du, Criccieth, LL52 0LY. Tel. 01766-522239).

From Aberdaron an unclassified road is taken east, this in *3m* reaching *Y Rhiw*, a hamlet on a miniature pass commanding a wide view, including the great four-mile-long sweep of Porth Neigwl, or Hell's Mouth, both arms of which are in large part protected as National Trust properties. From here the road drops steeply, at the foot of the hill being *Plas-yn-Rhiw* (NT. April–Sept: daily except Sat 12.00–17.00. Oct: Sun 12.00–16.00. Tel. NT, North 01492-860123), a small, part medieval, part Tudor and part Georgian manor house with beautiful gardens and woodland. *5m.* **Llangian**, where in the churchyard (roughly in line with the south centre window of the church) there is a particularly interesting 5C stone, inscribed Meli Medici/Fili Martini/ Jacit/ (Here lies Melus the doctor, son of Martinus), the earliest mention of a doctor in Wales.

1m. **Abersoch** is a still small but growing resort at the end of the coastal road from the north east. Attractively situated with its harbour at the mouth of the river Soch, with two large and sandy beaches, and important also as a yachting centre, the town can become overcrowded in summer. Boat excursions to the *St. Tudwal's Islands*, on the northern of which are the chapel remains of a small medieval priory. At *Llanengan*, one and a half miles southwest of Abersoch, there is a 15C church (but tracing its origin to a foundation of the 6C), with two naves, each crossed by a rood screen, one of which has an elaborately carved loft. Noteworthy also are the builder's 'credit' on the crossbeam of the vaulting of the south nave; the tower, with bells from Bardsey; the old return-stalls, the 17C altar rails, and a dugout chest. South of Llanengan, a road continues for two miles into the headland of *Mynydd Cilan* with good coastal scenery.

3m. **Llanbedrog** is a modest resort sheltering below the bold promontory of Mynydd Tir-y-Cwmwd (434ft), paths across which offer views of St. Tudwal's Islands.

Just before Pwllheli, A497 bears northwest, in two miles passing *Bodvel Hall*, the birthplace of Dr Johnson's friend Mrs Thrale. At *Boduan*, a mile beyond, the church of 1894 claims descent from a shrine founded in 595 by St. Buan, to whom a cross has been erected.

4m. **Pwllheli**, pronounced Pool-thelli and meaning Salt Water Pool (*Inf.*), today, as a popular and crowded resort, gives no hint that it received its first charter as long ago as 1355. The main town lies along A497, well back from the long sand and shingle beach area with a promenade opened in 1890. At its east end this seafront ends at a narrow hook of land forming one of the protecting arms of the almost landlocked harbour.

In *3m* a minor road branches north for **Penarth Fawr** (Cadw; see p. 11), a 15C hall-house; the single room which served as the home of a family of some substance, probably numerous and with their several servants also all under the same roof. But properly to picture those late medieval days the imagination must place a tall screen along the open passage below the platform, with the lord and his family living on one side, the servants on the other; and those elegant windows and fireplaces installed in the 17C must in imagination be replaced by slits and an open hearth. From Penarth Fawr, anyone with a feel for holy wells will continue north for two miles to *Llangybi*, a name recalling that Anglesey saint who founded his Christian church within the walls of the Roman fort at Holyhead. Here at Llangybi, Fynnon Gybi (300 yards from the church; path) is a holy well sheltered within a building generally accepted as being at least in part early Christian in origin; the beehive vaulting here is thought to be unique in Wales, though found in Ireland. The well is adjacent to another roofless building, which, although it does not look all that different, is in fact an 18C cottage.

Continuing east, A497 in *4m* reaches **Llanystumdwy**, the home during his early years of the Liberal leader and world statesman (during the 1914–18 war and the negotiations for the Treaty of Versailles) Earl Lloyd George of Dwyfor (1863–1945), never known in Wales as other than David Lloyd George. Here today a compact small park encloses the various features which together make up the *Lloyd George Museum* (Easter–Sept: daily 10.00–17.00. Oct: Mon–Fri 11.00–16.00. Tel. 01766-522071). The museum proper, originally a building designed by Clough Williams-Ellis to house gifts from foreign leaders, was in 1990 (to mark the centenary of the stateman's first election to parliament) much enlarged and now offers exhibitions, documents, an audio-visual presentation, and a Victorian schoolroom. Adjacent, reached through a Victorian garden, is Highgate, the cottage belonging to Lloyd George's uncle and in which, after the death of his father, he lived until the age of seventeen; alongside the cottage is the uncle's shoemaking workshop. A short walk deeper into the small park reaches, above the river, Lloyd George's simple tomb with, on top, a rough boulder on which he often sat.

2m. **Criccieth**, a family resort near the corner of Cardigan Bay, here Tremadog Bay, enjoys a particularly fine outlook down the Lleyn, northeast towards Snowdonia, and across the water to Harlech and the mountains behind. The *Castle* (Cadw; see p. 11), perched on a rocky green hill above the town, is interesting for being a native Welsh stronghold built in c 1230, strengthened by Edward I in 1284, and Welsh again in 1404 when taken by Owen Glendower. The ruins consist mainly of a curtain enclosing the small rectangular inner ward (the oldest part of the castle) and the bold north gatehouse flanked by towers. The large outer ward, of which less remains, dates from c 1260. The Leyburn Tower (west) was probably the home of the constable, while the Engine Tower (north) was the launching site (from an upper floor, now disappeared) of missiles. The castle houses two exhibitions, one on the native Welsh castles, the other on Giraldus.

B4411 north out of Criccieth in *4m* joins A487, a short way southeast down which is *Dolbenmaen* with, opposite the church, a large motte, probably the 11C or earlier seat of the local rulers before they built their castle at Criccieth. A487 followed north in *6m* reaches *Pen-y-Groes*, until the beginning of the present century the centre for the slate and copper mines the forlorn traces of which litter the hills to the west. However, slate working survives at the *Inigo Jones Slate Works* (self-guided tour, café, shop. Easter–Sept: Mon–Fri 09.00–17.00; Sat, Sun, Bank Hol. 10.00–17.00. Oct–Easter: Mon–Fri 09.00–17.00; Sat 09.00–12.00. Workshop hours Mon–Thurs 09.00–16.30; Fri 09.00–15.30. Tel. 01286-830242). Opened in 1861, when the main product was slates for school use, the works here now turn out a wide variety of products both practical and decorative. The self-guided tour includes a video on slate mining, the workshop, an exhibition and a studio in which visitors can try their hands at engraving.

3m. Glanrhyd, where this circuit of the Lleyn is completed. *3m.* **Caernarfon**.

13

Chirk to Llangollen, Corwen and Betws-y-Coed

A5. Total distance 37m.—*6m.* **Llangollen**.—*10m.* **Corwen**.—*9m.* **Cerrigydrudion**.—*5m.* **Pentrefoelas**.—*7m.* **Betws-y-Coed**.

Mainly undulating agricultural country and moor, with occasional distant views of mountains.

Chirk, a pleasant small place on the English border, traces its origins to a castle built here in the 11C, of which all that remains is a small motte near the mainly 15C church. Beyond the south edge of the town and well seen from the A5, two adjacent viaducts impressively span the Ceiriog valley some 30ft below, one (1848) carrying the railway, while the other, Telford's aqueduct of 1801, carries the Shropshire Union Canal. (For a view from level or above, see Vale of Ceiriog below.)

Chirk Castle (NT. April–Sept: daily except Mon and Sat, but open Bank Hol. Oct: Sat and Sun 12.00–17.00. Tel. 01691-777701), two miles west of the town, stands massively and splendidly within a large park entered (from the east) through ironwork gates of 1719 which are an outstanding example of the work of the Davies brothers. Originally these gates stood in front of the castle, a complete and still inhabited pile, possibly designed by James of St. George c 1290–95 and completed c 1310 by Roger de Mortimer, on whom the land had been conferred by Edward I. The estate was bought in 1595 by Sir Thomas Myddelton, Lord Mayor of London and brother of the engineer, Sir Hugh. Originally square, the castle early lost its southern wall and is now rectangular in plan with a round bastion at each corner and a half-bastion at the centre of each face. The interiors have been frequently rebuilt and today's visitor sees decorative styles ranging from the 16 to the mid 19C. The park has a lake, north of the castle, near which a stretch of *Offa's Dyke* is clearly seen.

VALE OF CEIRIOG (B4500. 6m from Chirk to Glyn Ceiriog). Leaving Chirk the road offers a good view from above of the viaducts mentioned above, then ascends the Vale of Ceiriog cutting west into the *Berwyns*, a beautiful district of wooded hills reaching westward towards Bala and offering, to anyone not averse to steep and narrow lanes, unexpected tree-clad and pastoral glimpses and vistas. At **Glyn Ceiriog**, where B4500 turns south, the *Chwarel Wynne Slate Mine and Museum* (Easter–Oct: daily 10.00–16.30. Tel. 01691-718343) tells the story of the slate industry by means of a video film and a tour of the underground workings, and also offers a nature trail. From Glyn Ceiriog small roads wander southward through the eastern Berwyns to join Rte 19C in some ten miles at Llanrhaeadr-ym-Mochnant, while northward steep and narrow lanes provide a scenic approach to Llangollen.

A5 runs north out of Chirk, in a mile and a half crossing the Shropshire Union Canal. Visitors to Chirk Castle aiming for Llangollen may leave the park by the north exit and then follow a minor road to join A5 by the canal crossing.

3m (from Chirk, along A5) *Froncysyllte* where a side road north drops down to the Dee far below Telford's *Pontcysyllte Aqueduct* (1795–1805) which, 1007ft long and supported by 18 piers, carries the Shropshire Union Canal across the valley at a height of 121ft. There are boat excursions from Llangollen (tel. 01978-860702) and the footpath is a section of the Offa's Dyke Path.

3m. **Llangollen** (*Inf.*), in summer crowded and often a traffic bottleneck, lies mainly on the south bank of the Dee, here flowing below wooded hills on one of which, to the north, is perched the conspicuous Castell Dinas Bran.

Llangollen is the home of the annual (July) *International Music Eisteddfod*, first held in 1947 and now each year attracting around 150,000 visitors from all over the world. The competitions include events for choirs, soloists, folk singing, dancing and suchlike. For further information: Secretary, International Eisteddfod Office, Llangollen, LL20 8NG. Tel. 01978-860236.

Although a modest enough town, Llangollen, with its environs, is surprisingly rich in the number and variety of its places of interest.

SOUTH OF THE RIVER. A5 crosses the town as, successively, Queen Street, Regent Street, and Berwyn Street. Butler Hill, south off Queen Street, leads to *Plas Newydd* (April: daily 10.00–17.00 or 16.00 on Sun. May–Sept: daily 10.00–19.00 or 17.00 on Sun. Oct: daily 10.00–17.00. Tel. 01978-860828), a picturesque half-timbered house which was the home from 1780 of Lady Eleanor Butler (died 1829) and the Hon. Sarah Ponsonby (died 1831), better known as the 'Ladies of Langollen'.

The two 'Ladies of Langollen' were eccentric Irishwomen, who left their homes secretly in order to devote their lives to 'friendship, celibacy, and the knitting of blue stockings'. They became famous for their peculiarities of dress, their beneficence, and their collection of old oak and curios, to which it became recognised practice that their many visitors should contribute. Wellington, De Quincey (as a boy), Walter Scott (who made the house a scene in 'The Betrothed'), and Wordsworth were among such visitors; Wordsworth's somewhat tactless sonnet, with its description of the house as a 'low browed cot' and its oblique reference to the ladies' age, is said to have given offence. A third member of this distinctly odd household was Mary Carryl, the ladies' maidservant, who somehow managed to buy the freehold of Plas Newydd with her savings, leaving it to her employers on her death in 1809.

Sadly, the greater part of the collection was dispersed in 1832, but some memorabilia survive and the house in any case merits a visit for its carved panelling, stained glass and Spanish leatherwork gifted by the Duke of Wellington.

Church Street, opposite Butler Hill, leads to the *Church of St. Collen*, dedicated to a 6C saint whose cell survived here until 1747 when it was demolished, its stones being incorporated in the construction of the tower. Important in its own right during the 12C, the church was made subordinate to Valle Crucis (see below) early the following century. Inside the church the main features of interest are a 14C tomb-niche and the 15C hammer-beam roofs, while in the churchyard there is a monument erected by the Ladies of Llangollen to their faithful servant Mary Carryl, this also later serving to mark their own burial place.

Castle Street descends north from the point where Regent Street becomes Berwyn Street, passing on the left the *European Centre for Traditional and Regional Cultures* (Mon–Sat 10.00–17.00 or 18.00 on Sat. Sun 12.00–18.00. Tel. 01978-861514), a centre presenting the heritage of Europe's regions by means of a programme of exhibitions and performances, together with a book and craft shop selling both Welsh and continental regional products. Just beyond, the Town Hall, with *Tourist Information*, is on the corner of Castle and Parade streets, along the latter being the *Victorian School* (Easter–Oct: daily 10.30–17.00. Tel. 01978-860794) providing an insight into the schooling of a century or more ago. From Tourist Information, Castle Street continues to the river, crossed by *Llangollen Bridge*, dating in part (east side) to the bridge built in 1347 by John Trevor, later Bishop of St. Asaph. Rebuilt in Tudor times, the bridge was in turn widened for 18C coaches and then strengthened for modern traffic.

NORTH OF THE RIVER. Immediately north of the bridge there are two features of interest (Llangollen Railway and Llangollen Wharf), while beyond are the grounds of the International Musical Eisteddfod, a motor museum and the abbey of Valle Crucis. High above are the ruins of Castell Dinas Bran.

Llangollen Railway (daily 10.30–17.00. Tel. 01978-860951) represents enthusiasts' work which since 1975 has brought back to life both the station and some of the track (over four miles of Glyndyfrdwy; extension planned to Corwen) of the Ruabon to Barmouth line which operated between 1865 and 1968. The station is a museum in itself and the trains (daily in April–Oct. Weekends in Nov–March) are mainly steam.

Llangollen Wharf (Easter–Oct: daily 10.00–17.20. Tel. 01978-860702) offers canal boat trips and, in a former warehouse, a canal exhibition using models and audio-visual.

The ruin of *Castell Dinas Bran* (1000ft), conspicuous to the north above Llangollen, can be reached by a waymarked route from near the wharf. An Iron Age hillfort, and, later, a Welsh and for a brief period Norman wooden castle probably preceded the stone castle which seems to have been built in about 1236 and which, apparently little used, is known to have already been a ruin by 1578. In legend, though, this was the home of the lovely Myfanwy Fechan who spurned the love of the poet Hywel ap Einion and drove him to write a love poem, set to music in the 19C by Joseph Parry and now in the repertoire of male voice choirs. The climb is rewarded more by the views than by the ruin, which consists chiefly of the wall surrounding the hilltop, together with the entrance passage, flanked by towers, at the northeast angle. Much of the stone came from the ditch hacked out of the rock on the east and south.

A542, followed west and north, passes the International Musical Eist-eddfod ground, with its Royal International Pavilion opened by the Queen in 1992, and reaches Pentrefelin, with the *Llangollen Motor Museum* (Easter–Oct: daily. Nov–Easter: Mon–Fri 10.00–17.00. Tel. 01978-860324) with collections spanning the 1920s to 1960s. From here B5103 continues beside the river for half a mile to Telford's *Horseshoe Weir* and to *Llantysilio Church* (for both of which see below), while A542 leaves the river and heads north, quickly reaching the ruins of Valle Crucis Abbey.

• Valle Crucis Abbey (Cadw; see p. 11) was a Cistercian house founded in 1201 by Madog ap Gruffydd, an ambivalent prince of Powys who tended to side alternately with his own people and the English. A serious fire later in the same century led to major alterations, and the tower collapsed in 1400. The abbey was dissolved in 1535, but, despite centuries of neglect, the surviving ruins are quite extensive and include both the church and some of the domestic buildings.

The church adheres to the common early Cistercian plan of aisled nave, transepts with east chapels, and short aisleless choir; the north transept has been walled off from the crossing. In the walls of the north aisle can be seen the original masonry, heightened by small flat stones added after the fire. The west front is a beautiful composition (c 1250–75), with three fine plate-tracery windows enclosed in a common frame, and with a delicate rose-window in the gable. The east end (c 1240) is notable for the manner in which its external pilaster buttresses split above the bottom row of lancets so as to embrace an upper pair. To be noted in the church are the remains of the pulpit (including the stairway) under the vanished west arch of the crossing; the base of the altar; the curious recess, with remains of a shafted screen, on the north side of the choir; the bases of altars in the two chapels on the east side of the south transept; and the arch (at the end of the south transept) by which the dormitory was entered from the now vanished night-stairs. The piers of the crossing were heavily buttressed after the tower fell in 1400. In front of the choir there are six mutilated tombs, said to include those of Myfanwy Fechan, the legendary beauty of Castell Dinas Bran, and Iolo Goch, the bard of Owen Glendower.

Domestic Buildings. The south transept is adjoined by the Sacristy, to the south of which is the vaulted *Chapter House (rebuilt c 1315–50), in three parallel aisles. In the central one of these is the door from the Cloister, south of which is the day-stair (blocked) to the dormitory, while to the north the curious little vaulted space may have been for books. The passage immediately south of the chapter house led perhaps to the infirmary. To the south of the Dormitory, which occupies the whole length of the upper floor, is the Reredorter, while the northeast corner of the dormitory was apparently the Abbot's Lodging. The south and west cloister ranges are no more than foundations.

Eliseg's Pillar, a quarter of a mile north of the abbey, a tall broken shaft 8ft high, stands atop what may well be a burial mound. The pillar's interest lies in its Latin inscription, originally of 31 lines but now so badly weathered that parts only of 15 remain. Luckily a scholar of 1696 made a record, so it is known that the cross was erected early in the 9C by Cyngen (Concenn), who died c 854 on a pilgrimage to Rome, in memory of his great-grandfather, Eliseg, who annexed Powys from the English. It may be that the mound marks Eliseg's grave, and it may also be that it is from this cross that this valley and the abbey take their names.

To the east of the valley rises the range of *Eglwyseg Mountain*, at the south end being the ridge of the Eglwyseg Rocks, a series of terraced limestone cliffs of rounded promontories with gullies between. Offa's Dyke Path runs much of the length of the mountain, as does also a small road from Pentrefelin to World's End. The ridge is well seen from *Horseshoe Pass* on A542 beyond Valle Crucis, this road continuing north to join Rte 14.

This Route now continues westward from Llangollen along A5. Visitors to Valle Crucis may return to Pentrefelin, there taking B5103 to join A5.

2m (from Llangollen) *King's Bridge (Berwyn)* crosses a delightful stretch of the Dee, above Chain Bridge, the earlier crossing here, restored 1929. Just across King's Bridge are Telford's *Horseshoe Weir*, built in 1806 to supply water to the Llangollen branch of the Shropshire Union Canal, and Norman *Llantysilio Church*. Robert Browning worshipped here in 1886, a fact recorded by a brass on the south wall placed here by Lady Martin (Helena Faucit, the actress; died 1898), herself commemorated in a more modern chapel north of the choir. Sir Theodore (died 1909) and Lady Martin lived at the adjacent house. The road runs between two high areas of moorland, the Berwyns being to the south and Llantysilio Mountains to the north, in *4m* reaching *Glyndyfrdwy*, once an estate owned by Owen Glendower and the place from which he derived his name. A mound, between the road and the river, may well have been the site of his fortified manor. *Carrog*, just beyond across the river, is reached by a fine stone bridge of 1660.

4m. **Corwen**, a small town below a steep wooded hill, has its place in history as Owen Glendower's headquarters, where he gathered his forces before the battle of Shrewsbury. The Church (part 13C, restored) contains in the choir a curious raised monumental slab (14C) to a former vicar, and a Norman font. On the outer lintel of the priest's door (south choir) is an incised dagger, known as Glendower's Sword and supposed to mark the point of impact of a weapon thrown by Glendower from the hill above in a moment of anger with the townsfolk. In fact it dates from the 7–9C. There is another dagger-mark on a 12C cross outside the southwest corner of the church. Across the river, the hill of *Caer Drewyn*, with a stone rampart, probably dates to the immediate post-Roman period.

For Corwen to *Rhyl*, see Rte 5; to (north) *Wrexham* and *Chester*, and (south) *Bala, Dolgellau* and *Barmouth*, see Rte 14.

Beyond Corwen, A5 crosses the Dee, and within the next two miles the junctions with the above Routes 5 and 14 are passed. The valley of the Alwen is followed to (*4m*) *Maerdy*, where A5 enters that of the Ceirw. *5m* **Cerrigydrudion** is a village on a loop off the main road. The name, often wrongly written as 'druidion', means Place of the Brave and has no connection with Druids. Here B4501 leads north for Llyn Brenig (see Rte 4). *Caer Caradog*, a mile east of Cerrigydrudion, is a hillfort where the British chief Caractacus (Caradog) is said to have been betrayed to the Romans by Cartismandua, Queen of the Brigantes, after his final defeat by Scapula in 51. For the next five miles the road crosses rather dull moorland, relieved however by distant views of Snowdonia. A mile farther on Snowdon itself comes into view.

5m. **Pentrefoelas**, quietly sited and somewhat scattered, survives as an example of what was once an upland estate village. Today Pentrefoelas is becoming a focus for crafts or skills growing out of the former maintenance needs of the parent estate, a working mill being among the attractions.

Several roads converge near here, including A543 which, as Rte 4, joins from Denbigh; also B5113 which, running northwest for Llanwrst, crosses a high point of 1056ft, and commands exceptional views.

One mile west of Pentrefoelas, B4407 bears south, ascending the narrow valley of the Upper Conwy and in two miles reaching the secluded village of *Yspytty Ifan*, which once belonged (yspytty = hospitium) to the Knights Hospitaller of St John. In the church (rebuilt 1858) there are recumbent effigies (15–16C) of the Rhys family, one of these being of Rhys ap Meredydd who carried Henry Tudor's Red Dragon standard at Bosworth. The road continues southwest, following the Conwy almost to its source in *Llyn Conwy*, about four miles beyond Yspytty Ifan and half a mile north of the road. Until the Dissolution this upper valley was officially sanctuary and, despite the presence of the Hospitallers, notorious for its lawlessness. Beyond, traversing open moor, the road joins Rte 15 at *Pont-ar-Afon Gam*.

A5 soon crosses the river, following it down a deepening wooded glen and soon passing a small road which ascends northwest to reach in one and a half miles *Capel Garmon Burial Chamber* (c 1500 BC), the remains of a long barrow with three chambers, one with its capstone still in position. The stone base which surrounded the mound can be seen, with the long entrance passage. In rather over another mile A5 reaches a road junction (B4406) above Conwy and Machno Falls (paths) by the confluence of these rivers in the steep, wooded valley below.

DIVERSION TO PENMACHNO. B4406, running southwest above the tight wooded valley of the Machno, soon reaches *Penmachno Woollen Mill* with a shop and a café specialising in Welsh teas (Easter–mid Nov: daily 09.30–17.30, but in early and late season opens on Sun at 12.00. Weaving only Mon–Fri. Tel. 01690-710545). Here, is a lovely setting, a small road bridge crosses the river just above a packhorse bridge, the road beyond descending through woods above the left banks of the Machno and Conwy (not visible from the road) to join the Betws-y-Coed to Ffestiniog road (Rte 6C). B4406 soon reaches *Penmachno*, where the church houses a *Collection of Early Christian Stones*, one of the most important in Wales. One stone is inscribed with the sacred Chi-Rho (Christos) monogram; a second commemorates 'a citizen of Venedos' (an ancient name for Gwynedd), cousin of Maglos the Magistrate; and a third states that it was erected during the time of the Roman consul Justinius. Inscribed in Latin and dating from the 5–6C, the stones suggest that some form of Roman administration was surviving here even at this late date. For *Ty Mawr*, which can be approached from Penmachno, see Rte 6C. Beyond Penmachno B4406 rounds the west side of Llyn Conwy to meet Rte 15 at *Pont-yr-Afon-Gam* (8m from A5).

7m (from Pentrefoelas) **Betws-y-Coed**, see Rte 6C.

14

Wrexham to Bala, Dolgellau and Barmouth

A525 and A5104 to Corwen. B4401 to Bala. A494 to Dolgellau. A496 to Barmouth. Total distance 56m.—*10m*. **Llandegla.**—*9m*. **Corwen.**—*12m*. **Bala.**—*5m*. **Llanuwchllyn.**—*12m*. **Dolgellau.**—*4m*. **Bont-ddu.**—*4m*. **Barmouth**.

Pleasant if unexciting scenery as far as Bala, after which there is higher moor and mountain on both sides. From Dolgellau to Barmouth the road fringes the wooded Mawddach estuary. Views of Cader Idris (2927ft).

Wrexham (see Rte 4). *10m*. **Llandegla**, from where this Route follows A5104 which traverses a district once known as the Hundred of Ial (Yale), in two and a half miles reaching *Plas-yn-Yale*, former home of the Yale family and birthplace of Elihu's father, and, a short way beyond, *Bryngeglwys* where the church has relics of the family—*9m* (from Llandegla) Junction with Rte 5 (A494) from Ruthin and, just beyond, with Rte 13 (A5) from **Corwen**, which is half a mile east.

Here there is a choice of roads onward to Bala, A494 being the main approach (10m), though this Route takes B4401 out of Corwen, an approach some two miles longer and slower but more attractive along the fertile Vale of Edeyrnion below the slopes of the Berwyns. *4m*. *Llandrillo* is a starting point for walks into the hills. The fine mass of Arenig Fawr comes into view ahead before the river Dee is crossed to (*4m*) *Llandderfel* where the 15C church has a contemporary rood screen and one parapet of its loft, and also two curious wooden relics, a headless animal and a piece of a pole. Known as St. Derfel's Horse and St. Derfel's Staff, these are said to be all that is left of an equestrian figure of the saint the rest of which was taken to London to form part of the fire in which Friar Forest, Catherine of Aragon's confessor, was martyred in 1538.

4m. **Bala** (*Inf.*), set back from the north end of Bala Lake, is a pleasant local and holiday centre fortunate in having an attractive tree-lined main street (High Street, A494) broad and straight enough to ease the flow of through traffic.

History. The town's name derives from the Welsh 'bala', meaning 'outlet', because the Dee here flows out of Bala Lake. The motte in the town, as also the smaller one at the northeast corner of the lake, is probably Norman, though some opinion suggests that it is Iron Age and that the Romans, who were certainly in this district (e.g. at Caergai, see below), made use of it. The town was the centre of the more or less independent district of Penllyn within the principality of Powys, and when the castle was taken in 1202 by Llewelyn the Great he annexed Penllyn to Gwynedd. Little else is known of Bala's history until the 18C when it became prosperous as a centre of the woollen industry, Pennant writing of a 'vast trade in woollen stockings' and of women and children 'in full employ, knitting along the roads'. This prosperity died in the early 19C with the Industrial Revolution. Bala's repute as a religious centre was more enduring, the town's best known figure being the Rev. Thomas Charles (Charles of Bala, 1755–1814), pioneer of the Methodist movement in north Wales, founder of the British and Foreign Bible Society, and a leader of the Sunday School movement. Other local religious figures were Hywel Harris (1714–73), a Dissenter whose persecution here was marked by riots in 1741 (see also Trefecca); Dr Lewis Edwards, who in 1837 started an academy for young preachers, later the Theological College for Calvinist Methodists and today a Christian Movement Centre; and the Rev. Michael Jones, who in 1865 fitted out a ship which took 153 people, most of them from Bala, to Patagonia where they could be free to practise their nonconformism. They founded the town of Trelew, with which Bala still keeps close touch. In 1967 the National Eisteddfod was held in Bala.

East of A494 on the north edge of the town the large car park was once part of the Green, the town's market and the scene of large Methodist gatherings. Gorsedd stones nearby recall the National Eisteddfod in 1967. To the west, a short way up A4212, stands the former *Bala Theological College*, while the ancient, perhaps Iron Age motte, *Tomen-y-Bala*, is just east of the north end of High Street. Farther on (right) stands a bronze statue (Goscombe John) of Thomas Ellis (1859–99), long Member of Parliament for Merionethshire. Roughly opposite the White Lion Hotel is the house (tablet) where Thomas Charles lived. From here Tegid Street leads to the north extremity of Bala Lake, on the way passing, in front of the Welsh Presbyterian Church, a statue of Thomas Charles.

For *Bala Lake*, see below. For Bala to *Ffestiniog* and *Porthmadog*, see Rte 15; to *Lake Vyrnwy*, see Rte 19B; to *Bwlch-y-Groes* and *Dinas Mawddwy*, see Rte 20B.

Bala Lake is known in Welsh as Llyn Tegid, a name deriving from Tegid Foel (Tegid the Bald), a shadowy figure who in the 5C was Lord of Penllyn, the ancient local district, and perhaps husband of Ceridwen, mother of the bard and seer Taliesin. The lake, lying pleasantly though undramatically below green hills backed by mountains, is several times mentioned in literature. Tegid Foel is a character in the 'Mabinogion'; Giraldus, who calls the lake Penmelesmere, possibly from the old English 'pemmel' meaning 'pebble', records that it 'rises by the violence of the winds'; it appears in Spenser's 'Faerie Queen'; and Tennyson in 'Geraint and Enid' refers to the sudden floods in the Dee valley caused by the southwest wind 'that blowing Bala Lake fills all the sacred Dee'. This flooding has now been checked by the building of sluices below the river outlet, but in strong winds Bala can still be very rough. The lake, four miles long and half a mile broad, is the largest natural sheet of water in Wales, though it is smaller than the artificial Lake Vyrnwy. It is fed by several streams, one being the Dyfrdwy (Little Dee) at the south end, and empties into the Dee which flows through Llangollen to its estuary northwest of Chester. Bala is thought to be the only lake in which are found gwyniad, white fish of salmon species.

The main road, skirting the west bank, is described below. Along the east bank run a narrow, rather enclosed road, and also the *Bala Lake Railway* (Easter–Oct. Tel. 01678-4666), which operates along a section of the former Great Western Railway's Ruabon to Barmouth line. In 1972 a local company laid 1ft 11½ inch track, and today both steam and diesel trains run the length of the lake between Llanuwchllyn (the main station) and Bala (station at northeast tip of the lake). It should be noted that it is not possible to make a return trip using the last departure from Bala.

1m. **Llanycil**, where the churchyard contains the graves of Thomas Charles, Lewis Edwards, and the Rev. John Parry (1812–74), compiler of a Welsh encyclopaedia. In another two miles the road crosses the Llafar, by the lake being *Glanllyn*, a main centre of the Welsh League of Youth (see below), then leaves the lake and passes below *Caergai* (no adm.), a 17C manor standing within the earthworks of a Roman camp occupied c 98–117 and also traditionally site of the home of Sir Kay of Arthurian romance; Sir Rowland Vaughan (1590–1667), Royalist, hymnologist, and translator, lived here. Beyond, the Lliw, Bala Lake's longest feeder, is crossed. For the lonely and beautiful road ascending this river and crossing high moor and afforestation to Bronaber, see Rte 16. *Castel Carndochan*, south of the river one and a half miles up the valley, is a Norman motte, still with something of its foundations, and a 14C effigy in the church at (*4m*) **Llanuwchllyn** is probably that of one of the castle's owners. The *Bala Lake Railway Station* (workshops etc.) is at the far end of the village, while at the main road entrance to Llanuwchllyn stand statues of Sir Owen M. Edwards (1858–1920) and of his son, Sir Ifan, both active in helping youth, the father as an educationalist and writer of children's books and the son as founder of Urdd Gobaith Cymru, the Welsh League of Youth, broadly an amalgam of youth movements and organisations, and practically concerned with activities which range from an annual eisteddfod to all manner of outdoor endeavours (see also Glanllyn above). For the high scenic road through Llanuwchllyn to *Bwlch-y-Groes* and *Dinas Mawddwy*, see Rte 20B.

Generally following the course of its Roman predecessor, A494 now ascends the river Dyfrdwy through rather desolate country overshadowed on the south by Aran Benllyn (2901ft) and Aran Mawddwy (2970ft), volcanic peaks the names of which recall the semi-independent districts of Mawddwy (see Rte 20B) and Penllyn (see Bala, History, above). Reaching the watershed at 770ft, the road descends the wooded Wnion valley, with Cader Idris prominent ahead. *9m* (from Llanuwchllyn) *Bont Newydd*, where a road south through Brithdir, avoiding often-crowded Dolgellau, connects to the main roads to Dinas Mawddwy and Machynlleth. *3m.* **Dolgellau**, see Rte 16.

For the first three miles beyond Dolgellau there is a choice of roads, north or south of the Mawddach Estuary, the southern road being slightly shorter but crossing a tollbridge.

The northern road reaches the bridge over the Mawddach, just before which are the modest but evocative remains of *Cymmer Abbey*, a Cistercian house founded in 1199 by monks from Cwmhir (the name, pronounced Kummer, was in full once Kymer deu dyfyr, meaning Meeting of the Waters). The ruins are principally those of the abbey's never completed 13C church, survivals being the north nave arcade, three lancets at the east end, battered sedilia, and a piscina in the south wall. Of the cloister and domestic buildings little remains, but something of the chapter house is in the local farm's yard, and the farm itself is probably on the site of the guest house, important at an abbey where travellers must frequently have been delayed by river floods. For Precipice Walk, which can be reached from here, see Rte 16, Dolgellau. For the Mawddach valley northwards, also see Rte 16. In the churchyard at *Llanelltyd*, across the bridge, is buried Frances Power Cobbe (1822–1904), social writer and suffragist. Beyond, and running below the ridge which carries New Precipice Walk, A496 reaches the north end of the Mawddach tollbridge referred to above. At *Penmaenpool*, at the south end of the bridge, the signal box of the old railway (1865–1965, originally the Aberystwyth and Welsh Coast Railway) has been converted by the Royal Society for the Protection of Birds and the North Wales Naturalists' Trust as a Nature Information Centre (Easter week and week-ends between Easter and Whitsun: 12.00–16.00. Whitsun to about mid Sept: daily 11.00–17.00. Tel. 01341-422071). Rte 21, from Machynlleth and Ty-wyn, joins here from the south.

4m (from Dolgellau) *Bont-Ddu* lies below hills through which runs a gold seam. Intermittently worked since Roman times, the mines have long been commercially abandoned though gold from here has been used in recent royal wedding rings, including that of the Queen. The road briefly leaves the shore, regaining it for a fine view of the Cader Idris massif across the estuary. *4m*. **Barmouth**, see Rte 17.

15

Bala to Ffestiniog and Porthmadog

A4212 and B4391 to Ffestiniog (Pont Tal-y-Bont). A496 and A487 to Porthmadog. Total distance 23m.—*3m*. *Frongoch.*—*7m*.
Pont-yr-Afon-Gam.—*3m*. **Ffestiniog**.—*3m*. **Maentwrog**.—*4m*. **Penrhyn-deudraeth**.—*3m*. **Porthmadog**.

Moor and mountain. After Pont-yr-Afon-Gam fine views down to the Vale of Ffestiniog and the coast.

Leaving **Bala** (see Rte 14) A4212 ascends the pleasant open valley of the Tryweryn, in *3m* reaching a road fork at *Frongoch* from where an upland road bears north for Cerrigydrudion on Rte 13. *2m*. **Llyn Celyn**, in a beautiful setting of moor and mountain, is a reservoir completed by Liverpool Corporation in 1965 to regulate the flow of the Dee and supply water largely to Liverpool and the Wirral. The dam (2200ft long) is at the east end, and fish, which formerly swam up the river, are now collected in a trap and spawned for stocking. The main road runs with the north shore, by the northwest arm passing a chapel and memorial garden commemorating the chapel and burial ground drowned by the lake; some of the stone from the submerged chapel is incorporated into this new one.

About one and a half miles beyond the west end of Llyn Celyn a road fork is reached, the road to the left (A4212) following the track of the old railway past little Llyn Tryweryn to *Trawsfynydd* on Rte 16. The old bridge near this road fork is said to be Roman in origin.

Almost due south rises *Arenig Fawr* (2800ft) which, isolated and barren, prompted George Borrow to write that of all the hills he saw in Wales none made a greater impression. On the summit a tablet on a cairn commemorates the crew of a United States Air Force Flying Fortress which crashed here in 1943. The mountain can be climbed by following A4212 for a mile, and then a track which ends about three quarters of a mile below the summit.

Now following B4391 across rather desolate moor, this Route reaches a watershed at 1507ft (*2m* from the fork) and, in another *3m*, *Pont-yr-Afon-Gam*, where the moorland road (see Rte 13) from Penmachno and Yspytty Ifan comes in from the north. A short distance beyond this junction there is a car park beside a *Viewpoint high above the deep slate cleft of *Rhaeadr Cwm* with its several cataracts.

Llyn Morwynion (Lake of the Maidens. 1292ft) is a quarter of a mile north over the hill. The story goes that the men of Ardudwy, who had made a foray into Clwyd, were returning with their captive women when they were overtaken here by the pursuing men of Clwyd and slain. But so enamoured had the women become of their captors that, rather than return with their own men, they drowned themselves in the lake. Another story is that this is where the maidens of Blodeuwedd were drowned, after their mistress, who had murdered her husband in order to be with her lover, had been turned into an owl.

The descent into the Vale of Ffestiniog affords a superb view across Traeth Bach to Tremadog Bay and the long line of the Lleyn. *3m*. **Ffestiniog**, at 600ft, is boldly situated on a bluff between the Vale of Ffestiniog and the valley of the Cynfal. The knoll behind the church, reached by a path beside the south wall of the churchyard, affords a view which, though now marred by the Trawsfynydd power station, still includes the full perspective of the valley and the sea and coast beyond. A hill southwest of the village, on which is the tomb of the 4th Baron Newborough, is another viewpoint, while a local walk (sign by the church) is to the *Cynfal Falls*, just south below the town; above the falls a rock is known locally as Pulpud (pulpit) Huw Llwyd, recalling a local mystic who preached from here. The walk can be continued up the valley via Bont Newydd to Rhaeadr Cwm.

For Ffestiniog to *Blaenau Ffestiniog* and *Betws-y-Coed*, see Rte 6C; to *Dolgellau*, see Rte 16; to *Harlech* and *Barmouth*, see Rte 17; for the *Ffestiniog Railway*, see Porthmadog, below.

The Porthmadog road descends to the valley, at *Tal-y-Bont* merging with A496 from Blaenau Ffestiniog and in *3m* reaching **Maentwrog** (see Rte 17 which here comes in from Barmouth and Harlech). A487 crosses the river Dwyryd, on the farther side, at the foot of the old road from Beddgelert, being *Tan-y-Bwlch*. The estate (Plas Tan-y-Bwlch) formerly belonged to the Oakley family, owners of the Blaenau Ffestiniog quarries, but is now the Snowdonia National Park Residential Study Centre, with, in summer, an information facility. Here, too, are nature trails, one of which (Llyn Mair) runs through a part of the nature reserve which protects something of the original oak woods that once covered much of Wales.

4m. **Penrhyndeudraeth**, see Rte 7. *1m*. *Minffordd*, for *Portmeirion* (daily 09.30, or 10.00 for shops–17.30. Opening hours may be shortened in Nov–March. Tel. 01766-770228), an astonishing and, in other than sunny weather, somewhat incongruous private village and tiny harbour in Italianate style, the achievement of the Welsh architect Sir Clough Williams-Ellis (1883–1978) who, acquiring this then run-down estate in 1925, determined 'to show that one could develop even a very beautiful site without defiling it and indeed ... even enhance what nature has provided for your background'. Sir Clough's work here has generally been of two periods, one before the 1939–45 war and the other from 1954 onwards, the more conspicuous buildings being the Campanile, half-Romanesque and half-Baroque, and the Bath House Colonnade (18C), brought from Bristol in 1957 when the house itself was in danger of demolition (every half hour

Portmeirion. View towards the campanile

there is a video presentation narrated by Sir Clough). The site is surrounded by grounds notable for their rhododendrons; and gardens are integral with the village, the slopes and steps of which, however, make it difficult for some disabled. Other features include a large beach area, notorious, though, for strong currents and swift tides; the hotel, and cottages of unique character for renting; a licensed restaurant and several shops. The famous Portmeirion pottery is not made here, but is sold at two shops, one of which is a popular 'seconds' shop, the only such in Wales.

2m. **Porthmadog** (*Inf.*) is reached by crossing *The Cob* (toll), the mile-long embankment carrying the road and the Ffestiniog Railway across the mouth of the Glaslyn which was built by W.A. Madocks (1774–1828), the local Member of Parliament, as part of the reclamation of the 7000 acres of Traeth Mawr (see towards the end of Rte 10). Today primarily a holiday and sailing centre, Porthmadog was once important as a port (largely for the Blaenau Ffestiniog quarries) and this past is recalled at the *Maritime Museum* (Easter, June–Sept: daily 10.00–16.00. Tel. 01766-513736) in a

Ffestiniog Railway, Porthmadog

surviving slate shed on one of the harbour wharves. *Porthmadog Pottery* (April–Sept: Mon–Fri 10.00–17.30. Also open Sun in July and Aug and Bank Hol. weekends. Tel. 01766-512137) offers exhibitions and demonstrations and also encourages visitors to try their hand at the wheel or with the paint brush, while for train enthusiasts Porthmadog is the home of two railways.

The *Ffestiniog Railway* (March–Nov: daily. Also limited winter service. Tel. 01766-512340. Museum, shop, travel centre and restaurant at the station), climbing and running high above the estuary and the Vale of Ffestinog and affording exciting coastal and mountain views, reaches Blaenau Ffestiniog (see Rte 6C) in 13½ miles and one hour. Opened in 1836 as a horse-drawn tramway for the Blaenau Ffestiniog slate quarries, and adapted for passengers in 1865, the line had a gauge of 1ft 11½ inches and, with a total rise of 700ft, was skilfully engineered so that the gradient (maximum 1:70) enabled laden trains to descend by gravity. Closed in 1946, the line has been re-opened in stages since 1954, one major achievement being the construction of nearly three miles of new alignment, made necessary by the drowning by the Tanygrisiau Reservoir of a section of the original course. Trains may be steam or diesel and there are a number of stations along the route. The *Welsh Highland Railway* (Easter–Oct: most days. Tel. 01766-513402), represents the restored survival of a short section of the scenic narrow-gauge line which from 1923 to 1937 linked Porthmadog (via Aberglaslyn, Beddgelert and Rhyd-Ddu) with Dinas near Caernarfon. At present about a mile of track from Porthmadog is open, served by steam or diesel locomotives. The sheds and workshops are open to visitors.

For Porthmadog to *Caernarfon* and *Bangor*, see Rte 10. For the *Lleyn*, see Rte 12.

16

Dolgellau to Ffestiniog

A470. Total distance 17m.—*2m. Llanelltyd.*—*3m. Ganllwyd.*—*5m. Bronaber.*—*2m.* **Trawsfynydd.**—*3m. Junction A470/A487 (for* **Maentwrog**).—*2m.* **Ffestiniog.**

The first half of the road is up the beautiful Ganllwyd valley, beside the rivers Mawddach and Eden and through the forest of Coed-y-Brenin. Afterwards the country opens up giving some views of mountains. For much of the way the road runs just west of the Roman Sarn Helen.

Dolgellau (*Inf.*), its name pronounced Dol-gethly and meaning perhaps Meadow of the Hazels, is the chief centre for a wide surrounding mountain district and thus very Welsh in both custom and language. Pleasantly situated on the south bank of the Wnion, crossed by a seven-arch bridge largely of 1638, at the foot of the mass of Cader Idris, within easy reach of varied but always beautiful scenery, and at the junction of several main roads, the town can be a magnet for tourists and its narrow streets and bridge a traffic bottleneck in summer.

History. Owen Glendower held a Welsh parliament here in 1404, and later in the same year here signed an alliance with Charles VI of France, but otherwise Dolgellau figures little in history. The Vaughan (Fychan) family were long the most important land-owners, their seats being at Nannau (2m N) and Hengwrt (1m NW). One distinguished member of the family was Robert Vaughan (1592–1667), the antiquary, who lived at Hengwrt and was known for his priceless collection of manuscripts, now in the National Library of Wales.

The town centre is Eldon Square, the name recalling the Lord High Chancellor of the early 19C who legally represented the Vaughan family. Here in the same building are *Tourist Information* (Snowdonia National Park) and, reflecting this district's association with the Quakers, an inter-pretive exhibition, *Merioneth Quakers* (Easter–Oct: daily 10.00–18.00. Tel. 01341-422888). In the mainly 18C *Church of St. Mary*, successor to one of the 13C if not earlier, there is an effigy (1350) of Meurig ap Ynyr Fychan, a Vaughan of Nannau ancestor.

Dolgellau is perhaps best known for its choice of local walks, two favourites being Precipice Walk and Torrent Walk. *Precipice Walk*, about three miles to the north, is a path some three miles in total length encircling the steep high ridge of Foel Cynwch, 1000ft above the river Mawddach and with on its east side the wooded small Llyn Cynwch. The walk affords superb views of Cader Idris and the length of the Mawddach estuary towards Barmouth. One approach is from Cymmer Abbey (see Rte 14), but the shorter one is from a parking area on the Dolgellau to Llanfachreth road near the entrance to Nannau Park, ancient seat of the Vaughans. *Torrent Walk*, two miles east of the town, is a two and a half miles walk up the mossy, fern-clad glen of the Clywedog, starting from the point where this stream runs into the Wnion and ending at the bridge at the junction of A470 with the road to Brithdir.

For Dolgellau to *Barmouth* (W) and to *Bala* (NE), see Rte 14; to *Machynlleth*, see Rte 20A; to *Machynlleth* via the coast (*Tywyn*), see Rte 21; to *Dinas Mawddwy*, see Rte 20B.

CADER IDRIS, lifting high (2927ft) to the southwest of Dolgellau, means Chair of Idris, who was according to tradition and the bards a giant variously celebrated as warrior, poet and astronomer. Tradition further insists that anyone sleeping the night in the chair, the precise position of which is obscure, may expect to wake up as either a poet or a lunatic. More historically, if still shadowy, it seems that Idris was a descendant of Cunedda, through Meirion (who gave his name to Merioneth), and that he was killed in about 630 fighting the Saxons. A hoard of Iron Age ornaments, found under a boulder on the mountain in 1963, is now in the National Museum of Wales.

Though exceeded in height by many Welsh peaks, Cader Idris, thanks largely to its accessibility, almost levels with Snowdon in visitor popularity. The main core of the mass is a ridge, some eight miles long, the summit being *Pen-y-Gadair*, while the ridge itself, steep on all sides, presents almost perpendicular walls of rock towards the north with an average drop of 900ft. To the south the ridge descends, for the most part in abrupt grassy slopes, down to the Dysynni valley, part of the fault (geologically known as the Bala Fault) which includes Bala Lake and Tal-y-Llyn. On this south side there is also an impressive cwm, enclosed by Craig-y-Cau and Pen-y-Gadair and containing the dark lake of *Llyn-y-Cau*. Of the massif's lesser heights, *Mynydd Moel* (2804ft) is a mile northeast of the summit, while *Tyrau Mawr* (2167ft), two and a half miles west, commands a view at least equal to that from Pen-y-Gadair. To the northwest of Pen-y-Gadair there is another deep cwm in which lies *Llyn-y-Gadair*, the narrow wall of rock, 1000 to 1300ft high and separating the basin of this lake from that of Llyn-y-Cau, being the most striking feature of the mountain. Cader Idris has been a national nature reserve since 1955, of particular interest to geologists for its Ordovician lavas and to botanists as one of the most southern areas in Britain for arctic-alpine plants.

There is a choice of paths to the top, some from the north from near Dolgellau, others from the south from the area of Tal-y-Llyn lake. Local advice should be sought regarding current conditions and as to which path best suits individual requirements.

For Dolgellau to (*2m*) *Llanelltyd*, see Rte 14. A470 (but see alternative road below) ascends the lovely *Ganllwyd Valley*, following the west bank first of the Mawddach and then of the Eden, the ridge above the opposite bank of the former being Foel Cynwch, with Precipice Walk high up on its slope. In a couple of miles, where the Wen and Las streams flow into the other side of the Mawddach, the road enters the wooded Ganllwyd Valley proper, soon, just beyond the Tyn-y-Groes Hotel, passing above the bridge by which the alternative road (see immediately below) joins this main road.

A quiet and pleasant alternative is provided by the small road which ascends the east bank of the Mawddach, passing, first, close to Cymmer Abbey (see Rte 14). In a little over two miles, with the Mawddach bearing away northeast, the Las stream is crossed, just the other side being a road which leads east for Forest Enterprise's *Glasdir Arboretum*. Returning west, the Mawddach is crossed, the Eden then being followed north to the next bridge across to A470.

3m (from Llanelltyd) *Ganllwyd*, the hamlet which gives this valley its name and immediately west of which is the National Trust's Dalmelynllyn estate, best known for the waterfall of *Rhaeadr Ddu*. Continuing beside the west bank of the Eden, A470 soon reaches *Pont Dolgefeiliau* (picnic site), the name meaning Meadow of the Smiths and recalling that in the early 19C this was where the drovers had their cattle shod before starting the long drive towards London.

From Pont Dolgefeiliau a branch roads leads in half a mile to Forest Enterprise's **Maesgwn Visitor Centre** (Easter–Sept: daily 10.00–17.00. Tel. 01341-422289) in the heart of the *Coed-y-Brenin*, a forest most of which was part of the ancient Nannau Estate. The first owner (c 1100) was Cadwgan, Prince of Powys, the property later passing to the Vaughans. After land had been bought from the Vaughans, the Forestry Commission started planting in 1922, and in 1935, to celebrate the Silver Jubilee of George V, the name was changed from Vaughan Forest to Coed-y-Brenin, the Forest of the King. The total area of forest, on both sides of A470 and with a number of outlying sections, is some 21,700 acres, of which about 15,500 are planted, most of the remainder being agricultural land. The Maesgwm Centre provides an admirable survey of all the main aspects of the forest—past, present and planned—and includes also much about local gold mining.

The varied scenery—the most accessible area being that to the east of A470—includes forest proper, pasture, moorland and the wooded glens through which tumble the Eden, Gain, Mawddach and Wen. A map obtainable at the Visitor Centre describes a network of many miles of paths and some motorable roads, particularly popular objectives being the cascades of *Rhaeadr Mawddach* and *Pistyll Cain*, both near former gold workings. For an alternative approach from the north (from Bronaber), see below.

A470 crosses the Eden at Pont Dolgefeiliau, gradually leaving the river's east bank and in one and a half miles, at *Bryn Eden*, exchanging the forest for open moor, with views of the Rhinogs to the west. *5m.* (from Ganllwyd) *Bronaber* is a scattered hamlet from which a choice of small roads traverse the lonely moorland to the east.

A road ascends east through a holiday village, on the hilltop above which a fork offers a choice. The righthand road, soon passing a chapel, leads across moor and through forests to (3m) a farm where the road ends. From here a path descends (25 minutes) to the cascades of *Rhaeadr Mawddach* and *Pistyll Cain* (see above). The lefthand road soon arrives at another fork. Here the righthand road (Abergierw) drops to the river Gain with, before the bridge, two antiquities. *Llech Idris*, to the right, is a tall standing stone, probably set up in prehistoric times though later given the name of the 7C warrior of Cader Idris. To the left is *Bedd Porius*, the grave of Porius, now no more than broken fragments marking the site of a 5–6C inscribed stone (in Latin, 'Porius, a simple man, lies here') now housed in the National Museum of Wales. The lefthand road at the fork wanders across remote high moor and afforestation to (12m from Bronaber) Llanuwchllyn (see Rte 14) at the south end of Bala Lake.

2m. **Trawsfynydd** is a village beside the lake of the same name created in 1930 as part of the Maentwrog hydro-electric scheme and now dominated by a nuclear power station (Sir Basil Spence, 1959–64; now closed). In the village there is a statue to Hedd Wyn, a shepherd poet whose winning of the bardic chair at the 1917 Eisteddfod was declared after he had been killed in Flanders; and from here A4212 bears northeast to meet Rte 15 in eight miles just west of Llyn Celyn.

Just beyond the power station, and just before the A470/A487 junction, a small road leads east to reach in a mile a spot which, however bypassed and insignificant today, nevertheless has its roots in the Roman and Norman past as also in Welsh legend. Here is a tiny *Roman Amphitheatre*, interesting for being the only example in Britain serving an auxiliary fort, while, a short way southwest, the mound of *Tomen-y-Mur* (Mound of the Wall) was probably an early Norman motte raised inside the walls of this 1C Roman auxiliary fort on Sarn Helen. And in legend, in those shadowy years between the departure of the Romans and the arrival of the Normans, this was a seat of the princes of Ardudwy; the place, too, from which the men of Ardudwy set out on that raid into Clwyd which ended in the drowning of the maidens in Llyn Morwynion (see Rte 15).

3m. (from Trawsfynydd village) Junction of A470 and A487. For **Maentwrog**, two miles along the latter, see Rte 17. A470, crossing the Cynfal at Bont Newydd, in *2m* reaches **Ffestiniog**, see Rte 15.

17

Barmouth to Maentwrog

A496. Total distance 21m.—*8m*. **Llanbedr**.—*2m*. **Llanfair**.—*2m*. **Harlech Castle**—*3m*. **Llanfihangel-y-Traethau**.—*6m*. **Maentwrog**.

At first the road runs through the district of Ardudwy, the narrow land between the mountains and the sea which was the home of a people who, after the departure of the Romans, seem to have moved to Tomen-y-Mur (Rte 16). Beyond the flat coast with its many caravan sites, there is a seaward view across to the Lleyn, while ahead, beyond Llanfair, appear the mountains of Snowdonia. Inland there is moorland, dull as seen from the road but, deeper in, with some wild scenery; the best parts of this inland country, with many prehistoric remains, are indicated below as diversions eastward off A496.

Barmouth (*Inf.*), in Welsh Abermaw or Y Bermo, is a popular and at times uncomfortably overcrowded resort which manages to preserve something of its 19C origins amid an extrovert ambience. Situated at the north extremity of the estuary of the Mawddach, on a narrow strip between the sea and the hills, the town's most obvious attraction is its waterfront and beach with two miles of sands. This area is rather awkwardly separated from the rest of the town by the railway.

A496—here from south to north the sequence Church Street, High Street and King Edward Street—represents, together with Jubilee Road (parallel to and just seaward of Church and High streets) the main street on the railway's landward side. On the steep slopes above, and especially above Church Street, cluster the houses of the old town. Above, again, is *Dinas Oleu*, four and a half acres of cliffland of particular interest as the first property acquired by the National Trust, the gift, in 1895, of Mrs. F. Talbot.

The fine beach is backed by the Promenade, a wide motor road and walk extending some two miles between Llanaber to the north and the harbour, near the latter being *Ty Gwyn* (tel. 01341-280787), a house, largely rebuilt but still showing an old door, reputedly used by a Vaughan when plotting with Jasper Tudor to put Henry Tudor on the English throne; today the house has a Tudor exhibition and shows material from medieval shipwrecks. Barmouth also offers a *RNLI Museum* (tel. 01341-280787).

Three walks are popular, one being the *Railway Bridge* footpath across the estuary. The bridge is 800 yards long, with an iron swingbridge at its north end where the navigable channel hugs the shore, and the view, which embraces the massif of Cader Idris, is striking enough to have prompted Wordsworth, who was here in 1824, to write of this 'sublime estuary'. The estuary can also be crossed by ferry (not cars) to Penrhyn Point, terminal of the Fairbourne small-gauge railway (see Rte 21). *Panorama Walk*, reached by a lane off the main road 150 yards short of the railway bridge, undulates for some three miles along a steep slope 300–500ft above the estuary, while a third walking area is provided by the high ground above the town, which, municipally owned, has been laid out with paths.

Leaving Barmouth, A496 in *2m* reaches *Llanaber* where the church, between the road and the sea and dating from the early 13C, is well worth a visit, if only for the interior work which is surprisingly elaborate for what was, at the time of the church's building, a remote corner of Wales. Note, for example, the choir and the south doorway with its clustered shafts. There are some unusual features here, too, such as the single east lancet, the contemporary outer door to the porch and the construction, due to the sloping site, on three levels, with five steps from the nave to the choir and two more to the sanctuary. Noteworthy also are an old alms chest; the 16C roof timbers; a cross on the west wall which is part of an ancient graveslab; and two venerable stones (before 10C), one of which, inscribed 'Caelexti Monedo Regi', though mentioned by early writers on Wales, is of undetermined provenance. *3m. Llanddwywe* is associated with a branch of the Vaughan family, one of whom, Gruffyd, in 1615 founded a chapel in the church (west side of the road), both the chapel and its monument to Gruffyd being ascribed to Inigo Jones. Opposite the church a driveway leads to the one-time Vaughan mansion of *Cors-y-Gedol* (1593), largely remodelled but with a gatehouse of 1630 said to be a design by Inigo Jones. The small gated-road round the south of the house soon reaches, on the right beside the road, *Cors-y-Gedol Burial Chamber* (or, on some maps, Arthur's Quoit), now little more than a large perched capstone.

The road westward beside the church is the motor approach to the area of *Morfa Dyffryn National Nature Reserve*, within an inverted triangle (apex at the car park) which fringes the shore for almost two miles northwards.

The straggling built-up area of **Dyffryn Ardudwy** begins immediately beyond Llanddwywe, at the south end, off the east side of the road, being *Dyffryn Cairn*, one of the more important burial chambers in this part of Wales and one from which excavation in 1962–63 produced pottery and other finds, now in the National Museum of Wales. Calculated to have been 100ft long, narrowing in width from 54ft at its west end to 35ft at its eastern, the surviving visible remains are simply some of the base stones of the cairn and the two burial chambers. The west chamber, with its own cairn, traces of which can be seen, is thought to have been the first built and to have later been covered by the cairn of the larger east chamber. In the church at *Llanenddwyn*, the western part of Dyffryn Ardudwy, is buried Colonel Jones of Maes-y-Garnedd (see below); brother-in-law of Oliver Cromwell, he signed the death warrant of Charles I and was himself executed as a regicide at the Restoration.

3m. **Llanbedr**, beside the river Artro, is the home of *Maes Artro Village* (Easter–Sept: daily 10.00–17.00. Tel. 01341-23467), a tourist complex set up in a RAF wartime camp and today including a RAF wartime museum, a 'village of yesteryear', an aquarium, craft shops, woodland walks, café and much else, especially for children. But connoisseurs of ancient stones will also visit Llanbedr church in which a stone, bearing a spiral design probably of the Bronze Age, interestingly indicates religious use spanning pagan to early Christian times.

From Llanbedr diversions can be made both west and east, the latter being into some wild country.

The WESTWARD DIVERSION is to *Shell Island* (mid March–Oct: daily. Fee) beyond a tidal causeway covered at high water (no attempt should be made to cross at times other than as posted on boards). Formed during the 19C when the local landowner, intent on increasing his holding, diverted the river Artro, this area of grassy and sandy dunes, beach and rocks has become popular largely on account of the many shells washed up here (over 200 different kinds), the wild flowers and the variety of birds. An informal place, visitors are free to explore along a network of small roads, while practical needs are met by restaurants, tidal slipways for boats, fishing facilities, camping sites and shops. From here, exposed at low tide, extends Sarn Badrig, or St. Patrick's Causeway, rocks running away southwest and fabled as having once been a road to the Lowland Hundred.

The EASTWARD DIVERSION (11 miles return; narrow road) gradually ascends the valley of the Artro, which, with its tributary Cwmnantcol, embraces *Rhinog National Nature Reserve*, in large part a wild area of ledges, scree and boulders building up to Rhinog Fawr (2362ft). There are several tracks and a walk circuit may be made by way of Bwlch Tyddiad (Roman Steps, see below) and Bwlch Drws Ardudwy.

The lane up Cwm Nantcol, with a nature trail, finishes at *Maes-y-Garnedd*, birthplace of the regicide Colonel Jones (see above), a track continuing northeast and in a mile reaching Bwlch Drws Ardudwy, the pass below Rhinog Fawr (N) and Rhinog Fach (S).

The narrow road up to the Artro in four miles (from Llanbedr) skirts the beautiful tarn of *Llyn Cwm Bychan* before ending at a farm (parking), whence a path (once a packhorse trail) in what can seem a long mile reaches the start of the so-called *Roman Steps* (Bwlch Tyddiad), a strange broken ascent of flat unhewn slabs, in places edged by smaller uprights. Of obscure origin, the steps are variously attributed to British, Roman and medieval builders.

2m. **Llanfair** was between 1853 and 1906 prosperous with deep slate quarries, recalled today by *Chwarel Hên* slate caverns (Easter–mid Oct: daily 10.00–17.00. Tel. 01766-780247) for guided tours through underground workings, as also café, picnic area and shop. Ahead now is a view of the Snowdon mountain group.

2m. ***Harlech Castle** (Cadw; see p. 11), backed by its small town, rises four-square on its rock platform some 200ft above the marshes of Morfa Harlech. The castle is a notably complete and well-preserved example of Edward I's system of concentric fortification. Access is from either above or below, the latter (summer only) being much easier for parking but involving a long steep climb up from the old watergate.

History. The name means Bold Rock, a name and a place known in legend which tells that Bendigeidfran, the King, sat with his siblings upon the rock of Harddlech and watched 13 ships coming from Ireland, 'beautiful, seemly and [with] brave ensigns of brocaded silk'. In those Dark Ages days the estuary waters, now some three miles to the north, would have lapped this towering rock, as indeed was still the case when this site was chosen by Edward I in 1283.

Edward's castle was started by James of St. George in 1283 and completed by 1289, its builder staying on as constable until 1293. The town received its charter as an English Borough in 1285. With a garrison of only 37 men the castle withstood a siege by Madog in 1294–95, but was not again besieged until 1404 when it was taken, but only after some treachery and bribery, by Owen Glendower. For four years, until retaken for the English in 1408, Harlech served as Glendower's capital. In 1460 Margaret of Anjou took refuge here after the battle of Northampton, and, although she soon moved on to Scotland, the castle remained in Lancastrian hands until taken by the Yorkists in 1468. It was the last stronghold in England and Wales to fall, and then only after enduring a siege of seven years. Among the survivors was a boy of 12, later to become Henry VII. The castle's stubborn resistance is said to have inspired the song 'The March of the Men of Harlech'. By the 16C Harlech had become a ruin, but during the Civil War, defended by Colonel William Owen, it held out for Charles I until, the last Welsh fortress to fall, it was taken by General Mytton in 1647. The castle was then allowed to lapse further into ruin.

The upper ENTRANCE is across the wide moat from the site of the barbican to a doorway flanked by two towers in the outer curtain. The outer defence here consists of a revetted terrace with a breastwork, rather that the full wall found at some other castles. Another surprising feature is that the gateways of the outer and inner defences are in line, there being no attempt, as for example at Denbigh and Beaumaris, to construct an oblique approach. The GATEHOUSE, three storeys high and housing an exhibition, is the principal feature of the castle. The residence of the constable, it had living rooms on the upper floors. It has two huge half-round towers facing outwards, and two large drum-towers, rising a further storey, at the inner corners. The rooms include an oratory, which was also a portcullis chamber, and a second oratory above that. This gatehouse, and the northeast tower, were the only parts of the castle still roofed in the later 16C, the former then being used as judges' lodging and the tower as a prison.

A central passage admits to the INNER WARD, which is roughly oblong, enclosed by walls 40ft high with a round tower at each corner. The rampart walk is corbelled across the flattened inner faces of these towers, the outer two of which carry circular watch-towers. The southeast and northeast towers are similar, each having a dungeon entered originally by trapdoor from the room above. The rooms, not uniform in shape, are approached by wall stairs, at the top being privies. The outer towers represent the last part of the castle to be built and contain pentagonal rooms of one size. Various rooms can be traced around the interior of the ward. On the west side are the Kitchen (S) and Great Hall (N). On the south side are the Granary (E) and, adjoining the kitchen, the site of a room known as the Ystumgwern Hall, so called because it was brought here complete from the residence of that name (four miles away) of Llewelyn the Last. Opposite, against the north wall, are the Chapel (W) and Bakehouse (E).

Between the chapel and bakehouse a passage with a postern leads to the OUTER WARD with, straight ahead, another postern, flanked by towers, that gave access to the precipitous CASTLE ROCK. On the north and west sides of the castle, following more or less the lower edge of the rock and connected by steep walls to the northeast and southwest corners of the outer ward, was a third line of defence, a wall added c 1295 after Madog's unsuccessful siege. The west part of the rock is now reached by a gate behind the northwest tower. Beyond can be seen the remains of a wall which ran from the tower to the precipice; also, to the south of this wall and a little below the castle, platforms on which stood defensive engines. A path descends to the Upper Gate, once with a drawbridge, and thence, with a protecting wall, down to the Watergate.

3m. **Llanfihangel-y-Traethau** is reached either by A496 across the flat Morfa Harlech, or, more pleasantly, by the higher B4573 which, just outside Harlech, skirts *Coed Llechwedd*, a woodland property given to the National Trust in 1937 in memory of the Irish writer A.P. Graves (1846–1931). At Llanfihangel-y-Traethau a narrow lane climbs to the small church above the village. When first built the church stood on a tidal island, and, although the sea receded in the later Middle Ages, there was still flooding until the building of a seawall in 1805. In the churchyard, close to the porch, stands a 12C stone, its Latin inscription recording that it marks the grave of the mother of the builder of the church during the time of King Owain Gwynedd (1137–70). Portmeirion can be seen across the water.

A496 crosses the railway, passes the hamlet of *Talsarnau*, and reaches the head of the Traeth Bach estuary, where a road branches north and west to cross the Dwyryd by tollbridge and in a mile reach *Penrhyndeudraeth. 5m.* (from Llanfihangel-y-Traethau) *Maentwrog Power Station* is a small power station in woods, linked by pipe with Llyn Trawsfynydd; it is open to visitors Mon–Fri 09.30–16.30.

A path here follows a glen for a mile and a half to *Rhaeadr Ddu*, the Black Cascade, a twisted water slide set among rocks and trees.

1m. **Maentwrog**, a pleasant village below wooded hills, gets its name from its ancient stone, the 'maen' of Twrog, which stands in the churchyard and traditionally commemorates (there is no inscription) a 7C holy man known to have been a companion of St. Beuno. The stone, though only 4ft high, may be a prehistoric standing stone. Also in the churchyard is the grave of Archdeacon Prys (died 1624), once minister here and author of the Welsh translation of the Psalter still in use.

For Maentwrog to (W) *Porthmadog* and (E) *Ffestiniog* and *Bala*, see Rte 15; to *Trawsfynydd* and *Dolgellau*, see Rte 16.

18

Shrewsbury to Machynlleth and Aberystwyth

This Route cuts across central Wales at the principality's narrowest part, within which, however, there are three roads. There is little to choose between the three, but Rte 18A is marginally shorter than the other two, while Rte 18C is the most scenic. A fourth route (but cutting out Machynlleth) would be the straight line provided by A470 and A44 from Llanidloes on Rte 18C. For this choice, see Rte 23A.

A. Via Welshpool and Mallwyd

A458 to Mallwyd. A470 to Cemmaes Road. A489 to Machynlleth. A487 to Aberyswyth. Total distance 70m.—*18m.* **Welshpool.**—*9m.* **Llanfair Caereinion.**—*16m.* **Mallwyd.**—*11m.* **Machynlleth.**—*6m.* *Furnace* (*Eglwysfach*).—*2m.* *Tre'r Ddol.*—*2m.* *Talybont.*—*6m.* **Aberystwyth**.

In large part agricultural scenery, but some moor between Llanfair Caereinion and Mallwyd. Green valley of the Dyfi to Machynlleth. After Machynlleth, wood and moor inland and estuary flats to seaward.

Shrewsbury, see 'Blue Guide England'. *12m. Middletown*, a village just in Wales, lies below the Breidden Hills (1234ft) which derive the second syllable of their name from the forts (duns) found on two of the hills, Middletown immediately north of the village, and Breidden beyond. The latter, thought to have been the site of a battle between the Welsh and the English in 1292, bears an obelisk commemorating Admiral Rodney's victory over the French off Domenica in 1782. At (*4m*), *Buttington*, traditionally the site of a battle in 894 between the Saxons and the Danes, the church has a font made from a capital from the abbey of Strata Marcella, now disappeared. The Severn is crossed just beyond the village.

2m. **Welshpool** (*Inf.* at Leisure Centre at east edge of town on A458), enjoys the Welsh name of Y Trallwng, as such being granted a charter by the Prince of Powys in 1263. This, however, was largely a confirmation of earlier privileges, notably the already long-established Monday market for which the town is still known today. The town is entered by Salop Road, just before St. Mary's Church being a cottage said to have been a gift to Grace Evans from a grateful Lord Nithsdale after she had helped her mistress Lady Nithsdale, daughter of the Marquess of Powis, in the romantic rescue of her husband from the Tower of London in 1716. *St. Mary's Church*, restored by Street in 1871, shows work dating from the 13–19C, the earliest parts being the west tower and the choir, the roof of which is decorated with armorial designs. Farther into the town, at Canal Wharf, the *Powysland Museum and Canal Centre* (Whitsun–Sept: daily except Wed. Oct–Whitsun: daily except Wed and Sun. Times are Mon–Fri 11.00–13.00, 14.00–17.00; Sat and Sun in summer 10.00–13.00, 14.00–17.00; Sat in winter 14.00–17.00. Tel. 01938-554656) was founded in 1874 and moved in 1990 into this former canal warehouse. The ground floor covers the story of Montgomeryshire from prehistoric to modern times and has agricultural, canal and railway exhibitions while the upper floor shows archaeological and social history galleries.

Welshpool is about half-way along the 35-mile-long *Montgomery Canal* which comes in from the northeast and continues southwest to end at Newtown. Dug in three stages—1796, 1797 and 1821 when the extension to Newtown was completed—the canal was intended to support agriculture as also to move limestone, coal and other goods. Abandoned by 1944, considerable lengths have now been restored by volunteers and the waterway now offers towpath walks and narrowboat cruises from Canal Wharf (April–Oct: daily. Tel. 01938-553271).

Also of interest in Welshpool are the Cockpit, the only one in Wales on its original site (behind the National Westminster Bank in Broad Street), and, just north of the station, traces of the early Norman motte-and-bailey castle, the bailey now being a bowling green.

For the *Welshpool and Llanfair Railway*, see below.

Guilsfield, three miles north, is worth a visit for its large 15C church, of particular interest here being the unusual upper chamber over the south porch; the clustered pier shafts; the carved heads on the beams in the south aisle, these coming from a predecessor church; the 19C vaulting, with each panel different; and a Jacobean or earlier churchwarden's chest.

Long Mountain stretches for some four miles along the Welsh side of the border to the east of Welshpool. It is crossed by Offa's Dyke, and the highest point, *Beacon Ring* (1338ft), on the east side and commanding a length of Roman road, is a hillfort.

*Powis Castle** (NT. April–June and Sept and Oct: daily except Mon and Tues, but open Bank Hol. Mon. July and Aug: daily except Mon but open Bank Hol. Mon. Hours for *Castle* 12.00–17.00. Hours for *Clive Museum* and *Garden* 11.00–18.00. Tel. 01938-554336), a mile southwest of Welshpool, has been inhabited for some 500 years, and, although in part rebuilt during the 16 and 17C, still keeps the general aspect of its 13–14C origin. Standing in fine grounds which include famous terraced gardens, Powis shows late 16C plasterwork and panelling, a 17C staircase, early Georgian furniture, tapestry, some notable portraits, and its important Clive (of India) Museum.

History. It seems probable that the remains of a Norman motte-and-bailey in the park are those of the original castle here (c 1100), destroyed by Llewelyn the Great in 1233 during his struggle with his rival, the local Gruffydd ap Gwenwynwyn, and again and finally in 1275. Under the Treaty of Conwy (1277), Edward I granted the Gwenwynwyn family the barony of De la Pole, but required that they renounce Welsh princely titles. Agreeing, the family then built the castle which is the nucleus of today's. The barony died out in 1551, and in 1586 the castle was bought by Sir Edward Herbert, a younger son of the Earl of Pembroke, and it was he who put in hand the conversion to Elizabethan taste and standards. Sir Edward's son, William, created Baron Powis in 1629, defended the castle for Charles I during the Civil War, but it fell to Parliament in 1644. The 3rd Baron (1667) undertook further rebuilding, but, as a supporter of James II, had to flee the country in 1688, and it was his wife who, as a Lady of the Bedchamber, attempted to smuggle out the future Old Pretender shortly before his father's hurried departure.

In 1784, through marriage, the estate passed to Edward Clive (later, in 1804, Earl of Powis), son of Lord Clive of India, and in 1807 the family took the name of Herbert. It was the 4th Earl who was responsible for much remodelling of the interior (by G.F. Bodley in 1891–1904), and it was in 1952 that Powis came to the National Trust.

The *Clive Museum* shows the complete collection of Indian and Far Eastern art and arms and armour assembled by Robert, 1st Lord Clive ('Clive of India', 1725–74), his son Edward (1754–1839), who was Governor of Madras, and his daughter-in-law Lady Henrietta Herbert.

In a tour around the castle—some 12 rooms including the museum and the 17C Great Staircase—visitors see numerous examples of the internal decorative work of such craftsmen as J-B Lanscroon (the walls of the Great Staircase and the ceilings of the Library and the Blue Drawing Room), William Winde (design of the Great Staircase), G.F. Bodley (plaster and panelling in the Oak Drawing Room), the cabinet maker Pierre Langlois and many others, while the tapestries include 16C Tournai, 16 and 17C Brussels and 17C Mortlake. Also of great interest, and bringing to life, if formally, the men and women who lived here, are the many family portraits by such artists as Batoni, Romney, Reynolds, Kneller and Nathaniel Dance.

The *Gardens*, of the later 17C and a mix of terraces, formal, informal and woodland (18C), and believed to have been designed by William Winde, are best known for their four terraces, nearly 200 yards long. The Orangery, at the centre of the terraces, carries a balustrade with urns and early 18C lead statues (? Van Nost, or Cheere) of shepherds and shepherdesses. Within the grounds, but outside the gardens, a Douglas fir (185ft) is the tallest tree recorded in Britain.

Welshpool is left by A458, descending into the valley of the Einion (also called the Banwy) and running close to the line and stations of the *Welshpool and Llanfair Railway* (tel. 01938-810441), the headquarters of which are at the station at *9m* **Llanfair Caereinion**. This railway (2ft 6in. gauge) linked Welshpool and Llanfair Caereinion from 1903 to 1931 (passengers) and 1956 (goods). Re-opened by enthusiasts in 1963 to Castell Caereinion, and in 1972 to Sylfaen, the extension to Welshpool was achieved in 1981. The *Church* of this small town was rebuilt in 1868 as successor to a derelict 13C predecessor, of which, however, the doorway survives. Other survivals include the font, the oak vaulting of the choir, and the recumbent effigy (?14C) of a knight, unusual for being hollow as also for having the inscription on the low-slung sword-belt rather than on the shield. Outside the porch, the sundial of 1765 is the work of Samuel Roberts, a local clockmaker, while below the church, on the river bank, *St. Mary's Well* was once known for its healing properties.

Meifod, four miles northeast of Llanfair Caereinion, a village in a tranquil pastoral and wooded valley, is celebrated in Welsh poetry, because here, or nearby, there was once a summer residence (maifod) of the princes of Powys. The *Church* here, consecrated in 1155, is of several periods ranging from the 11 to the 19C, the oldest part being the 11C piers ahead and left of the entrance. But older still (9–10C) is a graveslab in the south aisle, bearing the early Christian XP symbol and also some Norse features. The churchyard is exceptionally large and is thought once to have included at least one if not two other churches.

5m. Llanerfyl with, in the village churchyard beneath a yew, a 5C or 6C gravestone. From here the road ascends the north bank of the river, in *3m* crossing the tributary Twrch and in another *4m* the watershed (957ft) between the Severn and the Dyfi. From here the pleasant valley of the Dugoed is descended, the road soon making a sharp curve where it crosses a glen. The name *Llidiart-y-Barwn* (Baron's Gate) here recalls that it was in these woods that Baron Owen was murdered in 1555 (see Rte 20B, Mallwyd).

4m. **Mallwyd,** see Rte 20B, which describes the road north to *Bala* and also south (*11m*) to **Machynlleth,** for which town see Rte 20A.

Beyond Machynlleth this Route, now A487, drops gently with the wooded valley of the Dyfi to reach (*6m*) *Furnace* (*Eglwysfach*) where, beside the road, the Dyfi Furnace (Cadw; see p. 11) is now preserved as industrial archaeology. Using the power of the Einion cascade, this site was first used during the 17C for refining silver, this being followed in the mid 18C by the construction of the present building as an ironworks blast furnace, the water driving the bellows. From here a small road leads up through the pretty *Cwm Einion*, or Artists' Valley, with, in about a mile, a forest walk, while bird enthusiasts will make for the *RSPB Ynys Hir* reserve (daily 09.00–21.00 or sunset, whichever earlier. Tel. 01654-781265) with an information room, shop and a choice of often rewarding woodland and estuary walks and hides. *2m. Tre'r Ddol* where Hen Gapel, a Wesleyan chapel of 1845, was in 1961 bought by Mr R.J. Thomas to house his growing collection of folk objects. Left on his death in 1976 to the National Museum of Wales, the chapel and its collection are now administered by Aberystwyth's Ceredigion Museum. Hen Gapel is open Easter–mid Sept: Mon–Sat 10.00–17.00. Tel. 01970-634212.

From Tre'r Ddol there is a choice of roads to Aberystwyth; either direct along A487, or, using B4353, by a westward loop around Dyfi Nature Reserve.

To ABERYSTWYTH DIRECT (A487. 8m). *2m. Talybont*, at the foot of the scenic drive via Nant-y-Moch reservoir to Ponterwyd (see Rte 23A). Also from Talybont a lane climbs northeast on to moorland, in rather over a mile reaching, on the right, *Bedd Taliesin*, the stones seemingly of a burial chamber and traditionally the grave of Taliesin, a (possibly mythical) bard and seer of the 6C. *6m.* **Aberystwyth,** see Rte 22.

To ABERYSTWYTH BY WESTWARD LOOP (B4353 and A487. 11m). From Tre'r Ddol B4353 heads west across *Dyfi National Nature Reserve* (restricted access: dangerous tidal paths), established in 1969 and 1972 and comprising the Estuary, with wildfowl and migrant waders; Cors Fochno, or Borth Bog, either side of the road, an area of raised bog much used for botanical research; and, where the road curves at the northwest, Ynyslas Dunes, with parking, information and a nature trail.

Southward, beyond the straggling resort village of *Borth*, there is a road choice between B4572 or B4353. The former crosses hills above cliffs, below which, at Wallog, *Sarn Cynfelyn* is a rock causeway said to be the remains of a road leading to the drowned Lowland Hundred (see Rte 21). The latter runs through the village of *Llandre*, in the woods above which is Castell Gwallter, the motte of an early Norman castle (destroyed by the Welsh in 1137) the name of which recalls its builder, Walter de Bec. Beyond, B4353 joins A487 for the four mile run into **Aberystwyth**, see Rte 22.

B. Via Welshpool, Newtown and Cemmaes Road

A458 to Welshpool. A483 to Newtown. A489 to Caersws. A470 to Cemmaes Road. A489 to Machynlleth. A487 to Aberystwyth. Total distance 73m.—*18m*. **Welshpool**.—*13m*. **Newtown**.—*5m*. **Caersws**.—*16m*. **Cemmaes Road**.—*5m*. **Machynlleth**.—*16m*. **Aberystwyth**.

After Welshpool the general course of the valley of the Severn is followed as far as Caersws. Beyond, there is increasing moorland, this, beyond Machynlleth, giving way to mixed wood and moor inland with estuary flats to seaward.

For **Shrewsbury** to (*18m*) **Welshpool**, see Rte 19A. *5m*. *Berriew*, a pleasant half-timbered village on the Rhiew, is traditionally associated with St. Beuno after whom a large glacial boulder is named. It is said that, when communing by the Severn, he heard English voices across the water and successfully warned the villagers of this pagan threat. Near *Garthmyl*, *1m* farther, the Severn can be crossed; beyond the bridge, a road running north parallel to the railway in a mile reaches the remains of a small Roman fort, probably a stage between Viroconium and Caersws and apparently in use until the 4C.

Montgomery, in Welsh Trefaldwyn, two and a half miles southeast of Garthmyl, is a small town, attractively Georgian in character and straddling a hill below the ruins of its castle; this castle, a preserved length of Offa's Dyke, and the basically 13C church are the three sites of specific interest.

History. Offa's Dyke cut through here in about 784 (a section is preserved in Lymore Park, east of the town). Some 300 years later, in c 1072, another fortification was started, Roger de Montgomery's Norman castle, the site of which is almost certainly the motte-and-bailey a mile northwest and known as Hen Domen (see below). The present castle was built by Henry III in 1223 and the town received its charter four years later. Both town and castle are closely associated with the Herbert family. The 1st Lord Herbert of Cherbury (1583–1648), philosopher and diplomat, spent his youth here and .t was he who in 1644 surrendered the castle to Parliament. But it was demolished in 1649 because the 2nd Lord Herbert was a Royalist. Another Herbert, the 1st Lord's brother George Herbert (1593–1633), the poet, was born either in the castle or in the town. What was left of the castle pretty well collapsed during the 19C.

Of Henry III's *Castle* not much survives—something of a twin-towered gatehouse, the lower courses of wards, a ditch, a deep well—but the site is as it should be: a long, narrow and rocky ridge projecting boldly towards the north and, accessible virtually only from the south, of unusual strength. Inside the mainly 13C *Church* (tower rebuilt in 1816) the most noteworthy feature is a double *Screen and Loft, the original 15C part being the west side of panels with traceried tops, five each side of the door. The loft is thought to be made up of sections from the mother priory at Chirbury

(2½ miles northeast in England) where the church preserves the 13C nave arcades of a small priory of Austin Canons founded c 1180, probable provenance also of Montgomery's church's 15C stalls and misericords. Also in the church are the fine Renaissance tomb (1600) of Sir Richard Herbert and two recumbent effigies, the smaller figure probably being Sir Edmund Mortimer (died 1409), grandson of Owen Glendower, and the other Sir Richard Herbert (died 1534), grandfather of the occupant of the Renaissance tomb. Less distinguished, but of more interest perhaps, is the occupant of the Robber's Grave on the north side of the churchyard; for here the grass is said never to grow above the grave of John Newton Davies, an innocent man hanged in 1921.

On the adjacent hill to the west is the hillfort of *Fridd Faldwyn* (750ft), while *Town Hill* (1050ft), a short mile southwest of Fridd Faldwyn and crowned by the county war memorial, commands a view which includes Cader Idris.

A483 may be regained by B4385 and B4386. Just north of the former (a mile from Montgomery, in trees on the left side of a road leading north from a small crossroads) the motte of *Hen Domen* probably represents Roger de Montgomery's castle of 1072.

B4386 meets A483 near where the latter crosses the Severn (*4m* from Garthmyl), near here, on the steep narrow ridge to the northwest, being the slight remains of *Dolforwyn Castle*, started by Llewelyn the Last in 1273. **Kerry**, two and a half miles south and reached by B4368, is a small place in the heart of a sheep-rearing countryside and the origin of the name of a well-known breed distinctive for the black spots on their faces and legs. The *Church* here was dedicated in 1176 amid, it is said, disorderly scenes as the retainers of Giraldus and those of the Bishop of St. Asaph disputed over local episcopal jurisdiction. Of this early Norman church, however, there survive only the north arcade and, possibly, part of the tower (most of which was rebuilt in the 14C), with its buttresses of varying pattern and picturesque boarded top. Inside are a chained Welsh Bible (1690); a 15C font, with the Instruments of the Passion; a 14C piscina (south choir); and a pulpit which, though modern, bears some 15C tracery.

3m (from A483 Severn bridge), **Newtown** (Drenewydd. *Inf.*) is a busy but pleasant enough market town on the Severn and with several places of varied interest to visitors. Because of one-way streets, visitors are advised to walk the tour described below, the total distance being under a mile.

History. Despite its name, Newtown traces its origins to about 973 and to a motte-and-bailey castle. Edward I granted the associated borough a charter in 1280, this marking the start of a commercial progress which peaked in the 19C by which time the town was a weaving and textiles centre and the home of the Welsh flannel industry. Notable dates include 1648 when Charles I sheltered here after defeat at Naseby; 1771, birth of Robert Owen (see below); 1821 when the Montgomery Canal reached Newtown; and 1859–63 which saw Newtown served by railways to Llanidloes, Oswestry and Aberystwyth.

Just beside Tourist Information (Central Car Park) stands the 1960s *Davies Memorial Gallery*, commemorating the art collecting sisters of nearby Gregynog Hall and used for a variety of touring and temporary exhibitions, to the south of this, and near the Council Offices, being the motte of the motte-and-bailey to which Newtown traces its origins.

From the Central Car Park, Wesley Place leads northeast into Broad Street, about 150 yards northwest up which Long Bridge crosses the Severn. Just across the bridge, at 5–7 Commercial Street, in a building which in the days of handloom weavers served as both dwelling and workshop, is the *Textile Museum* (May–Oct: Tues–Sat 14.00–17.00. Tel. 01686-554656), telling the story of Newtown's one-time key industry.

From opposite where Wesley Place meets Broad Street, Old Church Street leads to ruined *St. Mary's Church*, built in the 13C but abandoned in 1856 because it was too small and also liable to flooding. The tower and other remnants were restored in 1939, and in the yard, beside the church wall, is the tomb of Robert Owen (1771–1858), factory reformer, founder of the cooperative movement, and Newtown's most cherished native. Owen was born at what is now the *Robert Owen Memorial Museum* (Mon–Fri 09.45–11.45, 14.00–15.30; Sat 10.00–11.30. Hours may be extended in summer. Tel. 01686-626345), farther southeast along Broad Street on the corner with Severn Street. Here there is a reconstruction of the room in which Owen was born, while displays record his life, starting with his birth here, tracing his many wanderings and experiments (notably in Scotland at New Lanark), and concluding with his return to and death in Newtown in 1858. Just round the corner in High Street there is a museum of a very different kind, namely the *W.H. Smith Shop and Museum* (Mon–Sat 09.00–17.30. Tel. 01686-626280), the former in part restored, as a contribution to European Architectural Heritage Year (1975), to its elegant style of 1927, while the museum tells the story of the firm from its beginnings in 1792 in London's Little Grosvenor Street.

Broad Street, continuing southeast, becomes Short Bridge Street. Here, on the left, is a small triangular *Robert Owen Memorial Park* with a charming figure of the reformer.

This Route leaves Newtown by A489, in *5m* reaching **Caersws**, on the site of a 1C Roman station, well defended by the Severn and the Carno and at the hub of road links with Castell Collen, Y Gaer, Pennal and, away to the north, Deva (Chester). The fort, the earthworks of which survive on the northwest side of the town, is known to have been garrisoned by troops from Spain. A more modern claim to interest is that Caersws was for 20 years the home of the poet John Ceiriog Hughes, then manager of the local Van Railway (plaque on house just south of the station).

For the more scenic 'Mountain Road' to Machynlleth via Llyn Clywedog, see Rte 18C.

Caersws is left by A470, this soon passing just west of the village of *Llanwnog*, with, in the churchyard, the grave of John Ceiriog Hughes. The church itself has a 15C rood loft, still with its stairs, and also some fragments of 15C glass in a window on the north side. The scenery now starts to become moorland in character as the road follows the glen of the Carno to (*5m*) *Carno*, which has its place in history, for it was here in 1081 that Gruffydd ap Cynan and Rhys ap Tewdwr, both returning from exile, joined forces, defeating their rivals and winning respectively the crowns of northern and southern Wales. *3m. Talerddig*, just before which the watershed (731ft) between the Severn and the Dyfi is crossed. *3m Llanbrynmair*, a mile south of which is *Llan*, birthplace of Abraham Rees (1743–1825), the encyclopaedist, and long the home (1806–57) of the Rev. Samuel Roberts, social reformer and tireless advocate of postal innovations. The early 15C church here is a curiosity, with its wooden tower enclosed inside the nave. *5m* **Cemmaes Road**, from where to (*5m*) **Machynlleth** see Rtes 20B and 20A. For Machynlleth to (*16m*) **Aberystwyth**, see Rte 18A.

C. Via Welshpool, Llanidloes and Llyn Clywedog

A458 to Welshpool. A483 to Newtown. A489 to Caersws. A470 or B4569 to Llanidloes. B4518 and unclassified to Machynlleth. A487 to Aberystwyth. Total distance 76m.—*18m*. **Welshpool**.—*13m*. **Newtown**.—*5m*. **Caersws**.— *7m*. **Llanidloes**.—*17m*. **Machynlleth**.—*16m*. **Aberystwyth**.

After Welshpool the general course of the valley of the Severn is followed as far as Caersws. The 'Mountain Road' between Llanidloes and Machynlleth, across high, remote moorland. After Machynlleth wood and moor inland, estuary flats to seaward.

For **Shrewsbury** to (*18m*.) **Welshpool**, see Rte 18A. Beyond, to (*18m*.) **Caersws**, see Rte 18B.

There is a choice of roads between Caersws and Llanidloes. Along A470, the more southerly choice, *Llandinam*, was the home of David Davies (1818–90), a local lad who became a leading industrialist, developing the coal industry and founding the docks at Barry; he is remembered by a bronze statue (by Sir Alfred Gilbert, best known for London's Piccadilly Eros) at the east end of the bridge over the Severn, now little more than a stream and here usually given its Welsh name Hafren. Along B4569, the northerly choice, *Trefeglwys* was the birthplace of Benjamin Piercy (1827– 88), an engineer who built many of the railways in Wales and also those in Sardinia.

7m. **Llanidloes** (*Inf*.), at the confluence of the Severn (or Hafren) and its larger tributary the Clywedog, has roots deep in the religious and social upheavals of the 18 and 19C. John Wesley preached here in 1748, 1749 and 1764, and in the following century, in 1839, the town was a centre of the Chartist riots, a time recalled by a plaque on the wall of the Trewythen Arms Hotel. The main feature of Llanidloes, however, is the half-timbered free-standing *Old Market Hall* of c 1600. The upper floor, originally used as a court house, became in the 18 and 19C the meeting place for Quakers, Methodists and Baptists before they built their own chapels (a local museum, formerly here, may be reopened), while against the building's exterior stands a stone from which John Wesley preached during his three visits. The *Church*, dedicated to the 7C St. Idloes, was restored and enlarged in 1881 but nevertheless retains much of its early structure, though the early 13C north arcade, with heavily moulded arches and clustered piers, and the 15C hammer-beam roof may both have been brought here from Cwmhir Abbey. The 14C tower also merits attention, for its pronounced external batter and, inside, the vaulted base with curious slate masonry.

From Llanidloes A470 and A44 lead direct to Aberystwyth (see Rte 23A).

Hafren Forest, on the east slopes of the massif of Plynlimon and covering over 17 square miles, is some six miles west of Llanidloes and offers several waymarked walks ranging from one to eight miles through the forest, along the upper Severn and up on to Plynlimon.

B4518, the start of what is sometimes called the 'Mountain Road', heads northwest out of Llanidloes, in two miles reaching a fork offering a choice between skirting the east or west shore of **Llyn Clywedog**, a beautiful reservoir created between 1964–68 to regulate the flow of the Clywedog and Severn, thus both meeting water demand and, by catching and storing winter rain, preventing flooding along the Severn's lower reaches. For the west bank road, see below. On the east side, B4518 runs some distance from the reservoir's shore, on the road's right rising *Fan Hill* (1580ft) on the slopes of which can be seen (a road rounds the hill) the chimneys of the now disused Van Lead Mine, once one of the most prosperous in this part of Wales and still with the forlorn remnants of terraced houses and even chapels. To the road's left, crowning a promontory which now juts into the reservoir, is the hillfort of Dinas (1461ft), and some two miles beyond this, at the north end of the narrowing finger where the river Clywedog becomes a reservoir, the hamlet of *Staylittle* (*7m* from Llanidloes) owes its odd name to three blacksmiths who shod horses so quickly that their smithy came to be called Stay-a-Little.

The road along the west shore of Llyn Clywedog, only some two miles longer, is scenically rather more rewarding and also offers picnic sites, view points, the dam (237ft high), and walks, one of these, just below the dam, being the Clywedog Gorge Trail which includes the remains of Bryntail lead mine, an early mine, which was reopened in the mid 19C (the period of today's remains) but finally closed in 1884. Immediately beyond the dam the road rounds the hillfort of *Pen-y-Gair* (1250ft), then, continuing round the lake, enters *Hafren Forest* (see above), at a T-junction here bearing right and in another two miles rejoining B4518 just north of Staylittle.

A little farther north of Staylittle a road junction is reached from which B4518 continues due north to meet Rte 18B in seven miles at Llanbrynmair. This Route, though, bears west along an unclassified road to reach in half a mile a view point above *Ffrwd Fawr*, with an awesome barren abyss. Beyond, the road makes its lonely way across high open moor, in two and a half miles, on the left, reaching a track down to *Glaslyn* (parking and information board) at the heart of Glaslyn Reserve (Montgomeryshire Wildlife Trust. Tel. 01938-555654). In fine scenery, the reserve comprises some of the best heather moorland in Wales, as also the lake, bog, rough grassland and a ravine (dangerous; do not enter), and a walk which makes the circuit of the lake. Beyond, the unclassified road descends along the north flank of the Plynlimon plateau to reach (*10m.* from Staylittle) **Machynlleth**, for which see Rte 20A. For A487 to (*16m.*) **Aberystwyth**, see Rte 18A.

19

Lake Vyrnwy and its Approaches

A. Lake Vyrnwy

Lake Vyrnwy (pronounced Verny), or Llyn Efyrnwy, at a height of 825ft and scenically situated below wooded hills, is a narrow strip nearly five miles in length and less than half a mile wide. The lake (dam at south end), a reservoir for the water needs of Liverpool, was formed in 1886–90; tablets in the roadside rock-face at the north end of the dam record the various stages of the work and of the associated pipeline projects. Prior to the construction of the reservoir, the river Vyrnwy, a chief Welsh tributary of the Severn, was here a small stream meandering across a marshy flat formed by the sands and gravels which had silted a lake basin scooped out in glacial times. The present dam, 390 yards long and 144 feet high, rests on the bar of glaciated rock that retained the early lake, and the reservoir can thus be regarded as the restoration of an ancient natural feature. The lake's surface area is 1121 acres, its storage capacity is 12,131 million gallons, and the catchment area covers some 36 square miles. A short way north of the dam, a picturesque tower marks the entrance to the Hirnant Tunnel, over two miles long and representing the first section of the 75-mile-long aqueduct that carries the water to Liverpool.

Around the lake the RSPB manages some 16,000 acres of moor and woodland, by the western end of the dam (Llanwddyn) being a joint *Severn Trent Water and RSPB Visitor Centre* (April–Christmas: daily. Christmas–March: weekends 10.30–17.30. Tel. 01691-73278). Here there is RSPB information and a shop while, alongside, modern techniques present the history and legends of this district. The nearest RSPB trail will be found farther down the road.

A small wooded road makes the circuit of the lake, passing several parking places close to walks, and there is another RSPB trail at the north tip of Vyrnwy, near where the road comes in from Bala via Cwm Hirnant.

Approaches to Vyrnwy from Bala and Oswestry (see 'Blue Guide England') are described below, those from Bala being very scenic.

B. Approaches from Bala

VIA LLANGYNOG. B4391 and B4396. 19 miles. The road skirts the north tip of Bala Lake, almost immediately afterwards passing the road to Cwm Hirnant (see below). Beyond, in another three miles at the junction with B4402, it climbs through woods, reaching open moor and (*8m* from Bala) *Milltir Gerig Pass* (1595ft), a saddle in the long Berwyn range. The descent is above the precipitous valley of the Eirth. *3m* **Llangynog**, a name recalling Cynog, son of the 5C prince, Brychan, is a long village beautifully set below mountains at the meeting of the Eirth and Tanat glens. The lead mines and slate quarries are now closed, the former due to flooding.

The valley of the upper Tanat, cutting northwest as a wooded and pastoral finger into the mountains, in two miles reaches the little Norman church of *Pennant Melangell*. Inside are two 14C recumbent effigies, one said to be of a Welsh prince and the other of St. Melangell; an 18C wooden candelabrum; and a rood screen of c 1500. The loft of the screen has on its bottom beam mutilated carvings illustrating the 7C legend of St. Melangell (or Monacella), according to which a hare, hunted by Brochwel Ysgythrog, Prince of Powys, took refuge under her robe. As a result Melangell became the patron saint of hares, thenceforward known as 'St. Monacella's lambs' and treated as sacred in the district. Recent excavations have revealed, below the rebuilt apse and in line with the original, a grave which may well be that of the saint, while fragments identified as parts of her shrine are incorporated in a reconstruction. The valley ends in a rounded cwm, with the white thread of *Blaen-y-Cwm* waterfall.

The valley below Llangynog is that of the middle Tanat. *2m*. **Penybontfawr**, where the Tanat Valley and Llansilin approaches from Oswestry are met. For *Llanrhaeadr-ym-Mochnant* and *Pistyll Rhaeadr*, see Rte 19C. From

Penybontfawr B4396 ascends Cwm Hirnant (not to be confused with the other Cwm Hirnant described immediately below), in 6m reaching **Lake Vyrnwy**.

VIA CWM HIRNANT, unclassified road. 9 miles. A beautiful drive through remote wood and moorland scenery. B4391 is taken east out of Bala, then, soon after leaving the lake, an unclassified road which climbs south up the thickly wooded *Cwm Hirnant* (FE picnic site). Emerging from the woods, the road continues to climb across high moor (1641ft) before, again in woods, descending beside the tumbling Nadroedd stream to reach the north extremity of **Lake Vyrnwy**.

VIA BWLCH-Y-GROES. A494 or B4403 to Llanuwchllyn, then unclassified roads. 14 miles. *5m.* **Llanuwchllyn** may be reached either by A494 along the west shore of Bala Lake (see Rte 14 for this road as also for the village) or by B4403 along the east shore. From Llanuwchllyn an unclassified road ascends high up on the side of Cwm Cynllwyd for (*5m.*) *Bwlch-y-Groes* (1790ft. Rte 20B), the highest road pass in Wales. Just beyond the summit a road branches east away from the Dinas Mawddwy road to descend beside the Eunant stream, first across moor and then through woods, to (*4m.*) **Lake Vyrnwy**.

C. Approaches from Oswestry

VIA LLANSILIN. B4580 and B4396. 18 miles. *3m.* *Rhyd-y-Croesau*, where the Welsh border is crossed. *2m.* *Llansilin*, where Hugh Morris (1622–1709), the Royalist satirical poet, is buried. *5m.* **Llanrhaeadr-ym-Mochnant**, of which Bishop Morgan (1545–1604), who in 1588 here made his translation of the Bible into Welsh, was vicar. In the church there is a Celtic cross-slab (9–10C).

From the village a narrow, and in summer crowded, road leads in under four miles northwest to **Pistyll Rhaeadr** (parking), said to be the highest falls in Wales and of which Borrow wrote 'I never saw water falling so gracefully, so much like thin beautiful threads as here'. The falls descend some 240ft by a series of leaps, of which the first is an unbroken drop of more than 100ft, falling into a cauldron from which the second cascade issues through a gap in the rock.

2m. Penybontfawr to (*6m.*) **Lake Vyrnwy**, see Rte 19B.

VIA TANAT VALLEY. A483, A495, and B4396. 22 miles. A483, south out of Oswestry, in *4m* reaches *Llynclys*, from where A495 and B4396 are followed to (*2m*) *Llanyblodwel*. Soon the road reaches the north side of the Tanat and crosses into Wales. At *Sycharth*, a mile north and reached by the first road beyond the border, a motte is all that marks the site of a principal residence of Owen Glendower, described in a poem by the bard Iolo Goch as having nine halls, many guest rooms, and a church. It was destroyed in 1403 by the future Henry V. *7m.* Junction with B4580, up which (1m) is *Llanrhaeadr-ym-Mochnant* (see above). *3m. Penybontfawr* to (*6m.*) **Lake Vyrnwy**, see Rte 19B.

VIA LLANFYLLIN. A483, A495, A490 to Llanfyllin: B4393 to Lake Vyrnwy. 23 miles. *14m.* **Llanfyllin**, a town which received its first charter in 1293, straggles along the upper Cain valley below wooded hills. At *Llanfyllin Bird and Butterfly World* (Easter–Sept: 10.00–18.00. Tel. 01691-84751) there are 50 aviaries with birds from most parts of the world, a large tropical house for butterflies and also practical facilities such as cafeteria, shop and play area.

The road to Lake Vrynwy is through country well known to Ann Griffiths (1776–1805) a name probably unknown to the majority who visit here but deeply respected by many Welsh. Although she died at the age of 29 and probably never travelled farther than Bala (to listen to Thomas Charles preach), this simple Calvinist Methodist countrywoman wrote no fewer than 70 highly sensitive Welsh hymns. She is buried at Llanfihangel-yng-Ngwynfa, on B4393 *5m.* from Llanfyllin, and was born and lived at Dolwar Fach, a farm near Dolanog (just south of Llanfihangel by B4382) where there is a memorial chapel. After an ascent, B4393 drops to (*4m.*) **Lake Vyrnwy**.

20

Machynlleth to Bala

A. Via Dolgellau

A487 and A470 to Dolgellau. A494 to Bala. Total distance 32m—*5m.* **Corris**.—*3m. Minffordd*—*4m. Cross Foxes.*—*3m.* **Dolgellau**.—*17m.* **Bala**.

The narrow wooded valley of the Dulas is followed by moor, a fine view of Cader Idris, and a craggy stretch along the mountain's east foot.

Machynlleth (*Inf.*), pronounced Mahun'hleth, in the green valley of the Dyfi, is a centre serving a wide district, and also, being at the heart of much lovely scenery, a popular but generally not overcrowded holiday base. The town centre is the *Clock Tower* of 1872, from which Maengwyn Street, the broad main street, runs east to reach on the left side the *Owen Glendower Centre* (Easter–Sept: daily 10.00–17.00. Tel. 01654-702401), a 16C building said to be on the site of a predecessor in which Glendower held his first parliament in 1404. Today the building houses Tourist Information and exhibitions. Opposite is the entrance to *Plas Machynlleth* (1653), which, with its fine grounds, was presented to the town by Lord Londonderry. The hall now houses local government offices while the grounds are a public park and recreation area. Farther east, on the south side of Maengwyn Street, the so-called *Mayor's House* is a half-timbered building of 1628. The *Tabernacle*, a redundant 19C chapel, now serves as a cultural centre (performing arts), adjacent being the *Museum of Modern Art, Wales*, offering both a permanent collection and also touring exhibitions (Mon–Sat 10.00–16.00. Tel. 01473-737-468).

For Machynlleth to (S) *Aberystwyth* and (E) *Llanidloes, Newtown, Welshpool* and *Shrewsbury*, see Rte 18; to *Dinas Mawddwy* and *Bala*, see Rte 20B below; to *Tywyn* and *Dolgellau*, see Rte 21.

A487 (Doll Street) passes the station and crosses the Dyfi by a bridge first built in 1533 but rebuilt c 1800. Beyond, A493 bears west as Rte 21, while this Route heads north, climbing the wooded, narrow and winding valley of the river Dulas to reach in *3m* the •**Centre for Alternative Technology** (daily 10.00–17.00 or 16.00 in winter. Tel. 01654-702400). Of particular interest in a world increasingly concerned with its environment, this Centre is an independent educational charity; not a museum, but a community actually living and working with alternative technology. Among the functioning themes are solar power; windmills and water-wheels; a water-powered cliff railway; a conservation house, with super-insulation, heat pumps and quadruple glazing; organic horticulture; fish culture and bee keeping. A short way farther up the road, *Tan-y-Coed*, a Forest Enterprise picnic site, is the starting place for forest walks (Cwm Cadian) which may be extended to the moorland ridge (2187ft) beyond and thence down to the valley of the Dysynni.

The 'Windpower Pavilion' at the Centre for Alternative Technology, Machynlleth. This is one of many displays about renewable energy, building and organic gardening techniques at this internationally renowned demonstration site

2m. **Corris**, a village sharply below the road at the junction of the Dulas and a small tributary, was in the 19C a part of a district busy with slate quarrying, associated with this being a rail line between Aberllefenni and Machynlleth. Now long disused, the line is recalled by a small museum in Corris, while some of the quarry buildings can be seen along a trail which starts from a Forest Enterprise picnic site between Corris and Aberllefenni. After Corris, A487 turns away from the Dulas, soon passing the *Corris Craft Centre* (daily, but some units may close Sun especially in winter. 10.00–18.00 in summer or 16.00 in winter. Tel. 01654-761249) with a variety of craft units and most facilities, including Tourist Information (April–Oct: daily 10.00–17.30). Climbing past slate workings the road reaches 666ft with a splendid view of Cader Idris.

3m, *Minffordd*, at the junction with B4405 which has ascended the Dysynni from near Tywyn. For this beautiful road (with the Talyllyn Railway, Castell-y-Bere, Llanfihangel-y-Pennant and Tal-y-Llyn lake) see Rte 21. Minffordd is immediately below Cader Idris, the road now climbing northeast, with craggy heights on either side, to reach a pass at 938ft. *4m*.

Cross Foxes, where A470 comes in from the east from Dinas Mawddwy. In another mile and a half, at the head of Torrent Walk (see Rte 16), B4416, diverging northward through Brithdir, offers a shortcut avoiding Dolgellau, which can be a bottleneck in summer. *3m.* **Dolgellau**, for which, with Cader Idris, see Rte 16. For Dolgellau to *(17m)* **Bala**, see Rte 14.

B. Via Dinas Mawddwy and Bwlch-y-Groes

A489 to Cemmaes Road. A470 to Dinas Mawddwy. Unclassified over Bwlch-y-Groes to Llanuwchllyn. A494 or B4403 to Bala. Total distance 30m.—*5m.* **Cemmaes Road.**—*8m.* **Dinas Mawddwy.**—*7m.* **Bwlch-y-Groes.**—*5m.* **Llanuwchllym.**—*5m.* **Bala**.

As far as Dinas Mawddwy the road follows the pastoral valley of the Dyfi, with high ground on either side. Beyond Dinas Mawddwy the narrow and steep unclassified road climbs through wild scenery across Bwlch-y-Groes (1790ft), the highest road pass in Wales. Motorists preferring the main road can continue on A470 to Dolgellau, and thence to Bala.

Machynlleth, see Rte 20A above. *2m.* **Penegoes** was the birthplace of the painter Richard Wilson (1714–82), and is today the home of Felin Crewi (Easter–Oct: daily 10.30–17.30. Tel. 01654-703113), a restored and working 17C water-mill at which stoneground flour, local muesli and other products can be bought, or a walk enjoyed along the river. *3m.* **Cemmaes Road**, where A470 (Rte 18B) comes in from the east. *6m*, **Mallwyd**, where A458 (Rte 18A) joins from the east and where the name of a hotel, the 'Brigands Inn', recalls that in the middle of the 16C this neighbourhood was terrorised by a large gang, known from the colour of their hair as the 'Red Robbers of Mawddwy'. Eighty of these brigands were seized and executed in 1554, mainly through the efforts of Baron Lewis Owen, who, the following year, was murdered by the gang's survivors at Llidiart-y-Barwn (the Baron's Gate), about two miles up A458. After this, the gang was exterminated. The church here, dating from 1641, but certainly on much older foundations, is also of modest interest. The rib of some unidentified prehistoric beast, dug up locally during the 19C, hangs over the wooden east porch, while John Davies (1570–1644), the lexicographer and assistant to Bishop Parry in producing the Welsh Authorised Version of the Bible, is buried in the churchyard. Minister here from 1604–44, John Davies was also something of a practical engineer, building Pont Minllyn, a picturesque twin-arched foot and packhorse bridge about half-way between Mallwyd and Dinas Mawddwy close to *Meirion Mill* (March–Oct: daily 10.00–17.00. Tel. 01650-531311), a working wool mill which, in part occupying the buildings of what was once Dinas Mawddwy station, is just the other side of the main road river bridge. The mill includes a shop, while the railway (the Cemmaes-Mawddwy Line, opened in 1868) is recalled by the station buildings, the reconstructed fine wrought-iron gates and a section of track maintained as a walk.

Dinas Mawddwy village, rather under *2m* from Mallwyd, was long ago the centre of one of two more or less independent districts within the princedom of Powys, the other being Penllyn to the north (see Rte 14, Bala Lake). Mawddwy remained with Powys until the Edwardian conquest, when it became a part of the shire of Merioneth, although retaining the dignity of its own mayor and council until 1668. Today a walking and fishing centre, the village nestles in a lovely amphitheatre below wooded hills and mountains at the junction of the Dyfi and the Cerist. Much of the hillsides is covered by rhododendrons, and in season the colour across the valley to the east can be breathtaking.

Motorists not wishing to take the direct Bala road across Bwlch-y-Groes can use the longer main road route via Dolgellau (10m). This road, for its first part very scenic, with steep cwms and waterfalls, ascends the valley of the Cerist, above the north bank in a mile being National Trust property, given in 1947 by Squadron Leader J.D.K. Lloyd and his brother Dr W.E.B. Lloyd as a memorial to the men of Bomber Command who lost their lives during the war. Beyond, the road climbs steeply to the top of *Bwlch Oerddrws* (Cold Door Pass; 1178ft), beyond which the country, though becoming open and bleak, is backed by a magnificent view of Cader Idris. At *Cross Foxes Hotel*, Rte 20A is joined.

1m. **Aber-Cywarch**, from where a small road ascends the narrow valley of the Cywarch for two miles. From the end of this road a path climbs northeast up the steep slope of Hengwm valley for Dyrysgol and the range of the Arans. Near (*3m.*) *Llanymawddw*y there are some fine waterfalls, notably Pistyll Gwyn, rather over a mile west (path) on the Pumryd. The scenery grows wilder, the Dyfi is crossed, and the valley ends in a cwm of precipitous mountain slopes, 800–1000ft high, deeply scarred by watercourses. The Dyfi, from its source in the tarn of Craiglyn Dyfi (2½ miles northwest), comes in through *Llaethnant* (Milk Valley) in a succession of cataracts, and the black, rocky peak of Aran Mawddwy stands out beyond the head of the glen. The road now climbs the steep side of the deep *Glen of the Rhiwlech* (over 1000ft in under two miles), passing the eastward road to Lake Vyrnwy and reaching the summit of (*3m*) **Bwlch-y-Groes** (1790ft; parking), the highest point on any road in Wales. To the west the dominant feature is the range of the Arans, a volcanic ridge running between Bala Lake and Dinas Mawddwy, the names of the peaks of which—Aran Benllyn (2901ft) and Aran Mawddwy (2970ft)—recall the two semi-independent districts referred to under Dinas Mawddwy above.

The descent is down the precipitous wall of Cwm Cynllwyd to (*5m*) the lake level at **Llanuwchllyn**, from where **Bala** can be reached in *5m* either by A494 along the north shore of Bala Lake, or by B4403 skirting the south shore and accompanied by the little Bala Lake Railway (for Llanuwchllyn, the above roads, and Bala, See Rte 14).

21

Machynlleth to Tywyn and Dolgellau

A493. Total distance 34m.—*11m.* **Aberdyfi**.—*4m.* **Tywyn**.—*2m.* *Bryncrug* (for the Fathew and Dysynni valleys).—*9m.* **Fairbourne**.—*8m.* **Dolgellau**.

A pleasant coastal road with some good views. Interesting and scenic diversions from Bryncrug up the valleys of the Fathew and Dysynni rivers towards the south foot of Cader Idris. Beyond Fairbourne the main road runs between the Mawddach Estuary and the northwest side of Cader Idris.

Machynlleth (see Rte 20A) is left by the bridge across the Dyfi (first built 1533, rebuilt c 1800), on the far side of which A487 (Rte 20A) continues north, while this Route bears west along A493 to (*4m.*) *Pennal*, a village near the site of a Roman fort, traces of which, with a later motte, can be seen south of the road. *3m.* *Gogarth*, where the estuary of the Dyfi is reached. For the Dyfi National Nature Reserve, see Rte 18A. *4m.* **Aberdyfi** (*Inf.*), the name frequently anglicised to Aberdovey, is a modest small resort with good sands and well known for golf and, more particularly, sailing, the latter the theme of the *Outward Bound Sailing Museum* (Tel. 01654-767464) on the waterfront.

The song, 'The Bells of Aberdovey', became popular through Charles Dibdin's opera 'Liberty Hall' (1785). The legend is that of the Lowland Hundred, or Cantref-y-Gwaelod, a low-lying land protected by dykes. On one stormy night its prince, Seithenyn, was so drunk that he forgot to close the sluices, and the cantref, or hundred, was drowned. But its bells still peal below the water, and Sarn Badrig (Rte 17) and Sarn Cynfelin (Rte 18A), geologically glacial deposits, are said to be ancient roads which once led to this lost land. The earliest mention of this catastrophe is in a 13C manuscript, but the story held a strong attraction for writers of the 17–19C who added their own romantic embellishments. See also James Elroy Flecker's poem 'The Welsh Sea'.

4m. **Tywyn** (*Inf.*), or Towyn (the yw or ow pronounced as in 'now' and the name meaning Sand Dune), is essentially an inland small town which has grown into a seaside resort, with a sand and shingle beach reaching south as far as Aberdyfi's golf links, and caravan parks and holiday camps to both the north and the south. Tywyn's ancient roots live on in the *Church of St. Cadfan* at the north end of the town. Named after the founder (in 429) of the monastery on the island of Bardsey off the tip of the Lleyn, the church has an early Norman nave (probably 11C), with massive short piers, curiously primitive whitewashed arcades, and tiny splayed windows in the clerestory. There is also some early work in the north aisle, though the rest of the church is rebuilding of 1844. But the church's most interesting feature is the so-called St. Cadfan Stone, probably of the 7C and bearing an inscription thought to be the oldest example of written Welsh and certainly older than any extant manuscript. Also interesting, inside the church, are, north of the choir, two recumbent effigies of the 14C, one of a knight seemingly in the act of drawing his sword, the other of a vested and hooded priest, while on the church's exterior there are two old horizontal slabs curiously incorporated into the 19C tower, the one on the south side showing a cross.

Tywyn is probably best known for the *Talyllyn Railway* (generally, late March–Oct: daily. Tel. 01654-710472), the principal station of which, Tywyn Wharf, is at the southwest end of the town on the Aberdyfi road. The line, opened for freight in 1866 and for passengers the following year (over 23,000 were carried in 1877), was built to carry slate from the quarry above Abergynolwyn (7m NE) down to Tywyn, where it was transferred to main line trains. The quarry closed in 1947, after which (in 1950) the Talyllyn Railway Preservation Society was formed, the result being a railway service which was the first in the world to be operated by volunteers. With a gauge of 2ft 3ins, with venerable and historic steam engines (1865 and later), and with carriages of many shapes, sizes and origins, the track ascends the pleasant valley of the Fathew (for the road, see below) as far as Nant Gwernol (no road access; forest walks), the full return journey requiring some two hours. With several stations and halts (parking and other facilities at Abergynolwyn and Dolgoch), however, the timetables permit a good deal of individual choice and flexibility. Other attractions of the railway include a letter service with special stamps and postmarks; and, at Tywyn, a shop and the Narrow Gauge Railway Museum with a notable collection of material, including engines and rolling stock, relating to narrow gauge railways generally.

Beyond Tywyn, while the main line railway and a minor road skirt the shore crossing the mouth of *Broad Water*, a lagoon into which the Dysynni flows, the main road runs inland to (*2m.*) *Bryncrug*, burial place of Mary Jones (see Dysynni Valley just below) and starting point for diversions up the interesting and scenically pleasant Fathew and Dysynni valleys. A circuit may be made.

FATHEW VALLEY. The road is B4405 which in three miles at *Dolgoch*, with a waterfall, meets the Talyllyn Railway which it accompanies to *Abergynolwyn*, reached in another two miles. Above was the Bryneglwys Slate Quarry (closed 1947), for which the line was built. Here the upper course of the Dysynni is met and a road follows the river northwest through a cut in the hills to its main valley just south of Castell-y-Bere (see below). B4405 continues northeast, ascending the upper Dysynni for two and a half miles to the river's source in *Tal-y-Llyn Lake*, below the southern slopes of Cader Idris. The village of the same name, at the south end of the lake, has a little church with a timbered roof, perhaps of the 15C, curiously boarded and painted in the choir. A short way north of the lake the road meets Rte 20A.

DYSYNNI VALLEY. The unclassified road up the south side of the valley in three miles reaches the bold buttress of *Craig Aderyn* (Bird Rock) which, though now well inland, is a breeding place for cormorants, an interesting natural continuation from the times when this valley was an arm of the sea. In rather over a mile farther, the Dysynni valley, with its road to Abergynolwyn, turns southeast, the ancient Welsh fortress of *Castell-y-Bere* being a short way north of the turning. Started by Llewelyn the Great in about 1221, and taken by the Earl of Pembroke in 1283, the castle was rebuilt by Edward I who, however, held it only until 1285 when it was retaken by the Welsh by whom it was apparently razed. The now only fragmentary remains on a defensive ridge form a long narrow enclosure, at the end of which a postern protected by a tower can be traced. The borough established here in 1285 by Edward I seems not to have survived the retaking of the castle by the Welsh. The scattered hamlet of *Llanfihangel-y-Pennant* is a short way beyond Castell-y-Bere. Here, in a beautiful setting below mountains, the road crosses the Cader river by a modern bridge beside an old one, on the far side being the ruin of *Mary Jones's Cottage*, with a memorial. Daughter of a weaver, Mary Jones was born in 1784. When ten years old, she started to save for a Welsh bible, a task which took her six years. She then walked barefoot across the mountains to Bala where, so she had been told, she would be able to buy a bible from Thomas Charles, only to find that none was available. Thomas Charles, however, gave Mary his own bible and, as a result of this incident, founded the British and Foreign Bible Society. Mary Jones lived to the age of 88 and is buried at Bryncrug, while her bible is preserved in the Society's headquarters in London. The cottage marks the end of the road.

After Bryncrug A493 crosses the Dysynni, just beyond the bridge being a motte, all that survives of an early seat of the princes of Gwynedd, in use before the construction of Castell-y-Bere. *2m. Llanegryn*, where the little church, on a hill to the northwest, has a Norman font and also a magnificent *Rood Screen and loft, according to one tradition, brought here by the monks of Cymmer Abbey at the Reformation but more probably an example of superb local craftsmanship of somewhere between the early 14 to 16C. Note also, on the south exterior wall of the choir, to the left of the window, an incised cross, possibly a consecration cross from an earlier church. The road reaches the coast shortly before *(2m.) Llangelynin Church*, a very primitive mainly 12C structure above the sea, dedicated to St. Celynnin, a local saint of the 7C, and containing several curiosities: a unique double horse-bier; murals of ancient but unknown date, discovered during restoration in 1917; old pews with painted names; and a stoup, once reputed to be miraculously kept filled with water.

5m. **Fairbourne** is a growing holiday resort with sands stretching away north for two miles to Penrhyn Point, marking the south side of the narrow entrance of the Mawddach Estuary. Barmouth, on the other side, can be reached either by ferry (not cars) or by footpath across the main line railway bridge (see Rte 17), access to this being by a road a mile to the northeast along A493. The *Fairbourne Railway* (April–Sept. Tel. 01341-250362), with a gauge of only 15 inches the smallest of Wales's little trains, started in the 19C as a horse-drawn tramway (2ft gauge) used for carrying materials for the construction of the village. The gauge was changed to 15 inches in 1916, and, rescued by enthusiasts after disuse during the last war, the train today carries passengers in a choice of 1st or standard class carriages between Fairbourne Station (a Victorian replica with tearoom and shop) and the ferry.

2m. Arthog, to the east above which, surrounding twin lakes, is the National Trust property of Cregennan (705 acres), given in 1959 by Major C.L. Wynne-Jones in memory of his two sons killed in the war. *4m. Penmaenpool* with its nature information centre (see Rte 14). *2m.* **Dolgellau**, see Rte 16.

22

Aberystwyth

ABERYSTWYTH combines several features, being the main town on Cardigan Bay and thus a general centre serving a wide area; a lively seaside resort; the base of the Vale of Rheidol Railway; with its castle, a place of some historical interest; and the home of the National Library of Wales and of the University College of Wales.

Tourist Information. Terrace Road (below museum). Tel. 01970-612125.

History (Town and Castle). The present suburb of Llanbadarn Fawr is on the site of a 6–8C bishopric and settlement, which can be regarded as the parent village of Aberystwyth, in fact known as Llanbadarn until the 15C. In 1110 Gilbert FitzRichard of Clare built a primitive castle, the earthworks of which can still be seen about a mile and a half south of the present castle on a site which at that date was near the mouth of the Ystwyth. For over a century this early castle endured a violent history, being burnt down no fewer than five times, usually in disputes between Welsh princes, the last recorded incident being the taking of the castle by Llewelyn the Great in 1221. The present castle, dating with its associated borough from 1277, was started by Edmund of Lancaster, brother of Edward I. Progress, slow in any case, was halted in 1282 when the Welsh took and briefly held the castle, but by 1284 the place was fit enough to receive a visit by Edward I, and, ten years later, in 1294, strong enough to withstand a Welsh siege. During Owen Glendower's revolt the Welsh destroyed the town in 1401 but failed to carry the castle until 1404, after which it remained a Glendower headquarters for four years. During the Civil War Aberystwyth was held for Charles I until the castle was surrendered in 1646 and blown up in 1649. At the close of the 18C the discovery of a chalybeate spring sparked a short-lived attempt to turn Aberystwyth into a fashionable spa.

The general pattern of the town is a seafront, running north to south and broken by the castle headland, backed by a zone of pleasant and mostly small streets (the main axis of which is Great Darkgate Street linking Terrace Road at the northeast with Pier Street and Bridge Street at the southwest), with to the east the station and to the southwest the harbour. The district of Penglais (National Library, and new University College) is on rising ground to the northeast.

From the seafront there can be a view embracing virtually the whole of Cardigan Bay, from Snowdon and the Lleyn in the north to Strumble Head and the Presely Hills in the south. Beyond the north end of the town rises *Constitution Hill* (400ft), climbed by a path or by the Aberystwyth Electric Cliff Railway, 'a conveyance for gentlefolk since 1896' (Easter–Oct: daily, frequent 10.00–18.00 or 21.00 in Aug. Tel. 01970-617642), from the top being an even wider view, this, since 1985, enhanced by a camera obscura (times as for railway).

Along the curve of Marine Terrace are the bandstand and, farther southwest, the Pavilion and Pier, while, just west again and beside New Promenade—and the most conspicuous feature along the seafront—is the old building of the *University College of Wales* (see below). Originally intended to be a hotel, the building was restored after a fire of 1885 and now houses various departments of the university. In front, both in their robes of office, stand Thomas Charles Edwards (1837–1900), the first Principal, and the Duke of Windsor who was Chancellor when Prince of Wales.

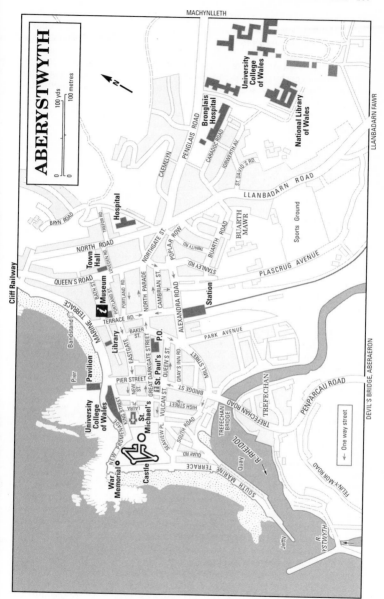

The **Castle** ruins occupy the low hill of a promontory immediately south-west of the college. For the castle's history see above. The open site is an unusual diamond shape, with a large inner ward above and surrounded by a narrow outer ward. Of the outer ward there survive most of the length of the curtain (but much restored) and remains of the east and northwest gates and of the angle towers. The inner ward, its line marked by an embankment, has virtually disappeared except for its east and northwest gates and fragments of angle towers. To the east of the east angle of the outer ward there was a barbican, now marked by a mound, and it is thought that the War Memorial at the tip of the promontory may stand on the site of outlying defences. The *Harbour*, south of the castle and fed by both the Rheidol and the Ystwyth, is used by both fishing and private craft.

In the town proper the **Ceredigion Museum** (Mon–Sat 10.00–17.00. Tel. 01970-634212) is interestingly housed in the Coliseum, a restored Edwardian theatre (1905) in Terrace Road. The basic theme here is the story of Ceredigion (Cardigan), this being told through a good folk collection which includes material illustrating local crafts, mining, seafaring, agriculture, housing (a cottage interior of 1850), and much else. Additionally there is a gallery with an exhibition on the geology and archaeology of this district, while temporary exhibitions show the works of local artists. Another, though more modest place recalling the past is *Aberystwyth Yesteryear* (April–Nov: Mon–Sat, and also Sun June–Sept 10.00–17.00. Tel. 01970-617119) at the British Rail station, a small private collection of all manner of items recalling the last 100 years or more.

The **University College of Wales** was founded in 1872, mainly through the efforts of Sir Hugh Owen (1804–81). For the original buildings on the seafront, see above. Other buildings lie to the east of the station, but the main recent development (buildings generally dating from 1959 onwards) has been on Penglais Hill in the northeast outskirts of the town. Here the *Aberystwyth Arts Centre* (tel. 01970-623232), which includes a concert hall and the university theatre, throughout the year mounts a programme of wide-ranging exhibitions and events.

The ***National Library of Wales** (tel. 01970-623816) occupies a commanding site on Penglais Hill, the land of which was presented by Lord Rendel. Begun in 1911, the buildings span from that date to modern times. There is a regular programme of exhibitions.

The movement for a national library was contemporary with the founding of the University College in 1872, and a Royal Charter was granted in 1907. Under this, the task of the library is to collect, preserve and make available all books, manuscripts etc. in Welsh and other Celtic languages, or which deal with the Welsh and other Celtic people; also to hold works on all subjects and in all languages which help to achieve the purpose for which the University of Wales and other Welsh educational institutions were founded. In 1912, under the Copyright Act, the library became one of six libraries entitled to claim a copy of all books, pamphlets, maps etc. published within the British Isles.

Among the library's chief treasures are the 'Black Book of Carmarthen' (12C), the oldest manuscript in Welsh; the 'Book of Taliesin' (13C); the 'White Book of Rhydderch' (13–14C), containing the oldest known versions of the Mabinogion tales; Latin and Welsh manuscripts of the Laws of Hywel Dda; early manuscripts of Geoffrey of Monmouth's 'Chronicle'; the Henwrt manuscripts of Bede's 'Ecclesiastical History of Britain' (12C) and Chaucer's 'Canterbury Tales' (c1400); the so-called 'Bangor Missal', really a Sarum missal of the late 14C or early 15C and finely decorated; one of the only two vellum copies of 'The Great Bible' of 1539; a 15C 'Passionale' probably made for Henry VII.

As noted above (History), the suburb of **Llanbadarn Fawr**, a mile southeast off A44, was the ancient parent village of Aberystwyth, its origins dating to the founding here in the 6C of a monastery and bishopric by St. Padarn. The actual date was 546 when St. Dubricius (or Dyfrig), Celtic Bishop of all Wales, divided his see into three, appointing Deiniol to Gwynedd, Padarn to central Wales and Teilo to the south. By the 11C this had become an important centre of learning, but by 1188, when Giraldus visited here, the place was in decline and by the mid 13C it had disappeared. At about this time, though, work had started on today's church, a plain early 13C building (except for the sanctuary which may be a 15C extension) which is one of the largest churches in Wales, its size reflecting that of its parish which embraced some 140 square miles.

Today the south transept—beyond a screen incorporating etched glass with themes from the poems of Dafydd ap Gwilym, said to have been born in this parish in c 1340—houses an elegant small exhibition area the central feature of which is a granite altar flanked by two venerable Celtic crosses which until 1916 stood in the churchyard. The smaller cross, much mutilated, is the older, tradition insisting that, before its Christian shaping, it was a prehistoric standing stone. The larger may date to the 7 or 8C. Legend associates both stones with St. Samson, agriculturist brother of St. Paternus. Samson, it is said, was threshing corn on a farm two miles or so away, using the stones as a flail, when the head flew off and landed at Llanbadarn, whereupon, losing his saintly patience, Samson hurled the shaft after it. To one side of the granite altar is a Chapel of St. Padarn, interestingly to the scale of a typical Celtic monastic cell, while in the small rooms on the other side are panels depicting themes from Llanbadarn's story from the 11C onwards.

The **Vale of Rheidol Railway** (adjacent to British Rail station. April–Oct: daily. Tel. 01970-625819 or 615993), gauge 1ft 11½ins and steam hauled, was opened in 1902 by a private company partly to carry lead from the Rheidol valley mines and partly in response to tourist demand. Later operated by British Rail, the railway was in 1988 acquired by the Brecon Mountain Railway (see also Rte 31).

The line ascends the lovely Vale of Rheidol from Aberystwyth to Devil's Bridge and is the best way to enjoy the Vale as the main roads (Rtes 23A and 23B) run well above and clear of the valley. For the minor road along part of the north side to Rheidol Power Station, see Rte 23A. After Llanbadarn, the line keeps to the south bank of the river, beyond Capel Bangor, as the valley narrows and winds, affording constantly changing views, including, after Aberffrwd, the Rheidol Falls. For *Devil's Bridge*, see Rte 23B.

For Aberystwyth to *Machynlleth* and beyond, see Rte 18; to *Rhayader* and *Builth Wells*, see Rte 23; to *Carmarthen*, see Rte 41.

23

Aberystwyth to Rhayader and Builth Wells

Between Aberystwyth and Rhayader there is a choice of roads, both scenic with moor, forest and the beautiful valley of the Wye. These alternatives are either via Ponterwyd (near a silver-lead mine museum) and Llangurig, (31m to Rhayader); or a more southerly choice via Devil's Bridge, followed by a wild and remote mountain road (29m to Rhayader). The two Routes, here only three miles apart, are linked by a road between Ponterwyd and Devil's Bridge.

A. Via Ponterwyd and Llangurig

A44 to Llangurig. A470 to Builth Wells. Total distance 44m.—*10m.* **Ponter-wyd.**—*5m. Eisteddfa Gurig.*—*4m. Pant Mawr.*—*3m.* **Llangurig.**—*9m.* **Rhayader.**—*7m. Newbridge-on-Wye.*—*6m.* **Builth Wells.**

For **Aberystwyth** and (*1m*) *Llanbadarn Fawr,* see Rte 22. *3m. Capel Bangor,* from where a minor road ascends the Vale of Rheidol beside the north bank of the river, in about four miles reaching *Cwm Rheidol Visitor Centre* (Easter–Oct: daily 11.00–16.30 to 30 Sept, or 12.00–16.00 in Oct. Tel. 01970-84667), the focus of a number of attractions this side of the valley, these including power station tours, a fish farm and walks around or above Cwm Rheidol reservoir. For the Vale of Rheidol Railway, across the river, see Rte 22. *4m. Bwlch Nant-yr-Arian,* with a Forest Enterprise Visitor Centre, starting-point for walks in Rheidol Forest. *1m.* *Llywernog Silver-Lead Mine* (April–Oct: daily 10.00–18.00, but 10.30–dusk in Oct. Tel. 01970-85620), describing itself as a 'boom-days museum', is based on the mine which opened here in the 1740s and reached its greatest prosperity during the 19C, albeit only to be abandoned in the 1880s. Restoration started in 1973 and the museum now offers a Miners' Trail embracing working water wheels, 18 and 19C mining and agricultural machinery, exhibitions, underground workings and much else. *1m.* **Ponterwyd** is a hamlet where the upper Rheidol is crossed and from where roads north and south enable two diversions, both scenic and interesting, to be made. The name of an inn here, the Borrow Arms, recalls that it was here that George Borrow dried out after floundering through peat bog, much of which is now covered by the reservoirs of Dinas and Nant-y-Moch (see immediately below).

NORTHWARD DIVERSION. 13m to Talybont on Rte 18A. This 'Scenic Route' through a bare mountain landscape below the west flank of Plynlimon passes above the small *Dinas Reservoir* and in four miles reaches *Nant-y-Moch Reservoir,* an irregular, narrow crescent of water some three miles long representing the upper part of the Rheidol hydro-electric scheme. The reservoir (named after a chapel drowned here), with its dam (170ft high and 1150ft long), was inaugurated in 1965. The dam is crossed and the road skirts the south and west shores, the scenery here being broken and softened by plantations. Leaving the reservoir, the road bears west, crossing a watershed at 1300ft and then dropping down the scenic Cwm Ceulan to reach Talybont.

SOUTHWARD DIVERSION. A4120. 3m to Devil's Bridge on Rte 23B. The place of interest along this road is the church of *Ysbytty Cynfyn*, set within the remains of a stone circle (only five stones survive) and thus providing on the same site a fascinating continuity of ritual building, pagan, and Christian, spanning from prehistoric to present day times. Cynfyn was a hospice (Ysbytty) of the abbey of Strata Florida. A path from the church leads in ten minutes to the *Parson's Bridge*, below which the Rheidol forces through a narrow passage.

Beyond Ponterwyd, A44 rises steadily along the south slopes of **Plynlimon** (2468ft), a large moorland dome on which are the sources of five rivers: Severn, Wye, Dulas, Llyfnant and Rheidol. Featureless, notorious for its bogs and mists, and with several abandoned mines, Plynlimon is not for the inexperienced or ill-equipped walker. *5m. Eisteddfa Gurig* (1359ft) is the road pass and watershed. Beyond, the road descends beside the Tarenig, with Ystwyth forest on the south. In another mile the Wye, dropping down from the north, is crossed and then followed past *Pant Mawr* to (*7m*), in gentler scenery, the village of **Llangurig**, the name recalling St. Curig, a holy man who died in 550. The church (dedicated to the saint), although a rebuilding of 1879 by George Gilbert Scott, nevertheless preserves some older parts, notably the 14C tower and, from the 15C, the arcade between the nave and the north aisle, the choir arch, and the tracery of the east window. For *Llanidloes*, four miles northeast, see Rte 18C.

Keeping to the east bank A470 continues to descend the now narrowing and increasingly beautiful Wye valley. *9m.* **Rhayader** (*Inf.*) is in Welsh Rhaeadr Gwy, the 'Waterfall of the Wye', a name which recalls falls here that virtually disappeared when the river bridge was built in 1780. The castle built here by Rhys ap Gruffydd in the 12C has also long disappeared, and Rhayader today is a country centre much used by holiday visitors attracted by pony trekking, fishing, walking, and the beautifully situated reservoirs a short distance to the west. There are two popular visitor objectives on the edges of the town. *Gigrin Farm* (Easter–Nov: daily 10.00–20.00. Tel. 01597-810243), immediately south on A470, is a working hill farm which offers a scenic farm trail of variable length (up to two miles) as also a picnic and play area. In contrast, there is *Welsh Royal Crystal*, just to the east on A44 (factory tours: Mon, Tues, Thur, Fri 09.00–12.00, 13.00–16.00. Shop: Mon–Fri 09.00–17.00; Sat 09.30–17.00; Sun 10.00–16.30. Tel. 01597-811005).

The diarist Francis Kilvert was in 1876–77 vicar of *St. Harmon*, three miles north, where his church preserves a Norman font.

The ***Elan Valley and Claerwen Reservoirs**, completed respectively 1892–96 and 1952 and supplying water to the Birmingham district, are reached in three miles by B4518 southwest out of Rhayader. An alternative approach, from the north, is from Pont-ar-Elan on B4574 towards the end of Rte 23B, this and the approach from Rhayader allowing a scenic circuit to be made. In a setting of mixed woodland and rocky, bare hills, the Elan reservoirs comprise a chain of five narrow lakes, each with its dam, extending some nine miles from north to south. The flooding of the valley provided the theme for Francis Brett Young's novel, 'The House under the Water'.

Claerwen reservoir, aligned roughly east–west and nearly four miles long, fills its own river's valley to the west.

Roads skirt the entire length of the reservoirs, and there are a number of parking areas. The road from Rhayader in three miles reaches *Elan Valley Visitor Centre* (Easter–Oct: daily 10.00–18.00. Tel. 01587-810449) where the story of the valley is told and local information provided. Also here are café, shop and a particularly pleasant picnic area. Just beyond is the dam on the east side of the reservoir of *Caben Coch*, and in another mile comes the *Garreg Ddu Viaduct* (built above a part-submerged dam wall) where there is a choice of roads, either south and then west to Claerwen reservoir or northward beside the Elan chain.

The Claerwen road skirts the west shore of Caben Coch, towards the south of which, if the water is low, can be seen the garden walls of Nant Gwyllt, the house in which Shelley and Harriet lived in April–June 1812 and which also inspired Francis Brett Young's novel. At the lake's end the road curves west, to follow the river Claerwen and in two miles reach *Claerwen Reservoir* with its dam 1166ft long. The other road from Garreg Ddu viaduct heads north beside this narrowing reservoir, below which lies Cwm Elan, the house where, after his expulsion from Oxford in 1811 because of his pamphlet 'The Necessity of Atheism', Shelley visited his cousin Thomas Grove and wrote that 'all was gloomy and desolate'. Next, the *Pen-y-Garreg* reservoir dam (528ft long, 123ft high) is reached, with a car park from which an attractive short walk leads to the foot of the dam. The roads along either side of this reservoir meet at the dam (513ft long, 120ft high) at the foot of *Craig Goch* reservoir, clear of woodland and in open moor. From here the road north runs above and a short way back from the reservoir, at its head (*Pont-ar-Elan* on B4574) meeting Rte 23B.

Southward from Rhayader, A470 descends the glen of the Wye which in two miles is joined from the west by the Elan. *3m. Llanwrthwl*, where the church is successor to one built by St. Gwrthwl, an early Christian holy man who surely knew the ancient stone which still stands in the churchyard near the porch as a reminder of ritual of millennia ago. Doldowlod House, between the road and the river a mile and a half farther south, was once the home of the engineer James Watt. The valley opens out before (*4m*) the straggling village of *Newbridge-on-Wye*, just south of which the river cascades into one of its most broken and beautiful reaches. *5m. Llanelwedd*, site of the Royal Welsh Agricultural Society showground (July). Rte 24 comes in from the east, and the road crosses the Wye by a bridge of six arches, built in 1779 but since widened.

1m. **Builth Wells** (*Inf.*), in Welsh Llanfair-ym-Muallt, lies on the south bank of a pastoral stretch of the Wye.

History. The town probably originated as a settlement below the early Norman motte-and-bailey castle, thought to have been built by Bernard of Newmarch in 1091. The castle was partly destroyed by Llewellyn the Last in 1260, and in 1282 the refusal of the garrison (in Welsh history the 'traitors of Bu-allt') to allow Llewelyn sanctuary led to his death at nearby Cilmeri. At about this time Edward I built a stone castle here, known to have still been in good repair in the time of Henry VIII, it was probably destroyed under Elizabeth I. Later, Builth became an important stage along the cattle route to England (it still has a cattle market), and for a period the town was known for mineral springs.

Of Edward's stone castle virtually nothing has survived and *Castle Mound*, just beyond the south end of the bridge, really represents Bernard of

Newmarch's large motte-and-bailey of 1091. The earthworks are notable for the unusual width of their ditches, and for the way in which the bailey is divided by another ditch. The *Church*, west of the riverside car park, was rebuilt after 1875 except for the restored 12C tower. In the porch there is an effigy of John Lloid (died 1585), one of Elizabeth I's squires.

For Builth Wells NE to *Llandrindod Wells* and *Knighton* and SW to *Llandovery* and *Swansea*, see Rte 24; to *Abergavenny*, see Rte 25.

B. Via Devil's Bridge

A4120 to Devil's Bridge. B4574 to Rhayader. A470 to Builth Wells. Total distance 42m.—*11m*. **Devil's Bridge**.—*2m*. **The Arch**.—*11m. Pont-ar-Elan.*—*5m*. **Rhayader**.—*13m*. **Builth Wells**.
 For the Vale of Rheidol Railway, see Rte 22.

Aberystwyth, see Rte 22, is left by A487/A4120 which, after crossing the Rheidol, skirts the east side of a hill crowned by a hillfort and a monument to the Duke of Wellington. *1m. Penparcau*, a suburban village and cross-roads from which A487 (Rte 41) leads south while this Route continues east, gradually ascending along the south side of the Rheidol valley, with occasional views down to the river and across to the steep north side. The highest point reached is 989ft; beyond, during the descent, hills mask the valley.

10m. Devil's Bridge, a popular beauty spot with a hotel, a huge car park, and the terminus of the Vale of Rheidol Railway, is in a romantic landscape of wooded glen, rocks and torrent. Here the Rheidol abruptly changes direction, at the bend being joined by the Mynach, which drops 300ft through a rocky chasm in a series of cataracts which in spate become an almost continuous fall. An iron bridge (1901) spans the stream at the lip of the falls. Just below this is the stone bridge of 1753, and, lower still, the original and ancient *Pont-y-gwr-Drwg* (Bridge of the Evil One), traditionally ascribed to the Devil. It may in fact have been built by the monks at Strata Florida (the abbey is eight miles south, and its hospice of Ysbytty Cynfyn under two miles north), and Giraldus writes of crossing a bridge here in 1188, a few years after the founding of the abbey. The *Mynach Falls* (fee for non-residents) are in the grounds of the Hafod Arms Hotel. Paths offer views of the basin above the falls, of the three bridges, and of the distant Gyfarllwyd Falls up the Rheidol. Farther down, the whole series of the Mynach Falls is seen from a platform, from where steps descend steeply to a foot-bridge across the river at the foot of the falls.

For Devil's Bridge to *Ysbytty Cynfyn* and *Ponterwyd*, see Rte 23A.
 B4343, leading south from Devil's Bridge and crossing the valley of the Ystwyth, in eight miles reaches the abbey of *Strata Florida*, see Rte 41B.

Devil's Bridge is left by B4574 which climbs into woodland to (*2m*) **The Arch**, with a Forest Enterprise picnic site, trails and a view point. The stone arch was put up in 1810, to honour the Golden Jubilee of George III, by Thomas Johnes (1748–1816) of Hafod Uchtryd (demolished 1958), two miles south. When in 1783 Johnes inherited the estate, in, apparently, neglected condition, he resolved to transform the place through sound farming and afforestation, in the latter context becoming a pioneer and between 1786 and

Devil's Bridge. On top, the iron bridge of 1901; below, stone bridge of 1753; at the bottom, the Bridge of the Evil One, ascribed to the Devil but more prosaically probably built in the 12C by monks of Strata Florida

1813 planting over four million trees, mostly larch. He can thus be said to have anticipated the present Forest Enterprise estate. Johnes was also a scholar and published his own translations of Froissart's and Monstrelet's 'Chronicles' from his private press.

After The Arch the road leaves the forest for lonely, open moor, ascending the Ystwyth and passing large abandoned lead mines, notably at (*4m*) *Cwmystwyth* where lead was mined first in Roman times, later by the monks of Strata Florida, and finally during the 17–19C when this was one of the most advanced lead and silver mines in Europe. The desolate site—with remains which include workshops, a mill of 1898, a turbine house and tramways—is dangerous because of concealed adits and shafts, but much can be seen from the road. Still in remote and desolate country, B4574 crosses the watershed at 1320ft to descend the Elan to (*7m*) *Pont-ar-Elan*, a road junction above the head of Craig Goch reservoir into which the Elan flows. The small road leading south offers an alternative approach to Rhayader via the beautiful Elan Valley reservoirs (see Rte 23A). *5m.* **Rhayader**, for which, as also for Rhayader to (*13m*) **Builth Wells**, see Rte 23A.

24

Knighton to Llandrindod Wells, Llandovery and Swansea

A488 to Penybont. A44 to Cross Gates. A483 to Llandovery. A40 to Llandeilo. Choice of roads to Swansea. Total distance excluding diversions 82m.—*5m. Monaughty.*—*9m. Penybont.*—*2m.* **Cross Gates.**—*3m.* **Llandrindod Wells.**—*7m.* **Builth Wells.**—*12m.* **Llanwrtyd Wells.**—*10m.* **Llandovery.**—*12m.* **Llandeilo.**—*22m.* **Swansea**.

Gradually increasing moorland and afforestation, the road running below the Cambrian Mountains to the north and Mynydd Epynt and Black Mountain to the south. Several worthwhile diversions.

Knighton (*Inf.* Offa's Dyke Heritage Centre, The Old School. Easter–Oct: daily 09.00–17.30. Oct–Easter: Mon–Fri 09.00–17.00. Tel. 01547-528753), today a quiet border town on the steep Welsh bank of the small river Teme, recalls a more turbulent border past through two mottes—one, first mentioned in 1181, at the top of the town; the other, Bryn-y-Castell and possibly an outlying defence of the first, in the valley just east of the station—and through *Offa's Dyke* which crosses the southwest of the town and gives it its Welsh name of Tref-y-Clawd, the Cantref on the Dyke. The Heritage Centre (Offa's Dyke Association, Knighton, LD7 1EW. Tel. as above), close to a good section of the dyke, provides information and publications on both the dyke and its popular accompanying path.

5m. Monaughty (no adm.), to the west of the road, is a stone Tudor farm which was once a monastery grange. It is said that a tunnel once ran between the grange and Pilleth (see immediately below), this being used as an escape route by the monks when attacked, a not uncommon occurence in this border district.

MONAUGHTY TO PRESTEIGNE. (B4356. SE, 7m.) *Pilleth*, reached in a mile, was in 1402 the scene of an important battle in which Owen Glendower defeated and captured Sir Edmund Mortimer, fighting for Henry IV, thus establishing his claim to be the Welsh national leader. Mortimer, advancing from the east along the flank of the hill, seems to have been ambushed by Glendower, who was hiding on the reverse slope above, the English (according to Shakespeare's 'Henry IV, Part One') losing a thousand men whose bodies were so mutilated by the Welsh women 'as may not be without much shame retold or spoken of'. Probably wisely, Mortimer then sided with Glendower. *Castell Foel-Allt*, beside the river below Pilleth church, is a motte-and-bailey remain dating from the 11C.

From *Whitton*, a mile farther, B4356 continues southeast for Presteigne, but a diversion may be made south and then, at the first crossroads, northwest to (three miles from Whitton) the hamlet of *Cascob* where the church has a mound at its west end which is generally thought to represent the remains of a tower burnt by Glendower. The present tower is of unusual ground plan, being twice as long from north to south as from east to west. Inside the church are a triangular aumbry and a square piscina (both 13C), a 14C font, and a restored rather plain 16C rood screen.

Presteigne (*Inf.*) is an attractive and locally typical old border town—the Lugg which skirts the north edge of the town is the actual border—with half-timbered houses, notable among these being the *Radnorshire Arms* of 1616, once the home, it is said, of John Bradshaw (1602–59) whose signature headed those on the death warrant of Charles I. The Lugg bridge dates from the 17C. The *Church* is 14–16C, but has interesting earlier fragments; a jamb and segment of choir arch (east end of north aisle) are pre-Norman, and there are two early Norman window fragments in the north wall. Also noteworthy are a mosaic of old glass (south chapel); a late 13C sepulchral slab (north aisle); and an early 16C Flemish tapestry representing the Entry into Jerusalem. The low hill west of the town known as *The Warden*, now a public park, is the site of the Norman castle destroyed by Llewelyn the Last in 1261. At *Norton*, two miles north, the church has a bell-turret supported on timber framing, and a tree stump by the churchyard entrance still bears manacles suggesting its use as a pillory or whipping post.

2m. (from Monaughty) *Bleddfa* where, as at Cascob (see above), the church shows a mound at its west end. Excavation in 1962 revealed a small doorway and the base of a tower, probably that of the earlier church destroyed by Owen Glendower at about the same time as the battle at Pilleth. From here the road now climbs along the north flank of *Radnor Forest* before descending to (*4m*) *Llanfihangel Rhydithon*, two miles beyond which a road (sign) leads south for a mile to *The Pales*, a Quaker house of 1771. *3m. Penybont*, from where a diversion may be made eastward to historic New Radnor and Old Radnor, the return distance being some 22 miles.

DIVERSION TO NEW AND OLD RADNOR. A44 is followed south through *Llandegley* where the church has a 15C screen and a blocked priest's doorway with a curious seven-foiled head; the Pales (see above) is just to the north. Beyond, the road loops around the south of the moor and wooded upland of Radnor Forest to reach the junction with A481 to Builth Wells with, just to the north, a large tumulus (this A481 drops through open scenery into the upper valley of the Edw, which is crossed at Hundred House Inn, half a mile beyond which is *Maud's Castle*, a motte-and-bailey, now a farm, mentioned in the first half of the 12C). Along A44, just beyond Llanfihangel-nant Melan, a northward motorable lane leads into woods in which a cascade, attractively named *Water-break-its-Neck*, tumbles through a narrow ravine. A pleasant walk leads around the top of the ravine, and a track and path cross Radnor Forest to respectively Llanfihangel Rhydithon and Bleddfa on A488. **New Radnor** is a large village the most interesting feature of which, both visually and historically, is the large *Motte-and-bailey* beside the church. Visually this represents a castle built in the 11C, destroyed by King John, rebuilt by Henry III, and finally ruined by Owen Glendower in 1401; historically, the castle was the starting-point in 1188 of Archbishop Baldwin's tour through Wales with Giraldus to preach the Third Crusade. In the 13C the town was laid out to the Edwardian plan of square blocks, but of this street plan virtually nothing now survives, although just outside the southwest of the town something can be seen of the protective boundary earthwork.

Old Radnor, two and a half miles beyond New Radnor and on a hill to the south of the road, was once a base of Harold Godwinson, or King Harold, defeated and killed by William of Normandy (William the Conqueror) at Hastings in 1066. The small motte in a field some 300 yards southeast of the church represents the site of his castle, and must also have been the 'Cruker Castle' mentioned by Giraldus. The *Church, though essentially English in style (the border is little more than a mile away), is nevertheless one of the finest parish churches in Wales, with its imposing west tower a good example of late 14C work. Inside there is much of interest, such as the parclose screens north and south of the choir; the rood screen, still with the base of its loft; the ancient stalls and desks, one of the latter still with chain and clasp; the organ case of c 1500, with linenfold and Tudor roses; and the huge, rudely circular *Font, one of the largest in Britain, made from a glacial boulder which may once have served as a prehistoric pagan ritual stone. The floor slab with a floreated cross at the entrance to the choir is 13C; and in the north chapel are, at the east end, a late 15C St. Catherine window, an Easter sepulchre built into the north wall, and a massive medieval vestments chest.

2m. (from Penybont) **Cross Gates** (or Crossgates) is a road junction (A44 and A483) five miles northwest of which by A483 and a minor road are the fragmentary remains of **Cwmhir Abbey** in a beautiful pastoral setting in the winding valley of the Clywedog (Cwmhir means 'long valley'). The abbey was founded in 1143 for Cistercian monks from Whitland, and a second foundation followed in 1176. It was also twice destroyed, first by Henry III in 1231, and again in 1401 by Owen Glendower who is said to have suspected that the monks were Englishmen in disguise. Although after Henry III's attack an ambitious rebuilding was planned, in fact the choir was never built, the transepts were left unfinished, and the great nave was wrecked by Glendower. The 15C was one of steady decline and by the time of the Dissolution there were only three monks in residence. Today's remains comprise little more than the foundations of the nave and some battered lower courses of its wall, but visitors ready to accept tradition will accept also that the body of Llewelyn the Last was brought here from Cilmeri in 1282 for burial below the altar, a position today marked by a blackthorn.

From Cross Gates this Route follows A483 southward, almost at once passing the church at *Llanbadarnfawr*, with a 12C south doorway and fine carved *Tympanum of c 1140. The left supporting capital bears two naked figures, presumably Adam and Eve, with the Devil below, while another interesting feature is a Roman stone, inscribed with the name of Valerius Flavinius, inserted in the left wall of the porch. Almost certainly coming from Castell Collen, the stone was found embedded in the wall of the earlier church during rebuilding in 1878 and suggests that the original church in all probability used Castell Collen as a quarry.

3m. **Llandrindod Wells** (*Inf.*), though no longer a spa, is still a not-unfashionable holiday centre which, with its wide streets and large hotels, retains much of its spacious Edwardian character. The town is divided into two by the railway, Rock Park being to the west and the main street (Temple Street), with the town's museum, to the east.

History. Although today's Llandrindod Wells dates only from the late 19C, the town in fact has ancient roots. The Romans were nearby at Castell Collen and probably knew the springs (saline, sulphur, magnesian and chalybeate), and the parish church of the Trinity, which gives the town its name, traces its origins to the 12C. The saline spring is recorded in 1696, the sulphur spring in 1736, and in 1748 the springs were the subject of verses in the 'Gentleman's Magazine'. At this time, the place was no more than a scattered hamlet, but a hotel was built in 1749 and, until closed in 1787, gave Llandrindod a few years' notoriety as a haunt of gamblers and rakes. It was the arrival of the railway in 1867 that changed everything, and by the end of the century the spa had developed, welcoming as many as 80,000 visitors a year, a prosperity which was to last, if later in decline, until the Second World War.

The *Llandrindod Museum* (daily, but closed Sat afternoon and Sun in winter, 10.00–13.00, 14.00–17.00. Tel. 01597-824513), in Temple Street, is concerned with local history, principal themes being the Roman fort of Castell Collen and the town's period as a spa, while, beyond the railway, something more of Llandrindod's elegant past can be recaptured at *Rock Park Spa* with eighteen acres of park and the 19C *Pump Room* (March–Oct: daily 10.00–17.00. Tel. 01597-824307) where the visitor can sample the waters or enjoy a Welsh tea. Here too there are frequent craft markets while the former Bath House now offers an exhibition on this and other Welsh spas.

The Roman fort of **Castell Collen**, a mile and a quarter northwest of the town, is reached from A4081 (lane north, immediately west of the Ithon bridge). The fort seems to have known four phases, namely an original turf and timber site of 75–78, the work of Julius Frontinus during his campaign against the Silures; stone construction of the mid 2C; a contraction in size in the early 3C; and a strengthening in the late 3 or early 4C. Today the rectangular earthworks of a fort of between three and four acres are clearly detectable, while to the west can be traced something of the area abandoned in the 3C.

Llandrindod Wells is left by A483 southward. Between Llandrindod and (*2m*) *Howey*, to the west of the road and beyond the railway, aerial photographs have revealed evidence of a Roman road and temporary camp, while at *Disserth*, just west off the main road, the church has a curious three-level pulpit and a box-pew, both of the 17C. The *Carneddau Hills* (1430ft), to the east of the road, provide good walking and are of geological interest for the way in which the Llandovery and Lower Silurian flags here have been disrupted by volcanic intrustions, while ice markings, perched blocks and moraines indicate later glacial action. For *4m Llanelwedd* and *1m* **Builth Wells**, in the Wye valley, see Rte 23A.

Beyond Builth Wells A483 runs between the long ridge of Mynydd Epynt (1650ft; Ministry of Defence ranges) to the southeast and the southern end of the Cambrian Mountains to the northwest. Both areas include high moor and forest and are crossed by a number of motorable minor roads, those through the Cambrian Mountains serving some of the remotest country in Wales. *2m. Cilmeri* is where Llewelyn the Last, denied help by the garrison at Builth, was killed in 1282 during a skirmish with the English. A roadside monument (1956, replacing one of the 19C) stands on the spot where he is supposed to have fallen, one tradition holding that he is buried here, another that his remains were taken to Cwmhir Abbey. Glan Irfon, just south of the road, was a home of the eccentric Lady Hester Stanhope (1776–1839). *4m. Garth*, from where there is a choice of roads for the next five or six miles. The main road loops north through *Beulah*, a village which has given its name to a breed of sheep; from here an unclassified road northwest in five miles joins the drover road (see below) at Abergwesyn. The valley road passes through **Llangammarch Wells**, in parkland scenery at the confluence of the Irfon and Cammarch. The village gained its one-time reputation as a spa because its water was found to contain barium chloride, not found elsewhere in Britain and recommended for cardiac and rheumatic complaints; the now disused pump house and the well are in the grounds of the Lake Hotel. Somewhat surprisingly for so modest a place, Llangammarch claims association with a number of people who, if on the whole obscure, nevertheless have their niches in specialist segments of history. One such was John Penry, Puritan writer and publisher, born here in 1559 (traditionally at the farm of Cefn Brith, two miles south of the village) and hanged in London in 1593 after conviction for sedition. Another native was the Royalist Bishop Howell (1588–1646), while Theophilus Evans (1694–1767), author of a popular book on Welsh antiquities said to have achieved 30 editions, was vicar. The book, translated into English under the title 'View of the Primitive Ages', was highly imaginative and pleased the Welsh by its assertion that Arthur was as historic a figure as Alexander the Great.

6m. **Llanwrtyd Wells** (*Inf.*), once a spa known for its sulphur and chalybeate springs, is now a modest country holiday and pony trekking centre. The small modern town is on the main road and the old village about a mile northwest up the valley of the Irfon. The *Cambrian Factory*, a Welsh Tweed centre beside A483, was founded in the 1820s, then producing flannels which were marketed locally. But in its modern form the factory dates from 1918 when it was opened by the Royal British Legion for the benefit of war-disabled. Considerably extended in 1944, and again in 1970, the factory, now jointly managed by Powys County Council and the British Legion and giving employment to other disabled people, offers visitors a view of the production processes and also a high-class shop (factory: Mon–Fri 08.15–16.30. Shop: Mon–Fri 08.15–17.15; Sat 09.00–16.30 in May–Sept, or 12.00 in other months. Tel. 01591-3211).

From Llanwrtyd Wells a former drover hill road, today with Forest Enterprise picnic sites and walks, can be followed north and west through forest and across remote moorland to (18m) Tregaron on Rte 41B. The narrow rocky glen of the Irfon is ascended through *Abergwesyn*, some two miles beyond which the road bears west across a corner of Towy Forest before breaking out on to moor, passing a road south to the north tip of *Llyn Brianne* (see below), and reaching a watershed at over 1500ft. From here the road drops with the Berwyn down to Tregaron in the valley of the Teifi.

Beyond Llanwrtyd Wells, A483 ascends through remote country to cross in *4m* the *Sugar Loaf Pass* (949ft). *6m.* **Llandovery** (*Inf.*), a leading market town, owes its Welsh name of Llanymddyfri (Church amid the Waters) to its situation at the confluence of the Gwydderig and the Bran and about a mile and a half above that of the Bran and the Towy, this last, with a course of 68 miles, being the longest river entirely in Wales. Of the Norman *Castle* around which a settlement developed into a small town a few remains (an oval motte, a roughly square bailey, and some later masonry) stand beside the large parking area in the south of the town; partly burnt by Gruffydd ap Rhys in 1116, the castle does not seem to have been long held by the English. Two churchmen are associated with the town, one being Rhys Pritchard (1579–1644), celebrated for his preaching (he was known as the Vicar of Llandovery) and as the author of 'The Welshman's Candle', a paraphrase of the Gospels in Welsh quatrains; born in Llandovery, in 1602 he became vicar of the local parish of Llandingat. The other churchman was William Williams ('Williams Pantycelyn', 1717–91), a revivalist and hymn writer who was born at Cefncoed, four miles northeast.

LLANDOVERY TO LLYN BRIANNE. (N, 11m.) Ascending the upper Vale of Towy, roads follow either side of the river to meet in eight miles at *Craig Bron-y-Cwrt* where a minor road breaks away first northwest and then southwest to follow the Cothi down to Dolaucothi and Pumsaint on Rte 27. From Craig Bron-y-Cwrt the road up the Towy left bank is taken, this in two miles reaching the farm of Ystradffin, just west of which is *Twm Shon Catti's Cave*, the retreat of 'Tom John, son of Catherine' (1530–1620), a poet whose youthful freebooting escapades gained him the title of the Robin Hood of Wales. Later, he settled down, married the heiress of Ystradffin and even became a magistrate. *Llyn Brianne*, with a dam at its south end and over three miles long from the dam to the north tip of its long narrow east finger, boosts the water supply of Swansea.

For Llandovery to (E) *Brecon* and (W) *Lampeter* and *Aberaeron*, see Rte 27.

Beyond Llandovery, there is a choice of roads southwest either side of the Towy to (*6m*) **Llangadog**. A40, a straight Roman stretch north of the river, should be followed for Rte 27 (A482) to Dolaucothi, Lampeter and Aberaeron which bears away west at *Llanwrda*, four miles from Llandovery. From Llanwrda there is also a road northwest across to (5m) Talley Abbey (see Diversions from Llandeilo, below). Llangadog is a modest market town sandwiched between the rivers Sawdde and Bran just above where they join the Towy. *Mandinam*, two miles east, was the home of Joanna Bridges, Jeremy Taylor's second wife (1656), rumoured to have been a natural daughter of Charles I. *Carn Goch*, three miles south of Llangadog, is an exceptionally large hillfort, with a stone rampart and earthworks covering some 15 acres.

After Llangadog there is again a choice of roads, the more direct choice for Swansea being A4069 which ascends the Sawdde and crosses the long open moorland of Black Mountain before dropping to the industrial centre of Brynamman. But this Route takes the more interesting road through (*6m*) **Llandeilo** (*Inf.*) at the hub of a number of worthwhile diversions. Sprawled on the slope of a hill above the Towy, the town takes its name from St. Teilo who is said to have died in a monastery here in 560. Of this era there is no trace, but Llandeilo's *Church*, in origin 13C but largely a rebuilding of 1840, preserves the heads of two stone crosses of the 9 and 10C, while the little church of *Llandyfeisant* (Coed-y-Castell; wildlife visitor centre), reached in half a mile by a path leading west along the north bank of the Towy, or from Dinefwr park, is said to stand on a Roman site.

DIVERSIONS FROM LLANDEILO. As noted above, Llandeilo can be a hub for various diversions from this main route, these including the estate of Dinefwr, just west of the town; a westward circuit of 12 miles passing much of varied interest; Talley Abbey, seven miles north; and Carreg Cennen castle, four miles southeast.

The estate of **Dinefwr** (NT. Tel. 01558-822800), today comprising the park, the castle and mainly 19C Newton House, has roots deep in Welsh tradition and history.

Archaeology has revealed that the site of the castle was once an Iron Age hillfort; legend, as told by Spenser, places Merlin's grave 'amongst the woody hill of Dynevowre'; tradition tells that in 876 Rhodri Mawr built a castle here as a base in his stand against the Norsemen; and it is fact the Hywel Dda (died 950), grandson of Rhodri Mawr and great codifier of the law, was lord of Dinefwr. It is fact, too, that the books of the law refer to the white cattle, associated with Dinefwr since shadowy times (the breed may have been brought over by the Romans for sacrificial purposes) and today once again roaming the park.

Rhys ap Tewdr (died 1093), a descendant of Hywel Dda, ruled his princedom of Deheubarth from here, while the great Rhys ap Gruffydd (died 1197) is credited with building the first stone castle. As capital of Deheubarth, Dinefwr was a constant target for both the Normans and the English and an English siege of 1257 was raised by Llewelyn the Last. But not even Dinefwr could withstand Edward I and traces of his borough still survive near the castle.

Later, in the 15C, a manor house (on the site of the present Newton House) superseded the castle and by the 17C the family name of Rhys had become anglicised to Rice.

The *Park* (all year), in part landscaped by 'Capability' Brown in 1775, his main contributions being the strategically placed clumps of trees and the opening of elegant vistas, is home to the white cattle and also provides access to Llandyfeisant Church (see above) and the ruin of *Dinefwr Castle* (open when conservation work completed). *Newton House* (April–Oct: daily 10.00–17.00), with a Victorian garden, shows a small exhibition on the history of Dinefwr.

A **Westward Circuit**. A pleasant and varied round of 12 miles can be made either side of the Towy to the west of Llandeilo, starting along B4300, to the north of which the ruin of *Dinefwr Castle* can be seen on the hill above the valley. Soon afterwards, the mansion of *Golden Grove* (Gelli Aur) stands above the road on the south side. Now part of an agricultural college, the present building (by Joseph Wyatville, c 1824) is successor, though on a different site, to a mansion burnt down in 1769 in which Jeremy Taylor found a refuge with Richard Vaughan, 2nd Earl of Carbery, the mansion's owner, during the ten disturbed years of 1645–55. It was while he was here that Taylor wrote many of his best works, including 'Holy Living', 'Holy Dying' and 'Golden Grove', at the same time successfully running a school. The park is now an official Country Park, with nature trails, deer, an arboretum and a programme of events.

B4300 continues west—with a view ahead of *Paxton's Tower*, a folly built in 1811 by Sir William Paxton in honour of Lord Nelson and now owned by the National Trust—this circuit, however, bearing north along B4297 to cross the Towy for, just the other side of the river, the ruin of the early Welsh *Dryslwyn Castle*, on the site of an Iron Age hillfort (riverside picnic area with interpretive board). With traces of a chapel, a hall and a round keep (and with more excavation planned), the ruins are of particular interest for being to some extent the result of deliberate undermining by besiegers in the late 13C, an operation which, it is recorded, cost the lives of many of the sappers. The return to Llandeilo may be made along A40, with, on the south side before the turn to Llangathen, the hill of *Grongar* with a hillfort. The charms of this modest hill, as also of Dryslwyn, were sung by the poet John Dyer (1700–58) who was born at nearby Aberglasney.

The remains of **Talley Abbey** (Cadw; see p. 11), seven miles north of Llandeilo, are reached by B4302 up the pleasant valley of the river Dulais. Talley—the name deriving from Tal-y-Llychau, or Head of the Lakes, because of the abbey's situation on the more southerly of two small lakes—was founded in the late 12C by Rhys ap Gruffydd for Premonstratensian canons and was the only house in Wales of this Order. Although ejected as early as c 1200 by the powerful Cistercians of Whitland, the canons successfully appealed to the Archbishop of Canterbury and had returned by 1208. The skeleton of the abbey's church tower is the most significant remain, together with something of the nave, choir and transepts with their chapels, as also, to the south of the nave, the lower courses of cloisters. Talley claims, as does also Strata Florida, to be the burial place of Dafydd ap Gwilym (c 1320–80), described by Borrow as 'the greatest of his country's songsters'.

*Carreg Cennen Castle (Cadw; see p. 11), four miles southeast of Llandeilo, is dramatically sprawled along a precipitous limestone rock rising 300ft above the ravine of the river Cennen, a situation which means that there is a long, steep climb from the car park, rewarded, however, by a view over much of Brecon Beacons National Park and Black Mountain.

History. There must have been a fortress on a site such as this from very early times, and indeed tradition ascribes one castle here to Urien, a knight of Arthur's Round Table. The present castle, the name of its builder unknown, dates from the late 13C or early 14C. It was taken by the Lancastrians during the Wars of the Roses, but in 1462 was destroyed by William Herbert of Raglan because it had become a nest of brigands.

The castle, without a keep, was four-sided with inner and outer wards. The ruins are entered on the north by a gatehouse with a portcullis at each end. The solid tower at the southwest angle of the quadrangle is scarcely more than a buttress, and the southeast corner, above the cliff, is unprotected. Strangely, the hall is placed on the north and weakest sector of the curtain. Perhaps the most remarkable feature of the ruins is the long passage, cut through the rock and lit by loopholes, that leads to the so-called well, a kind of cave deep beneath the ruins which, though it may have served as a cistern, apparently contains no spring.

At Llwyndewi farm, a mile south of Trap, which is a mile west of Carreg Cennen's car park, barns and cowsheds have been converted to form *Trap Arts and Crafts Centre* (March–Christmas: Tues–Sun 10.30–18.00 or 19.00 in July and Aug. Tel. 01269-850362), a complex including a craft shop, art gallery showing work by local artists, tearoom, a visitor information point and a programme of exhibitions and demonstrations.

From Llandeilo, **Swansea** (see Rte 38) can be reached in some 22m. by a choice of roads, the shortest being A483 through Ammanford, beyond meeting the M4 motorway.

25

Builth Wells to Abergavenny

The alternative Routes described below run roughly parallel and up to eight miles apart, meeting at Tretower, with its medieval manor and ruined Norman castle, seven miles north of Abergavenny. Rte 25A, descending a particularly lovely reach of the Wye, is for its first dozen or so miles scenically the more attractive. Rte 25B, on the other hand, includes the interesting cathedral town of Brecon, with access to some beautiful country to its south. The best of both Routes will be achieved by choosing Rte 25A as far as Bronllys, then using a section of Rte 33 to cut across to Brecon, thence continuing to Tretower and Abergavenny by Rte 25B.

A.   Via Talgarth and Tretower. Wye Valley

A470 to Llyswen. A479 to just beyond Tretower. A40 to Abergavenny. Total distance 33m.—*8m.* **Erwood**.—*4m. Llyswen*.—*3m.* **Bronllys**.—*1m.* **Talgarth**.—*10m.* **Tretower**.—*2m.* **Crickhowell**.—*5m.* **Abergavenny**.

Between Builth Wells and Llyswen the road descends the wooded and pastoral valley of the Wye, this being followed, between Talgarth and Tretower, by the upland western slopes of the Black Mountains. Beyond Tretower, the pleasant valley of the Usk.

Builth Wells, see Rte 23A. A470 runs with the west bank of the Wye, offering, soon after (*4m.*) *Alltmawr*, a view across the river to *Aberedw Rocks*, an outcrop of the Silurian formation rising in terraces of slabs to a height of nearly 600ft. *4m.* **Erwood**, the name pronounced Errod and a corruption of the Welsh Y Rhyd (the Ford), recalling a past when the shallow crossing here was much used by drovers and their herds. *4m.* **Llyswen** and (by A479) *3m.* **Bronllys** where Rte 33 is crossed and where the church, a 19C rebuilding, has a detached 14C tower. *Bronllys Castle*, just southeast and balancing on an earlier motte, is a lone cylindrical tower of c 1200, with later alterations but a possibly earlier vaulted basement.

1m. **Talgarth**, a small town of some character, stood athwart the Norman thrust into Wales (under Bernard of Newmarch) and still shows defensive features, notably in the tower (14C in its present form) of the church and in another tower, this one of the 11–13C and later serving as the jail, beside the bridge and now incorporated into a house. Talgarth is associated with Hywel Harris (1714–73, and buried here), a Methodist revivalist who in 1752 established at Trefecca House, a mile and a quarter southwest by B4560, 'The Connexion', a community organised on communal religious-industrial lines. Today the house is a college (tel. 01874-711423) with a museum which includes rare books published by the Connexion press, field pulpits and much else relating to the community.

Llangorse Lake, rather over four miles south of Talgarth by B4560, is some four miles in circumference and, after Bala, the largest natural lake in Wales. Shallow and reedy, and today popular for water sports, the lake is the result of glacial action. It also has the distinction of being the only place in Wales where definite traces have been found (on a crannog-island off the north shore) of prehistoric lake-dwellings, an ancient settlement which may well have been the source of the local legend of a drowned township. The best general view of the lake is from B4560 above the lake's southeast end, the road from here continuing to Bwlch on Rte 25B.

A479, leading south out of Talgarth, now crosses the western slopes of the Black Mountains, representing the eastern extremity of Brecon Beacons National Park. *3m. Pen-y-Genffordd*, above which *Castell Dinas*, originally a hillfort, was later a motte-and-bailey castle complementing Tretower Castle at the foot of the glen. From here a track ascending the south bank of the Rhiangoll stream heads towards (3m) Waun Fach (2660ft), the highest point of the Black Mountains. *Ty Isaf Burial Chamber*, a quarter of a mile east of the road, three quarters of a mile south of Pen-y-Genffordd, is on private land, but the mound and stones can be seen from the lane. The road descends beside the Rhiangoll to (*5m*) *Cwm-Du*, where the church has a late 14C tower, a sanctuary arch (though none to the choir), a curious small porch towards the south, and (south exterior) an early inscribed stone.

   2m. **Tretower** is an Usk valley village known for its medieval manor and, adjacent, ruined Norman castle (both Cadw; see p. 11).

   •Tretower Court, entered through a gatehouse and an exceptionally complete and picturesque example of a late medieval manor house, was the seat of the Vaughans. The oldest part, the stonework on the north, is 14C, and the woodwork is possibly 15C, a time when Sir Roger Vaughan made extensive alterations, but preserving the house's earlier character. The wall-walk, originally a defensive structure, was given its roof and windows during the 17C. For today's visitor the outstanding features are the rich oak woodwork, well seen in the spacious empty rooms, and the unusually generous provision of garderobes. A medieval garden is being created. *Tretower Castle*, Norman-built early in the 12C, was, with Castell Dinas at the head of the Rhiangoll glen, intended to guard this pass against the incursions of the unconquered Welsh. Nevertheless it was successfully besieged by Llewelyn the Last and was partly destroyed by Owen Glendower in 1403, after which it seems to have been abandoned. The layout—a massive cylindrical tower of about 1235 planted within the enclosure of an earlier (mid 12C) square keep, which had been partially demolished—is unusual if not unique. The large ward, on the east, now encloses a farmyard.

   1m. Junction with Rte 25B, the onward road now being A40 along which, on the left in about another mile, at the entrance to the Manor Hotel and with a good information board, is *Gwernvale Chambered Tomb. 1m.* **Crickhowell** (*Inf.*) takes its name from the hillfort of Hywel on the hill known as Table Mountain a mile to the north. Worth noting on the way through the small town are, on the west of the road at the north entrance to the town, the picturesque 15C gateway of a now vanished mansion of the Herberts; the *Church* of the 14C, with a shingle spire unusual in Wales; and the motte and two shattered towers of the Norman *Castle*. The river Usk, to the west, is spanned by a medieval bridge of 13 arches.

Beyond Llangattock, across the river, the westward road in a mile and a half (first cattle grid) reaches *Craig-y-Cilau Nature Reserve*. Access is by a track from the grid, a path then running the length of the reserve (1¼m) below the 400ft escarpment. The reserve (157 acres) is one of the best botanical sites in the Brecon Beacons National Park, with over 250 recorded species, and is also known to be the breeding place of some 49 kinds of bird. The reserve also includes entrances to a cave system of about 12 miles, but access is only for members of approved clubs.

On the east side of A40, a mile south of Crickhowell and just behind the wall of a military establishment, there is a fine standing stone. Approaching Abergavenny, a steep and narrow road (National Trust sign) climbs up on to the *Sugar Loaf* (1955ft), a National Trust property of 2130 acres given in 1936 by Viscountess Rhondda. From a car park there is an easy upland walk of about a mile and a half to the highest point. *5m.* **Abergavenny**, see Rte 28.

B.   Via Brecon and Tretower

B4520 to Brecon. A40 to Abergavenny. Total distance 33m.—*5m. Mynydd Epynt watershed.*—*10m.* **Brecon**. *8m.* **Bwlch**.—*3m.* **Tretower**.—*7m.* **Abergavenny**.

From **Builth Wells** (see Rte 23A) B4520 climbs across the open upland of *Mynydd Epynt*, with Ministry of Defence ranges to the west. *5m.* From the watershed (1560ft), with a road across to Garth on Rte 24, the east edge of the ranges is skirted before the descent into the valley of the Honddu. *8m. Llandefaelog Fach*, where the church preserves a 10C Celtic cross-slab bearing the name and figure of one Briamail. *2m.* **Brecon**, see Rte 26A.

A40 is now followed southeast to reach, in *3m, Llanhamlach* where the church, although rebuilt, still houses an unusually well-preserved effigy of a lady, a 10–11C slab representing the Crucifixion, and, in the north porch, several graveslabs showing the floreated cross motif (see Rte 26A, Brecon Cathedral). Just beyond, *Ty Illtyd* (a quarter of a mile east, by foot, of the junction with minor road to Pennorth) is a prehistoric long cairn with a well-preserved mound containing a small chamber and capstone. The

Llangynidr Bridge over the river Usk

carved crosses on the capstone supports are medieval. *3m. Llansantffraid*, with, in the churchyard near the east wall, the tomb of Henry Vaughan (1622–95), self-styled the 'Silurist' (the Silures were the early tribe of this district), born at Seethog, a mile and a half farther on. The tomb bears the Vaughan crest of three heads, said to recall the birth in c 1100 of Vaughan triplets who survived despite some umbilical strangulation. Henry Vaughan was himself a twin. For *Talybont Reservoir*, two miles southwest, and beyond, see end of Rte 26B. *2m.* **Bwlch**, half a mile northwest of which (off B4560) is *Castell Blaenllynfi*, the fragmentary remains of a Norman castle of the De Braose family. *Llangynidr Bridge*, a mile south below Bwlch, is a particularly attractive four-arch bridge across a lovely stretch of the Usk.

The road now drops, rounding the wooded hill of Myarth, passing (*3m*) **Tretower** (see Rte 25A), plainly seen immediately east, and, just beyond, reaching the junction with A479. For Tretower to (*7m*) **Abergavenny** see Rte 25A.

26

Brecon and the Brecon Beacons

This Route, in two parts, first describes the city of Brecon, together with the Roman fort of Y Gaer, three miles to the west. The second part covers the Brecon Beacons, with Talybont and Taf Fechan forests, and suggests a motor circuit around the area.

A. Brecon

BRECON (*Inf.* Cattle Market Car Park. Tel. 01874-622485), in Welsh Aber-honddu, sprawls over raised ground north of the river Usk at its junction with the Honddu and the Tarell. Of ancient origin, the town is visited largely for its interesting 13–14C cathedral, and also as a base for touring the Brecon Beacons and the national park of the same name.

History. The Romans were here (at Y Gaer, three miles west) in about 75, and in the 5C, after the Roman departure, the Brecon area was controlled by the chieftain Brychan, from whom it derives its name. During the reign of William II, at the close of the 11C, the Norman Bernard of Newmarch built his castle here, and it was around this that the town began to grow, gaining its first charter, from Humphrey de Bohun, Earl of Hereford, in 1276. Brecon was besieged by Llewelyn the Last in 1282, and later the neighbourhood suffered raids by Owen Glendower, but by the 15C the town had developed a considerable cloth trade. During the Civil War Brecon's attitude was unequivocally neutral, the citizens even demonstrating this by demolishing the town walls and much of the castle.

Among natives of Brecon were Sir David Gam (fell at Agincourt, 1415), supposed to have been the original of Shakespeare's Fluellen; Dr Hugh Price (1495–1574), founder of Jesus College, Oxford; Dr Thomas Coke (1747–1814), founder of the American Methodist Episcopalian Church; Mrs Sarah Siddons (1755–1831), the actress, and her brother, the actor Charles Kemble (1775–1854). Henry Vaughan (1622–95), the 'Silurist', worked here as a physician for some years.

St. Mary's Church, at the town centre, has a 16C tower and a nave arcade which retains a single fluted Norman capital on the north side. Adjacent, the *Sarah Siddons Inn* was the birthplace of the actress in 1755 (it was at that time the 'Shoulder of Mutton'), and the actor Owen Nares died here in 1943, while, as a third theatrical link, it was in the *Roman Catholic Church* in Glamorgan Street that the opera singer Adelina Patti married Baron Cedarström, her third husband, in 1898.

Brecon has two museums. In the town centre, within the angle of Glamorgan Street and Captain's Walk, the **Brecknock Museum** (Mon–Sat, and also Sun in summer, 10.00–13.00, 14.00–17.00. Tel. 01874-624121) is a district museum concerned largely with the county of Brecknock or Breconshire and covering a wide field including archaeology, history, natural history, country life and much else. From here, Captain's Walk, descending towards the Usk and passing some remains of the old town wall, is said to have been a favourite promenade for French officers interned at Brecon during the Napoleonic wars. The other museum, farther east alongside barracks, is the *South Wales Borderers Regimental Museum* (Mon–Sat, or Mon–Fri in Oct–March, 09.00–17.00. Tel. 01874-623111. Ext. 2310), covering 300 years of the history of the South Wales Borderers and the Royal Regiment of Wales.

The ***Cathedral**, or the Priory Church of St. John the Evangelist, stands on high ground above the Honddu.

History. The priory was founded, very probably on the site of an earlier church, by Bernard of Newmarch at the close of the 11C as a cell of the Benedictine monastery of Battle in Sussex, an association recalled by a village called Battle three miles northwest. Giraldus was Archdeacon of Brecon in c 1172, but of the early church of this Norman period little remains other than parts of the nave walls immediately west of the crossing. The choir and transepts were entirely rebuilt in the first half of the 13C, the tower being added at the same time; and during the 14C the nave, together with the north and south aisles, was newly built and the east chapels of the transepts were reconstructed to a larger scale. The church was restored in 1862–65 by Sir Gilbert Scott.

In 1923 the church was promoted to be cathedral of the dioceses of Swansea and Brecon, and in 1927 such parts of the priory domestic buildings as had survived the Reformation were restored by W.D. Caröe and rededicated for cathedral chapter use.

The NAVE is normally entered by the northwest porch, above which is an upper chamber. The present beautiful vista up the whole length of the church was before the Reformation broken by a rood screen, reached by the still remaining staircases west of the crossing. The screen divided the church into two, the east part being for the monks and the west serving as parish church; above the screen was suspended a great rood, the Crog (Cross) Aberhonddu, of miraculous virtue, which gave the church its third title, Church of the Holy Rood, and which is celebrated by the Welsh bards of the 15C. At the west end of the nave are a Norman font; a remarkable stone cresset with 30 cups, unique in Wales and the largest found in Britain; a stone thought to have been used by archers for sharpening their arrows; and several sepulchral slabs, notable for their retention as late as the 17C of the medieval floreated cross, a practice common in this neighbourhood though rare elsewhere. Similar slabs will be found in other parts of the cathedral. The *North Aisle*, the former Chapel of the Corvisors (shoemakers) and Tailors, has a 14C tomb-niche and recumbent effigy; an old parclose screen; a dormer window portraying three early Welsh saints,

Cynog, Brychan, and Alud; and a case of old religious books, including a rare breeches-bible (this word used instead of fig leaf, for the covering of Adam and Eve). In the *South Aisle*, the former Chapel of the Weavers and Tuckers, are the tombs of Sir David Williams (died 1613) and his wife Elizabeth Vaughan; the wooden effigy of a lady (c 1555), the only surviving figure from a tomb made up of three tiers of oak beds; and, at the west end, a medieval cope chest. The *North Transept* was known formerly as the Chapel of the Men of Battle, and the *South Transept* as that of the Red Haired Men (the Normans).

The *CHOIR, the vaulting of which was first completed by Gilbert Scott, contains the most beautiful work in the cathedral. The east window, of five large lancets, completely fills the wall space, while at the sides are graduated triplets; the full effect of those on the north, however, is impaired by the later (14C) blocking of their lower parts. Also worth noting are the 13C sedilia; the rare triple piscina; and the sepulchral slab on the north wall of the sanctuary, with a curious carving of the Crucifixion. The reredos (W.D. Caröe, 1937) has figures of saints and others in relief. Archways at the west end of the choir open into the transept chapels on either side. In the *Havard Chapel* (N), with a 14C doorway to the sanctuary combined with a squint, is the tomb of Walter Awbrey (?1312), with an inscription in old Saxon and Norman French characters. Here also are four old benches (two now cut down for footstools) that formerly took the place of fixed altar rails at the celebration of Holy Communion. This is now the regimental chapel (1961) of the South Wales Borderers. The *Chapel of St. Lawrence* (S), after lying in ruins for 300 years, was rebuilt by Caröe in 1930; it contains a small 13C piscina.

The domestic buildings of the priory, after serving as stables etc. for three centuries, were skilfully fitted up by Caröe as the canonry, deanery, and chapter house. On the steep bank of the Honddu above the church are the pleasant *Groves*, a public park, once a retreat of Henry Vaughan.

There are two **Castles** (no adm.), between the cathedral and the Usk bridge. The main ruin, in the grounds of the Castle Hotel, dates from a reconstruction during the reign of Edward I and consists of one side of the Great Hall and of the *Ely Tower*. It was in this tower that in 1483 the Duke of Buckingham, a lord of Brecknock, held prisoner Morton, Bishop of Ely, who had been arrested on the accession of Richard III. Morton succeeded in persuading his gaoler to rebel, but the venture failed and Buckingham was executed though Morton escaped, to become, under Henry VII, Archbishop of Canterbury, Lord Chancellor and Cardinal. On the rise opposite the hotel are the motte and part of the bailey of Bernard of Newmarch's original 11C castle, still with fragments of keep and gatehouse (see also Y Gaer below).

The remains of the Roman fort of **Y Gaer**, three miles west of Brecon, can be reached on foot by the track of the Roman road south of the now disused railway. By car, the Cradoc road is taken west out of the town, this road running below the hill of *Pen-y-Crug* (1088ft) with a hillfort. At Cradoc the left fork (signed Aberyscir) passes, on the left by the railway bridge, a 13ft-high standing stone and soon reaches a small crossroads, the left turn from which leads to a farm where permission to park and visit Y Gaer should be asked. Probably known to the Romans as Cicutium, the fort occupies a site bounded on the south by the Usk, on the west by the Yscir stream, and on the other sides by a ditch. It was first built in c 75 at the time of the final Roman conquest of Wales, rebuilt in c 105 and again in c 140, and finally abandoned in c 290, among the garrisons having been the Vettonian

Spanish cavalry and the 2nd Legion. Some eight centuries later, much of what remained of the masonry was used by Bernard of Newmarch in the construction of his castle at Brecon. Excavated by Sir Mortimer Wheeler in 1924–25, most of what was exposed was later covered, but the outer face of the north wall, in good condition and up to 10ft high, can be seen; and the other walls, with the usual rounded angles, and something of the north, east and especially west gates can be traced. The village of *Battle*, a mile north of the fort, recalls that Brecon priory, later to become the cathedral, was originally a cell of Battle Abbey in Sussex. Dr Thomas Coke (see History, above) is buried here.

For Brecon to (N) *Builth Wells* and (S) *Abergavenny*, see Rte 25B; to *Aberaeron*, see Rte 27; to (E) *Hay-on-Wye* and (W) *Swansea*, see Rte 33; to *Merthyr Tydfil*, see Rte 26B below.

B. Brecon Beacons. Talybont and Taf Fechan Forests

Together the Brecon Beacons with Talybont and Taf Fechan forests make up a splendid area of mountain, forest, moor and water, bounded on the west by A470 (Brecon to Merthyr Tydfil, see below), on the south by A465 (Merthyr Tydfil to Abergavenny, see Rte 31), and on the east by A40 (Brecon to Abergavenny, see Rte 25B). There is a network of walks, and a Motor Circuit, suggested below, takes in much of the best of the scenery.

The BRECON BEACONS, which are only one relatively small part of Brecon Beacons National Park, fill much of the park's central area. The Beacons themselves—given, with over 6000 surrounding acres, to the National Trust in 1965 by Sir Brian Mountain—have two principal summits, barely half a mile apart, these being *Pen y Fan* (N, 2907ft) and *Corn Ddu* (S, 2863ft), a distinctinve pair of sandstone peaks facing sharply north and on this side broken by cwms. Southward the slopes are for the most part gentle, while a range extending east in nearly a mile reaches the lesser peak of *Cribyn* (2608ft). Continuing east from Cribyn the ridge is broken by *The Gap*, a col between the north–south ridges of Bryn Teg and Cefn Cyff across which runs the track which may once have been a Roman road and which later, until the 19C, became the main link between Brecon and Merthyr Tydfil.

The Beacons are very popular with walkers, being crossed by several recognised routes which, because of the relative compactness of the area, can be combined as wished. (Information from Brecon Tourist Information; or the Mountain Centre (see below); or, by post, with a large stamped addressed envelope, National Park Office, 7 Glamorgan Street, Brecon LD3 7DP.)

Talybont and **Taf Fechan forests**, with their long narrow reservoirs of the same names and, on the lower southeast slopes of the Beacons, the two beautifully situated *Neuadd Reservoirs*, angle as valleys across the middle of the area. The valleys, which are water catchment zones, were first planted by the Forestry Commission in 1937; large scale planting of conifers started in 1945, but the earlier oak, ash and other trees have been preserved. A number of car parks and picnic sites have been provided. Information from Garwnant Visitor Centre (see below).

MOTOR CIRCUIT FROM BRECON (37 miles). The first objective (*6m.*) is the National Park's **Mountain Centre** (named for Sir Brian Mountain. Daily 09.30–17.00 or 16.30 in Nov–Feb. Tel. 01874-623366), at 1000ft on the upland **Mynydd Illtyd Common** in the southwest angle between A40 and A470. The main access, suitable for larger vehicles, is by a minor road from Libanus on A470. A more leisurely approach is by way of a minor road (sign) off A40 just beyond the roundabout on the west outskirts of Brecon. Ascending on to the common, this latter approach passes (half a mile north from a road fork two and a half miles from the A40 roundabout) the earthworks of the hillfort *Twyn y Gaer*, with, to its east and south, mounds which are probably Bronze Age burial cairns. In another mile, after passing a pond, there is a small standing stone on the left, probably an ancient route marker since a line projected southwest from here hits two similar stones at the edge of the common. About 200 yards farther, by another little pond, *Bedd Illtyd*, now no more than two stones in a hollow, is nevertheless by local tradition the grave of St. Illtyd (born 425), founder of the monastery at Llantwit Major. Beyond, a left turn passes now disused *Illtyd Church*, built in 1858 on a site the circular shape of which suggests a very early Celtic foundation, possibly by Illtyd. The *Mountain Centre*, a quarter of a mile farther and with fine views, offers National Park information, café, picnic facilities etc. Across the west section of the common can be traced a length of the Roman *Sarn Helen*; and, by contrast, the underground oil pipeline from Milford Haven to the Midlands (1972) crosses the common.

A road from the Mountain Centre drops in under *2m* to *Libanus* on A470 which, ascending the valley of the Tarell and rounding the west flank of the Beacons, in *3m* reaches the nature reserve of *Craig Cerrig-Gleisiad* (Countryside Council for Wales. National Park picnic site), a 698 acre glaciated area of crags, gullies and mountain streams rising from 1200 to 2000ft. Here, more than 300 plant and 60 bird species have been recorded, some of which may be seen from the footpath (permit necessary for other access) which skirts much of the reserve's boundary. *1m*. The watershed is at 1440ft, just beyond being the Outdoor Education Centre *Storey Arms*, near which start the Y Gyrn and Pont ar Daf ascents to the Beacons' summits.

A470 now drops with the valley of the Taff, passing plantations and, in succession, Beacons, Cantref and Llwyn-On reservoirs, all providing water for Cardiff. Overlooking the north end of this last reservoir is *Garwnant Visitor Centre* (FE. Easter–Sept: Mon–Fri 10.30–16.45 or 18.00 on Wed and Thurs in July and Aug; Sat and Sun 14.00–16.00 or 18.00 in July and Aug. Tel. 01685-723060), with walks, picnic and play areas and providing information on the forests of the Brecon Beacons, Talybont and Taf Fechan.

In *8m.* (from Storey Arms) a major crossing with A465 (for Merthyr Tydfil, see Rte 31) is reached. Here, this Route follows a minor road northeast, this in rather over a mile passing below a crag on top of which are the scanty fragments—traces of two round towers, a vaulted basement and a deep pit, this last unfenced and dangerous—of late 13C *Morlais Castle*. The minor road continues northeast through increasingly wooded scenery (for the nearby Brecon Mountain Railway, see Rte 31, Merthyr Tydfil) to skirt the western length of first *Pontsticill* and then *Pentwyn* reservoir, in *5m.* (from the A470/A465 crossroads), at the north end of the latter reservoir, bearing right at a fork. Here, however, a short diversion (four miles return) should be made to the *Neuadd Reservoirs*, lying in wood and moorland below the Beacons. Above the east side of these two adjacent waters runs the old road, perhaps Roman in origin, until the 19C the main Brecon to Merthyr road and today, leading through The Gap, one of the most popular walkers' routes across the Beacons.

At *Pont Blaen*-y-*glyn*, less than *2m* beyond the road fork at the north end of Pentwyn reservoir, there are Forest Enterprise picnic sites marking the starting-points of short walks, the Waterfall Walk, though the most strenuous, being the most rewarding. The small road continues north, fringing the west side of *Talybont Reservoir*, two miles long and with a dam at its north end.

5m. Talybont village, whence Brecon can be reached in *6m* by B4558. Alternatively A40 can be joined at *Llansantffraid*, three quarters of a mile northeast.

27

Brecon to Aberaeron

A40 to Llanwrda. A482 to Aberaeron. Total distance 51m.—*9m.* **Senny-bridge.**—*12m.* **Llandovery.**—*4m.* **Llanwrda.**—*7m.* **Dolaucothi.**—*7m.* **Lampeter.**—*12m.* **Aberaeron**.

For **Brecon**, see Rte 26A. *2m. Llanspyddid*, with a 14C church in the graveyard of which a gravestone is reputed to be that of the local 5C chieftain Brychan or of Aulach, his father. *4m. Trallong* where the church houses an Ogham stone of the 5–6C, though its ringed cross may be two or so centuries later. *3m.* **Sennybridge** is a relatively modern place, dating effectively from the arrival here of the railway in 1872, though the slight remains of Castell Ddu just west of the town go back to the 14C and are believed to be on the site of the 11C home of Sir Reginald Aubrey, friend of Bernard of Newmarch. For Sennnybridge to Swansea, see Rte 33. *3m.* **Trecastle**, with a small Norman motte-and-bailey, was at its most prosperous during the coaching years of the 18 and 19C. But, many centuries earlier, both prehistoric people and, later, the Romans were active around here. Minor roads wandering west out of Trecastle in three miles reach the long wooded *Usk Reservoir*, a sheet of water unknown of course to the peoples who over millennia erected the several cairns, tumuli, lone megaliths and stone circles which survive around the lake. As to the Romans, they are represented by traces of a road running northwest from Trecastle (half a mile south of and roughly parallel to A40) to reach in four miles (of which the first two are motorable) the camps of *Y Pigwn*, earthworks thrown up in the early years of the Roman occupation, in perhaps 50 to 80, on a site only a few yards west of already ancient stone circles.

1m. Llywel, where, in the church, the Llywel Stone (a cast of the original now in the British Museum) is particularly interesting for bearing carving of three early periods. The Ogham probably dates from at latest the 5C; the Latin commemorates one Maccutrenus Salicidunus, believed to have been a local man of c 500; and a small cross between the two names—possibly carved by some pious descendant to confer belated Christian respectability and salvation on a forebear suspected of being a pagan—is probably of the 7C. Also in this church are another Ogham stone; parts of the 16C rood screen and loft, the latter, removed in 1869, now forming the entrance to the vestry; an ancient font; and the stocks of 1798. At about five and a half miles beyond Llywel, beside the south side of the road, the *Mail Coach Pillar* gives a dramatic warning from the past against driving and drinking. *8m.* (from Llywel) **Llandovery**, see Rte 26. *4m.* (by A40) **Llanwrda**, where A482 is now taken north while A40 continues south as Rte 24.

A482 ascends the Dulais to (*5m.*) *Felin Newydd Watermill* (Easter Sat–Oct: Tues–Sun, but open Bank Hol. Mon. Tours hourly between 10.30 and 17.30 inclusive. Tel. 01558-650375), generally of the 18C, when, despite its name (New Mill), it was last modernised, but successor to others on this site since perhaps the 14C. Alongside the mill are a crafts workshop, tearoom, shop and mill pond.

2m. **Dolaucothi Gold Mines** (NT. April–mid May and mid Sept–Oct: daily 11.00–17.00. Mid May–mid Sept: daily 10.00–18.00. Last adm. one hour before above closing times. Underground guided tours mid May–mid Sept: daily, hourly, or half-hourly in peak season. These tours last one hour, involve some rugged climbing and no children under five are accepted. Tel. 01558-650359). The mines—at the south end of the NT Dolaucothi Estate of 2522 acres, given in 1941–44 by Mr H.T.C. Lloyd-Johnes as a memorial to his family, owners since the time of Henry VII—today include a Visitor Centre and Miners' Way (the latter a self-guided surface trail) which combine to explain the remains of the Roman and other workings which cover some 30 acres. Also here are a shop, refreshments and opportunities for gold panning.

The complex evidence survives in the form of opencast pits, adits and water courses and is witness to the advanced mining technology of the Romans. The Roman mining remains are, however, overlaid with more recent evidence from the 19 and 20C, this including the 500ft shaft sunk in the early 20C and the foundations of the gold processing plant. In fact the mine saw two major exploitation periods between 1888–1910 (Mitchell Mine) and 1933–38 (Roman Deep Holdings. British Goldfields), but on neither occasion did the returns justify the cost, the mine being closed in 1938, British Goldfields dissolved in 1943 and the machinery and buildings then being scrapped. However, working mining machinery from the 1930s, donated to the National Trust, now helps to provide an insight into the more recent industrial heritage of this ancient site. Alongside the site stands an ancient boulder showing five depressions, the story being that five ('pump') saints—hence the name of the nearby village, Pumsaint—rested here and used this boulder as a pillow. Whether or not these five were the same five brothers associated with Llanpumpsaint (Rte 41B) the story does not reveal.

In the village of *Caio*, a mile to the east, a 4C Roman gravestone is built into the wall of the church. The small road passing the mines ascends the valley of the Cothi before dropping into that of the Towy and, in 11 miles from the mines, reaching Llyn Brianne (Rte 24).

Leaving the mines, A482 almost immediately runs through the village of *Pumsaint* (Five Saints), on the site of the Roman settlement busy with the exploitation of the mines (nothing visible today, though traces of baths have been excavated and covered), and then in another mile reaches a small northward road (to Ffarmers) which marks the line of the Roman Sarn Helen. *7m.* **Lampeter** on Rte 41B which is crossed here. Leaving Lampeter, A482 rises for four miles before dropping into the rich Vale of Aeron. *12m.* **Aberaeron**, see Rte 41A.

28

Abergavenny to Skenfrith and Grosmont

B4521 and B4347. Total distance 16m.—*5m.* **White Castle.**—*6m.* **Skenfrith.**—*5m.* **Grosmont**.

After leaving Abergavenny, the principal objectives are the three castles—White, Skenfrith and Grosmont—all in 1201 granted by King John to Hubert de Burgh and becoming known as the Welsh Trilateral. Except for 1205–19, when the castles fell into the hands of William de Braose and his son, the Trilateral continued to be held by Hubert de Burgh until his fall from favour in 1232 when the castles reverted to the Crown. All three castles are probably of early Norman origin, and all have adjacent churches of some interest.

Abergavenny (*Inf;* local and national park), a place of Roman and Norman origin, is today a busy centre at the confluence of the Usk and the Gavenny.

History. The town's origins go back to the modest Roman fort of Gobannium, one of those protecting their road up the Usk, but real civic development grew from the settlement which clustered below the Norman stronghold built by Hameline de Balun (1085–1138). This castle later came into the hands of the notorious William de Braose who at Christmas 1176, in revenge for the killing of his uncle by the Welsh, here murdered many of the Welsh lords of Gwent whom he had invited as his guests. The town was sacked by Owen Glendower in 1404, and again by Parliament (by Fairfax) in 1646, but Royalist Jacobite sentiment survived and, in 1688, the town demonstrated in favour of James II and against William III, the result being that its charter (granted 1639) was suspended.

The two principal places of interest, close to one another in the southern part of the town, are the large Church of St. Mary with its many fine monuments, and the slight remains of the castle, the home today of the town and district museum.

The *Church of St. Mary* was formerly the chapel of a small Benedictine priory, founded by Hameline de Balun as a cell of the abbey of St. Vincent at Le Mans in France. Of this, though, nothing remains, today's church, apart from the mainly modern nave, being largely of the 14C. The choir lost its clerestory and received the present lath-and-plaster groining during early 19C restoration. The *Monuments, spanning from the 13 to the 17C, combine as an outstanding series. First, in the south or Herbert Chapel, there are the recumbent effigies of the Herbert, Cantelupe and Hastings families, in the centre being Sir William ap Thomas (died 1446), father of the 1st Earl of Pembroke of the Herbert line, and of his wife. Here too is what is thought to be a 14C Herbert graveslab, found in 1961 buried in the churchyard. In the nave there is a fine wooden figure of George de Cantelupe, Baron Bergavenny (died 1273), and in the north or Lewis Chapel are effigies of Eva de Braose (died 1246) and of Eva de Cantelupe (died 1257), this latter (sometimes said to be Christina Herbert, died 1307) being a rare example of a figure of a woman with a shield. The monument of Dr David Lewis (died 1584), the first Principal of Jesus College, Oxford, was erected by himself, while the large 15C wooden recumbent figure evidently formed the root of a Tree of Jesse, probably once part of the reredos of the high altar.

Noteworthy in the choir are the old stalls, with latticed backs, and the seats for the prior and sub-prior beneath tall tabernacled canopies, mostly probably dating from the late 14C; on the north floor, a small brass to the Stephens (father and son), bearing an intriguing rhyming epitaph; and the font with a Norman bowl and ropework carving.

The slight remains of *Abergavenny Castle* are a short distance southwest. Of Hameline de Balun's early stronghold only the motte and the roughly pentagonal bailey remain, and of the later stonework defences, which were incorporated with the town walls, all that is left is part of the northwest curtain wall, with the ruins of the entrance gate and two mural towers. *Abergavenny Museum* (March–Oct: Mon–Sat 11.00–13.00, 14.00–17.00; Sun 14.00–17.00. Nov–Feb: Mon–Sat 11.00–13.00, 14.00–16.00. Tel. 01873-854282), housed in a Regency hunting lodge within the castle precincts, presents the town's story from prehistoric through Roman to modern times, two of the principal features being a Victorian farmhouse kitchen and a saddler's workshop. Abergavenny also has a second museum, the *Museum of Childhood and Home* (Mon–Sat 10.00–17.00, Sun 13.00–17.00. Tel. 01873-850063) in Market Street, one of the largest of its kind in Wales and showing bygones mainly of the mid 19 to mid 20C.

Blorenge (2½m SW. 1834ft) is capped by mountain limestone and known for its sink or swallow holes. A road leads to close to the summit where there are car parks, one of which, called Foxhunter, was presented by Colonel Llewellyn in memory of his champion horse (died 1959), buried near here. Foxhunter represented Britain 35 times and had 78 international wins.

For *Sugar Loaf* (2½m N), see Rte 25A.

For Abergavenny to *Raglan* and *Monmouth*, see Rte 29; to *Newport*, see Rte 30; to *Merthyr Tydfil*, *Neath* and *Swansea*, see Rte 31.

Leaving the town, B4521 runs across the south slopes of *Skirrid Fawr* (or Ysgyryd. 1596ft), 205 acres of the summit of which are National Trust property given by Major Jack Herbert in 1939. More than just a mountain, Skirrid Fawr is also a place of both legend and, for long, of religious significance. The cliffs on the west side, for instance, are popularly attributed to an earthquake at the time of the Crucifixion and, presumably because of this, the mountain early became treated as a holy place and, at times of persecution, Roman Catholics climbed to the summit to celebrate mass at St. Michael's Chapel, today little more than a hollow in the ground. From a small car park, a path climbs to the site of the chapel (under three miles return).

5m (beyond *Llanvetherine*), a small road leads south to the ruins of **White Castle** (Cadw; see p. 11), of two distinct 12C and 13C periods and once covered by white plaster. The general plan of the castle is a large outer ward to the north; an inner ward protected by a curtain and moat; and to the south a defensive hornwork, also protected by a moat.

History. Earthworks here are evidence of early Norman or other border fortification, but the present stone remains are of a 12C and 13C castle originally known as Llantilio, the title of the local manor, but in the 13C changing its name when its walls were coated with white plaster. In 1201 King John granted White, together with Skenfrith and Grosmont, to Hubert de Burgh, the three then forming what came to be called the Welsh Trilateral (see introduction to this Rte). In c 1263, at the time of the threat from Llewelyn the Last, White Castle, now owned by Henry III, was refortified, a major undertaking which included the transfer of the main entrance from the south to the north. After the subjugation of Wales by Edward I, White sank to become little more than an administrative centre, and already by the 16C it was roofless and abandoned.

The visitor enters the castle through the *Outer Gatehouse*, an addition (on the east side of the outer ward) of the 13C refortification. This structure was essentially a broad rectangular passage with gates at both ends; the portcullis groove can be seen by the outer gate, and the modern bridge crosses the pit formerly covered by the drawbridge. The large *Outer Ward* formed part of the original defences, these surviving today as a bank beyond the ditch (never a real moat and probably always dry) on the north and west. The wall and towers all date from the 13C, the northwest tower being rectangular and believed to have served as offices, possibly of the quartermaster. A recess in the west of the wall was a garderobe. The moat is crossed to the *Inner Ward*, the oldest part of the castle, with walls of the late 12C. The gatehouse and towers, however, represent the 13C refortification, the former of standard pattern with towers of four storeys flanking the passage; the portcullis groove can be found.

Inside the ward, only the outlines of the rooms survive. The Hall, with its kitchen on the opposite side of the ward, was against the northeast wall, the outer foundations representing the original 12C hall (a tall building which probably rose higher than the wall), and the inner foundations the successor hall known to have been built in 1244. South of the hall are the well and the east tower, with, beyond, the Constable's Solar and, south again, the latrine pit. The Chapel occupies the southeast corner of the ward, the choir being provided by the southeast tower, while the nave projected into the ward. The base course of the south of the ward, the oldest masonry of the castle (early 12C), is all that is left of the original small keep; only the inner part survives, the remainder being cut by a section of 13C wall linking the southeast and southwest towers. This was the site of the castle's main entrance prior to the refortification, the entrance being protected by the moat and the *Hornwork* beyond. Although a length of 13C wall crosses to the hornwork, it does not seem that this latter was ever given any stonework defences.

The village of **Llantilio Crosseny**, a mile and a half southeast, has an ancient and attractive origin. In 556 this was the land of a chief called Ynyr who, when threatened by pagan Saxons, appealed for help to St. Teilo. Teilo responded with prayer, Ynyr set up a large wooden cross and the Saxons were defeated. In gratitude Ynyr gave land to Teilo for the founding of a church, and hence the village's name, meaning Holy Enclosure of Teilo at the Cross of Ynyr.

The *Church* here, successor to several since 556, is mainly of the 12 and 13C. Originally cruciform, the church's north transept was absorbed by a 14C chapel (Cil Llwch, see below) and a clerestory was added in the 15C. The nave was originally considerably lower, as indicated by the low arches at the crossing, and the present structure (Perpendicular in style) is of the 15C. In the north aisle the main windows are modern restoration, but the small window of two lights at the east end, revealed during this restoration, is 16C. It carries the arms of two men thought to have been local manorial lords; a Herbert beheaded after the Battle of Banbury in 1469 during the Wars of the Roses (see also Raglan Castle, Rte 29), and Sir David Gam, killed at Agincourt in 1415 and said to have been the model for Shakespeare's Fluellen ('Davey Gam'). Steps in the wall of the tower, facing the nave, led to the now vanished rood loft. On the west pier of the central crossing arch, will be found a 'Green Man' with foliage coming out of his nostrils, an attractive reminder of the way in which a cautious Christianity adapted what had been a pagan fertility symbol into one of new life and resurrection. In the choir, some of the floor slabs are especially noteworthy, a particularly pleasing one being that of a father, mother, and three sons. There is also (north wall) a marble relief by Flaxman of Mary Ann Bosanquet (died 1819). The Cil Llwch Chapel, the former north transept, derives its name from a medieval manor, now Great Hillborough Farm, a mile southwest. Points of interest are the squints, suggesting that the chapel proper may have been private to the manorial family; and, either side of the altar, stone brackets in the shape of youths' heads, these representing, according to one local tradition, the murdered Princes in the Tower.

6m. **Skenfrith Castle** is an unusually small ruined castle, the main feature being a circular tower near the centre of an irregular four-sided ward.

History. There was almost certainly a Norman motte-and-bailey here, but Skenfrith as seen today (one of the Welsh Trilateral, see introduction to this Rte) was largely built by Hubert de Burgh, probably between 1229 and his fall from favour in 1232, and thereafter by the Crown to whom the castle reverted. The west tower seems to have been added in about 1263, at the time when Llewelyn the Last was threatening, but by the 16C Skenfrith was roofless and abandoned. The last Governor of the Trilateral (John Morgan, died 1557) lies in Skenfrith church.

The entrance is through what little remains of the Gatehouse in the north wall. Within the ward, the mound on which the Round Tower (completed by c 1244) stands is not, as might be thought, a survival of an early Norman motte, but a mound built from spoil from the moat and designed to give the tower sufficient height to enable defenders to fire beyond the curtain wall. The tower is of three levels, and it is interesting that there is no communication between ground and first floor, each having its individual entrance, while the second floor and the roof were reached by a stair, partly in the west wall and partly in a turret. The West Range of buildings was revealed by excavation in 1954. The central room here, reached by shallow steps, is divided from the north room by a wall, but it seems probable that the two were originally one; features are a blocked fireplace (perhaps blocked when it was found that flooding made these rooms unusable), and, at the south end, a recess which may represent the site of a stair to a floor above. It seems that virtually no East Range was built, though the kitchens were probably between the Round Tower and the east curtain.

Skenfrith Church. Although there was almost certainly an earlier church on this site, the present one is largely of the 13C, but with aisles which may be up to 200 years later. The church is dedicated to St. Bridget, and the ancient carving of the head of a nun over the porch is reputed to represent her. The tower is semi-defended, with thick walls, this and the upper storeroom suggesting its role as a refuge. In the north aisle is the *Altar-tomb of John Morgan (died 1557), last Governor of the Trilateral, and of his wife (died 1564), his four sons and his four daughters; the tomb is remarkable for its detail of the dress of the period. The church's stone altar is its original one of 1207; thrown down at the Reformation, it served as floor paving for several years until, comparatively recently, replaced as altar on new supports. The slab bears some small cut consecration crosses (e.g. front left corner). The front of the reading desk in the choir incorporates a part of the medieval rood-screen.

The village of **Grosmont**, also with its castle and church, is *5m* northwest of Skenfrith and reached by B4347. *Grosmont Castle*, on a hill as indicated by its Norman name, is the third and northernmost of the Welsh Trilateral (see introduction to this Rte). After reverting to the Crown in 1232, the castle was in the following year besieged by Llewelyn the Great, but saved by the timely approach of Henry III; and in 1402 it was again invested, this time by Owen Glendower who, however, was driven off by the future Henry V. Mostly of the early 13C, but with some 14C additions on the north, Grosmont is a rather fragmentary survival, the most interesting feature, perhaps, being the ruin of the Hall (c 1210), to the right on entering the castle; untypically large, it is also curious for being on the outer side of the later curtain of 1220–40.

In Grosmont *Church*, mostly 13C, noteworthy features are the late Norman arches of the nave, the Norman font, the Early English arcading in the choir, and the Decorated piscina. The church is associated with the enigmatic John Kent (fl. 1400), said to be buried here, also known as John of Kentchurch (Kentchurch Court, a mile northeast in England, was the estate of the Scudamores, one of whom married one of Owen Glendower's daughters). A bard—he enjoyed the patronage of the Scudamores who sent him to study at Oxford, afterwards giving him the living of Kentchurch—he became the focus of many stories; that he was a magician, that he lived to be 120, and that (presumably arising from the Scudamore marriage link) he was Owen Glendower in hiding. The large figure in the southeast of the nave is popularly thought to represent this John Kent.

29

Abergavenny to Raglan and Monmouth

A40. Total distance 16m.—*9m*. **Raglan Castle**.—*7m*. **Monmouth**.

From **Abergavenny** (see Rte 28), A40 briefly descends the valley of the Usk, with the heights of Blorenge to the west, in *6m*. passing the northern edge of the National Trust *Clytha* estate, with a riverside picnic area and waymarked walks. Clytha Castle, a 19C folly, is leased for holiday accommodation.

3m. **Raglan Castle** (Cadw; see p. 11), a stark and striking ruin on a knoll, interestingly combines medieval defensive requirements with the ever pressing demands of manorial elegance and comfort. Built mainly in the 15C and 16C the castle represents the last, though not the least impressive, example of medieval fortification in Britain.

History. The original motte, on which the Great Tower now stands, was raised by William FitzOsbern after the Norman conquest of Gwent in 1067–71. The present castle was started by Sir William ap Thomas, who had been knighted by Henry VI and made Steward of Usk and Caerleon. He built the Great Tower (c 1430–45), and probably also the south gate. His son was William Herbert, Earl of Pembroke, a leading Yorkist who helped to put Edward IV on the throne but was later (1496) defeated in battle and beheaded. It was he who completed the greater part of the present buildings. Later the property passed to the earls of Worcester, the 3rd Earl (William Somerset) between 1548-89 rebuilding the hall and enlarging the Pitched Stone Court to a mainly domestic pattern. In the Civil War Raglan, a principal Royalist centre, was defended for 11 weeks in 1646 against Fairfax by the 5th Earl, aged 84. The castle's fall in August marked the end of the first phase of the Civil War, Raglan later being slighted. At the Restoration the ruins were returned to the 6th Earl. Today Cadw provides a historical exhibition.

Approaching the *Gatehouse* the gargoyles above and the heraldic stone-work to the left are worth notice. Although this gatehouse was protected by a drawbridge and two portcullises, everything beyond, except for the Great Tower, is residential building in which the fine doorway arches and windows are pleasing features. Beyond the gatehouse the *Pitched Stone Court* is crossed to the *Kitchen* (north corner of castle) containing two large double fireplaces. To the left of the kitchen is the *Pantry*, and the rooms lining the west side of the court are the *Buttery* and the *Great Hall*, the latter with a fine oriel window. From the hall stairs descend to the huge cellars. On the west of the hall are the slight remains of the *Chapel*. The hall and chapel divide the Pitched Stone Court from the *Fountain Court*, occupying the site of the early Norman bailey. In the northwest corner the *Grand Staircase* ascended to living apartments, while at the southwest corner of the court a gateway leads to the *Bowling Green*, from where steps descend to the *Moat Walk*, with niches (late 16C) which once held statues of Roman emperors. The *Great Tower*, reached from Fountain Court, is a hexagonal detached keep, surrounded by a moat and designed as a self-contained last point of defence. One side was blown up by Fairfax, but the stairway to the top remains.

7m. **Monmouth**, see Rte 34.

30

Abergavenny to Newport

A. Via Usk and Caerleon

B4598 to Usk. B4596 to Caerleon. B4236 to Newport. Total distance 20m.— *11m.* **Usk.**—*7m.* **Caerleon.**—*2m.* **Newport.**

Running at first southeast, then, after crossing A40, due south, B4598 in a little under *7m* for the second time crosses the Usk. At *Bettws Newydd*, a mile northeast of this bridge, the church preserves a small but good rood loft, complete with its boarded tympanum, while, just north of the village, the height of *Coed-y-Bwynydd*, also known as Coed Arthur, is a National Trust property of 25 acres (gifted in 1945 by Captain Geoffrey Crawshay in memory of Sergeant Arthur Owen RAF) with a hillfort and affording some good views over the Usk valley.

4m. **Usk** (or Brynbuga), on the east bank of the river of the same name and in part spread over the site of the Roman Burrium, predecessor of Caerleon, is a market town much of which dates from the 18C, though the castle remains and the church span the 12–15C. The small *Castle* (12C;

private), belonging to the De Clares and the earls of March, was taken by Simon de Montfort in 1265; the ruins include the keep (1169–76, but altered in the 15C), a round tower on the 13C curtain, and a gatehouse. The parish *Church* was once that of a Benedictine nunnery (refounded by Richard de Clare, son of 'Strongbow', in 1236), the gatehouse of which survives by the churchyard gate. In the church, the nave is early 13C, but the arches of the crossing, the choir and the tower are of the first half of the 12C. The aisle was added during the 13C, but in the 15C rebuilt to a wider scale, its two quite elaborate porches being additions of the same period. Also worth noting are the large circular stair turret that projects into the aisle; the tall 15C rood screen; and a fine brass inscription of c 1400 in an early Welsh dialect.

This district's rural past lives on at the *Gwent Rural Life Museum* at the Malt Barn, New Market Street (April–Oct: Mon–Fri 10.00–17.00; Sat and Sun 14.00–17.00. Tel. 01291-673777), a museum which is a great deal better than some of its kind and noteworthy for the detail of the explanations. Housed in a 17 or 18C malt barn and an adjoining Victorian cottage, the material includes wagons, agricultural and craft and trade tools, vintage machinery, and, in the cottage, a kitchen, laundry and dairy.

7m ****Caerleon**, now to a great extent a dormitory town for Newport and farther afield, is visited for its Roman past, the four principal objectives, all close to one another, being the Amphitheatre, the Barracks, the Baths and the Legionary Museum (parking at Baths for baths and museum).

History. The Roman fortress, dating from c 75, was called Isca from the name of the river Usk, but to the Welsh this became Caerleon, a corruption of Castra Legionis, the Fort of the Legion. The legion was the 2nd Augustan which came here as a permanent garrison after its subjection of the Silures and remained until late in the 4C. The legion's normal strength was 5–6000 men, at first protected by earthworks and timber but soon, by about 100, living behind sound stone walls. Few fortresses such as this continued in isolation, and a civilian settlement beyond the walls soon began to grow into a town, and it is recorded that a Bishop of Caerleon was present in 314 at the Synod of Arles, the first general council of western Christianity. The bishopric seems to have lasted into the 6C when it is said to have been transferred to St. David's by St. David himself, as foretold by Merlin. It was also during this early post-Roman period (though only on the suspect authority of Geoffrey of Monmouth) that Arthur was both crowned and had his capital here, the Roman amphitheatre becoming known as King Arthur's Round Table. Be this as it may, Tennyson came to Caerleon in search of local colour for his 'Idylls of the King'. In 1188 Giraldus passed this way and enthusiastically described the Roman remains.

The Roman fort and town occupied the area immediately southwest of today's town, between the town and the Usk, access now being by a road opposite the museum. To the left of this road is the amphitheatre (parking) with, to its left, a length of Roman wall (originally a rectangle of c 540 by 450 yards), virtually all that can be seen of their town. To the right of the approach road, a short way along a path, is the site of the Barracks.

The *Amphitheatre* (Cadw; see p. 11), dating from 80 to 100 and with seating for the entire legion of 6000, is a hollowed oval area, surrounded by an earth bank and supported by stone walls. There are eight entrances (all originally vaulted so that no seating space was lost), two of these being for performers and six for spectators, those for the performers being the more elaborate ones at the northeast and southwest, both with traces of a small waiting room and stone benches. At the northwest entrance can be seen the drain which ran the length of the amphitheatre. The *Barracks*. The fort had 64 blocks, originally of wood but of stone from the 2C, these generally arranged in pairs. Of this sytem, the lower course ground plan of four blocks can today be seen.

The *Baths* (Cadw; see p. 11), by the Museum, were discovered only in 1964. Today, excavated and provided with admirable and imaginative visitor facilities, Caerleon's baths rank as the most complete example of their kind in Britain. Started with the first building of the fort in 75, and in use until about 230, the baths—which may be regarded as forerunners of today's leisure centres, and provided with similar exercise, catering and other facilities—were eventually a massive stone complex, the three halls (cold, warm, hot) rising to nearly 50ft and the whole on a scale which has been compared to that of a medieval cathedral.

The *Legionary Museum* (mid March–mid Oct: daily 10.00, or 14.00 on Sun, to 18.00. Mid Oct–mid March: 10.00, or 14.00 on Sun, to 16.30. Tel. 01633-423134), a branch of the National Museum of Wales, was re-opened in 1987 in a new, modern building, only the classical portico surviving from the museum's original home of 1850. Gone, too, is the dreary Victorian display, succeeded by modern lighting and imaginative presentation which together vividly and instructively bring Roman Isca to life, of perhaps particular note, and a practical help to the imagination in peopling the amphitheatre, barracks and baths, being the lifesize figure of an accoutred legionary. The museum shows also material excavated at Burrium, predecessor of Caerleon and covered now by the town of Usk. The church adjacent to the museum stands on the site of the legion's headquarters.

It was at the *Hanbury Arms*, a Tudor inn overlooking the river, that Tennyson stayed while in search of colour for his 'Idylls of the King' (1859). Roughly opposite, in private property surrounded by a wall, can be glimpsed an early Norman motte.

2m. **Newport**, see Rte 35.

B. Via Pontypool

A4042. Total distance 16m.—*10m.* **Pontypool.**—*2m.* **Cwmbran.**—*4m.* **Newport**.

The road skirts the east edge of the South Wales mountains and a main industrial area. It also runs just east of the Monmouthshire and Brecon Canal, dating from 1797–1812, closed to commercial traffic in 1932 and now used for recreational purposes (Tel. 01452-525524, British Waterways).

From **Abergavenny** (see Rte 28), A4042 heads south, with Blorenge high on the west. *10m.* **Pontypool**, today a diversified industrial town, was the home of the Welsh iron industry.

History. The first forge here was in operation as long ago as 1425. The first ironworks followed in 1577, and it is said that the first forge in America (1652) was built by Pontypool emigrants. In 1682 the first rolling mill is thought to have been started here by Thomas Cooke, and in the early 18C Thomas Allgood (died 1716) developed 'Pontypool Japan', a novel and attractive treatment of iron plates by a brilliant and heat-resistant lacquer. In 1829 Pontypool was a Chartist focus, the local leader, William Jones, marching to Newport to help in the assault on the Westgate Hotel; for this he was transported.

One of the town's attractions is Pontypool Park (once the home of the Hanbury family, owners of the local ironworks), the late-Georgian stables of which today house the *Valley Inheritance* (Feb–Dec: Mon–Sat 10.00–17.00; Sun 14.00–17.00. Tel. 01495-752036), where permanent and temporary exhibitions record the social and industrial past of the local Torfaen valley. Canals played a major role in this industrial story and something of this aspect is recalled at *Junction Cottage* (tel. 01452-525524), a canal tollkeeper's cottage of 1814 at the junction of the Monmouthshire and Brecon Canal and the river Lwyd within the north angle of A472 and A4042. *Llandegfedd Reservoir*, two miles east of Pontypool, doubles as a water supply and as a recreational area; picnic sites mark the start of walks.

2m. **Cwmbran** is a 'new town' immediately west of A4042. At *Llantarnam*, beyond the south of the town, a modern abbey stands on the site of a 12C Cistercian predecessor, a gateway of which survives. From near here, B4236 offers an alternative approach to Newport via Caerleon. *4m.* **Newport**, see Rte 35.

31

Abergavenny to Merthyr Tydfil, Neath and Swansea

A465 to Neath. Choice to Swansea. Total distance 44m.—*7m.* (by A465)
Brynmawr.—*9m.* **Merthyr Tydfil.**—*6m.* **Hirwaun.**—*4m.* **Glyn Neath.**—*8m.*
Aberdulais.—*1m.* **Neath.**—*9m.* **Swansea**.

Rather bleak, part industrial moorland as far as Glyn Neath is followed by the part wooded and part industrialised Vale of Neath.

From **Abergavenny** (see Rte 28) there is a choice of roads to Brynmawr: the direct A465 (7m), or a southerly loop (B4246 and B4248. 9m) through Blaenavon with its Ironworks and Big Pit mine museum.

DIRECT ROAD TO BRYNMAWR (A465). *4m. Gilwern*, a mile beyond which, just before A465 crosses the river Clydach (by the Clydach Gorge sign), a small road (Station Road) off left past a caravan park reaches the Clydach Gorge picnic area and, just beyond, *Clydach Ironworks*. This industrial archaeological site is that of a coke-fired ironworks which functioned between 1792 and bankruptcy in 1877; after over a century of collapse, a programme of clearance began in 1986 and many structures have now been identified. Clydach was the birthplace of Sir Bartle Frere (1815–84), distinguished colonial administrator and the first High Commissioner of South Africa (1877).

A465 (between here and Merthyr Tydfil known as the Heads of the Valleys Road, the valleys being Ebbw Fach, Ebbw, Sirhowy and Rhymney, for all of which see Rte 37) cuts through the Clydach Gorge, passes Cwm Clydach Nature Reserve, known primarily for beech woodland which survived the charcoal demands of the 18 and 19C furnaces and forges which lined the Clydach, and in *3m.* reaches **Brynmawr**, a town which grew with the iron industry. Although economically a part of the industrial valleys, geographically the town sprawls over high ground.

VIA BLAENAVON TO BRYNMAWR (B4246 and B4248). Reached in five miles **Blaenavon**, though associated with heavy industry, is, surprisingly, set in fine open countryside where, southward, upland moor meets the pastoral green valley which drops down to Pontypool. This is an area to be visited by anyone with a feel for the heritage of coal and iron. Ironworks were first established here in 1757—these, a century later, being only one of a string along the north of the South Wales coalfield—and coalmining started in earnest in c 1782 when it became clear that coal could meet the demands of the ironworks better than wood, supplies of which were in any case fast running out. The local ironworks had closed by the 1890s, and Big Pit coalmine closed in 1980, but both live on as visitor attractions.

Blaenavon Ironworks (April or May–Sept: Mon–Sat 11.00–17.00; Sun 14.00–17.00. Tel. 01495-752036), off the northwest edge of Blaenavon, were built in 1788 and were at their most prosperous in the 1820s, though it was much later, in 1876, that Gilchrist Thomas here solved the problem of separating phosphorus from iron. Today, though forlorn and ruined, the works survive as one of Europe's best preserved of their kind, and from a viewing platform visitors can study the remains of blast furnaces, casting houses, a water-balance lift and even the workers' cottages. In the town, iron features interestingly in 18C *St. Peter's Church*, here being an iron font, memorials to local ironwork pioneers, and, in the churchyard, iron graveslabs.

Big Pit Mining Museum (March–Oct: daily 09.30–17.00. Underground tours 10.30–15.30. Tel. 01495-790311 regarding winter opening), a mile west of Blaenavon off B4248, preserves a coalmine which functioned for just a century, from 1880 to 1980. Today the mine offers both surface interest—an admirably documented self-guided tour including, for instance, a geological introduction, winding engine house, blacksmith's yard (a smith is still often at work), pithead baths and suchlike—and an underground tour (not suitable for small children or the disabled). Kitted with helmet and lamp, underground visitors descend 300ft by cage to explore the workings, which include genuine coal faces, workshops, stables and haulage engines. The complex offers also a cafeteria (in the original colliery canteen) and an imaginative gift shop.

On the drive up to the mine, a site of the *Pontypool and Blaenavon Railway* (intermittent opening. Tel. 01495-792263) is passed. Originally linking Brynmawr and Pontypool, the line was closed to passengers in 1941 but in part continued to carry coal until Big Pit was closed in 1980.

Brynmawr is reached in four miles from Blaenavon.

Beyond Brynmawr, A465 fringes the northern edge of *Bryn Bach Park*, providing a striking example of how a wasteland resulting from pit and opencast mining can be converted into some 500 acres of grass and plantations. The focus of the park is the Visitor Centre (signed off A465. Tourist Information etc. Tel. 01495-711816), where the story of the ten or so years of reclamation is told, while the adjacent large man-made lake is a focus for the park's many and varied recreational opportunities.

9m (from Brynmawr) **Merthyr Tydfil** (*Inf.*), central in the story of Wales's coal, iron and steel (by 1831 Merthyr's population was larger than those of Cardiff, Swansea and Newport combined), and long dependent on these, is today a sprawling mixture of 19C and modern which has largely cleared the scars of a past now replaced by diversified activities which surround the town and tend to be associated with several modern housing estates.

History. The Romans were here first, with a fort on the site of today's Penydarren Park, but the town derives its name from St. Tydfil, a pious daughter of the chieftain Brychan. She was murdered here in the 5C and a settlement grew around her shrine, this settlement developing into a village dependent on Morlais Castle (Rte 26B), built in 1275. In the 17C, and by now a sizeable, scattered hill village, Merthyr became a centre for Dissenters, but it was the 18C that brought industry and, with it, explosive change; starting with the opening of John Guest's Dowlais Ironworks in 1759, and followed in smart succession by Crawshay's at Cyfarthfa in 1765, Hill's Plymouth Works in 1767, and Hamfray's Penydarren Works in 1784. The opening in 1795 of the Glamorganshire Canal between Merthyr and Cardiff (substituting water transport for slow and costly packhorses) gave a major boost to the town's prosperity, but soon the many locks between Merthyr and Abercynon proved a deterrent and in 1802 the Penydarren (horse) Tramroad was opened to bypass these (some sections and the tunnels survive). It was along this tramway in 1804 that the earliest steam locomotive to run on rails, built by Richard Trevithick (1771–1833) was tested. Then, in 1841, Brunel's railway to Cardiff was opened. By now—the largest conurbation in Wales, and with the Dowlais Ironworks, the world's largest, employing 10,000—Merthyr was a commercially prosperous but otherwise grim, smoke-laden complex of ugly iron and coal workings with their associated tips and slagheaps; a place, too, with one of the worst public health records in Britain.

But industrial decline came with the early years of the 20C as the import of cheaper ore from abroad not only killed ironstone mining but also led to the transfer of the steel mills (1928–30) to the coast with its fast-developing ports at which the ore arrived.

Joseph Parry (1841–1903), the composer, was born here; and Merthyr was the home of Lady Charlotte Guest (wife of the owner of the Dowlais Ironworks), translator in 1893 of the 'Mabinogion'. From 1900 the town's Member of Parliament was James Keir Hardie (1856–1915), founder of the Independent Labour Party and the first Labour member.

The town centre is, for the most part, the area between the railway station and the river, the northern edge being Castle Street. *St. Tydfil's Church*, built in 1809 and said to stand on the site of its patron's murder, is successor to possibly several others including the chapel-shrine around which the early settlement grew; inside the church there are two inscribed stones of the 6–9C. Nearby stands the *Robert and Lucy Thomas Fountain*, a cheerfully ornate cast-iron affair, built, rather curiously, in Glasgow and erected in 1907 in memory of Robert Thomas and his wife who in 1828 pioneered the export of South Wales steam coal, Thomas mining the coal while Lucy, clearly a remarkable woman for her time, developed the markets.

Other sites of interest are outside the immediate town centre and for the most part northward. Just across the river from the west end of Castle Street, behind the Technical College, is *Ynysfach Engine House* (Easter–Oct: Mon–Fri 11.00–17.00; Sat, Sun, and Bank Hol. 14.00–17.00. Nov–Easter: Mon–Fri 10.00–16.00; Sat and Sun 13.00–16.00. Tel. 01685-721858). Opened in 1801 (additions in 1836) as an extension of the Crawshay Cyfarthfa ironworks and with two blast furnaces, coke ovens and kilns, this was the first Crawshay furnace to use steam power and was soon producing more iron than Cyfarthfa. Closed in 1879, as steel production took over from iron, the site lapsed into ruin until rescued by Myrthyr Tydfil Heritage Trust (offices here. Tel. 01685-383704) and opened in 1989 as Heritage Centre for the Merthyr Tydfil and South Wales iron industry, with, today, an audio-visual presentation, exhibitions, a coffee shop and a local history bookshop.

Northward from here Dynevor Street and Nant-y-Gwenith Street reach (off to the right in rather over a quarter of a mile) Chapel Row in which is *Joseph Parry's Cottage* (Easter–Oct: daily 14.00–17.00. Or by arrangement. Tel. 01685-383704), the 19C ironworks cottage in which the composer was born in 1841. Restored by Merthyr Tydfil Heritage Trust, the ground floor is now furnished as in the 1840s and there are also exhibitions on Parry and the town's past. Outside the cottage, and both restored by British Steel, are a 19C cast-iron bridge (brought here from nearby Rhydycar and erected over an excavated section of the Glamorganshire Canal which once ran here) and a cast-iron tram found in old mine workings.

Cyfarthfa Castle (Mon–Sat 10.00–18.00; Sun 14.00–17.00. Closes one hour earlier in Oct–March. Tel. 01685-723112), in a large hillside park off A470 rather under a mile northwest of the station, was built in ostentatious castellated style in 1825, the mansion and its grounds enabling its owner, William Crawshay, to survey his nearby ironworks. Acquired in 1909 by the local authority, Cyfarthfa has long housed Merthyr Tydfil's distinguished museum and art gallery.

Mention was made in the History above of the tramway-tunnel along which in 1804 Richard Trevithick tested his early steam locomotive. The tunnel mouth, at Pentrebach, about a mile and a half south of Merthyr Tydfil by A470, has now been restored by the Heritage Trust with, today, interpretive panels and a large mosaic depicting the great event here of 1804.

Railway enthusiasts will make for the *Brecon Mountain Railway* (generally, April–Oct: daily. Tel. 01685-722988) at Pant Station, Dowlais, about three miles north of Merthyr Tydfil and signed off A465. Running almost entirely on the bed of the Brecon and Merthyr Railway of 1859–1962, this narrow-gauge line drawn by vintage steam locomotives offers a four-mile return ride (50 minutes, with 20 minute stop at Taf Fechan reservoir) through the forest and reservoir scenery of the southern part of Brecon Beacons National Park.

For Merthyr Tydfil to *Brecon* (Morlais Castle, two miles north; Brecon Beacons; Taf Fechan; Talybont), see Rte 26B.

Leaving Merthyr Tydfil, A465 in *6m* reaches **Hirwaun**, a one-time colliery town at the head of the Cynon valley (see Rte 37B). Just beyond, A4061 climbs south in a large loop over Hirwaun Common to descend into the Rhondda valley, see Rte 37A. *4m.* **Glyn Neath** marks the head of the Vale of Neath.

A NORTHWARD DIVERSION. From Glyn Neath (starting eastward along B4242 for rather over a mile) an unclassified moorland road (picnic sites and walks) heads north across Fforest Fawr, the arm of Brecon Beacons National Park to the west of the Beacons. The road runs above and to the west of the river Mellte, which tumbles in cataracts and falls through a wooded ravine, to reach (nearly five miles from Glyn Neath) *Porth-yr-Ogof* for car parking, picnic area and waterfall trails. Just beyond is the upland village of *Ystradfellte*, beyond which the road ascends the Llia into country known to the Romans whose Sarn Helen, here a track, comes in from the southeast just two miles north of the village. Half a mile back down this track stands *Maen Madog*, a particularly interesting tall standing stone placed here by prehistoric people and, some 2500 years later, given a Latin inscription recording that this is the stone of one Dervacus, son of Justus, who lies here. *Maen Llia*, a couple of miles farther north just west of the road, is another tall standing stone.

From Glyn Neath, A465 descends the Vale of Neath, a narrow but almost level valley, part afforested, part industrialised and once lovely enough to have been painted by Turner. *4m. Resolven* (across the water by B4434) for boat rides on the Neath canal (tel. 01639-641121), towpath walks, and, just south, *Melincourt* from where a short path leads to falls in a nature reserve. *4m.* **Aberdulais** can be reached either by the trunk A465 or by the quieter

B4434. Here, and within a few miles, there are several places of interest, the first and nearest being *Aberdulais Falls* (NT. Jan–March, and Nov–24 Dec: daily 11.00–16.00. April–Oct: Mon–Fri 10.00–17.00; Sat, Sun and Bank Hol. 11.00–18.00. Tel. 01639-636674. Parking at nearby Tourist Information. Site lift for disabled), a site which, because of the water power readily available, was since the 16C home to a variety of industries; in turn copper works (1584), corn and grist mill (c 1765–1819; painted by Turner), iron-works (c 1819–40) and tin-plate works (c 1840–90). Today, using Britain's largest electricity generating water wheel, the site is for its energy both self-sufficient and environmentally friendly. For visitors there is access, via the new turbine house, to the top of the falls (power equipment, fish pass, displays); also the great water wheel in the wheel pit of the restored Victorian tin-plate works; Information Centre; gift shop; and of course the powerful falls themselves.

Of the other three sites of interest in this general area, the closest, by Cilfrew just west of Aberdulais, is *Penscynor Wildlife Park* (daily 10.00–18.00 or 16.30 in winter. Tel. 01639-642189) with many exotic birds, monkeys, sea lions and other attractions, especially for children. The remaining two sites will be found along A4109 leading north from Aberdulais, the first, reached in about three miles, being *Cefn Coed Colliery Museum* (daily 10.30–18.00 or 16.00 in Oct–March. Tel. 01639-750556) preserving the story of a colliery which once was the world's deepest anthracite mine, a highlight here being the massive steam (but now electric) winding engine with its six boilers. *Seven Sisters Sawmill and Museum* (Easter–Sept. Tel. 01639-700288), about three miles farther along A4109, is a working sawmill with also a musuem showing a collection of miners' lamps and, for the children, Gunsmoke Cowboy Town.

1m. (from Aberdulais) **Neath**, a town with a long industrial background (it was a copper centre, and the first smelter in South Wales was built here in 1584 by copper men from Cornwall), grew around its *Castle* (remains northeast of the station) founded by Richard de Granville in c 1130 as successor to a motte-and-bailey which stood on the more vulnerable west bank of the river. Burnt by Llewelyn the Great in 1231, the castle was rebuilt in 1284 but today survives as little more than the outer face of the gateway with two towers linked by an arch. *Neath Museum* (Tues–Sat and Bank Hol. 10.00–16.00. Tel. 01639-645741), in the Old Mechanics Institute in Church Place, has both a permanent display on the town's history from prehistoric times through to the Act of Union of 1535 as also a programme of temporary exhibitions.

The town is largely on the east bank of its river, but two sites of visitor interest—the 13C abbey and the small remains of Roman Nidum—are on the west side.

The somewhat smoke-begrimed 13C ruins of *Neath Abbey* (Cadw; see p. 11) have the perhaps unique distinction of having in turn served religious, residential and industrial needs.

History. The abbey was founded by Richard de Granville, on land seized from the Welsh at the same time (c 1130) that he built his castle on the other side of the river. Originally for Sauvigniac monks, the abbey had already become Cistercian by 1147. Quickly achieving prosperity, mainly by trading in wool and hides (in 1291 the inventory is said to have included 5000 sheep), the monks built the present church between 1280 and 1330. Two centuries later, Neath had sunk deep into decline, supporting only eight monks and thus an obvious target for dissolution in 1539. Later in the 16C a part of the abbey was converted into a mansion for Sir John Herbert, a status lost in the 18C when, under the pressure of the accelerating local industrial development, the abbey was used for copper smelting while the Herbert mansion housed the workers.

Beyond the entrance, the Lay Brothers' quarters form the west range of the site, the chimneys on the east side of these quarters being relics of the period of industrial use. Moving northeast, the site of the main refectory (with at the north end the washing bays) is crossed to the cloister, beyond the north side of which is the Church, of which, though, little remains except the outer walls of the nave and part of the west front. It once comprised a nave of seven bays and two aisles, with a presbytery of three bays. The transepts were each of two bays, with two chapels, and in the south transept can still be seen two altars, a piscina, and, on the west side, the night-stairs. To the south, beyond the sacristy, there are traces of the chapter house, beyond this being the Herbert Mansion standing on the medieval foundations of the abbot's house. The Dormitory Undercroft, with good medieval vaulting, houses some abbey stones.

The remains of Roman *Nidum*, a fort built in 75–80 on the road from Caerleon to Carmarthen (Caer Maridunum), were discovered in 1949 during the building of a housing estate. What little there is to be seen (the lower courses of the east and south gates) can be found behind two sets of railings in a housing estate off the east of A474 a short way north of the A474/A4230 roundabout.

9m. **Swansea**, see Rte 38.

32

Hay-on-Wye to Abergavenny

Unclassified through Llanthony to Llanfihangel Crucorney. A465 to Abergavenny. Total distance 19m.—*10m.* **Llanthony Priory.**—*5m.* **Llanfihangel Crucorney.**—*4m.* **Abergavenny.**

From Hay-on-Wye to Llanfihangel Crucorney this Route, running immediately west of the English border and for much of the way accompanied by Offa's Dyke, crosses the BLACK MOUNTAINS, a large district of high moorland just straddling the border but wholly included within Brecon Beacons National Park and extending southward from Hay-on-Wye to end in the Sugar Loaf above Abergavenny. On the west—the higher side, with Waun Fach rising to 2660ft—the mountains are bounded by the Talgarth to Tretower road (Rte 25A), while to the east the massif, here in England, eases gently down to the lower ground across which lies the city of Hereford. From the south, from A465, the mountains are cut by several attractive valleys.

Hay-on-Wye (*Inf.*), on the south bank of the Wye, just in Wales, and with both Roman and Norman roots, is known for two contrasting activities. One is as a market serving a wide rural community; the huge market area, known as Smithfield, is home to general, country and sheep markets, this last mainly for the local Clun and Kerry sheep. The other and more recent activity is secondhand books, shops for which are scattered around the town. The Roman association is recalled by the traces of a fort (half a mile north across the river), while Hay's Norman roots live on both in its name ('haie' being Norman French for a hedged or wooded enclosure) and in its *Castle* (no adm.), originally an early 12C motte-and-bailey mentioned during the reign of Henry I and standing in the southwest part of today's town but soon, in the reign of King John, superseded (on today's site) by the stone stronghold of the De Braose family. This was destroyed in about 1400 by Glendower, but, despite much rebuilding instigated by Henry IV, little now remains beyond a ruined gatehouse (blown up during the Civil War) and parts of the walls, on to which an Elizabethan or Jacobean manor was grafted. *St. Mary's Church*, restored in 1834, incorporates part of the tower and porch of a church probably contemporary with the original motte-and-bailey.

For Hay-on-Wye to *Brecon* and *Swansea*, see Rte 33.

Leaving Hay-on-Wye the minor road in *2m.* reaches *New Forest*, little more than a fork from which the road to the left, crossing into England, in two miles reaches a farm lane leading northeast for half a mile to the small ruin of *Craswall Priory*, founded by Roger de Lacy in 1222. This Route takes the right fork, soon emerging on to open moor, crossing Offa's Dyke—clearly seen on the east side with Hay Bluff (2219ft) beyond—and, a few yards farther, reaching a stone circle. *Gospel Pass*, between Hay Bluff and Lord Hereford's Knob (2263ft), is next soon reached, the road from here starting its descent of the Honddu and in *5m* (from the New Forest fork) reaching *Capel-y-Ffin*, a remote spot which has tended to attract the pious. There are two chapels here, and it was here too in 1870 that the Rev. J.L. Lyne, an Anglican who took the name Father Ignatius, founded a monastery, which, however, did not long survive its founder's death in 1908. Later, in the 1920s, the buildings were for a while used by the sculptor, Eric Gill.

Continuing its descent, for much of the way blind between hedge-topped banks, the road in *3m* reaches **Llanthony Priory**, just before which, on the left beside the road, can be seen the old gatehouse, now forming part of a barn.

History. In 1100, the story goes, the Norman nobleman William de Lacy was hunting in this valley (on land owned by his brother) and sheltered in a ruined chapel dedicated to St. David. So pious was the atmosphere that De Lacy promptly decided to renounce the world and become a contemplative hermit. Three years later he was joined by one Erniseus, a former court chaplain, the two men and their followers then building a church and the community becoming Austin Canons. Soon, however, during the troubled years of Stephen's reign when the Welsh were able to regain much of their land, the De Lacy family lost their estates here and the community had to move first to Hereford and then to Gloucester, returning only in 1175 under the more settled conditions imposed by Henry II and building a new church, the ruins of which are those seen today. But, though initially quite prosperous, the priory constantly suffered the ravages of border warfare and was already in a sorry state (and administratively demoted to being a dependency of Gloucester) when dissolved in 1538.

The usual neglect and decay followed, the two main events of later years being the 18C conversion of the south tower to serve as a shooting lodge, and, in 1807, the purchase of the estate by the poet Walter Savage Landor. But his ambitious plans—embracing a school, 10,000 cedars of Lebanon, and merino sheep—soon put him at loggerheads with his tenants, his neighbours and the local authority, until, bankrupt, he assigned the estate to trustees in 1815.

The best overall view of the ruins—essentially the church, with on the south side some domestic remains—is from the field to the north, this view embracing the long and graceful north arcade of the nave. Of the great church (1175–1220) the west front, with its twin towers, and portions of the nave, transepts, central tower and choir remain, the architecture being a plain and almost severe Transitional combined with some Early English. The hotel here, originally built as the house of the steward of the 18C hunting lodge, represents the southwest tower of the church, various priory domestic buildings (west range) and, in the cellars, something of the remains of the prior's house. The adjacent *Parish Church* dates from the 13C and was probably the priory infirmary and associated chapel.

5m. **Llanfihangel Crucorney**, where A465 is joined and where *Llanfihangel Court* (by appointment. Tel. 01873-890217) is a Tudor and Stuart manor house remodelled on a medieval predecessor. Among noteworthy features here are the plasterwork ceilings of 1559, oak panelling and a yew staircase.

DIVERSION TO PARTRISHOW CHURCH AND GRWYNE FAWR RESERVOIR (NW, 11m). Minor roads lead first a mile northwest to Stanton, then two miles southwest through Cwm Coedycerrig, then (at a meeting of five roads) north up the valley of Grwyne Fawr, off which in under a mile is the short lane approach to remote little *Partrishow Church (or Patricio). The story goes that a holy man named Issui, or Ishow, had a cell near here, probably at the holy well just below the church, the approach to which is marked by a stone cut with a Maltese cross. In the early 11C a chapel was built, tradition says with money left by a pilgrim whom the well had cured of leprosy, and it has been suggested that the chapel (or cell) built on to the west wall of today's church may mark the site of this. Giraldus came here in 1188 and is said to have preached from the cross (in part original) which stands in the churchyard. The church, which was restored in 1908 when in danger of collapse, is of various periods, the earliest parts being the north wall of the chapel and the windows in its west wall, both 13C or earlier. The south wall of the chapel and its roof, and the nave porch, date from the 14C, while the remainder of the church seems to be of the 15C or 16C. Features of note inside the church are the small rood screen and loft (late 15C and probably local work); two very early stone altars in front of the screen, and a third in the chapel; the 15C cradle roof; and a decorated font which may be dated from the inscription round the rim recording in Latin that it was made 'in the time of Genillin', who has been identified as an 11C prince of Powys.

The minor road continues north with Grwyne Fawr to run through Mynydd Du Forest (walks), beyond the forest reaching *Grwyne Fawr Reservoir* in the heart of the Black Mountains.

From Llanfihangel Crucorney, A465 runs below (W) *Sugar Loaf* (1955ft. See Rte 25A) and (E) *Skirrid Fawr* (1596ft. See Rte 28) to reach (*4m*) **Abergavenny,** see Rte 28.

33

Hay-on-Wye to Swansea via Brecon and Sennybridge

B4351 to Clyro. A438 and A470 to Brecon. A40 to Sennybridge. A4067 to Swansea. Total distance 52m.—*1m.* **Clyro**.—*4m.* **Glasbury**.—*1m. Three Cocks.*—*2m.* **Bronllys**.—*8m.* **Brecon**.—*8m.* **Sennybridge**.—*10m.* **Dan-yr-Ogof Caves**.—*3m. Abercraf.*—*8m. Pontardawe*.—*7m.* **Swansea**.

Mixed scenery, including, to Glasbury, the pastoral Wye valley. High, open moorland after Sennybridge; and the largely industrial valley of the Tawe south of Dan-yr-Ogof.

From **Hay-on-Wye**, see Rte 32, this Route for about five miles follows the more interesting north side of the Wye, crossing the river for (*1m*) **Clyro**, with the scanty remains of a motte-and-bailey built by William de Braose. The diarist Francis Kilvert was curate here from 1865–72, living in the 18C house opposite the Baskerville Arms and here writing much of his homely record which describes the village and its surrounding countryside. He is commemorated by a tablet in the church. *2m.* **Llowes**, where the church houses a Celtic stone with two faces, the simpler cross dating from the 7C and the wheel from the 11C. Known as the Great Cross of St. Meilig, the stone is thought first to have stood on a nearby height until brought to the churchyard in perhaps the 12C; it was moved into the church in 1956. At *Painscastle*, or Castell Paen, three miles north of Llowes, there is an early Norman motte, first built by Payn FitzJohn (1130) and later, at the close of the 12C and by then rebuilt in stone, in the hands of the notorious William de Braose.

About a mile beyond Llowes a road to the north in half a mile reaches *Maesyronen*, a curious Nonconformist chapel of 1696 complete with its contemporary fittings. *2m.* **Glasbury**, or Clas-ar-Wy, was the site of a Celtic monastery (the clas on the Wye). Here the river is crossed for (*1m*) *Three Cocks*, named after a locally well-known coaching inn. *2m.* **Bronllys**, see Rte 25A which is crossed here. *2m.* At *Llanfilo*, south of the road, the restored little church has a good 15C rood screen and loft with its original plaster tympanum, box-pews of 1600 and a simple font that may be pre-Norman. *5m. Llanddew*, just north of A470, preserves some slight remains of a former palace of the bishops of St. David's; the village was also the official home of the archdeacons of Brecon and thus in about 1172 that of Giraldus. The church, of the 12 or 13C, shows the external batter (probably copied from military architecture) typical of many churches in this district, and the transepts, entered by unusually small arches and with very narrow squints, are also of interest.

1m. **Brecon**, see Rte 26A. Rte 25B is crossed here. For Brecon to (*8m*) **Sennybridge**, see Rte 27.

At Sennybridge this Route turns south on A4067, in three quarters of a mile reaching *Defynnog* with a church mainly of the 15C but founded as early as c 450. Externally, a curious feature is the 5–6C stone bearing a Latin inscription and traces of decorative work which has been built into the southwest angle of the tower, while inside the church the font bears a Runic (ancient Anglo-Saxon) inscription, believed to be the only Runic specimen in Wales. The road now climbs on to upland moor, passing Cray Reservoir and reaching (*7m* from Sennybridge) the pass of *Bwlch-y-Rhudd* (1212ft).

In a little less than two miles below Bwlch-y-Rhudd, a minor road ascends north up the valley of the Tawe. *Cerrig Duon* (or *Maen Mawr*), two miles up the valley and west of the road and river, is a prehistoric stone oval, a rather rare shape of which there are only some ten examples in Britain. The stones are small, and other curious features are the large standing stone just north of the oval and the rows of small stones starting from near the east side. There is another standing stone half a mile north to the east of the road.

3m. •**Dan-yr-Ogof Caves** (April–Oct: daily 10.00–17.00. Tel. 01639-730284) are the main feature of a tourist complex which includes Tourist Information, a small museum, an artificial ski slope, a Dinosaur Park with a short geological trail, an Iron Age farm and a Shire Horse Heritage Centre. Discovered in 1912, explored in the 1930s and opened to visitors in the 1960s, there are now three show caves—Dan-yr-Ogof, the longest in Britain; Cathedral, with the largest single chamber in any visitable British cave; and Bone—the tour of which is enhanced by the most modern interpretive lighting and sound system.

Craig-y-Nos Country Park (daily 10.00 to about 19.00. Tel. 01639-730395), just south of the caves and in a lovely setting of wood, water and meadow beside the Tawe, was the private park of its mansion, generally known as Craig-y-Nos Castle (1842). In 1878 the estate was bought by the opera diva Adelina Patti as a romantic home for herself and her second husband, the tenor Nicolini. Here, between tours, she arrived by special train, enjoyed the luxury of a private waiting room at the station and then, at Craig-y-Nos, relaxed with her aviary, winter garden (now the Patti Pavilion in Swansea's Victoria Park), and the small theatre which she built in 1891 as a miniature of London's Drury Lane. Later, after Patti's death, long a geriatric home, the castle is now open to the public (restaurant, functions room and suchlike) and the theatre is still used as such.

Henrhyd Falls (NT), where the Nant Llech plunges over a cliff into the Tawe, are reached by a road leading southeast off A4067 (to Coelbren) a miles south of Craig-y-Nos.

Beyond Craig-y-Nos the road starts to enter an industrial area, though there are increasing signs of reclamation. *11m. Pontardawe, 4m* beyond which A4067 crosses the M4 motorway to reach (*3m*) **Swansea**, see Rte 38.

34

Monmouth to Chepstow

A466. Total distance 13m. (Alternative B4293, unclassified and B4235. 22m.)—*5m. Bigsweir Bridge.*—*4m.* **Tintern Abbey.**—*4m.* **Chepstow.**

A466 descends the LOWER WYE VALLEY (for an informative exhibition, visit Tintern Old Station, see below), generally regarded as the stretch between Ross-on-Wye in England and Chepstow, the reach (see 'Blue Guide

England') between Ross-on-Wye and Monmouth, a distance of some 15 miles, being scenically the finest. Over many centuries, from about the 13C until 1900, the valley was industrially important, being a principal iron-producing district and known for its wire mills. Throughout these centuries, and particularly during the 18 and 19C, the river was a vital waterway (many places building ships), with ships of up to 90 tons ascending to Brocksweir (eight miles below Monmouth), from where goods continued upstream by barge. There was no valley road until the 19C, the road from Monmouth to Chepstow running across the higher ground to the west. The Monmouth to Chepstow railway, opened in 1876, closed in 1959. The forest of the valley was ruthlessly exploited from medieval times until the 1920s when the Forestry Commission took over with the associated aims of improving productivity while at the same time preserving the scenery and fostering recreational facilities. In 1938 the Wye woodland became a part of the *Dean and Wye Valley Forest Park*. For walkers there is the Lower Wye Valley Walk (Ross-on-Wye to Chepstow), in part above the valley and in part beside the river, and the Offa's Dyke Path runs with the east bank.

Monmouth (*Inf.*) is a border town of long history and some character. On the west bank of the Wye immediately north of where it is fed by the Monnow, the town's perhaps best-known feature is its rare 13C fortified bridge gateway.

History. Monmouth was the site of the Roman Blestium. Later (1068) came early Norman defences built by William FitzOsbern, these in turn by the 12C succeeded by a stone castle, and, typically, a settlement grew around this castle and the associated Benedictine priory. Among Monmouth's famous sons were (c 1100) the 'historian' Geoffrey of Monmouth, who was perhaps a monk at the priory, and Harry of Monmouth, later Henry V, born in the castle in 1387 and in 1415 the victor of Agincourt, at which battle, according to Shakespeare, Monmouth caps (woollen headgear worn by medieval soldiers) were prominent ('Welshmen did good service ... wearing leeks in their Monmouth caps').

Agincourt Square, once the market, is the town centre, with *Shire Hall* (1724) carrying a statue of Henry V placed here in 1792 when the Wye valley was becoming increasingly popular with tourists. It was in this hall that John Frost and other Chartists were tried in 1839, the sentence being death though this was later reduced to transportation. In front of the hall stands a statue (by W. Goscombe John) to the Hon. C.S. Rolls, who lived at nearby Hendre; one of the founders of Rolls Royce, he was killed in a flying accident in 1910. Of the *Castle*, approached by Castle Hill roughly opposite Shire Hall, little survives—it was slighted in 1646—beyond the early 12C keep, or Great Tower. Today the castle houses a *Castle and Regimental Museum* (summer, daily. Winter, Sat and Sun 14.00–17.00. Tel. 01600-712935), principal themes of which are the castle itself, the history of the Royal Monmouthshire Royal Engineers (Militia), and, increasingly, local archaeology. Adjoining is the King's Garden, restricted to plants known during the reign of Henry V. The adjacent *Great Castle House*, now Ministery of Defence property, was built in 1673 (largely with stone from the castle) by the 3rd Marquess of Worcester because, it is said, he wanted the birthplace of his grandson to be as close as possible to that of Henry V.

Priory Street, leading north out of Agincourt Square and constructed in 1837, represents the only significant addition to the town's generally still medieval street plan. Here the Market Hall, a 1969 rebuilding of a Victorian predecessor burnt down in 1963, houses the *Nelson Museum and Local History Centre* (Mon–Sat 10.00–13.00, 14.00–17.00; Sun 14.00–17.00. Tel.

01600-713519). The Lord Nelson collection consists largely of material assembled by the mother of C.S. Rolls, an admirer of the admiral, while the Local History Centre shows Monmouth caps, material on the Monnow bridge, Henry V and C.S. Rolls, as also local archaeological displays. *St. Mary's Church*, a short way northeast of the Market Hall and on the site of the church of the Norman priory, is mainly a rebuilding of 1881 by G.E. Street, though the tower and spire are older; inside the church there is a cresset stone, probably from an earlier church of c 1102 and thus roughly contemporary with the early priory. In the nearby *Roman Catholic Church* there are relics of John Kemble, a priest executed in Hereford in 1679.

From Agincourt Square, Monnow Street, leading southwest, represents very early Monmouth and has for several years been the focus of some of the principal activities of the Monmouth Archaeological Society. Some of the earliest Roman material found in Wales (associated with a mid 1C fort) has been excavated here, and, from a later period, there is clear evidence that this street was laid out along its present course as a planned settlement soon after the arrival of the Normans. Flooding, from the early 12C onwards, compelled the raising of floors, use often being made of domestic rubbish, the archaeological result being stratified floor sequences which have yielded some of the richest medieval deposits in Wales. Modern development cannot be halted indefinitely and in each instance the archaeologists have only limited time before sites have to be abandoned and then built over. But the Monmouth Archaeological Society (tel. 01600-714136) has a continuing programme and visitors are always welcome at any site under current excavation. Both of Monmouth's museums show local archaeological material and offer explanatory displays.

•*Monnow Bridge Gate*, at the foot of Monnow Street, is a simple and robust late Norman structure of 1262 and a rare example in Britain (and rare also in Europe) of a fortified gateway on a bridge. Just across the bridge the *Church of St. Thomas*, though much restored, retains its Norman choir arch and a north door (both c 1180) though the porch is mock-Norman of the 19C. To the south of Monnow Bridge, and with a small medieval bridge, is the *Clawdd Du*, an early earthwork (possibly 12C) thrown up to defend this outlying part of the town.

For Monmouth to *Abergavenny*, see Rte 29.

This Route now follows A466 down the Wye valley, passing famous Tintern Abbey. However an alternative, perhaps to be chosen by those with an interest in prehistory and some early churches, is offered by B4293, the main road to Chepstow prior to the opening of the valley road in about 1820. This alternative (with several roads linking across to A466) is described immediately below. Between these two roads—the Wye valley and the upper alternative—lies the extensive woodland of Tintern Forest with many walks and picnic areas and through which several small roads provide unspoilt and attractive links between river and upland.

TO CHEPSTOW BY B4293 AND B4235. 22m—5m. **Trellech** where the early 14C church is successor to one founded in the 7C or 8C, to which period the base of the preaching cross in the churchyard and the Saxon font may belong. Trellech means Three Stones and these large prehistoric ritual monoliths, inexplicably called the *Harold Stones*, will be found some 250 yards south of the church. Also of interest (southwest of the church) is a mound called the *Tump*, probably the surviving trace of a Norman motte-and-bailey.

Rather less than *4m* farther south, a road bearing generally west in *2m* reaches the *Wolvesnewton Model Farm Folk Museum and Countryside Centre* (Easter–Oct: daily 11.00–18.00. Tel. 01291-650231), set in remote, rolling pastoral scenery. Housed in unique cruciform 18C farm buildings, the complex includes a folklore collection (better than many such, of eclectic scope and with some emphasis on Victorian humour), a Victorian cottage bedroom, crafts and craft shop, waterfowl and farm animals, playground, picnic area and restaurant.

At *Llangwm Uchaf (Pentre)*, *2m* west of Wolvesnewton, the church of St. Jerome, at the road's end, is known for its 15C locally carved rood screen and loft, still with tympanum, as also for its three 'green men' at the base of the choir arch, two on the north and one on the south; with oak leaves in their mouths, they cautiously link pagan with Christian tradition. The road from Llangwm to Chepstow (B4235) in *3m* reaches a junction of six roads, immediately north of which, behind a hedge, is *Caer Llwyd Burial Chamber*, now, however, little more than collapsed stones. For *Wentwood Forest*, immediately southwest of here, see Rte 35. *6m.* **Chepstow**, see below.

TO CHEPSTOW BY A466. 13m.—From Monmouth A466 is followed down the east (English) bank of the Wye to pass in *2m Redbrook*, during the 17C and 18C a copper smelting centre and, from 1771 to 1961, the site of tinplate works. *3m. Bigsweir Bridge*, where the road crosses to the Welsh bank. *3m. Brocksweir Bridge*, during the industrial 18 and 19C the point at which cargoes were transferred from ships to barges. Just beyond, *Tintern Old Station* (April–Oct: daily 10.30–17.30. Tel. 01291-689566), a delightful pastoral and wooded corner, is today a modest visitor complex with tourist information; an exhibition in a railway coach, telling the story both of the Wye Valley Railway as also of the industrial past of the valley; a picnic area; and waymarked walks; a shop; and changing exhibitions in the original station building. Beyond the old station, the road loops with the river, just round the loop being a footbridge, interesting for having once carried an industrial tramway.

1m. **··Tintern Abbey**, beside the Wye below wooded hills, is the loveliest, most impressive and most complete of the abbeys of Wales (Cadw; see p. 11; self-guided cassette).

History. The Cistercian abbey was founded here in 1131 by Walter de Clare, the monks coming directly from Normandy, but of this early foundation little remains, today's ruins dating mainly from rebuilding of the 13 to 15C. During this period the 13C saw rebuilding of the refectory and church, the 14C that of the abbot's quarters, while in the 15C it was the turn of the infirmary. Concerned mainly with agriculture, Tintern was at its most prosperous during the 14C, the wealthiest abbey in Wales and a focus of wide power and influence. With the Dissolution, though, came despoiling and neglect—for instance the roofing lead was stripped off, melted and then used at Raglan and Chepstow castles—a process which continued until the then ivy-clad ruins beside the river caught the imagination of the romantically minded travellers of the 18C and 19C.

The principal survival is the great church, but much of the domestic complex can also be seen, though largely only as lower courses or foundations.

The car park and entrance are on the north of the ruins, immediately beyond the entrance being an introductory exhibition. From here the approach to the church passes on the right the *Reredorter*, with its drain, adjacent (just west) being the *Novices' Lodging*. If this is left by its south door, a right turn passes the Day Stairs and arrives at the north walk of the

Abbot's
Lodging

Infirmary

Great

Kitchens

Drain

Abbot's Hall

Infirmary
Cloister

Entrance and
Exhibition

Reredorter

Novices'
Lodging

Day Stairs

Great Drain

Warming
House

Monks' Refectory

Kitc

N

Lay Brothers' Refectory

TINTERN ABBEY

0   50   100 ft

0   20   20   30 metres

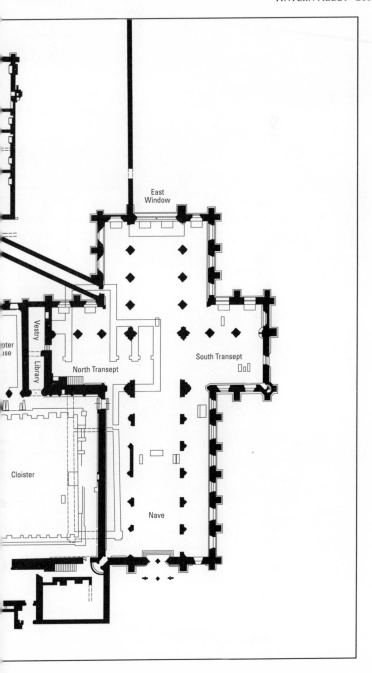

East
Window

Vestry

Library

pter
use

North Transept

South Transept

Cloister

Nave

main cloister. Along this walk are, in turn, the *Warming House*, the *Monks' Refectory*, the *Kitchen* (note the serving hatch) and the *Lay Brothers' Refectory*, this last larger than that of the monks since, with the Cistercian emphasis on agriculture, the lay brothers normally outnumbered the monks.

Tintern Abbey. The huge east window as seen from the crossing

From the northeast corner of the cloister (by the Warming House), the approach to the church is along the east walk, passing on the left the *Parlour*, the *Chapter House*, and then the *Library* and *Vestry*, now, because of the disappearance of the wall between them, a single room. Here the *Church* is entered by the Processional Doorway beside the north transept, the nave, beyond, being mainly of the late 13C and retaining its clerestory on the south side. Both the west and east ends are magnificent, the former, particularly the fine tracery of the great window of seven lights and the moulded arch enclosing the two-trefoil-headed opening of the doorway, best appreciated from the outside. The four large and beautiful arches of the crossing formerly supported a tower, and beyond is the huge and beautifully proportioned *East Window covering almost the whole of the wall.

Returning through the Processional Doorway and along the east walk of the main cloister, a walk along the north side of the Parlour reaches the *Infirmary Cloister*, across which is the *Infirmary*, with, to its north and west, its kitchens. To the north of the kitchens are the *Abbot's Quarters*, with his lodging and adjacent chapel on the east, and his hall to the west.

The abbey made much use of the river as a waterway, and the adjacent Anchor Hotel is on the site of the *Watergate*; a 13C arch leading to a slipway can be seen. Just west of the church, the *Guest House* and other buildings have been partially excavated.

2m. *Wyndcliff* (800ft) is a well-known lower Wye valley view point, reached either by 365 steps from a car park on the main road or by a path from another car park a short way up the road signed Wyndcliff. *Chepstow Racecourse*, just beyond, the largest and best known in Wales, was first developed in 1926.

2m. **Chepstow** (*Inf.*), an ancient walled border town on the west bank of the Wye two miles above where it flows into the Severn, is most visited for its Norman castle, forbiddingly sited high above the river.

History. The town's name, meaning simply Market Town, is Saxon; but to the Romans this was Castell Gwent (in Welsh today, Cas-Gwent) and to the Normans Striguil. From Norman times until the Civil War the town's story was largely that of its castle, under the protection of which, and of a priory of about the same period (1072), it developed not only as a market but also as a port and shipbuilding centre, an activity which was at its most prosperous during the late 18C and early 19C.

Chepstow Castle (Cadw; see p. 11), comprising three wards, a keep and a barbican, sprawls strikingly along a precipitous platform of rock washed by a broad reach of the Wye. There is a dramatic 'A Castle at War' exhibition.

History. Within a decade of the Norman Conquest, William FitzOsbern, later Earl of Hereford, thrusting into southern Wales, built a stone keep here, thus leap-frogging the usual timber and earthwork motte-and-bailey stage and making Chepstow the earliest stone Norman castle in Wales, and perhaps also in Britain. As the result of a rebellion FitzOsbern's son soon lost both castle and title, and in 1115 the Marcher lordship of Chepstow was granted to the De Clare family, in 1189 passing to William Marshal (also a De Clare) who, with his five sons, each succeeding in turn, progressively increased their castle's strength. In the 13C Chepstow was held by the Bigods, earls of Norfolk, and in the 15C it passed to William Herbert, Earl of Pembroke, remaining in this family until the present century. During the Civil War, and then owned by that staunch Royalist the Earl of Worcester, Chepstow was twice besieged, falling in 1645 but only after the starving garrison and their gallant commander, Sir Nicholas Kemeys, had fought to the death (memorial plaque in the Lower Ward).

Prisoners in Chepstow included Henry Marten, the regicide, who occupied what is now known as Marten's Tower from 1660 until his death in 1680, and Jeremy Taylor who was here for six months in 1655.

The entrance is through a Gatehouse (1225–45) flanked by towers, beyond being the Lower Ward (mainly 13C), a part of the castle which, overhanging the cliff, offers dizzying glimpses down to the river as also a view upwards to the Great Tower. Marten's Tower is at the northeast (see History), recalling an imprisonment which was perhaps not too arduous since Henry Marten managed to survive until the age of 78, during this time publishing his 'Familiar Letters to his Lady of Delight', the lady being his mistress. To the north are the remains of domestic quarters, including a hall and kitchens and, below the former, cellars. The defences dividing the Lower and Middle wards were built by William Marshal (c 1190). The Middle Ward is crossed to the Great Tower, the cellars and lower two storeys of which are survivals of FitzOsbern's original castle of 1067–72, the east door and the south and west wall arcades being the oldest features. Beyond are an Upper Ward and Barbican.

The *Chepstow Museum* (March–Oct: Mon–Sat 11.00–13.00, 14.00–17.00; Sun 14.00–17.00. Extended hours in July–Sept with Mon–Sat opening at 10.30 and Mon–Sun closing at 17.30. For Nov–Feb days and times tel. 01291-625981), across Bridge Street from the castle car park, provides many insights into the local history not only of Chepstow but also of the Wye valley and its once flourishing river trades.

The 13C *Port Wall*, which enclosed the medieval town (then primarily a port) on the south and west (the north and east were protected by the loop of the Wye), can be traced along much of its course. The west gate, however, though probably more or less reflecting the original 13C design, was rebuilt by the Earl of Worcester in 1524.

As was frequently the Norman practice William FitzOsbern built a priory, in his case Benedictine, as religious complement to his great secular stone keep, and the church of this priory lives on as *St. Mary's Church*, much rebuilt and restored but still with a partly Norman nave. This, though, is of later date than the original church (c 1072), traces of which are thought to survive as pillars and an arch by the west wall of the chapel (all that is left of the original nave aisles demolished in 1841) off the southeast end of the nave; in this chapel there is also a font of about the same early period. But St. Mary's is visited largely for two spectacular coloured *Memorial Tombs, restored in what is believed to be the original colouring. One of these, in the south transept, is that of Margaret Cleyton (died 1620) and includes effigies of her two husbands and twelve children; the 'dame' hats worn by two of the girls indicate that at least two of the ten daughters were married off. The other memorial tomb, at the northwest of the nave, is that of the 2nd Earl of Worcester (died 1549), shown here with his second wife. The grave of Henry Marten (see Chepstow Castle) is at the church's west entrance; but it is not visible although a wall notice tells about its occupant. Also of interest, in the north transept, is a picture recalling the winning of the Victoria Cross (at Gallipoli in 1915) by Able Seaman Williams of Chepstow, also remembered by a gun-memorial in the town's Beaufort Square.

For the south coast roads to *Newport, Cardiff, Swansea* and *Carmarthen*, see Rte 35.

35

Chepstow to Carmarthen

A48 to Cardiff. Choice to Penarth. B4267 and A4055 to Barry. A4226 and B4265 to St. Bride's Major. B4524 to Bridgend. A473 and A48 to Penllergaer. A484 to Carmarthen. Total distance 105m.—*5m.* **Caerwent**.—*9m.* **Newport**.—*11m.* **Cardiff**.—*3m.* **Penarth**.—*4m.* **Barry**.—*10m.* **Llantwit Major**.—*6m. St. Bride's Major.*—*8m.* **Bridgend**.—*13m.* **Port Talbot** (for **Cwm Afan**).—*3m.* **Briton Ferry** (for **Swansea**).—*8m. Penllergaer.*—*6m.* **Llanelli**.—*9m.* **Kidwelly**.—*10m.* **Carmarthen**.

For most of its length this Route runs through industrial South Wales. Nevertheless industry tends to occur only in pockets, and there are many stretches which are clear of it, while diversions either side of the road quickly lead either to an incidental coast or to scenic valleys slicing up towards often remote moorland. The M4 Motorway parallels on the north for much of the length of this Route. *Note:* Along or close to this Route a number of new road systems will be under construction during the 1990s, principally between Chepstow and Newport (second Severn crossing), around Cardiff Bay to Penarth, and in the Port Talbot–Briton Ferry area. While these works should not normally cause significant delays, motorists should be prepared for local changes in routing and road numbering.

Chepstow, see Rte 34. *5m.* ***Caerwent** is the site of an extensive Romano-Welsh town, a place of unusual interest for being essentially civilian and largely native as compared to most other contemporary Roman remains which are military.

History. The capital of the native Silures was the hillfort of *Llanmelin*, a mile to the north. On occupying new territory it was the Roman custom to transfer the inhabitants of capital hillforts to new towns, built of course to the Roman pattern, and this happened to the Silures in c 75. Their new town of Caerwent, or Venta Silurum, was easily controlled by the Romans whose main route London to Caerleon road (considerably wider than the present road) ran through its centre. The town would have been at its most prosperous during the 2C, at which time, or a little later, the original earthwork boundary was strengthened by a stone wall. Insecurity came with the 4C and in c 340 the town's defences were improved by the addition of bastions. With the departure of the Romans in c 400 Caerwent, though partially reoccupied from time to time, began to fall into ruin. Later, the Normans appeared, building their motte-and-bailey castle in c 1070. Finds from Caerwent are in Newport Museum and the National Museum of Wales in Cardiff. Much, however, remains unexcavated below today's village.

The village *Church* (13C, but probably successor to an earlier one), roughly halfway along the east–west (Roman) road, makes a good startingpoint, if only because in the porch there are two exceptionally interesting inscribed stones. One—recording the erection of a statue by the tribal senate of the Silures to Paulinus, successively commander of the 2nd Legion and governor of the Gaul provinces of Narbonensis and Lugdunensis—provides evidence of tribal autonomy combined with some loyalty to Rome, while the other, dedicated to Ocelus Mars, indicates how native and Roman gods become merged into one. Across the road from the church the village war memorial stands on a Roman platform, while a few yards west from here Pound Lane leads north to the remains of a combined shop and house and, just beyond, another house.

Farther west along the Roman road the *West Gate* is reached, a stone stile here giving access to the town walls which can be followed round to the east gate, the most interesting section being the *South Wall* with the remains of the bastions (the addition of c 340) attached to the outer face. From the *South Gate*, contemporary with the 2–3C wall, there is a choice between continuing round the wall, passing at the southeast corner the Norman motte; or a lane may be followed due north to its junction with the east–west road, opposite being the excavated *Temple*. The *North Gate* can also be visited.

Caldicot Castle (March–Oct: Mon–Sat 10.30–13.00, 14.00–17.00; Sun 13.30–17.00. Tel. 01291-420241. For medieval banquets tel. 01291-421425), a short two miles southeast of Caerwent and the main feature of a country park, stands on an early motte but was built as a stone castle during the 12–14C, its round keep being the oldest part. Restored during the 19C to be the family home of a wealthy Victorian, the castle today offers local history material displayed around the castle; in one tower a programme of temporary exhibitions; and, outside, gardens and the country park with walks and play and picnic areas.

3m. **Penhow Castle** (Easter–Sept: Wed–Sun, but also Bank Hol. and daily in Aug 10.00–18.00. In winter open Wed only. Tel. 01633-400800) is a neat fortified manor dating from the 12–16C and first held by the St. Maur family, a name which soon corrupted to Seymour. Later the manor several times changed hands until bought in 1973 and given the major restoration which has made possible today's claim that Penhow is the oldest lived-in castle in Wales. The *Church*, adjacent to the castle, restored in 1914 on its 13C plan, was within the castle's outer ward and thus contributed to defence; note the arrow slits in the tower.

Wentwood Forest, a mile and a half north of Penhow, originally belonged to the princes of Gwent, then, after the arrival of the Normans, to the Marcher lordship of Striguil (Chepstow), but at the end of the 15C passed to the 1st Earl of Worcester. By this time tenants' rights had become clearly defined, the law being applied twice yearly at a court held at *Foresters Oaks*, now a road junction just north of Wentwood reservoir. During the 17 and 18C the demand for timber for shipbuilding and for oak bark for tanning led to the enclosure of much of the forest and exploitation continued until well into the present century. Today the forest comprises some 3000 acres, over half of which is managed by the Forest Enterprise (several picnic sites, linked by waymarked walks).

A48 crosses M4 and runs through the eastern suburbs of (*6m*) **Newport** (*Inf.*). In these suburbs the road splits, the lefthand fork crossing the tidal Usk by George Street Bridge while the righthand fork soon reaches Newport Bridge, just across which are the castle and the city centre. Essentially a busy industrial and commercial centre and port which developed during the 18 and 19C, the town nevertheless has much older roots, evidenced today by its Norman castle and cathedral.

History. Robert FitzHamon built an early Norman motte-and-bailey here, the site of which, near his church on Stow Hill, disappeared when the railway tunnel was dug in the 1840s. This motte-and-bailey was in any event short-lived, in 1191 giving way to a stone castle built that year beside the river, and it was not long before a town and trading centre had developed called Novus Burgus or Castell Newydd (today, in Welsh, Cas Newydd) in distinction to the 'old port' at Caerleon. During the 13C the town was seized by Simon de Montfort, and in 1402 it was sacked by Owen Glendower. Major change came with the industrialisation of South Wales from 1750 onwards, this particularly affecting the docks, hitherto little more than riverside wharfs, and with the opening of the valleys' canals in the 1790s Newport became the principal coal port of the south. But industrialisation also brought unrest, and in 1839 the town was the

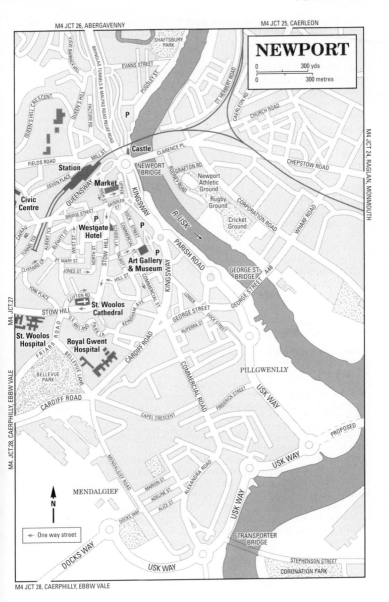

scene of Chartist riots when John Frost, a distinguished citizen and former mayor, led a large demonstration into the town, only to run into armed soldiery around the Westgate Hotel. The demonstrators broke and fled, leaving many dead, and Frost, at first sentenced to hang, was later transported.

In 1921 Newport was declared an episcopal see (Diocese of Monmouth).

The stone *Castle* of 1191, at the busy road intersection west of Newport Bridge, was rebuilt in the 14C, burnt by Owen Glendower, much modified in the 15C, slighted after the Civil War, and what survived was in part restored in 1930. What remains is the east side of a former ward rising direct from the tidal mud banks of the Usk, the ruins consisting chiefly of a square central tower (at the top the chapel, and at the bottom the watergate) between two octagonal towers with rectangular bases. Curving away from the bridge, High Street and Commercial Street are two main streets with, near the junction of the two with Bridge Street, the *Westgate Inn*, successor to the hotel which was the scene of the bloody Chartist defeat and with original pillars still showing bullet marks. The bright and well arranged *Museum and Art Gallery* (Mon–Sat 09.30–17.00 but closes 16.30 on Fri and 16.00 on Sat. Tel. 01633-840064), in John Frost Square, a pedestrian area off Commercial Street, has four main themes. The Archaeology displays include a wealth of important discoveries from Caerwent. Local History spans Norman to modern times, some emphasis being given to the industrial development of the 19 and 20C (the port, mining, iron and associated social aspects including the Chartist riots). Natural History covers the local flora and fauna, while the permanent displays in the Art Gallery include a distinguished collection of 18 and 19C English watercolours; local prints and drawings; a growing selection of Welsh paintings; examples of Welsh Japan ware; and sculpture by such as Rodin, Epstein and Goscombe John.

The *Civic Centre*, a handsome group of buildings half a mile northwest of John Frost Square beyond the railway, is known for its murals (Hans Feibusch, 1961–64), telling the story of Monmouthshire.

St. Woolos Cathedral, until 1921 the parish church, is at the top of Stow Hill, three quarters of a mile southwest of John Frost Square.

History. The name is a corruption of Gwynllwg, a local 5C lord who was suddenly converted to Christianity (when his dream that he would find a white ox bearing a black spot came true on this hill) and here built a church. Robert FitzHamon's Norman church followed in about 1171, lasting until the 15C when, after the ravages of Owen Glendower, the north and south aisles were rebuilt and the tower was added. With the creation of the Diocese of Monmouth, the church became a pro-cathedral in 1921 and a full cathedral in 1949. The east end was extended in the 1960s.

On the west exterior is a headless statue, said to be of Jasper Tu   (died 1495), uncle and guardian of the future Henry VII and reputedly builder of part of the tower. The Lady Chapel, immediately east of the tower, is thought to occupy the site of Gwynllwy's first church and is the oldest part of the present one, its east wall being 12C and the others 13C though, it has been suggested, perhaps embodying some pre-Norman material. The Nave (12C, with the 15C aisles rebuilt after the destruction by Owen Glendower) is entered through a particularly fine *Norman arch, the columns of which are thought to be of Roman origin from Caerleon. The nave itself is also typically Norman, with a clerestory of narrow round-headed windows.

Newport's perhaps most conspicuous feature is the curious *Transporter Bridge*. Built in 1906, there are only three others similar, one being at Middlesbrough and the other two in France. A movable platform carries loads up to a total of 120 tons. The *Docks* are to the south of the Transporter Bridge.

For Newport to *Caerleon*, *Usk*, *Pontypool* and *Abergavenny*, see Rte 30; to the *Ebbw* and *Sirhowy* valleys, see Rte 37E.

The town is left by A48, off which, in *2m*, is *Tredegar House and Country Park* (tel. 01633-816069 or 815880), the home of the Morgan family (later lords Tredegar) from 1402 until 1951, a school for the following 23 years, and in 1974 acquired by the Borough of Newport for restoration and development as a recreation area. The House preserves one stone medieval wing but is otherwise essentially 17C with some 19C additions, mainly service corridors and a servants' wing. Guided tours lead through some 30 period rooms, both 'upstairs' and 'downstairs'. The Country Park (Daily, 09.00–dusk) includes such attractions as a park trail, a boating lake, horse-drawn carriage rides, restaurant, shop and craft demonstrations.

A48 now skirts the marshes of the *Wentloog Level*, a fen district bordering the Bristol Channel. *5m. St. Mellons*, where there is a road fork, the left-hand prong (B4487) providing the more direct approach to the centre of (*4m*) **Cardiff** (see Rte 36).

In addition to the M4 motorway, there is a choice of three routes between Cardiff and Bridgend. This Route proper takes the more interesting though rather longer sequence of southerly roads through Barry and Llantwit Major. The other two routes—A48 through Cowbridge and a northerly loop via Llantrisant—are described first, immediately below.

CARDIFF TO BRIDGEND VIA COWBRIDGE (A48. 20m.). With the castle on the right, Cardiff is left by Cowbridge Road which, meeting A48, in rather over six miles reaches *St. Nicholas*, half a mile south of which is *Tinkinswood Long Cairn*. Excavated in 1914, this large and quite well preserved burial chamber has, from the grave goods discovered (flint tools, pottery and the bones of some 50 people), been dated to about the middle of the third millennium BC. The weight of the capstone has been estimated as some 50 tons. *Dyffryn House Gardens* (daily from 10.00. Tel. 01222-593328), just beyond, are spread around some 55 acres and include sweeping lawns, many small theme gardens, heather gardens, a cactus collection, and temperate, plant and butterfly houses. About a mile farther, beyond the gardens, a left turn almost immediately reaches *St. Lythan Long Cairn*, smaller and not in such good condition as Tinkinswood.

Cowbridge is a small town of some character and of Norman origin. A turning (Church Street) south off the long main street leads to the town's 14C walls and gatehouse, with, adjacent, a school founded in 1609 but now housed in 19C buildings. A short way beyond the walls, a right turn at a T-junction soon reaches the small ruin of *St. Quentin's Castle* with a 14C gateway; started by Gilbert de Clare, the castle remained unfinished after its owner's death fighting the Scots at Bannockburn in 1314. At *St. Hilary*, a mile and a half southeast of Cowbridge, memorials in the Norman church remember the Basset family, owners of ruined nearby Beaupré Castle, reached by footpath (not Sun. Tel. 01446-773034). A straight stretch of Roman road reaches **Bridgend** (see below) in under seven miles.

CARDIFF TO BRIDGEND VIA LLANTRISANT (A4119 and A473. 19m.). Cardiff is left by Cathedral Road and Llandaff, **Llantrisant** being reached in ten miles. Picturesquely sited in a saddle between two steep hills, the town takes its name (Three Saints) from Illtyd, Gwyno and Dyfod, to whom its church (in origin Norman, but rebuilt in the 16 and 19C) is dedicated. The *Model House* (May–Christmas: Tues–Sun 10.00–17.00. Jan–April: Wed–Sun 12.00–17.00. Tel. 01443-237758), in the town centre, is a craft and design centre with studios, a Royal Mint display (the Royal Mint transferred in 1967 from Tower Hill, London, to a Llantrisant trading estate), a shop, a café and a programme of special exhibitions and events. In an adjacent car park will be found a fragment of a round tower, all that survives of Richard de Clare's 13C castle, to which, in 1326, Edward II and Hugh Despenser were probably brought after falling into Queen Isabella's hands. The 13C church at *Coychurch*, seven miles west of Llantrisant, has several architectural peculiarities, these including a blank bay before the crossing; lobed quatrefoil windows in diamond frames at the west of each aisle; a cinquefoiled clerestory in the nave; and unusual buttresses to the choir and north transept. The tower collapsed in 1877 destroying the south transept (rebuilt; both transepts are the only parts of the church not original 13C) and shattering one of the two Celtic crosses of interlaced pattern which then stood in the churchyard. Fragments of the damaged cross, bearing the name Ebisar, and the undamaged cross are now inside the church. **Bridgend** (see below) is reached in two miles.

With a choice of roads out of Cardiff, main Rte 35 in some *3m.* reaches **Penarth** (*Inf.*) sprawling over Penarth Head, the view from which is steadily changing with the progress of the Cardiff Bay Development Project. Leisurely and rather Victorian and Edwardian in character, Penarth is both a respectable suburb of Cardiff and a summer resort, among the attractions being the Esplanade with its Bristol Channel views; the 19C pier, starting point for cruises (tel. 01446-720656); and the string of seafront gardens and parks. Penarth is also home to the *Turner House Art Gallery* (Tues–Sat 10.00–12.45, 14.00–17.00; Sun 14.00–17.00. Tel. 01222-708870) built in 1888 by James Pyke Thompson as a gallery in which to show selections from his personal collection. Now a branch of the National Museum of Wales, the gallery is used largely for changing exhibitions from the museum's collections. Another attraction, immediately south of the town off B4267, is *Comeston Lakes Country Park and Medieval Village* (daily 10.00–17.00. Tel. 01222-701678) with all the usual country park facilities—visitor centre, picnic areas, café, shop—but also, outstandingly, the recreation, on the excavated original remains, of a medieval village (14–15C) complete with farm buildings, bakehouse, peasants' homes and even wandering domestic animals. *Lavernock Point*, a mile or so southeast of the country park, was the scene in 1897 of Marconi's early experiments in transmitting radio waves across water and of the historic reception of the words 'Are you ready?', transmitted from the island of *Flat Holm*, three miles to the southeast. Over the centuries this island has been a Viking anchorage (in 917; hence the Norse name), a lighthouse, a quarantine hospital and, during the Napoleonic wars, a Bristol Channel defence.

4m. **Barry** (*Inf.*). The town is named after the 7C St. Baruch, said to have been buried here, and owes its modern development (between 1881 and the 1920s the population leapt from about 100 to some 40,000) to its *Docks*, founded between 1884–99 by David Davies, a coal exporter who resented paying the port dues levied by Cardiff. To most of today's visitors, though, Barry is a holiday objective, the emphasis being on *Barry Island*, the stubby peninsula projecting between the docks to the north and the shore to the south and largely given over to a large Pleasure Park (tel. 01446-741250) and a holiday camp. The latter spills southward to Nell's Point, until the 19C known for a holy well much visited for the cure of eye diseases. *The Knap*, to the west, is a quieter and less brash resort area, with a pebble beach, gardens, boating lake, the foundations of a large 1 or 2C Roman building, and parkland. In the north of the area, beside Old Village Road, *Barry Castle*, dating from the 12–13C and the seat of the De Barri family, is known to have already been a ruin by the 16C; all that can be seen today is the ruined south gate and some wall of a fortified manor. Immediately west of the castle a road descends through *Porthkerry Country Park*, a green and wooded valley running down to the sea, while off A4226, some two miles north of Barry Island, there is the *Welsh Hawking Centre* (daily 10.30–17.00. Tel. 01446-734687), a pleasant and informal place showing over 250 birds of prey from many parts of the world. Breeding, and the care (leading, where possible, to release) of injured birds are among the centre's activities, and, weather allowing, birds are flown free during the afternoon.

3m. **Rhoose (Cardiff Wales Airport)**, adjacent to which is the *Wales Aircraft Museum* (May–Sept: daily 10.00–17.00. Oct–April: Sat, Sun 13.00–dusk. Tel. 01446-711141) showing a collection of post Second World War military and civil aircraft. From here the junction with B4265 is immediately north, just north again being *Penmarc* with, behind the church, the remains of a castle which originally belonged to the Norman Umfravilles; in 1664 it was acquired by the former parliamentarian Philip Jones. Although there is nothing to be seen at *Llancarfan*, a mile farther north, the place is of interest for having been the site of an abbey founded in the 6C which, before its destruction by Vikings in 987, had a school which rivalled that at Llantwit Major.

B4265, followed westward, in just over a mile passes *Fonmon Castle* (no adm.), a small late Norman keep with a 17C mansion; like Penmarc, Fonmon in 1664 was acquired by Philip Jones.

7m (from Rhoose) **Llantwit Major** (Llanilltyd Fawr) is a small town with roots deep in the early story of Christianity in Wales, roots recalled not only by the town's name but also, visibly, by an exceptionally interesting double church, the **Church of St. Illtyd* (parking behind the nearby very picturesque town hall, with local tourist information).

It was here in c 500 that St. Illtyd, a teacher and craftsman (he invented an improved plough) from Brittany, founded his monastery and school of divinity. An early 7C 'Life of St. Samson' of Dol in Brittany records that Samson was brought by his parents to the school of Illtyd 'the most learned of all the Britons in knowledge of the Scriptures'. Other pupils included Gildas, the historian; St. Paul Aurelian; the bard and seer Taliesin, and even perhaps St. David. The pupils were divided into 24 groups, each responsible for an hour of worship, a system ('laus perennis' or 'continual praise') traditionally also associated with Glastonbury and Old Sarum. The school did not survive the Normans, but the monastery continued until the Dissolution, though only as a cell to Tewkesbury Abbey.

The interesting and curious church is in two parts, and it seems that the Old (or West) Church, in origin Norman of c 1100 and probably occupying the site of St. Illtyd's early church, was the parish church, while the New (or East) Church of the late 13C was the monastery church. Of the original Norman Old Church there survive only fragments, notably the arched south doorway. The transepts disappeared about the middle of the 13C; aisles were added to the original chancel, which then became the nave of the New Church, and to this a new chancel was added on the east, while a chapel was built on the west of the original nave. In the 15C the Old Church was rebuilt on the original foundations, this becoming at least the third to occupy this site.

The Old Church contains a **Collection of Celtic stones* (9 and 10C), with interesting incised Latin messages (not easy to decipher, and a torch can help. The excellent church guide book, normally on sale in the New Church, clearly details the inscriptions, with drawings locating them). The Cross of St. Illtyd, or the Samson Cross, probably the shaft of a wheel-cross, originally stood in the churchyard and when lifted to be brought into the church was found to be covering two skeletons. The shaft bears the saint's name (Iltut) on the reverse while the opposite side records that Samson placed this cross here for his soul. The adjacent tall wheel-cross (the Houelt Cross) has interlaced carving on both sides and was erected by Houelt, probably a prince of Glwysing, for the soul of Res his father. Alongside, a cross-shaft, without inscription, includes four crosses in the elaborate interlacing. On the north side stands the Pillar of Samson, erected by Abbot Samson for his own soul and for those of Iuthahelo (possibly Ithel, a 9C king of Gwent), Artmail and Tecan. Also here are the 14C curfew bell, and the effigy of a lady in Elizabeth dress, the fragment of a baby by her shoulder perhaps indicating that she died in childbirth. The principal features in the New Church are some murals (14–15C; restored in 1950), especially noteworthy being St. Christopher carrying the Christ Child, the carved Tree of Jesse niche (13C) at the east end of the south aisle, and the squints.

The mouth of the little *Afon Colhugh* on which Llantwit stands is said to have once been a port, perhaps the place at which St. Illtyd landed from Brittany. On the cliffs immediately to the east *Castle Ditches* are Iron Age earthworks, while to the west *Tresilian Bay* with its caves has many associations with smuggling. *St. Donat's Castle*, two miles west of Llantwit Major and near the coast, is a restored 14–16C baronial mansion, long owned by the Stradling family, said to have prospered through the use of the castle for smuggling. Bought and restored in the 1930s by the American publisher Randolph Hearst, the castle has since 1962 housed the international Atlantic College. Within the castle grounds St. Donat's Arts Centre offers a programme of concerts, exhibitions and theatre in the converted 14C Tithe Barn theatre (tel. 01446-794848).

Leaving Llantwit Major B4265, passing close to several tumuli, heads northwest for (*6m*) *St. Bride's Major* where the church contains, immediately north of the altar, an elaborate 13C graveslab. B4265 provides the direct link to Bridgend, but this Route takes B4524 along the exposed coast and then up the estuary of the Ogmore river to (*4m*) **Ogmore Castle**, once the heart of the feudal lordship of Ogmore established in early Norman times by William de Londres. In addition to the early earthworks, the site comprises two rectangular wards, each surrounded by a moat, in the larger inner ward, enclosed by an early 13C wall, being an early 12C rectangular keep (probably built by William's son, Maurice), a 13C hall (NE), and a late 12C building (E) of unknown purpose. Ancient stepping stones across the river provide a further pleasant medieval touch.

2m. **Ewenny Priory**, to the east near Corntown off B4524, was founded by Maurice de Londres in 1141 (as a cell of the Benedictine abbey of Gloucester), its church having already been built by Maurice's father, William. The Benedictines, never integrating as successfully as did the Cistercians, were long regarded by the Welsh as no more than Norman intruders, if in religious guise. The monks therefore had always to be ready to repel attack, and, with its early Norman part ecclesiastical and part military character, Ewenny survives as a particularly interesting example of this requirement of those days. The defensive character appears in the crenellation (certainly not merely ornamental at this early period), in the remains of the strong precinct wall (12–13C) and in the gateways (c 1300), in both of which there are loopholes, that on the northwest also having a portcullis. At the Dissolution the domestic buildings were bought by Sir Edward Carne (British ambassador to the Vatican until Henry VIII broke off relations) who built a mansion within the walls. The priory *Church* is in two parts, separated by a 13C or 14C rood screen; the nave, which is the parish church and was probably always such, and the chancel which was for the monks. The nave, heightened in the late 12C, nevertheless shows much good early Norman work, notably in the arcade and in the arches of the crossing. The chancel, entered by a separate door (note the adjacent squint) from the churchyard, contains a 14C wooden screen, a double piscina, a leper squint, and, in the surviving transept, the (?13C) graveslab of the priory's founder, bearing the name Morice de Lundres and expressing, in Norman French, the hope that God will reward him for his labours. Outside the church, to the east of the demolished north transept, are traces of a mid 12C chapel.

A pleasant and interesting short diversion (5m) can be made westward from Ewenny, the road crossing the Ewenny river and in under a mile reaching a crossroads, just beyond which the Ogmore river flows below a narrow medieval bridge known as the Dipping Bridge because of the parapets arranged for sheep dipping. From the crossroads a minor road drops into the village of *Merthyr Mawr*, a period survival of whitewashed and thatched cottages. Beyond the village, the road continues for a mile to a car park and picnic site beside an area of dunes where evidence of Bronze Age, Iron Age and Romano-British occupation has been revealed (crouched burials, brooches, pins, pottery). *Candelston Castle*, at the car park, is the forlorn ruin of a fortified 15C manor the estate of which succumbed to the dunes although the house remained occupied until the 19C.

2m. (from Ewenny) **Bridgend** is in Welsh Pen-y-Bont ar Ogwr, or the Crossing of the River Ogmore; a crossing deemed by the Normans to be of sufficient importance to warrant the building of two castles, one on either side of the river. The Old Castle on the east bank has disappeared, recalled only by the fact that the town on this side of the river is known as Oldcastle. Similarly the district on the west bank is known as Newcastle, though here the 12C *Castle* survives high on the hill above. But, for all its Norman origins, modern Bridgend is essentially a diversified industrial development of the 19 and 20C.

The Norman presence is better recalled by the extensive ruins of **Coity Castle**, one and a half miles northeast of Bridgend.

History. Coity was probably first built around the end of the 12C by Sir Gilbert de Turbeville, who, the story goes, accepted and married the beautiful daughter prudently offered to him by the local Welsh chieftain. The castle remained in the family until the line died out during the 14C, subsequent successive owners being Sir Roger Berkerolles and Sir William Gamage, the latter surviving a long siege by Owen Glendower. When the Gamage line became extinct towards the end of the 16C, the estate passed by marriage to the 2nd Earl of Leicester and the castle was abandoned.

The plan is a large, irregular outer ward (14C), on the east of which is a circular inner ward. This latter is entered by the badly ruined Middle Gate, to the left being the keep and to the right against the curtain wall the domestic buildings. The walls of the keep date from the late 12C (and thus represent Gilbert de Turbeville's original construction), but most of what is inside it is 14C, and in Tudor times a four-storey addition was built on the north side. Most of the curtain wall is contemporary with the keep, but, again, the buildings inside it are mainly 14C. In these buildings, the principal rooms, reached by a stairway between the chapel and the hall, were on the first floor above small, vaulted ground floor rooms; the chapel is opposite the Middle Gate, with the hall to its west and then the kitchens. The large rectangular building which occupied much of the north part of the inner ward is of unknown date and purpose. *Coity Church* (14C, with a 15C tower) contains two small De Turbeville effigies, and a wooden chest with carving of the Passion, possibly a very rare example of a portable Easter Sepulchre (c 1500).

Bridgend is left by A473 which in *2m*, at *Laleston*, merges with A48.

DIVERSION TO PORTHCAWL. A round of some seven miles may be made, using A4106 into Porthcawl and then A4229 to rejoin A48. At *Newton*, reached in two miles, the church (13–15C), east of the road, offers some interesting features; for example, a door high on the east side of the tower, recalling the days when defence was a requirement even for churches. This door gave access to a wooden parapet that could be erected on the corbel immediately below, thus becoming an obvious vantage point for defenders. The south porch is another curiosity, the Norman pillars supporting the outer arch here being upside down, presumably as the result of having been brought from elsewhere. Noteworthy inside the church are the 13C floreated cross on the ledge north of the chancel arch; the east window by Burne-Jones; and, in the chancel, the stone altar, with original base and table, a rare pre-Reformation survival of Edward VI's order that all stone altars should be destroyed. **Porthcawl** (*Inf.*), in the earlier 19C a busy coal-exporting port (fed first by a horsedrawn tram and then, after 1865, by railway), declined in the face of competition from Barry and Port Talbot, until the dock was closed in 1907 and the inner harbour filled in during the 1920s. However, the decline was foreseen and already by the 1860s the development was under way which soon created what remains today a highly popular seaside resort with all the associated entertainment and facilities.

To the northwest of Porthcawl, a region of dunes planted with stabilising grass stretches almost to the Margam steelworks on the outskirts of Port Talbot. The area is divided into two by the river Kenfig (or Cynffig), the southern part being *Kenfig Burrows* (National Nature Reserve), marked by Kenfig Pool, a small freshwater lake formed in perhaps the 14C. Bronze and Iron Age peoples lived here, and in medieval times (12C) the river mouth boasted a port with, a short way upstream, a castle, a church and a village, all finally overwhelmed by the sands in the early 16C though traces survive about half a mile to the north of the pool. The village of *Mawdlam*, off the east side of the Burrows, owes its name to a church of St. Mary Magdalen, originally built in the 13C when old Kenfig's church was threatened by the sands. There are several footpaths, and roads off A4229 lead to Kenfig and Mawdlam from where a path reaches traces of the castle.

6m (from Laleston) **Margam Country Park** (April–Sept: daily. Park 10.00–19.00. Attractions 10.00–17.30. Last entry to park 16.00; to attractions 17.00. Oct–March: park only Wed–Sun 10.00–17.00. Last entry 15.00. On arrival, visitors are advised to take the road-train from the car park to the Visitor Centre and Coach House Theatre video presentation. Tel. 01639-881635 or for recorded information 01639-871131). Originally belonging to Margam Abbey (see below), at the Dissolution the estate passed to Sir Rice Mansel who in 1537 built a mansion here, this succeeded in about 1840 by the neo-Tudor 'castle' of the local magnate C.R.M. Talbot, a member of the family which acquired Margam during the 18C. Today Margam is a huge recreational area of some 800 acres offering a generous choice of attractions, these including the Visitor Centre, with the Coach House Theatre presentation; waymarked walks, and a farm trail; deer herds of five breeds; the Classical 18C Orangery designed by Anthony Keck in 1790; a Sculpture

Park for contemporary pieces; the largest maze in Europe; café and restaurant; and much for children, including an adventure playground and, for the under eights, the popular nursery rhyme village of Fairytaleland.

The park also includes (close to a magnificent lace-beech tree) the ruins of the 13C *Margam Abbey*, notably the Chapter House which, unlike most Cistercian chapter houses which were rectangular, is 12-sided outside but circular within. It was originally vaulted from a central shafted pillar (the foliated capitals of which survive), which, however, together with the roof, was destroyed in a storm in 1799. From here there may be access in summer by a side door to Margam Abbey Church, to which, though, visitors not interested in the park may drive direct.

1m. **Margam Abbey Church** (down a minor turn on the right). The abbey was a Cistercian house founded by Robert, Earl of Gloucester (natural son of Henry I), in 1147 near the site of a long vanished Celtic monastery. In 1206 the abbey underwent the possibly unique experience of a violent revolt by its lay brothers, a disturbance it clearly resolved since it went on to become one of the wealthiest houses in Wales. The greater part of the nave of the original abbey church survives in what is today the parish church (in fact the only Cistercian church still in use in Wales). The lower part of the west front (it was much restored in the 19C when the Italianate campaniles were added), the plain and massive arcades, and perhaps the groining of the aisles, date from the 12C. The windows at the west end contain glass by William Morris, and there are a number of Mansel and Talbot tombs. For the Chapter House see Margam Park above. The adjacent *Stones Museum* (Cadw; see p. 11), in a building which was one of the earliest church schools in Britain, shows an important collection of inscribed and sculpted stones spanning from Roman and Celtic through to medieval times. Most were found locally. *Capel Mair*, a ruined 15C chapel on a spur high above the church, may have been either a private oratory or a place for lay worship.

4m. **Port Talbot** is a name synonymous with steel, its great (Margam) steelworks sprawling southwards towards the Kenfig Burrows and dunes. The large harbour, separating the town from the steelworks, started as simple riverside wharfs. But with the Industrial Revolution and the increase in activity around the mouth of the Afan, it became necessary to provide a dock, so a new cut was made for the river and its former course was converted in 1837 into what is now called the Old Dock. No significant further expansion took place until the 1960s' construction by the British Transport Docks Board, together with the British Steel Corporation, of the modern deep-water harbour with a breakwater a mile long. Opened by H.M. the Queen in 1970, the harbour enables virtually the entire through-put of bulk iron ore for the steel industry, including Llanwern at Newport, to be concentrated here.

CWM AFAN SCENIC ROUTE (A4107) climbs northeast out of Port Talbot following a valley which from the 18C until recent times was largely given over to coal mining and industry. The South Wales Mineral Railway came in 1859, linking Briton Ferry with Glyncorrwg; a passenger rail service was opened in 1885; and A4107 was built in 1930–32 largely as a measure to relieve the unemployment of the depression. Today the railway and the pits have gone, but A4107 has been designated a Scenic Route (with picnic sites and other facilities), an increasingly afforested valley now linking the industrialised coast with the high moorland above Rhondda. The focal point along this Scenic Route is *Afan Argoed Countryside Centre* (April–Oct:

daily 10.30–18.00. Nov–March: Sat, Sun 12.00–17.00. After 1995 may open daily all year. Tel. 01639-850564), six miles above Port Talbot, within Afan Forest Park, and offering an exhibition on the district's social, industrial and woodland history; walks and cycle routes; play and picnic area and tearoom and shop. Here too is the interesting *Welsh Miners Museum*, telling both the technical and the social story of mining in Wales.

3m (from Port Talbot) **Briton Ferry** where viaducts carry a complex of roads across the dock and mouth of the river Neath. For **Swansea**, five miles west, and **Gower** beyond, see Rtes 38 and 39: for **Neath**, two miles north, see Rte 31. A48 heads northwest, soon passing (left) *Llandarcy*, with an oil refinery linked by pipelines to Swansea's Queen's Dock, and then rounding the northern and in part industrial outskirts of Swansea to reach (*8m*) *Penller-gaer*. Here (close to M4 Exit 47) A48, continuing northwest, provides an inland approach to Carmarthen, while this Route bears west on A484 for Gorseinon and (*3m*) **Loughor**, at the head of Burry Inlet where it is entered by the river Loughor. It was at this strategic point that the Romans established their station of Leucarum (1 and 2C), and here too, in c 1110, the Norman Henry de Newburgh built his castle at the southeast corner of the Romans' fort. All that is left, the ruin of a 13C square tower, stands on its motte beside the road before it drops to the river, today crossed by rail and road bridges. Between here and Llanelli, to the south of A484 and signed, is the *Wildfowl and Wetlands Centre* (daily 09.30–17.00 in summer or 16.00 in winter. Tel. 01554-741087), a large area of salt marsh with easy walks including wheelchair access, bird hides, and exhibition area, shop and café, this last popular for its view over the marsh.

3m. **Llanelli** (*Inf.*), essentially industrial with steel, chemical and engineering works, owes its name to the Celtic St. Elli to whom the parish church is dedicated. The *Public Library* (tel. 01554-773538) shows works by local artists and also receives touring exhibitions, while farther north, in Park Howard off Felinfoel Road (A476: no cars in the park), the *Parc Howard Art Gallery and Museum* (Mon–Fri 11.00–13.00, 14.00–18.00; Sat and Sun 14.00–18.00. Closes 16.00 between end Sept and Easter. Tel. 01554-772029), also with travelling exhibitions, shows material of local interest, including a good collection of Welsh pottery and works by Welsh artists.

Beyond Llanelli, A484 skirts *Burry Inlet*, here some three miles wide and of aviation interest; in June 1928 Amelia Earhart, the first woman to fly the Atlantic, arrived here after a flight of 20 hours and 40 minutes from Trepassy Bay in Newfoundland.

9m. **Kidwelly**, at the head of the estuary formed by the confluence of the Gwendraeth Fawr and the Gwendraeth Fach, grew around the castle and priory established here in the early 12C, the latter being Benedictine and founded in c 1130 by Roger, Bishop of Salisbury, as a dependency of Sherborne Abbey in Dorset. The town, which received a charter as early as the reign of Henry I, now lies mainly on the south bank of the latter river, here being the *Church of St. Mary*, successor to the original priory church. The present structure dates principally from c 1320, but was restored in 1884 after the spire, which had already crashed twice, had been struck by lightning. Features of the interior are the unusually broad nave, originally longer and extending west; the squint discovered in the sanctuary wall in 1973; and the mural stair in the vestry leading up to an anchorite's cell, with a loophole to enable him to hear services.

Kidwelly was long associated with tinplate (iron or steel rolled wafer-thin), starting with a forge in 1719 and followed by production in 1737 which lasted until 1941. Today this past lives on as the *Kidwelly Industrial Museum* (Easter–mid Sept: Mon–Fri 10.00–17.00; Sat, Sun 14.00–17.00. Tel. 01554-891078), based on the old works to the north of the town on the east bank of the Gwendraeth Fach. Opened in 1988 by the Prince of Wales, the museum includes an exhibition area (with video presentation) occupying the former Sorting and Boxing rooms; the hot rolling mill; the cold rolls engine house; a section devoted to the local coal industry, with colliery pit-head gear; and various steam and diesel locomotives.

From the town the Gwendraeth Fach is crossed by a bridge originally constructed in the 14C, beyond being the site of the original town which lay within the defences of *Kidwelly Castle* (Cadw; see p. 11). Built by Roger, Bishop of Salisbury, at about the same time as his priory, the castle, sometimes Welsh and sometimes Norman and English, several times changed hands until passing to the Crown during the reign of Henry IV. Of Roger's original castle virtually nothing survives (bar possibly the earthworks to the north and south), the oldest part seen today being the rectangular inner ward dating from c 1275. In plan the castle comprises this inner ward, surrounded by a semicircle of outer ward ending at either end at the river. The wall walk around the outer curtain affords a good general impression.

The Gatehouse (south end of the castle) dates from the 14C and is unusual for being sited on the outer rather than the inner curtain, as also for being a part of the defences of the original town; it contains dungeons, including (northeast corner) an oubliette. The outer curtain is also 14C, as are the upper parts of the inner ward's towers, all this, including the gatehouse, being the work of Henry of Lancaster, nephew of Edward I. In the Outer Ward a later period hall of c 1500 lies outside the inner ward between its southwest and northwest towers, this hall's kitchen being beyond against the outer curtain. At the northeast corner of the outer ward, beyond the north gate, are the stables. In the Inner Ward, the oldest part of the castle, the solar and hall (both late 13C or early 14C) are along the east side, beyond being the chapel of the same period occupying the third storey of a tower which projects boldly towards the river. The large kitchen is at the southwest corner of the ward.

Tregoning Hill, three miles west on the east headland of the Towy estuary, is a National Trust cliff property of ten acres offering good views of Carmarthen Bay.

10m. **Carmarthen**, see Rte 40.

36

Cardiff

CARDIFF (Caerdydd. 290,000 inhab.), in 1955 officially confirmed as the capital of Wales, is an exceptionally elegant and progressive city and port which successfully combines such varied roles as national and county capital; home of a historic castle and, at Llandaff, of an equally historic cathedral; cultural and educational focus (University College); and shopping, commercial and industrial centre. The spacious central area of the city is as interesting as it is dignified and striking with its walled and imposing castle, its extensive green riverside parks, its pleasant pedestrian precincts and arcades, and, in Cathays Park, one of Europe's most distinguished groups of public buildings.

Sweeping change is coming to the southern areas of the city, and indeed to the whole arc of Cardiff Bay round to Penarth, with the progress (throughout the 1990s and beyond) of the bold *Cardiff Bay Development Project*, the key to which is a barrage to link Cardiff's Alexandra Dock with Penarth Head and thus create a 500 acre lake to become the focus of high- quality waterside residential and leisure investments. Indeed, and particularly to the north and east, the project's scope extends well beyond the actual bay and, in addition to the residential and leisure aspects, embraces a pattern of industrial, commercial, professional, retail and other mostly purpose-built zones. For more about Cardiff Bay, including its Visitor Centre and two museums, see the concluding paragraphs of Section A of this route. Visitors to Cardiff and its southern environs as far as Penarth during the 1990s must expect major road layout change.

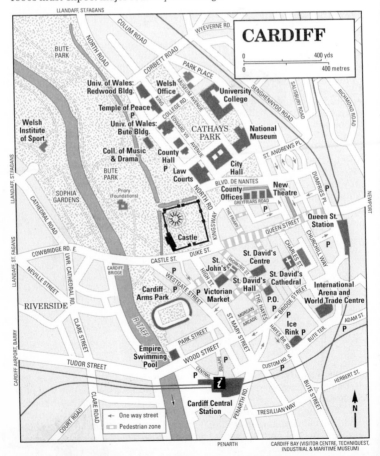

City Centre. Castle Street—Queen Street—Bute Terrace—Central Station—Westgate Street.

Tourist Information. Central Station. Tel. 01222-227281. *Tours*. Open-top bus tours of city and surrounds from Wood Street, just north of Central Station (July–Sept).

Airport. Cardiff Wales Airport, Rhoose; ten miles west.

Entertainment. *St. David's Hall*: concerts, including Welsh Promenade concerts (July) and Welsh Festival of Music (Sept–Oct). *New Theatre:* Welsh National Opera. Plays. Ballet. *Sherman Theatre:* Sherman Company. University and other productions. *Chapter Arts Gallery:* Theatre. cinemas and art gallery. *Cardiff International Arena:* events. Pop and other concerts. *Ice Rink:* championship ice hockey. Basket ball. Pop concerts. *Cardiff Arms Park:* international rugby and soccer. Pop concerts. World choir (May).

History. The Romans are known to have settled here in c 60–90 after their defeat of the Silures, a small civil settlement developing to the south of their fort. Of the period between the Roman withdrawal and the arrival of the Normans virtually nothing is known, though by one tradition Lancelot is said to have fled by sea from here, and there must also have been some association with the chieftain Morgan Mwynfawr (died c 975), from whose name the modern Glamorgan derives. In 1091 the Norman Robert FitzHamon arrived, building his primitive fortress on the site of its Roman predecessor, and in 1158 the later castle was successfully stormed by Ifor Bach, ruler of Senghenydd, the district to the north of Cardiff. It was not long before a town began to grow within the castle's protection. By the late 13C there were 2000 inhabitants, already enjoying a charter, confirmed by others in 1340, 1421, 1581, 1600 and 1608, this last continuing until the Municipal Corporations Act of 1835 which brought to an end municipal dependence on the lord of the castle.

Cardiff was overrun by Owen Glendower in 1404, and in 1488 both castle and town came into the hands of Jasper Tudor, uncle of Henry VII. In 1550 Cardiff was presented by Edward VI to Sir William Herbert. During the Civil War the place, with Royalist sympathies, was held alternately for the King and Parliament, but afterwards remained in the possession of the Herberts and their descendants, the marquesses of Bute.

Modern Cardiff was born of the Industrial Revolution, its population increasing from 1000 in 1801 to 30,000 by the middle of the century and over 180,000 in 1911. Important steps were the construction of the Glamorganshire Canal (Merthyr Tydfil to Cardiff) in 1794; the digging of the first dock, on the initiative and at the personal expense of the 2nd Marquess of Bute, in 1839; the arrival of the railways between about 1840–64; and the opening of further docks between 1859 and 1907. By the latter part of the 19C Cardiff, largely through being the leading port handling iron and coal, was at the height of its prosperity. At the turn of the century Cathays Park was acquired, the first building, the City Hall, being opened in 1905 by Edward VII who at the same time granted Cardiff the status of city. In 1922 the city's boundary was extended to include Llandaff with its cathedral.

After the First World War there was a serious drop in the trade through the docks, and in the last war the city, its docks and Llandaff cathedral were all severely damaged in air raids. The coal trade declined and disappeared and the docks shrank, until, in more recent years, a new pattern has come with the replanning of the docks for oil, timber and general cargoes and with the diversification into new industries. In 1955 Cardiff was officially confirmed as the capital of Wales; the 1980s saw the opening of progressive features such as the St. David's Centre and the associated St. David's Hall, while in 1993 came the opening of the 5000-seat Cardiff International Arena and World Trade Centre. For the remainder of the 1990s the chief activity will be the continuing and dramatic regeneration of Cardiff Bay.

For Cardiff to (E) *Severn Bridge* and (W) *Carmarthen*, see Rte 35: to *The Valleys*, see Rte 37.

A. Cardiff City

* ***Cardiff Castle** (daily 10.00–17.00 in March, April, Oct, to 18.00 in May–Sept, to 16.30 in Nov–Feb. Tel. 01222-822083. Medieval banquets, tel. 01222-372737). Conveyed to the city in 1947 by the 5th Marquess of Bute, the castle is contained within 19C walls, generally following the line of the Roman enclosure, and architecturally spans from Roman to modern times. The castle's history is essentially that of the town. The principal stages of its construction are c 1093 when Robert FitzHamon threw up the motte, this being followed by the first stone building, probably erected by Robert of Gloucester ('The Consul'), a natural son of Henry I; the building on the motte of the keep in the late 12C; the building by Gilbert de Clare in the later 13C of the Black Tower (today's entrance), the wall linking it to the keep, and the keep gateway, this work dividing the castle into two wards; during the 14C and 15C the move from the keep to more roomy and purely residential apartments along the west wall, this range being extended in Tudor and Stuart times; the removal in the late 18C of the outer buildings of the keep and of the wall dividing the wards; and finally the reconstruction in 1869–81, by William Burges for the 3rd Marquess, of the castle apartments, these including the addition of a spire to the Octagonal Tower and the erection of the 150ft high Clock Tower in the place of a small turret. At the same time the internal decoration was redesigned throughout in fantastic and colourful style.

The castle is entered by the *Black Tower* where, to the right, a fine length of Roman wall, probably of the 3C, can be visited. From the tower the line of Gilbert de Clare's wall runs across to the *Motte* and *Keep*, this last offering a good view. The Castle Apartments can only be visited by conducted tour (45 min.). In the *Clock Tower* the rooms are the Winter Smoking Room (first floor), the Bachelor Bedroom and, at the top, the Summer Smoking Room, designed on the theme of the firmament. The *Herbert Tower* (16C) is the southernmost of the projecting towers along the west wall. Here is the Arab Room (1881), with a decorated ceiling in gold leaf and a chimney-piece of white marble and lapis lazuli. Beyond is the *Banqueting Hall*, with murals depicting the life of Robert of Gloucester. The windows represent the various lords of Cardiff. Next comes the *Octagon Tower* (early 15C), forming part of the medieval defences. Here the Chaucer Room (decoration 1889) contains windows illustrating the 'Canterbury Tales', the floor is tiled as a maze and there are alphabet tiles in the hearth. A decorated staircase leads down to the frescoed *Chapel*, formerly a dressing room but converted after the death of the 2nd Marquess. In the *Bute Tower* the Dining Room has a fine ceiling in gold leaf in Moorish style. At the top of the tower is the Roof Garden (1876), open only May–September. The *Library* contains window bays inserted by Jasper Tudor, but the room's decorations are 19C. The carved and inlaid bookcases are noteworthy. The *Entrance Hall* has stained glass windows depicting English monarchs who have owned the castle.

The castle also houses two *Regimental Museums*—of the Welch Regiment (tel. 01222-229367), and of the Queen's Dragoon Guards (tel. 01222-222253) and hosts public events throughout the year, these including open-air concerts and an annual (May) Hot Air Balloon Festival.

WEST OF THE CASTLE. Castle Street skirts the south side of the castle, to the west soon crossing the Taff with, to the north, parks and gardens on both sides of the river. On the west bank are, from south to north, Sophia Gardens, the Welsh Institute of Sport, Glamorgan County Cricket Ground, and Pontcanna with sports grounds and the municipal caravan site. Cathedral Road, fringing the west of these open spaces, leads to Llandaff (Cathedral) and St. Fagans (Welsh Folk Museum). *Bute Park* stretches along the east side of the river, here, between the castle and the river, being the marked-out foundations of a medieval priory. Beyond the Taff, Castle Street becomes Cowbridge Road East, off which, in Market Road (a short mile beyond the river bridge), is the *Chapter Arts Centre* with two cinemas, a theatre, exhibition areas, studio artists, a restaurant and several workshops.

SOUTH OF THE CASTLE AND WEST OF HIGH STREET. Westgate Street, leading southeast from Castle Street, soon passes *Cardiff Arms Park* (named after a former pub), home of Welsh rugby. Beyond, and close to one another, are the bus and central railway stations and the *Empire Swimming Pool*, built in 1958 for the British Empire and Commonwealth Games.

Roughly opposite the castle entrance, at 25 Castle Street, the *Lovespoon Gallery* (Mon–Sat summer 09.00 or winter 10.00–17.30. Tel. 01222-231742) offers a generous choice of designs of lovespoons, the traditional Welsh courting gift up to about the 17C and today a popular souvenir.

To the northeast of the castle is Cathays Park, representing administrative and educational Cardiff and with the National Museum of Wales, one of the finest and largest museums in the United Kingdom; immediately to the southeast is downtown Cardiff. Each of these districts is now described.

NORTHEAST OF THE CASTLE. ***Cathays Park** (about a quarter of a mile north and northeast of the castle), Cardiff's distinguished Civic Centre, is a spacious and superbly balanced area of white Portland stone buildings (most dating from the early years of this century) set along broad avenues broken by gardens. The *City Hall*, the central of the three buildings marking the southeast flank, was built in 1905 by Lanchester, Stewart and Rickards in Renaissance style with a dome surmounted by a Welsh dragon and with a lofty clock tower. The fountains and the pool in front were completed in 1969 to commemorate the investiture of Prince Charles as Prince of Wales. Inside, in the Marble Hall on the first floor, which has pillars of Siena marble, is a series of eleven statues presented by Lord Rhondda (died 1918) illustrating Welsh history. These include St. David (Goscombe John), Owen Glendower, Henry Tudor, and Sir Thomas Picton, one of Wellington's leading commanders. The Council Chamber contains a collection of city treasures; the Assembly Hall has a rich segmented ceiling; and in the Lord Mayor's Parlour there is a mosaic of 86,000 marble pieces. The *Law Courts* (1906, Lanchester, Stewart and Rickards) stand to the left of City Hall, while to the right is the National Museum of Wales (see below). To the south of the museum are the Gorsedd Gardens, with a stone circle commemorating the National Eisteddfod of 1899. The statues here include one of David Lloyd George and four by Goscombe John. The *Welsh National War Memorial* (J. Ninian Comper, 1928), behind City Hall in Alexandra Gardens, bears a plaque commemorating also those who fell in the 1939–45 war.

Museum Avenue runs along the northeast side of Cathays Park, with, beyond the National Museum of Wales, buildings of the *University of Wales College, Cardiff*. The west wing (W.D. Caröe) dates from 1903–09, while the north wing (1930s and 1950s) and the south wing (1960s) are additions in the same style. To the north of Alexandra Gardens is the *Welsh Office* (P.K. Hanton, 1938), and at the northwest of the park is the university's *Redwood Building*. From here King Edward VII Avenue leads southeast with, from north to south, the *Temple of Peace and Health* (Percy Thomas, 1938), built as a headquarters for Welsh people fighting war and disease and now housing a variety of organisations concerned with international affairs and health; the university's *Bute Building* (Ivor Jones and Percy Thomas, 1916); *County Hall* (Vincent Harris and T.A. Moodie, 1908–12), with a south extension of the 1930s by Ivor Jones and Percy Thomas; and the *University Registry* (Wills and Anderson, 1901–03), extended in 1931 by Alwyn Lloyd. The modern *Cardiff College of Music and Drama* is off the southwest side of the park.

SOUTHEAST OF THE CASTLE is downtown Cardiff, roughly defined by, on the north, the spacious pedestrian precinct of Queen Street; on the west by High Street which merges into St. Mary Street; on the east by Churchill Way; and on the south by Bute Terrace. The heart of this downtown area is the large **St. David's Centre** (1983), filling the angle between Queen Street and Working Street and incorporating at its southwest corner *St. David's Hall*, opened in 1983 by the Queen Mother and accepted as one of Britain's finest concert and conference facilities; here too will be found restaurants, bars, gift shop and art and craft exhibitions. St. David's Hall flanks Working Street across which, just northwest, are the *Victorian Market* (1886–91) and, beyond, *St. John's Church*. Restored in 1890–99, the church dates largely from 1453, although its most ancient part, a survival from a predecessor, is the 13C south chancel aisle. The tower of 1473 was built by Ann Neville, wife of the future Richard III. Inside, the church is unusual for having a clerestory in the chancel but not in the nave, while other noteworthy features are the altarpiece in the south aisle by Goscombe John and the north (or Herbert) chapel with a monument to two Herbert brothers (Sir William, died 1609, Keeper of Cardiff Castle; and Sir John, died 1617, secretary to Queen Elizabeth I and James I).

Off the southeast of St. David's Centre is the Roman catholic *St. David's Cathedral*, while farther south, on Bute Terrace and within the angle with Churchill Way, are the *Ice Rink* and the *Cardiff International Arena and World Trade Centre* (1993).

CARDIFF BAY. As already mentioned and outlined at the beginning of this Route, the Cardiff Bay Development Project will over the second half of the 1990s transform much of southern Cardiff, and the approach to the heart of the project—around the Inner Harbour—will change dramatically as the long and drab Bute Street is superseded by a new dual-carriageway tree-lined Bute Avenue.

Described as 'Europe's most exciting waterfront development' and already well advanced, the project will over the second half of the decade be moving steadily towards completion. With the basic aim of revitalising an area long regarded as Cardiff's industrial heart—but in broader concept to embrace not just industry but also commerce, the professions, housing, recreation and culture (ranging from marinas to an opera house) and much else—the venture, the key to which as mentioned earlier is the barrage creating a 500-acre lake, includes among principal features an urban motorway, part raised and part tunnel, sweeping for some four miles across the area from Pengam in the east to cross the Taff and then, following the course of today's A4232, head for the M4.

For the visitor the key area is, and will remain, around the south end of Bute Street (Avenue) beside the Inner Harbour, here being the National Museum of Wales: Industrial and Maritime, Techniquest, the Cardiff Bay Visitor Centre, and the site for an opera house (planned for the turn of the century).

The **Welsh Industrial and Maritime Museum** (Tues–Sat 10.00–17.00; Sun 14.30–17.00. Tel. 01222-481919), a branch of the National Museum of Wales, focuses on the story of industrial and maritime Wales and includes a Hall of Power and transport and railway galleries. Among out-of-doors exhibits are ships, railway vehicles, an air-sea rescue helicopter, and a full-scale working replica of Richard Trevithick's locomotive of 1804. The Cardiff Bay project includes plans for major expansion of this museum. **Techniquest** (Tues–Fri 09.30–16.30; Sat, Sun, Bank Hol. 10.30–17.00. Also open some Mon during school holidays. Tel. 01222-460211), alongside the Industrial and Maritime Museum and also targeted for expansion, is a 'hands-on' science and technology centre covering an ever-widening field and enabling young and old to make things work and see why and how they do. A café and a Science Shop are among the attractions. The **Cardiff Bay Visitor Centre** (Mon–Fri 09.30–16.30; Sat, Sun, Bank Hol. 10.30–17.00. Tel. 01222-463833), housed in a strange tube, vividly explains the bay development project with a three-dimensional model, a multi-screen video wall, several informative displays and actual views across the Inner Harbour.

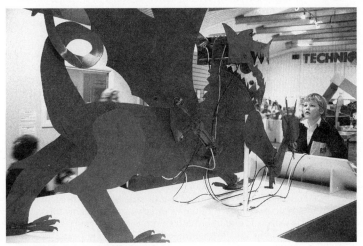

Welsh Dragon at Techniquest

B. **National Museum of Wales

The National Museum of Wales (Tues–Sat and Bank Hol. 10.00–17.00; Sun 14.00–17.00. Tel. 01222-397951) comprises the main building in Cardiff's Cathays Park (the subject of this description) as also several branch museums as outlined below. One of the finest and largest museums in the United Kingdom, the museum here contains important archaeological, art, botanical, geological, industrial and zoological collections. Although the emphasis is on the story of Wales, there is a much broader scope and interest, notably the outstanding collection of modern European art.

Branch Museums. *Welsh Industrial and Maritime Museum*. Cardiff. See Rte 36A above. *Welsh Folk Museum*, St. Fagans, Cardiff. See Rte 36D below. *Turner House*, the art gallery at Penarth, see Rte 35. *Roman Legionary Museum*, Caerleon. See Rte 30A. *Museum of the Welsh Woollen Industry*, Dre-Fach Felindre. See Rte 42. *Segontium Roman Fort Museum*, Caernarfon. See Rte 10. *Welsh Slate Museum*, Llanberis. See Rte 8A. *Power of Wales, Museum of the North*, Llanberis. See Rte 8A. *Graham Sutherland Gallery*, Picton Castle, near Haverfordwest. See Rte 43.

The proposal for a national museum was aired in parliament in 1903, and a Charter of Incorporation was granted by Edward VII in 1907. In 1910 the design by the architects Smith and Brewer was chosen out of 130 entrants in an open competition, but, although the foundation stone was laid by George V in 1912, subsequent work was delayed by the 1914–18 war and it was not until 1922 that the western part of the main hall and the galleries off it were opened to the public, and it was only in 1927 that George V formally opened the museum. The east and west wings date from later.

More recently the years 1988 to 1993 saw further major rebuilding, with extensions and new galleries, modern air conditioning and the provision of greatly improved visitor facilities. Facilities and activities now include programmes of temporary exhibitions, as also a major annual theme exhibition; a large specialised library; a bookshop selling a wide range of books published by the museum as well as a selection of other titles; a schools service; a lecture programme; free lunchtime concerts; restaurant and snack bar.

The MAIN HALL contains the permanent **Collection of Sculpture**, this including, by *W. Goscombe John:* St. John the Baptist. David Lloyd George. Boy at Play. Lady Goscombe John. Morpheus. The Drummer Boy. By *Peter Lambda*: Aneurin Bevan. By *John Gibson*: Narcissus. Meleager, or The Hunter. Wounded Amazon. Aurora. By *John Evan Thomas*: Death of Tewdric, King of Gwent. George Price Watkins. By *Auguste Rodin*: St. John, the Baptist. The Kiss. The Earth and Moon. Eve. By *Henry Moore*: Upright Motif, No. 8.

During recent years, the museum has received a number of portrait-heads of eminent contemporary Welshmen. The commissions by the Welsh sculptor *Ivor Roberts-Jones* include personalities from the worlds of literature, law, politics and the arts.

SCIENCE GALLERIES. **Discover the Countryside of Wales** presents, with the help of scenic paintings, simulated environments, sound effects and other means, a dramatic and informative picture of the Welsh countryside. Themes include Cwm Idwal; open moorland; bog, with Tregaron as the example; woodland and forest; grassland; lakes and marshes, Llangorse being the example; dunes, cliff and the shore. The **Animal Kingdom** is a largely specialist exhibition dealing with modern thinking on animal classification. **Botany in Wales** includes themes such as an introduction to the identification of flowering plants, illustrated by lifelike wax models; the history of plant hunting in Wales; forestry, pollution and reclamation. Recreational facilities such as Nature Trails, Country Parks, Picnic Sites, National Parks etc. are also featured.

ZOOLOGY. Whales and dolphins. The world's largest leatherback turtle. Reptiles. Birds, with dioramas illustrating various environments. A section on the Great Auk, and a giant egg of the extinct bird, Aepyomis. British mammals. Also, a display of wild animals (including some endangered types) features such as the bison, the snow leopard, impala, wolf, tiger, cheetah and zebra.

There is also a section illustrating concepts interesting modern scientists, e.g., the evolution of animal life, including the role played by inheritance; the relationship between man and animals, with some emphasis on conservation.

INDUSTRY. The museum's main industrial exhibits are now at Cardiff's Welsh Industrial and Maritime Museum.

ARCHAEOLOGY. The archaeological story of Wales is told more or less chronologically. *Prehistory.* Old Stone Age material includes an axe of local quartzite from Cardiff (perhaps 200,000 years old), and stone implements and ivory ornaments from Paviland and other sites. From the New Stone Age are a model of Bryn Celli Ddu, finds from Mynydd Rhiw axe 'factory', and simple grave goods from communal tombs. The Bronze Age is represented by a cist from Brymbo (near Wrexham), with bones; grave goods from other cists and from round cairns, including early metalwork, flint arrowheads, and faience beads, these last probably imported from the Mediterranean around 1400 BC. The increasing wealth and skill of the Bronze Age are well illustrated by gold ornaments, outstanding being neck-rings, bracelets and the *Caergwrle Bowl, with elaborate gold decoration and representing a boat on the waves. From the later Bronze or early Iron Age are a sheet-bronze bucket from Arthog and two cauldrons from Llyn Fawr. It was also at about this time (say 300 BC and later) that the first Celts were arriving in Wales, bringing with them metalwork in the La Tène tradition (La Tène: a site in Switzerland at which were first discovered ornaments and other objects produced by a culture spanning roughly the last 600 years BC), especially noteworthy being shields; a wrought-iron *Firedog from Capel Garmon; and ornaments from Tal-y-Llyn and Llyn Cerrig-Bach. Much other Iron Age material comes from the many hillforts of Wales.

Roman Period military equipment is mainly in the museums of Caerleon and Segontium, though here in Cardiff there is an instructive model of a typical auxiliary fort. Other material includes a 4C mosaic pavement from Caerwent; pottery and tiles from Holt where the 20th Legion had its kilns; and evidence of Roman mining activities. The *Early Christian Period* is principally represented by the *Gallery of Stone Monuments, a collection of some 23 stones and 14 casts ranging from the earliest inscribed stones of the 5C, through the sculptured high crosses introduced in the 9C, to the locally developed styles which probably survived into the 12C. The stones are arranged in a stepped circular setting, with clusters representing different chronological groups. Each stone is numbered and information boards are provided. *Medieval Period* material includes rood figures (14–15C); one leaf from an ivory *Diptych (14C, French) from Llandaff; a comparative display of decorated floor tiles (13–16C), and finds from castles, mostly pottery and metalwork reflecting Anglo-Norman influence.

BOTANY. Although the collections have a strong Welsh bias, the department's policy has nevertheless been to take a broad view. Thus plants from all continents are represented, even if the majority come from Britain and Europe. As early as 1920 the department began to commission models, a practice which was continued until 1937 when the first full-time botanical artist was appointed. Since then a large number of plant models have been created out of silk, wire, wax and paper, forming a *Collection of Plant Models acknowledged to be one of the world's finest. At the same time it has always been policy to display both wild and cultivated living specimens.

The collections are in two main parts. One covers the Vascular Plants, these including flowering plants, conifers and ferns and their allies; the other covers the Lower Plants or Cryptograms, with mosses, liverworts, lichens, fungi, slime moulds and algae. There are also collections of Economic Plants, woods, seeds and fruits.

GEOLOGY. The displays in this department are arranged as collections of fossils, minerals and rocks. There is also a collection of maps and manuscripts.

The *Fossil Collection* is arranged stratigraphically and represents all fossil groups throughout the stratigraphical column. The most notable elements (from oldest to youngest) are the very small but also significant set of early Cambrian fossils from The Lleyn; the large collection of brachiopods from the type area of the Ordovician System in Meirionnydd; the small but internationally important collection of the world's earliest vascular plants, from the Upper Ludlow strata of South Wales, and the equally small collection of early plants from the Old Red Sandstone; three major collections from the Coal Measures of South Wales; a small collection of Triassic micro-fossils (the so-called triconodonts), the remains of the earliest mammals, found in fissures in the Vale of Glamorgan; and a group of over 30 ichthyosaurs from the Charles Moore Collection.

The *Minerals Collection* is arranged according to chemical composition. There is a large display of garnets of worldwide provenance, and the representative Welsh specimens include a suite of Welsh gold. The *Rocks Collection* shows specimens from most Welsh geological formations, these including representative sets of rocks of economic importance. *Maps and Manuscripts* include several examples of early cartography, both topographical and geological. The collection of manuscripts is made up almost entirely of the letters and diaries of Sir Henry Thomas De la Beche, founder of the Museum of Practical Geology and of the Geological Survey of Great Britain.

FINE ART. The most notable collection is that of the sisters Gwendoline and Margaret Davies of Gregynog, bequeathed to the museum in 1952 and 1963. The collection includes Old Masters, works by the Barbizon School, British paintings and drawings, and, above all, French art of the late 19C with particular emphasis on the Impressionists.

Northern Art (c 1500–1650). *Marc Gheeraedts*: Queen Elizabeth. *Anon.*: 2nd Earl of Pembroke. *Lucas Cranach*: Portrait of a man. *Anon.*: Sir Roger Mostyn. *Anon.* (Antwerp): Katheryn Tudor of Berain. *I. Laudin*: Mater Dolorosa (Limoges enamel).

Italian Religious Art (1450–1580). *Giovanni Cima (da Conegliano)*: Madonna and Child (c 1505). *Alessandro Allori*: Virgin and Child, with Saints Francis and Lucy (altarpiece). *Studio of Botticelli*: Virgin and St. John adoring the Child. *After El Greco*: Christ led to Calvary.—Also the *Nynehead Tabernacle (c 1460, Florence) in marble. Originally made for the small church of Santa Maria alla Campora, outside Florence, the tabernacle was brought to England in the 19C and given to the church at Nynehead, Somerset. The door is not the original, but is part of an altarpiece of 1520 by *Francesco Granacci*.

Seventeenth Century. *Jusepe de Ribera*: St. Jerome in the desert. *Frans Hals* and *S. de Bray*: Family group in a landscape. *Nicolas Berchem*: Figures by a well. *Anthony van Dyck*: Portrait of a man. *Aelbert Cuyp*: River landscape with horsemen and peasants. *Benjamin Cuyp*: The blind leading the blind. *Jacob van Ruisdael*: Waterfall. *Jan van Goyen*: River scene.

Dunes scene. *Meindert Hobbema:* River scene. *Rembrandt:* Catrina Hooghsaet. *Karel Dujardin:* Travelling musicians. *Andrea Sacchi:* Hagar and Ishmael. *P.P. Rubens* and *Frans Snyders:* The fig. *Gaspard Poussin:* Hilly landscape with classical figures. *Nicholas Poussin:* The body of Phocion carried out of Athens. *Louis* and *Mathieu Le Nain* (?): A tavern quarrel. *Jan van de Cappelle*: *The Calm (acquired 1994).

But perhaps the most striking as also the most interesting of the works of the 17C are what are now generally known as the *Cardiff Cartoons, four large tapestry cartoons, first documented in 1650 and bought by the museum in 1979. There is room for opinion as to whether these are by *Rubens* himself of by his School (*Jan van Boeckhorst*, 1605–68, has been suggested), but so far as the average visitor is concerned this will matter little and he will be content simply to enjoy these bright and sumptuous works.

Eighteenth Century. The emphasis is on the Welsh landscape artist *Richard Wilson*, many of his works showing the influence of Claude Lorrain of a century earlier. Wilson was more concerned with the emotion aroused by a landscape than with detail. Paintings to be seen include Pistyll Cain; Landscape with banditti round a tent; Penn Ponds, Richmond Park; A Maid of Honour; Rome and the Ponte Molle; Landscape with Banditti, the murder; Pembroke town and castle; Caernarfon Castle; Dolbadarn Castle; and View of Dover. Also in this gallery are Roman ruins, by *Giovanni Panini;* Viscountess Bulkeley as Hebe, by *George Romney;* and Llanthony Priory, by *William Hodges*, a pupil of Richard Wilson. Also porcelain and furniture of the period, and a silver-gilt Rococo toilet service made by *Thomas Heming*, goldsmith to George III, for the marriage of Sir Watkin Williams-Wynn who appears on the left in the portrait group by *Pompeo Batoni.*

Nineteenth Century. *J.M.W. Turner:* Tobias and the Angel. Thames backwater, with Windsor Castle. Fishing boat in a mist. *John Constable:* Landscape near Dedham. *E. Landseer:* Encampment on Loch Avon. The ratcatchers. Landscape with waterfall. *David Cox:* Moorland landscape. *D.G. Rossetti:* Fair Rosamund. *Ford Madox Brown:* King René's honeymoon. *J.-F. Millet:* The Good Samaritan. Faggot gatherers. The shooting stars. The little goose girl. The storm. The peasant's family. *Honoré Daumier:* Head of a man. Workmen in a street. Lunch in the country. A famous case. By the Seine. Don Quixote reading.

The *Collection of Impressionists. *Van Gogh:* Rain at Auvers. *Henry Moret:* Village in Clohars. *Pierre Bonnard:* Sunlight at Vernon. *C.-F. Daubigny:* Morning on the Oise. *Eugène Boudin:* The port of Fécamp. River at Bordeaux. Village fair. Venice, jetty at the mouth of the Grand Canal. Beach at Trouville. *J.B.C. Corot:* Fisherman moored to the bank. Distant view of Corbeil, morning. Castel Gandolfo. The pond. *Pierre August Renoir:* Head of a girl. Peasants resting. La Parisienne. *H. Fantin Latour:* Immortality. Larkspurs. *Camille Pissaro:* Pont Neuf, Paris. Sunset at Rouen. *Alfred Sisley:* View in the village of Moret. *Edgar Degas:* Woman putting on a glove. Ballet dancer, aged fourteen (sculpture). Dancer looking at the sole of her foot (sculpture). *Edouard Manet:* Argenteuil, 1874. The rabbit. The church of Petit-Montrouge, Paris. *Auguste Rodin:* The fallen Caryatid (sculpture). *Claude Monet:* Water lilies (1905, 1908, 1906). Rouen Cathedral, sunset. Twilight, Venice. Charing Cross Bridge, London. Palazzo Dario, Venice. San Giorgio Maggiore, Venice. *Paul Cézanne:* Edge of a wood in Provence. Still Life with a teapot. Mountains seen from L'Estaque.

Twentieth Century. Welsh artists are well represented, these including the following. *Augustus John:* Study of a woman's head. A peasant family. Study of a boy. Grace. Aran Islands. La désespérance d'amour. Old Ryan. Dylan Thomas. Madame Suggia. Romany folk. Portrait of Dorelia. *Gwen John:* Dorelia John (drawing). Girl in blue. Girl in profile. Study for 'The brown teapot'. Study of a seated nude. *J.D. Innes:* Pembroke coast. Canigou in snow. *Frank Brangwyn:* Venice, St. Mark's. *David Jones:* Annunciation in a Welsh hill setting.

The major European movements also find a place here. Pure Cubism is represented by a small bronze of 1912 by *Archipenko,* and its influence can perhaps be traced in the bronze head of Henriette III, by *Matisse* (1929), and the painting Loom + a Woman, by *Natalia Goncharova* (1913). German Expressionism is represented by Lake near Moritzburg, by *Erich Heckel* (1909), and Coast scene with red hill, by *Alexei Jawlensky* (1911). Surrealism is seen in The empty mask, by *René Magritte,* and something of abstract art in Three figures with black, by *Willi Baumeister* (1920). Sculptures in the circular gallery and the small gallery adjoining it include Head of Augustus John by *Jacob Epstein* (1916) and Madame Chia Pi by the same artist (1942).

APPLIED ART is generally shown on the first floor balconies round the main hall. The Welsh ceramic is of particular distinction, with the Joseph Gallery of Welsh Ceramics (named after the collector Sir Leslie Joseph), opened in 1992, at long last giving the museum space in which to show more of its collection. This gallery is the first of four ceramics galleries (others being British, European and Far Eastern) planned for the 1990s. The museum also shows Swansea snd Nantgarw ceramic of the Nance Collection (E. Morton Nance, died 1953, auther of 'The Pottery and Porcelain of Swansea and Nant Garw'). Other Applied Art material includes British and European glass and the Jackson Collection of Spoons, including a unique Anglo-Saxon spoon, a spoon bearing perhaps the earliest extant example of the London hallmark, and a complete set of 13 Apostle Spoons (Sir Charles Jackson, died 1922, author of 'History of English Plate' and of 'English Goldsmiths and their Marks'). There is also an exhibition (changed monthly) showing the work of modern artist-craftsmen.

C.   Llandaff Cathedral

Llandaff Cathedral (12–13C), in the suburb of the same name rather over two miles northwest of the city centre, is reached by Cathedral Road or, by walkers, through the parks either side of the Taff.

History. That this was once a pagan site is known from the evidence of pre-Christian probably Romano-British burials discovered under the west part of the cathedral. Tradition connects the founding of the church with St. Teilo (died c 580), appointed Bishop of South Wales by St. Dyfrig (died c 546), and it is known that a pre-Norman church stood here or near here. Another saint, associated with Teilo and Dyfrig, was Euddogwy, the trio being the reason for the three mitres on the present coat-of-arms of the see. The existing church was begun c 1120 by Bishop Urban who, though probably a Welshman, would have been appointed by the Normans. Of this early church the chief remains are the Norman arch dividing the presbytery from the Lady Chapel and some traces of blocked windows in the south wall of the presbytery. It seems that the completion of the nave was delayed by some 50 years, for the north and south doorways (perhaps no longer *in situ*) date from c 1170. Two events of the

12C may be mentioned, one being the death of Geoffrey of Monmouth at Llandaff in 1154, and the other the visit in 1188 by Archbishop Baldwin, accompanied by Giraldus, preaching the Third Crusade (the next visit by an Archbishop of Canterbury would not be until 1972). The present nave and chancel arcades, as well as the west front, which was flanked by towers, date from the earlier 13C, and the chapter house was completed in 1250. In 1266 the cathedral was the scene of a great dedication service, which coincided with the enthronement of Bishop William de Braose, during whose time the Lady Chapel was added in Geometrical style. During the 14C the nave walls and aisles, which on the north had apparently begun to lean outwards, were rebuilt, and large windows with pointed heads were inserted. The presbytery was also remodelled by the cutting of arches through Urban's outer walls and windows, and the medieval history of the fabric closed with the rebuilding of the northwest tower by Jasper Tudor.

There followed nearly 300 years of neglect. The building was already in dangerous decay by 1575; Cromwell's soldiers used the nave as a tavern and post office, and the font as a pig trough, and burnt the cathedral's books at a formal ceremony at Cardiff Castle; after storms in 1703 and 1723 the southwest tower collapsed and the nave roof fell in; and in the 18C 'restoration' took the strange form of an Italian Temple, built within the walls by John Wood, better known for his work at Bath.

Real restoration began in 1835 when Precentor Douglas devoted two years of his stipend to this purpose. Later years saw the removal of Wood's temple (all that remains are two urns outside the northwest of the cathedral); the restoration of the Lady Chapel, presbytery, choir, and part of the nave; and the reopening of all these parts for divine service in 1857, Much of the later restoration was under the care of John Prichard, son of a priest of the cathedral and a pupil of Pugin, who rebuilt the southwest tower, gave the chapter house its distinctive roof, added the row of sovereigns' heads (south wall; modern heads north wall), and carved four Evangelists on the east face of the tower, It was Prichard's partner, J.B. Seddon, who brought in the Pre-Raphaelite work in glass, carving, and painting. In 1880 Dean Vaughan refounded the Cathedral School (perhaps founded in the 9C), abandoned in the 17C. In January 1941 a German landmine destroyed virtually the whole of the previous century's work, Llandaff being, next to Coventry, the worst damaged of Britain's cathedrals. Restoration, completed in 1960, was largely by George Pace, who added the parabolic concrete arch, the Welch Regiment Memorial Chapel (David Chapel), and the Processional Way.

EXTERIOR. Llandaff is unique among British cathedrals in having no transepts, and the absence of a triforium is also remarkable in so early a building. Externally the most notable feature is the irregular west front with its 13C centre. The curious pendent tympanum of the doorway (there never was a central shaft) has an original statue (St. Dyfrig or St. Teilo), and in the apex of the gable there was a Majesty, now, and very weathered, standing in the David Chapel. Along the south side of the cathedral the south door of the nave (c 1170) is a rich example of Norman Transitional work, while, beyond, there is a Garden of Remembrance in which a stone marks where the landmine fell in 1941. Immediately east of the garden juts out the Chapter House of c 1250. Along the cathedral's north side the line is broken by the 1950s David Chapel and Processional Way; the exterior stonework of the former is of stone recovered from two local cottages built in the time of Elizabeth I and destroyed in an air raid.

The INTERIOR is at once striking, the dominant feature being Pace's concrete arch, surmounted by a cylindrical organ case (with gilded Pre-Raphaelite figures, formerly in the niches and canopies of the pre-war choir stalls) bearing Jacob Epstein's huge Christus in unpolished aluminium. The effect is to separate nave and choir while not interfering with the lower level vista. The long arcades of the *Nave* and *Choir*, with foliated capitals, are 13C; the flat-panelled ceiling is modern, the hardwood being from Africa and Malaysia. At the northwest corner of the nave is the *Illtyd Chapel*, in which the Rossetti Triptych (1846–64), forming the reredos of the high altar until 1939, illustrates the Seed of David; Swinburne, Burne-Jones, and William Morris and his wife were the models. The font, at the southwest corner of the nave, is by Alan Durst (1952) and depicts Man's fall, Christ's Redemption, and scenes from the lives of SS. Dyfrig and Teilo. Most of the windows in the south aisle are Pre-Raphaelite, but the small panels in the second window are English 17C glass. Above the south door hangs a Madonna and Child, attributed to Murillo. In the *South Presbytery Aisle* a 10C Celtic Cross is the only relic of the pre-Norman church. The *Teilo Chapel*, at the east end of the south aisle, contains an albaster figure of Lady Audley (?early 15C).

The *Lady Chapel* (c 1287), finely proportioned and with lovely vaulting, contains in its northeast corner the tomb of the builder, Bishop William de Braose. The east window tracery is 19C, and the glass is modern. In the niches of the 15C reredos are bronze panels, each with a wild flower named in Welsh in honour of Our Lady. The (on the west side) richly carved *Urban Arch* dividing the Lady Chapel from the *Presbytery* is a remnant of Bishop Urban's church of c 1120. On the south side of the presbytery, on the site of St. Teilo's shrine, is a 13C effigy of a bishop. The silver-gilt shrine, a centre of pilgrimage, stood here until the Reformation when the canons dismantled it rather than have it destroyed, the various pieces soon disappearing. Note the remains of the old Norman window on the south wall. On either side of the altar are heavy Florentine candlesticks (17C), and the windows above the Urban Arch contain stained glass by John Piper and Patrick Reyntiens (who together also did a huge window in Coventry cathedral). In the *Choir* the Bishop's Throne and the stalls are 19C work (restored 1960).

The *Dyfrig Chapel*, the east end of the north aisle, is so called because Urban is said to have buried the saint's bones here in an attempt to boost his cathedral's reputation. It contains the badly broken 14C reredos (originally three-tiered), removed from its place behind the high altar during the 19C restoration, and, roughly opposite, the tombs of Sir David Mathew, standard bearer to Edward IV at Towton in 1461, and of Sir Christopher Mathew (died 1500). The family had the right to burial in this north aisle until the 18C when they failed to continue to maintain the roof. Six porcelain panels on the west Organ Case were designed by Burne-Jones and are from the Della Robbia pottery at Birkenhead; the model was Elizabeth Siddal, wife of Rossetti and inspiration to the Pre-Raphaelites. West of the organ case is the *Euddogwy Chapel*, commemorating the third saint traditionally associated with the founding of the cathedral and now the memorial chapel of 614 (County of Glamorgan) Squadron, Royal Auxiliary Air Force. Here, opposite a painting of the Assumption (15C, on board), is the marble monument of Dean Vaughan (died 1897) by Goscombe John.

The Norman *Teilo Doorway*, formerly an external door matching that on the south, now leads into Pace's *David Chapel* (1956), the memorial chapel of the Welch Regiment, with furnishings that are gifts from Commonwealth regiments. In the *Processional Way* (also 1956) there hang four medieval gargoyles, rescued from the damage caused by the 1941 landmine.

CATHEDRAL CLOSE. On the green, immediately south of the cathedral, are a restored *Cross* and the remains of a 13C *Bell-Tower*, a ruin since the early 15C; traditionally Exeter cathedral's bell known as 'Great Peter' came from here. Beside the green are the modern Deanery and Canon's Residence, while to the east a garden (1972) is surrounded by fragments of the former *Bishop's Palace*.

In the village, near the main crossroads, is *St. Michael's Theological College* (1907), with a chapel by George Pace.

Francis Lewis, a signatory of the American Declaration of Independence, was born in Llandaff in 1713.

D. **Welsh Folk Museum

The Welsh Folk Museum (10.00–17.00. Daily in April–Oct, Mon–Sat in Nov–March. Tel. 01222-569441), the largest of the branch museums of the National Museum of Wales, is at St. Fagans, some four miles west of central Cardiff (M4 Junction 33). Long a requirement, a museum on this scale became possible in 1946 when the Earl of Plymouth offered St. Fagan's Castle to the National Museum of Wales, at the same time transferring 80 acres of park on generous terms.

From the main entrance (car park and picnic area) the museum is toured as three individual parts—the Galleries, with exhibitions, shop, restaurant, offices and other facilities; the Outdoor Museum, with its superb range of re-erected buildings; and the Elizabethan St. Fagans Castle.

Working craftsmen may be seen, and the museum also stages four major annual festivals: May, Mid Summer, Harvest, Christmas.

The three indoor GALLERIES are devoted to Agriculture, Costume, and Material Culture, this last comprising several small sections illustrating aspects of the domestic, social and cultural life of Wales.

The OUTDOOR MUSEUM, with its fine range of buildings—a Celtic village, cottages, school, chapel, farms, smithy and much else, from many parts of Wales and spanning from Celtic times into the early years of the current century—is in two adjacent parts, the Park and the Castle Grounds, linked by a short tunnel. New buildings are added as opportunity offers. Visitors may wander at will (see plan), starting from the rear of the Galleries and

Pony and trap ride at the Welsh Folk Museum

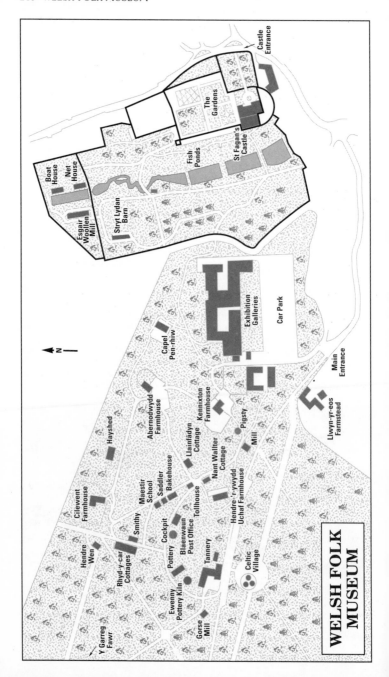

WELSH FOLK MUSEUM

ending at St. Fagan's Castle. From here it will be necessary to return through the tunnel to regain the car park. For visitors in search of architectural detail, the museum's illustrated guide can be strongly recommended.

ST. FAGAN'S CASTLE is an attractive Elizabethan mansion, built between 1560 and 1590 on the site of a 12C stronghold the 13C curtain wall of which survives. The house has been whitened to restore it to its probable early appearance.

History. The early castle was built by Sir Peter le Surs, on whom Robert FitzHamon, the Norman conqueror of Glamorgan, bestowed the lordship of St. Fagans (Fagan, or Fugatius, may have been a missionary sent to Britain by Pope Eleutherius during the 2C). By the early 16C the castle was already a ruin, but in 1560 a part of the estate came into the possession of Dr John Gibbon, who built the present house, incorporating something of the old north wall. In 1616 Sir Edward Lewis of Caerphilly bought the estate; in 1648 the parish was the scene of a battle in which Parliament under Horton and Jones decisively defeated the Royalists under Poyer and Laugharne; and in 1730 the estate passed by marriage to Other Windsor, 3rd Earl of Plymouth. By the early 19C the place was in serious disrepair, but in the 1860s considerable restoration was carried out, the main staircase was probably inserted, and the tower and servants' hall were built. In 1946 the Earl of Plymouth donated the castle to the National Museum of Wales which in 1981–83 carried out major refurbishment, largely restoring the castle's 17C appearance and period-furnishing the rooms.

The formal **Gardens**, to the north of the house and within their old wall, are generally 18C in landscaping and include topiary, and herb, knot and rose gardens, this last once a part of the village green. There are two bronzes by W. Goscombe John (Joyance and the Elf); and in front of the house stands a massive lead cistern dating from 1620.

Visitors tour the period-furnished rooms, of particular interest being the Long Gallery with its 17C Mortlake tapestries, and the Kitchen, left largely as it was when first built with its two large open 16C fireplaces. The utensils and furnishings span the 16C to the 18C, particularly noteworthy being the spits (especially the dog-driven one), and the bacon rack and bread crate suspended from the ceiling.

St. Fagan's Castle (1560-90)

37

The Valleys

The Valleys covered by this Route are Rhondda, Cynon, Taff, Rhymney and Ebbw. The first four are described as from Cardiff; Ebbw, which includes Sirhowy, as from Newport. The Rhondda river (the joined Rhondda Fawr and Rhondda Fach) and the Cynon river are both tributaries of the Taff and there is therefore some overlap along their respective Routes (37A, B and C).

Until the second half of the 18C these valleys, a fan of often steep-sided and quite narrow clefts reaching some 20 miles into the South Wales mountains, were virtually untouched wild countryside. Change came with the Industrial Revolution which in this part of Wales exploded through the combination of high grade coal in the valleys, the plentiful iron ore along their heads and the several ports that could readily be developed at their feet. Communications were at first primitive; by packhorse or mule along atrocious tracks. But soon canals were dug, the Glamorgan Canal between Merthyr Tydfil (and later Aberdare) and Cardiff being opened in 1794, closely followed by the Monmouth Canal in 1796 and the Swansea Canal in 1798. A measure of the speed of industrial development can be judged from the fact that the 50,000 tons carried on the Glamorgan Canal in 1820 had increased to 350,000 tons by 1839. The usefulness of the canals lasted some 50 years, until the railways took over; the Taff Valley railway was authorised in 1836, and the Rhymney dates from 1854–64. By the middle of the 19C the valleys, though untouched on their heights, had below been transformed into disfigured strips along which jostled towns, mines, iron and associated works, canals, roads and railways.

The first step in a long decline came with the invention of improved processes for the large-scale manufacture of steel. These processes demanded better quality iron ore, this in turn meaning either the closure of iron works or their transfer from the heads of the valleys to the coast with its fast-developing ports where foreign ore could be imported and treated. The depression, two wars, the replacement of coal by oil and the need for steelworks to be near the ore ports combined to bring about an accelerating decline, and after the last war it became clear that two related steps demanded urgent attention. The first was the substitution of diversified industry for the mining and heavy industry of the past, an aim now in large part achieved, with modern industrial estates now proliferating and continuing efforts by the Welsh Development Agency (set up in 1976) to attract increasing investment. The second requirement was reclamation, the removal or at least the softening of the scars of the past. This task began to be tackled seriously in the 1960s, although progress was slow and by 1966 only some 99 acres had been treated. The Aberfan tragedy of 1966, when a sliding tip killed 144 people, including 116 children, shocked public opinion and subsequent achievement, now largely the responsibility of the Welsh Development Agency, has been notable with many thousands of acres converting to industrial estates, recreation areas, country parks, new forests and suchlike.

The opinion, still sometimes heard, that these valleys are a 'black country' is today far wide of the mark. Admittedly there are often seemingly endless urban stretches and even some ugly industrial patches, but increasingly common features of the 1990s are the long, low terraces of houses, built in local stone, frequently brightly painted and lining the contours; the modern industrial estates; the country parks; and the smooth, green landscaped slopes that not so long ago were hideous slag. Contrasts can be as frequent as unexpected, and from most places there is quick access on foot or by car to the generally untouched moorland above. But, despite the brave if still early attempts being made to sell the Valleys as tourist country, it would be misleading to suggest that there are many significant sites. Six, though, emphatically do merit inclusion in this category, these being Castell Coch and Rhondda Heritage Park on Rte 37A; Caerphilly Castle, Gelligaer and Llancaiach Fawr on Rte 37D; and Cwmcarn Forest Drive on Rte 37E. Nevertheless the several roads ascending the valleys do provide convenient, not uninteresting, and even scenic links between the coast and Brecon Beacons National Park.

A. Rhondda Valley (Cardiff to Hirwaun)

A470 to Pontypridd. A4058 to Treorchy. A4061 to Hirwaun. Total distance 29m.—*5m*. **Castell Coch**.—*6m*. **Pontypridd**.—*3m*. **Porth**.—*15m*. **Hirwaun**.

Once synonymous with the word coal, but with all its pits now closed, Rhondda, today increasingly turning hopefully towards tourism, climbs as a main valley and an offshoot from roughly Pontypridd to, in the case of Rhondda Fawr, Hirwaun Common or, in the case of the offshoot Rhondda Fach, Maerdy.

With Cathays Park on the east, Cardiff is left by North Road, followed, after crossing the inner bypass (A48), by Northern Avenue. The valley of the Taff is then ascended. *5m*. **'Castell Coch** (Cadw; see p. 11), to the east of the main road and romantically perched on a steep wooded slope guarding a glen, is a folly built in 1875–79 by William Burges for the 3rd Marquess of Bute. But, unlike many, this is a folly claiming historical ancestry, for it stands on the massive foundations of a 13C stronghold, recorded as having already been in ruins centuries ago but today still with fragments surviving in the base of the tower nearest to the car park and in its dungeon. The name, too, Red Castle, is that of the early castle which was built of red sandstone. Today's building, a fantasy both in construction and interior decoration, is triangular with at each angle a round tower crowned by a conical roof. Drawbridge and portcullis are working copies of the originals, and the castle's rooms are decorated with romantic murals with scenes from Aesop's fables and Greek mythology, birds, animals and suchlike. There is an exhibition on the architectural partnership of Bute and Burges. *1m*. *Taff's Well* was at one time noted for its tepid medicinal springs. At *Nantgarw*, just beyond, a porcelain, now greatly valued by collectors, was produced for a short period in the early 19C. Beyond Nantgarw the road passes *Treforest Trading Estate*, founded in 1936 and the first such in Wales.

Approaching (*5m*.) **Pontypridd** (*Inf*.) A470 skirts (left) *Ynysangharad Park*, within the loop of the river Taff, before a left cut-off crosses the river by Bridge Street. Immediately across the bridge, on the right and close to

Castell Coch, a folly built in 1875-79 by William Burges for the 3rd Marquess of Bute

one another, are the graceful *Old Bridge*, built in 1736 by a local mason in what was then a wooded, rural setting, and the *Historical and Cultural Centre*, with *Tourist Information* (Mon–Sat 10.00–17.00. Tel. 01443-402077).

Rtes 37B and 37C continue north, while this Route bears northwest, now ascending the valley of the lower Rhondda and soon reaching the **Rhondda Heritage Park** (daily 10.00–18.00. Last adm. 16.30. Tel. 01443-682036) where, in refurbished buildings of the Lewis Merthyr colliery (closed 1983), dramatic interpretive presentations tell the story of the men and women and of the 'black gold' of the south Wales valleys and, in particular, of Rhondda, 'the most famous mining valley in the world'. Ambitious plans include more presentations, a village of the 1920s, a country park, a Valleys' chapel and much else. *3m.* **Porth**, the name meaning Gateway, a reminder that Porth is at the junction of the Rhondda Fawr and Rhondda Fach valleys, this Route following the former.

2m. **Tonypandy** was the scene of mining riots in 1910. *6m. Treherbert*, beyond which the road, built in 1930–32 by unemployed miners, climbs the northeast flank of the head of the valley, crossing Forest Enterprise land with several waymarked paths. *4m.* **Hirwaun Common Pass** (1600ft) affords a sweeping view northwards towards the Brecon Beacons beyond the partly industrialised valley below. Late Bronze and early Iron Age finds at Llyn Fawr (below) are in the National Museum of Wales; and a sign indicates the start of the Coed Morgannwy Way walk to Afan Argoed (13m) and Margam Park (23m), both on Rte 35. Descending in a large loop, the road in *3m* reaches **Hirwaun** on Rte 31.

B. Cynon Valley (Cardiff to Hirwaun)

A470 to Abercynon. A4059 to Hirwaun. Total distance 24m—*11m.* **Pontypridd**.—*3m.* **Abercynon**.—*7m.* **Aberdare**.—*3m.* **Hirwaun**.

For Cardiff to (*11m*) **Pontypridd**, see Rte 37A. *3m.* **Abercynon** is, in industrial historical terms, known as the southern end of Richard Trevithick's tramway along which in 1804 he ran his famous steam locomotive (see Rte 31, Merthyr Tydfil). A470 (Rte 37C) continues north, while this Route bears northwest up the valley of the Cynon to reach (*7m*) **Aberdare**, a typical Valleys' town which a century and a half ago was no more than a village although the Abernant Ironworks started up in 1802. But Aberdare's roots reach far back and *St. John's Church* is a centuries-old foundation, surviving parts of which are of the late 12C; the unusual ironwork gates outside the west door were made at the Abernant works. Victoria Square is the town centre, and here stands the blacksmith Griffith Rhys Jones (or Caradog; his first choir was called Cor Caradog), alert with poised baton, a vivid recall of the days (1872 and 1873) when under his leadership the South Wales Choral Union twice won the Crystal Palace Cup. *Dale Valley Country Park* (Easter–Sept: daily Oct–Easter: Mon–Fri 10.00–17.00 or 18.00 at weekends. Tel. 01685-872475), to the west of the town, has been created on land that formerly was ugly colliery and tips; today, and with a Visitor Centre, picnic sites and suchlike, this is a valley of trees and waymarked trails touching both natural history and some local industrial archaeology. *3m.* **Hirwaun**, see Rte 31.

C. Taff Valley (Cardiff to Merthyr Tydfil)

A470 (or, after Pontypridd, A4054). Total distance 22m.—*11m.* **Pontypridd.**—*3m.* **Abercynon.**—*3m.* **Aberfan.**—*5m.* **Merthyr Tydfil.**

For Cardiff to (*11m*) **Pontypridd**, see Rte 37A. From here either A470 or the adjacent A4054, both along the east side of the Taff valley, may be used as far as *3m.* **Abercynon** (see Rte 37B) at the northeast corner of which A470 reaches the major intersection with A472 and A4059, the latter heading northwest as Rte 37B. For the 'living history' mansion and museum of *Llancaiach Fawr*, a mile and a half northeast on B4254 to the north of Nelson, see Rte 37D.

From the intersection a choice of roads ascend the valley of the Taff, the trunk A470 on the west side or the quieter A4054, which should be chosen for Aberfan, along the east. *Quakers Yard*, which is soon passed, takes its name from a Quaker burial ground, while adjacent Treharris recalls the principal shareholder in Harris's Navigation Pit, a mine opened in 1894. *3m.* **Aberfan**, the place where in 1966 Pontglas School and a row of houses were engulfed by a sliding coal tip. Of the 144 dead, 116 were children, and a memorial garden now softens the site. The valley becomes more upland in character and at *Terodyrhiw* it widens considerably. A mile farther, at *Pentrebach*, by the junction of A470 and A4060, may be seen the tunnel-entrance mosaic (see Rte 31) commemorating Richard Trevithick's first steam locomotive to run on rails. *5m.* (from Aberfan) **Merthyr Tydfil**, see Rte 31.

D. Rhymney Valley (Cardiff to Rhymney)

A469. Total distance 19m.—*5m.* **Thornhill.**—*2m.* **Caerphilly.**—*7m.* **Bargoed.**—*5m.* **Rhymney.**

For those willing to walk 27 miles, or at any rate shorter sectors, the **Rhymney Valley Ridgeway Path** makes a circuit of the valley's hills. Information from Caerphilly Mountain Countryside Service, Taff Gorge Countryside Centre, Heol-y-Fforest, Tongwynlais, Cardiff, CF4 7JR. Tel. 01222-813356.

With Cathays Park on the east, Cardiff is left by North Road, followed, after crossing the inner bypass (A48), by Caerphilly Road, passing through the suburb of *Llanishen*. *5m.* **Thornhill**, a mile to the east of which is *Parc Cefn-Onn* (acquired by the city of Cardiff in 1944), some 200 acres of open country and wooded hillside noted for rhododendrons and azaleas and affording good views. *The Wenallt* (750ft. 140 acres), a mile southwest of Thornhill and also belonging to the city, is a rolling expanse of woodland and heath with views across Cardiff to the Bristol Channel. From the watershed (888ft), half a mile north of Thornhill, there is a panoramic view down to Caerphilly and the valleys beyond.

2m. **Caerphilly** (*Inf.*) is an industrial and market town which seems to have started as a Roman station (Caer) and later added the name of St. Fili (6 or 7C), who may have been the son of that St. Cenydd who founded a priory at Llangenydd on Gower. The town was long famed, possibly as long ago as the 13 or 14C, for a bland, white cheese. However the market closed in the early 1900s and the cheese is now made in various other places, notably in Somerset.

Caerphilly Castle (Cadw; see p. 11), the model for the concentric plan adopted by Edward I, is, after Windsor, the largest castle in England and Wales. The castle's defences are notable for their elaboration and ingenuity, and for today's visitor interest is added by full-size working replicas of medieval artillery pieces, as also by two exhibitions; one of these, in the Great Gatehouse, describes how Caerphilly developed, while another, in the Northwest Tower, has as its theme the Castles of Wales.

History. The earliest fortification here was the Roman fort of c 75, the site of which is now occupied by the Civil War earthwork (the Redoubt) to the northwest of the castle. In 1268 Gilbert de Clare, fearful of the threat to Cardiff from Llewelyn the Last, began to build a castle here, but this was destroyed in 1270 by Llewelyn when he invaded the surrounding district of Senghenydd. The following year Gilbert de Clare started again, continuing to build despite a siege by Llewelyn, whom he eventually forced to withdraw. From the Clares Caerphilly passed in 1317 to the Despensers, Edward II finding brief refuge here from Isabella. After this the castle lost its military value and before the middle of the 16C had already fallen into decay. During the Civil War a redoubt for artillery was built beyond the northwest of the castle, but later Cromwell drained the lakes and blew up the towers, his attempt on one of which clearly being only partially successful. Later Caerphilly passed via the earls of Pembroke to the Butes, the 4th Marquess in 1935–37 making careful and extensive restoration before handing the castle over to the Crown.

Caerphilly: the largest castle in Wales and a model for the concentric plan adopted by Edward I

The castle is a magnificent example of the concentric plan, borrowed, largely through the experience of the Crusades, from Europe and the Near East. It comprises four separate groups of fortification, these being the castle proper, a complex of two concentric wards completely surrounded by a lake; a large barbican system to the east of this, defended by an outer moat; a large hornwork on the west; and, to the northwest, the outlying Civil War redoubt. The lake (c 15 acres), created by damming the small

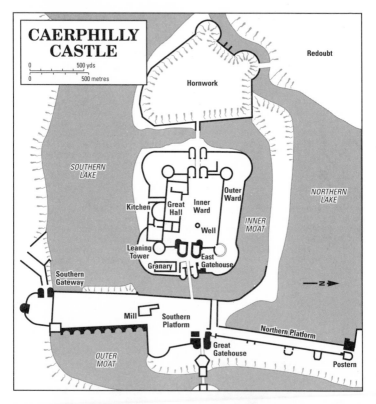

CAERPHILLY CASTLE

0 — 500 yds

0 — 500 metres

Redoubt

Hornwork

SOUTHERN LAKE

NORTHERN LAKE

Outer Ward

Inner Ward

Kitchen

Great Hall

INNER MOAT

Well

Leaning Tower

East Gatehouse

Granary

Southern Gateway

Mill

Southern Platform

Northern Platform

Great Gatehouse

OUTER MOAT

Postern

N →

Nant-y-Gledr, together with the moats which it fed, directly protected all the defences, an earth bank on the north, linking the Hornwork with the East Barbican, separating the lake from an inner moat.

The visitor's approach is across the EAST BARBICAN, a line of curtain wall, in places 60ft high, stretching north and south. This wall, sheltering a raised earthen platform and strengthened by several bastions, also formed a dam for the lake. Approximately in the middle there is a large Gatehouse, which was approached by two drawbridges resting at their ends on the hexagonal stone pier that still survives in the outer moat. The two halves of this barbican could be defended independently, as they were divided by a transverse wall, 20ft high, across the platform. The doorway that connected them was sealed by a portcullis and by a drawbridge over the adjoining overflow channel, which controlled the amount of water in the lake. At the north end of the north platform there is a postern. On the south platform are the remains of a mill, worked by water from the lake, and beyond, at the south end, a large gateway, facing west to prevent the barbican being outflanked and commanding the brook at the point where it was dammed.

The Inner Moat, formerly with a drawbridge, is crossed to the castle proper, the OUTER WARD being reached through the ruins of its east gate. This ward, which surrounds the inner with a wide terrace, was defended by water on all sides. Its outer boundary was little more than a breastwork above the revetted scarp of the moat, but it was reinforced by wide semicircular bastions at the corners. Just south of the outer ward entrance there are the ruins of what may have been a granary, and, against the wall of the building next to the leaning tower, are the remains of an oven.

The INNER WARD has massive gatehouses on the east and west, both with half-drum-towers. The East Gatehouse is the more impressive and contains on its second floor a hall and an oratory. Of the drum-towers at the angles of the ward, blown up by Cromwell, that on the northeast has largely disappeared, while that on the southeast survives as a 50ft high segment overhanging its base by 11ft 6ins. The other towers have been restored. The Great Hall is along the south side of the ward. It was probably rebuilt c 1317 by Hugh le Despenser. Note the ball-flower ornament inside. Now restored, the hall is sometimes used for official and charity functions. To the east of the hall are the buttery and a small chapel, together now used as modern kitchen and boiler house; and to the west is a range of state apartments. The Kitchen, very unusually placed, projects south into the outer ward, which, with the adjoining watergate, it effectively blocks on this side.

Opposite the west gatehouse of the outer ward, perhaps originally the castle's principal entrance, is the large revetted HORNWORK, once defended by yet another moat and drawbridge. Beyond, to the northwest, is the REDOUBT, the site of the Roman fort, possibly also the site of Gilbert de Clare's first castle, and in the Civil War used for artillery.

4m. **Ystrad Mynach** (meaning, for reasons unknown, the Valley of the Monk) stands at the crossing with A472 leading west to the Taff and Cynon valleys and east to the Sirhowy and Ebbw valleys. *Hengoed Viaduct*, just north, with its lofty curve of 16 arches, dates from 1857; once carrying one of the busiest rail stretches in southern Wales, its line has now long been closed but the viaduct survives as a listed reminder of Victorian energy. In *2m.* out of Ystrad Mynach A469 crosses B4254 offering a varied and interesting westward diversion.

GELLIGAER CIRCUIT AND LLANCAIACH FAWR. The circuit below (to Bargoed) is one of under five miles. If Llancaiach Fawr is included, this adds two miles.

At *Gelligaer*, a small upland town of Roman if not earlier origin, the 13C church stands adjacent to a Roman fort. The church, almost certainly successor to an earlier one, houses the St. Gwladys stone, of the 9–10C and formerly standing with Capel Gwladys (chapel) on Gelligaer Common (see below). The Roman fort, to the right of the road and its traces visible from a layby a short way beyond the church, probably dates from the early 2C and stood guard here on this tactically high ground between Cardiff and Brecon's y Gaer. A few yards farther along B4254, at the Cross Inn, the small road northwest, which this circuit follows on return from Llancaiach Fawr, represents the Roman Heol Adam.

Llancaiach Fawr (daily 10.00–17.00 or 18.00 on Sat and Sun. Tel. 01443-412248), a mile farther along B4254, is a 'living history' museum (set in the Civil War year, 1645) in a semi-fortified manor house of c 1530. The history of the house and family is told with an audio-visual experience of Charles I's visit in 1645, after which the owner, Edward Pritchard, turned Parliamentarian. Llancaiach Fawr is also an educational 'hands-on' experience where children can, for instance, don period clothing or try sitting in the stocks.

Other facilities include banquets, a candlelit ghost tour, 17C gardens, restaurant, picnic area and shop.

Returning to the Cross Inn, this diversion follows the narrow once Roman road on to the open upland of Gelligaer Common and in just over a mile turns east along an open unfenced road. Within half a mile this road curves downward, just on the left, but over the brow of a rise and not easily seen from this direction, being a tall cross standing within the foundations of Capel Gwladys, once home to the stone now in the church at Gelligaer. This chapel was founded in the 6C by St. Gwladys, pious daughter of Brychan and thus a sister of the equally pious but martyred Tydfil. Under a mile farther on, a rough track southward quickly reaches traces of Roman practice camps.

1m (by A469) **Bargoed**, long a valley village, grew rapidly during the 19C and especially after the opening of its colliery in 1897; today the town is notable for its rows of contoured terraces. At *Stuart Crystal* (factory tours: Mon–Fri 09.00–15.00. Shop: daily 09.00–17.00. Tel. 01443-820044), at Aberbargoed on A4049 just east of Bargoed, self-guided tours allow many aspects of glass manufacture to be appreciated. *5m*. **Rhymney** was an important iron town—the first works opening here in 1800—but little survives though the past is recalled by pub names such as the Puddlers' Arms and the Blast Furnace. St. David's Church (1843) was endowed by the ironworks company.

Beyond Rhymney, in a mile and a half, A469 joins Rte 31.

E.   Ebbw and Sirhowy Valleys (Newport to Ebbw Vale)

A467 or B4591 to Aberbeeg. A4046 to Ebbw Vale or A467 to Brynmawr. Total distance 17 or 18m—*6m*. **Sirhowy Valley**.—*1m*. **Cwmcarn**.—*5m*. **Aberbeeg**.—*5m*. **Ebbw Vale** or *6m*. **Brynmawr**.

Leaving Newport, A467 and B4591 both in *6m*. reach the area of **Crosskeys** at the junction of the Sirhowy and Ebbw valleys.

A4048, off A467 at Newtown near Crosskeys, serves the 14 miles length of the SIRHOWY VALLEY, soon reaching *Sirhowy Valley Country Park* (daily dawn to dusk. Visitor Centre open summer only. Tel. 01495-270991), one of the largest and most recent in Wales. There is little if anything of interest farther along this valley, although **Tredegar** (*Inf.* at Bryn Bach Park, see Rte 31) offers a town and environs walk (pamphlet), the interest being essentially local and largely in the context of the industrial, trades union and social conditions of the 19C. Bedwellty House, surrounded by public park and now local authority offices, is a fine example of a 19C ironmaster's home.

1m. **ˑCwmcarn Forest Drive** (FE. Easter–Oct: daily 10.30–19.00. Tel. 01495-272001), with a small visitor centre and shop at the entrance, will for many people be the most worthwhile objective along this Route. Along some seven miles of high forest road, and with several well-sited parking places (many with picnic tables), the drive provides not only constantly changing views but also an adventure playground at Park 3 and, at Park 6, a superb overview across the Severn estuary. *Twmbarlwm Hillfort*, the most interesting feature around the drive and reached by a short walk from Park 7, shows evidence of man's activity over many remote centuries: a small cairn near the northeast corner almost certainly represents Bronze Age burial; in the Iron Age people chose this obviously defensive position and raised the large hillfort rampart to protect their settlement; and the mound at the northeast corner beyond the cairn may well have been a Roman signal station before serving as a Norman motte.

Over the remainder of this Route, there is little if anything of specific interest, the road linking a succession of towns each coming to terms with the lean 1990s after the industrial peaks of the past. From 1907 to 1968 *Crumlin* (*3m.* north of Cwmcarn) lived from its Navigation Colliery, the large fan-ventilation engine of which has now gone to the Welsh Industrial and Maritime Museum in Cardiff, while Pen-y-Fan Pond, a mile and a half northwest, once a colliery feeder lake, is now a country park. At (*2m.*) *Aberbeeg* there is a choice of valleys, the west fork (A4046) being Ebbw Fawr and the east (A467) being Ebbw Fach.

Along EBBW FAWR the town of **Ebbw Vale** is reached in *5m.* A crowded industrial town once dependent on coal and steel, Ebbw Vale was seriously affected by British Steel Corporation's problems during the 1970s and steel making ended in 1978.

Along EBBW FACH the industrial town of **Abertillery** is reached in *1m. 5m.* **Brynmawr**, see Rte 31.

38

Swansea

SWANSEA (Abertawe. 187,000 inhab.)—a commercial, residential and academic city and port, as also the main shopping centre of southwest Wales—sprawls along and above the northwest shore of Swansea Bay, mostly on the right bank of the river Tawe, while the docks stretch away from the lower left bank. The city centre, largely reconstructed after air raid damage during the 1939–45 war, is spacious and modern, development both past and more recent having allowed for several pedestrians-only streets with, adjacent, large shopping precincts, while to the immediate southeast of the centre imaginative use has been made of the area beside South Dock and Tawe Basin (the Maritime Quarter), here being a leisure centre, marinas, museums, theatre and arts workshops. The city's central expansion continues, notably in the Parc Tawe area to the east between Castle Street and New Cut Road.

City Centre. The Kingsway—Circus—Princess Way—Oystermouth Road—Westway.

Tourist Information Singleton Street. Tel. 01792-468321.

Airport. Fairwood Common (5m W).

Entertainment. *Grand Theatre:* touring productions. *Brangwyn Hall:* concerts. *Dylan Thomas Theatre:* amateur and professional productions.

History. The name probably derives from Sweyn's-ey, suggesting that Swansea originated as a Viking settlement, possibly founded by Sweyne Forkbeard who is known to have been active in the Bristol Channel. The castle was first built by the

Norman Henry de Newburgh, or Beaumont, who in 1099 led an expedition into Gower, and the town which grew around it received a charter from William de Braose in 1210. Later, the castle was destroyed by Owen Glendower. Shipbuilding and coalmining began in the Swansea district in the 14C, if not before, and trade was early established with Ireland, France, and the Channel Islands. Swansea furnished ships for coast defence for Elizabeth I. In the Civil War the town was Royalist until 1645, when Colonel Philip Jones, a native Parliamentarian, was made governor; the town later received a charter from Cromwell.

By 1700 Swansea was the largest port in Wales. Smelters were attracted to the district (many from Cornwall) by the rich coal, and in the 18C numerous copper works were developed (mostly a little inland; the first at Landore), Nelson's ships being sheathed with Swansea copper. In the 19C not only copper, but silver, lead, tin, nickel, zinc, cobalt, and iron ores were imported for smelting and refining on a large scale. For a short time too, in the early 19C, Swansea porcelain was a noted local manufacture. The Swansea Canal, opened in 1798, had a rapid effect on the trade of the port, which increased from 90,000 tons in 1799 to 500,000 tons by 1839, and the first of the enclosed docks (North Dock) was opened in 1852, South Dock following in 1859. Both these docks were on the west bank of the Tawe. As steelmaking developed in the area, and as tinplate and coal became the principal exports, pressure grew for more docks and two were built on the east bank between 1879 (Prince of Wales) and 1909 (New King's). The copper smelting industry began to decline from c 1880, and later, with the rest of South Wales, Swansea suffered from two wars, the depression, and the ousting of coal

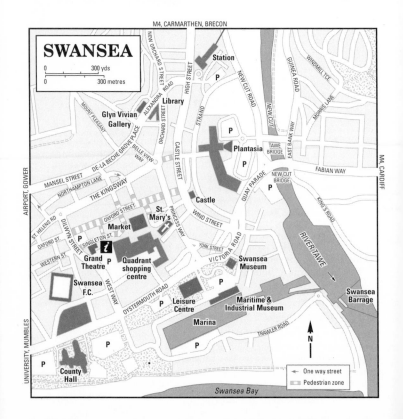

by oil. This last, however, was turned to good account when in 1918 the first oil refinery in Britain was opened near Swansea, the associated Queen's Dock for tankers following in 1920. During the Second World War (1941), the town centre was so badly damaged by bombing that rebuilding afterwards was to a new plan.

Among eminent natives are Bishop Gower (died 1347), who founded and endowed the original Swansea Hospital; Philip Jones (1618–74), the Parliamentarian; Beau Nash (1674–1762); and Dylan Thomas (1914–53), the poet.

CENTRE. The heart of modern Swansea clusters within a square (each side some 500 yards long) bounded by four streets: Princess Way on the east, Oystermouth road on the south, Westway on the west and The Kingsway along the north. Within this square will be found Tourist Information, the Grand Theatre, the Covered Market (food) and two shopping precincts, the Quadrant Centre and St. David's Square.

NORTH OF THE CENTRE. At its east end The Kingsway runs into The Circus, out of which, on the opposite side, the pedestrian College Street quickly reaches High Street, Swansea's pre-war main street, which leads north to the *Railway Station*.

Belle Vue Way, out of the northwest of the Circus, soon meets Grove Place with, a short distance to the right in Alexandra Road, the **Glynn Vivian Art Gallery** (Tues–Sun, also Bank Hol. 10.30–17.30. Tel. 01792-655006). Here the emphasis tends to be on temporary exhibitions and workshop activities, including activities for children, the permanent collection displays depending to a large extent on the space left available. However, pictures by modern Welsh artists, including Augustus John and Ceri Richards, are likely to be found, while Applied Art will probably include Swansea and Nantgarw porcelain, 17C and 18C glass, and collections of English and Continental paperweights and miniatures.

EAST OF THE CENTRE. On its east side the modern centre is defined by Princess Way, parallel to the east being Castle Street and Wind Street, with, beside the former, the remains of the *Castle*. However, this is not the ruin of Henry de Newburgh's castle, destroyed by Owen Glendower, but of a fortified manor built on the old castle's site. Below the castle, generally to the northeast and occupying the filled-in site of Swansea's first enclosed dock (the North Dock of 1852), is Parc Tawe with car parking, a ten-screen cinema, a shopping precinct and **Plantasia** (Tues–Sun 10.30–17.30. Tel. 01792-474555), devoted to tropical flora and smaller fauna.

SOUTH OF THE CENTRE. Here, immediately south of Victoria Road and its westward extension, Oystermouth Road, there are two museums and the **Leisure Centre** (tel. 01792-650351), opened by HM The Queen in 1977 while on her Jubilee tour. Behind the Leisure Centre, beside the Marina Main Basin, is the **Maritime and Industrial Museum** (Tues–Sun and Bank Hol. 10.30–17.30. Tel. 01792-650351), also opened in 1977 and a principal feature of Swansea's marina and maritime quarter concept. The museum is devoted to the history of the port of Swansea and of the industry of the city and its environs, together with material on transport and agriculture. Among the exhibits are locomotives, vehicles, the Mumbles tram and ship models. There is also a Woollen Mill, brought here from Neath and still producing, while various boats are moored alongside in what was once the South Dock of 1859 and is now the Marina Main Basin.

Swansea Museum (Tues–Sun and Bank Hol. 10.30–17.30. Tel. 01792-653763), a hundred yards to the north, was founded in 1835 as the Swansea Philosophical and Literary Institution; in 1838, when Queen Victoria became patron, it changed its name to the Royal Institution of South Wales;

and in 1993, when taken over by the city, it assumed its present name. The oldest museum in Wales and unashamedly old-fashioned, broadly the themes of the collections are archaeology, natural history, some geology and Welsh history. Archaeological material includes finds from the Paviland caves; a Roman milestone from the military road between Nidum (Neath) and Bovium (Boverton); the Gwindy and Penard Roman coin hoards; a Roman altar with traces of Ogham inscription; the Gnoll Stone, the shaft of a Celtic cross of c 1100; and a collection of medieval heraldic tiles from Neath Abbey. The Natural History section offers several good dioramas, while within the wide scope of Welsh History may be mentioned exhibits as diverse as Swansea and Nantgarw ceramics; a reproduction of an early 19C Gower kitchen; a coracle; a horrendous man-trap; a fascinatingly practical preaching chair; and souvenirs of the Mumbles tramway.

The *Dylan Thomas Theatre*, just south of Swansea Museum, stages both amateur and professional productions, while the nearby *Swansea Arts Workshop Gallery* (Tues–Sun, and also Mon in July and Aug, 11.00–16.30. Tel. 01792-652016), with a sales area, mounts exhibitions of contemporary art and craft.

WEST OF THE CENTRE most places of interest are strung along Oystermouth Road and its continuation, Mumbles Road, which run west close to the shore, the latter reaching Oystermouth (see Rte 39) in some four miles from the Leisure Centre. The **Guildhall** (tel. 01792-301301), built by Sir Percy Thomas in 1934, is set back but nevertheless conspicuous for its lofty tower. Here the *Brangwyn Hall* (concerts) shows the British Empire Panels by Sir Frank Brangwyn, originally painted as a war memorial for the House of Lords, and Brangwyn sketches also hang in the corridors. *Victoria Park*, immediately west of the Guildhall, includes the Patti Pavilion, once the opera singer Adelina Patti's Winter Garden at Craig-y-Nos (Rte 33).

The **University College of Wales**, in the large Singleton Park a mile farther west, includes Singleton Abbey, formerly the seat of Lord Swansea, and adjacent modern buildings. One of the constituent colleges of the University of Wales, the college was founded in 1920. Here the *Taliesin Arts Centre* (all year except Aug and Christmas, Mon–Sat 11.00–18.00 but closes 17.00 on Mon. Tel. 01792-296883) is a modern arts centre with theatre, cinema, art gallery, bookshop and programmes of events. *Singleton Park*, behind the university, reaches a good half mile northwards and includes botanical gardens, hothouses, a boating lake, play area and café. *Brynmill Park*, immediately east of Singleton, offers a lake and a children's zoo, while *Cwmdonkin Park*, three quarters of a mile farther northeast, was a favourite of the poet Dylan Thomas (memorial).

Mumbles road, curving south, in rather over half a mile from University College, passes *Clyne Gardens*, famous for azaleas and rhododendrons ('Clyne in Bloom', May). For **Oystermouth** and **Mumbles**, some two miles farther south, see Rte 39.

For Swansea to *Llandovery, Llandrindod Wells* and *Knighton*, see Rte 24; to *Merthyr Tydfil* and *Abergavenny*, see Rte 31; to *Brecon* and *Hay-on-Wye*, see Rte 33; to (E) *Cardiff, Newport* and the *Severn Bridge*, and to (W) *Carmarthen*, see Rte 35; for *Gower*, see Rte 39.

39

Gower

Tourist Information. The principal office is Tourist Information, Singleton Street, Swansea. Tel. 01792-468321. Also, but summer only, Oystermouth Square, Mumbles. Tel. 01792-361302.

The **GOWER PENINSULA**, a mass of carboniferous limestone some 15 miles long by four to eight miles broad projecting from Swansea into the Bristol Channel, is officially designated an Area of Outstanding Natural Beauty, known for its south coast bays, beaches and rocky cliff scenery. The bays, often with limited and expensive parking, can be very crowded in summer. The natural features along the peninsula's spine are, from east to west, Fairwood Common (with Swansea's airport), Cefn Bryn and Rhossili Down, these last two being old red sandstone uplands (over 600ft) affording long vistas. In the west the peninsula ends at the great sandy sweeps of Rhossili and Broughton bays, while the north shore is largely salt marsh. Much of Gower's scenic land, whether cliff, common or marsh, is owned by the National Trust, and there is nearly always footpath access. Indeed, walking is one of the best ways to see many parts of Gower, perhaps the most popular stretches being those between Port Eynon and Rhossili, and from Rhossili northward along Rhossili Down to Llangennith and Llanmadoc.

Once Gower was the home of lions, elephants, rhinoceros, hippopotamus, mammoth, bison, bear and others; animals whose bones have been discovered in the peninsula's many caves. And primitive man was here too, as evidenced by Palaeolithic remains (c 17th millennium BC) found in some caves, notably Paviland. The fact that access to these caves is now often difficult (and even dangerous) and subject to the tide indicates a major change in sea level, or, in some cases, that the carcases of larger animals could have been dragged in by, perhaps, wolves or hyenas. Finds from the caves may be seen in the National Museum of Wales (Cardiff) and at Swansea Museum.

Also of interest on Gower are prehistoric burial chambers, Iron Age hillforts, ruined medieval castles, nature reserves, and churches (usually basically 13C) notable for their small chancels and battlemented towers, the latter recalling the days when churches rather than castles were the ordinary person's places of refuge.

In the 12C Henry I planted Flemish colonists in Gower, a source to which some local people still trace their ancestry.

The description that follows starts at Oystermouth-Mumbles, then making a meandering clockwise circuit of, including diversions, some 40 miles to return to Swansea.

Oystermouth is known for its ruined *Castle*, strikingly placed on a green hill above the town (April–Sept: daily 11.00–17.00. Tel. 01792-368732).

History. There appear to have been a series of Norman wooden structures here, the first perhaps put up by Henry de Newburgh in c 1099. The first mention of a castle is 1215 when, the lordship having been given to the De Braose family by King John, a castle was burnt by the Welsh. Rebuilt, it was again destroyed by the Welsh in 1256–57 when Llewelyn the Last was in Gower. The keep, the nucleus of today's ruin, probably dates from c 1280 as it is known that Edward I visited here in 1284; the gatehouse and the ward walls are of a few years later. Afterwards the lands passed to the Mowbrays, who during the 14C converted the castle to residential use (the wings to the east and west of the keep dating from this period), and eventually to the Beauforts who presented the castle to Swansea in 1827.

The Gatehouse, originally flanked by two towers, of which traces remain, gives access to a single ward. Immediately on the left is the guardroom, beside which steps lead up to one of the governor's apartments, popularly though for no apparent reason known as the White Lady's Chamber. The ruins of the barracks are on the right of the ward, and those of kitchens on the left. At the top of the ward is the Keep, the oldest part of the castle, to its left being a three-storey building with a cellar, rooms, and, on the middle floor, the hall. To the right is another three-storey building, comprising a basement kitchen (note the roasting-jack holes by the fire), what may have been either a priest's or retainers' room, and, at the top, the chapel, with an aumbry and a piscina.

Oystermouth *Church*, reputedly built on the site of a Roman villa, has a battlemented 13C tower and an Early English east window. In the church-yard is the tomb of Dr Thomas Bowdler (1754–1825), who by expurgating Shakespeare added his own name to the English language.

Mumbles, the name deriving from the French 'mamelles' meaning 'breasts', strictly refers only to the two islets (accessible at low water) off the promontory beyond Ostermouth, but today the name is applied to the whole promontory town, a popular area with a pier. On the outer islet are a lighthouse of 1793 and a fort of 1861, and to the west of Mumbles are popular *Langland Bay* and *Caswell Bay*.

3m. Bishopston (on B4436), from where the National Trust's narrow and wooded Bishopston Valley (footpath) winds for nearly two miles down to Pwlldu Bay. At **Pennard** the church, with the usual castellated tower, spans the 13 to the 17C, the 13C claim being supported by the two lancets in the chancel, one with Norman dog-tooth moulding. From the church the westward road in about a mile reaches *Pennard Burrows* (footpaths), with traces of a castle and church, both victims of the sand, while to the south *Pennard Cliffs* is a fine National Trust estate reaching from Pwlldu Head west to Southgate. Below the cliffs are Bacon Hole and Mitchin Hole, two caves in which ancient animal bones have been found (c 1850), and Mitchin Hole also providing evidence of human occupation during Roman and Dark Ages times.

From Pennard B4436 kinks briefly north to meet A4118, a mile west along which, in the village of Parkmill, is the attractive small *Y Felin Dwr Craft and Countryside Centre* (daily 10.00–18.00. Tel. 01792-371206) with craft units clustered around a 14C water mill; also café and picnic area. From the western end of the village a lane leads north to a meadow in which lies prehistoric *Parc le Breose Burial Chamber*, discovered in 1869 and, on excavation, found to contain the scattered bones of some two dozen people within the four chambers off the long passage. The name of the site is of course more modern and recalls the early 13C De Braose owners of Oystermouth Castle. In Cathole, a cave a few hundred yards north of the burial chamber, flint tools found in 1968 suggest human occupation in around 12,000 BC. *1m. Penmaen*, to the south of which are Penmaen Burrows, with traces of a Norman earthwork, an ancient chapel and a prehistoric burial chamber (follow path signed Tor Bay for some 500 yards).

2m. Penrice Park (no adm.), within which is Penrice Castle, a ruin of the middle and late 13C (it was built by the Mansel family, of Norman origin).

From Penrice Park entrance the road dropping south to (*1m*) **Oxwich** crosses a part of *Oxwich National Nature Reserve*, with freshwater marsh on the west and saltmarsh followed by dunes on the east. Of both botanical and ornithological interest, the Reserve also includes, on the north, Crawley Wood and, on the south, Oxwich Wood. Parking is only allowed in the official car park, where there is an information point; there is no restriction on access to the beach and dunes, but for elsewhere a permit is needed. The small church, a little south above the shore, dates from the 13C and has a tiny chancel which may be a Celtic cell, and tradition holds that the ancient font was brought here by St. Illtyd. The so-called Castle remains are those of a Mansel manor built in c 1541.

From Oxwich, A4118 can be rejoined by following the minor road along the west flank of Penrice Park through (*1m*) the village of *Penrice*, with an early Norman motte or other earthwork and, on the green, the base of a medieval cross. On reaching A4118 a left turn, soon followed by a right turn, leads in about *1m* to **Reynoldston**, whence a road heading east climbs on to **Cefn Bryn**, a ridge (610ft) of open common affording fine views. To the north, and visible from the road, is *Arthur's Stone*, a large burial chamber capstone, while farther along the road, just south of where it kinks northeast, there is a holy well.

1m (from Reynoldston) **Knelston**, where there is a ruined 12C church, and, just beyond, **Llanddewi**, with a church in which the nave and chancel are curiously out of line, presumably due to different building periods.

From Llanddewi this Route now travels south to Port Eynon and then west to Rhossili and Worms Head. From here walkers may cross Rhossili Down to Llangennith, but motorists must return to Llanddewi to continue the Gower circuit.

2m. **Port Eynon** is a village at the end of A4118. From here (parking at the road's end beside the beach) a walk of just under three miles (but care must be taken with cliffs, rocks and tides) wanders through Overton and then across Port Eynon Point (NT), a limestone headland affording long coastal views. Of interest along the walk are Culver Hole (a largely man-made cave, said to have sheltered the local prince from the marauding English and later, in the 15C, to have been used by smugglers before conversion to a pigeon house), and the remains of a 16C salt factory. It is thought that sea water, trapped at high tide in specially built cisterns, was pumped up to the factory where it evaporated, allowing the factory to dry and sell the deposited salt.

Returning to (*2m*) *Scurlage*, B4247 is now followed west to (*1m*) *Pilton Green*. From here there is a footpath to Pilton Cliff, below being *Paviland Caves* (access dangerous), famous for having been the home of man at around the end of the Ice Age, for it was here, in Goat's Hole in 1823, that Dr Buckland found part of the skeleton of a young man, since scientifically dated to the 17th millennium BC (the bones, stained with ochre, were at first incorrectly identified, their owner becoming known as the Red Lady of Paviland). This man would have been a member of one of the groups of hunters who over centuries moved along this coast as the ice receded, while flints and ornaments also discovered here are evidence that men continued to use these caves over a span of millennia. *1m. Pitton*, less than a mile south of which is *Thurba Head* (200ft), with the remains of an Iron Age hillfort settlement, the head marking the south arm of Mewslade Bay, one of the most scenic of the bays along this coast. Red Chamber, a cave just east of Thurba, is so called from the ochre colouring of its walls.

1m. **Rhossili**, a village at the west end of B4247, lies above the south end of the five-miles-long great sandy crescent of remote and often windswept Rhossili Bay which marks the west extremity of Gower. One tradition is that the village is named after St. Fili, possibly a son of St. Cenydd (see below). In the church, with a 12C doorway, there is a memorial to Petty Officer Evans, born here, who perished with Scott in the Antarctic in 1912.

The land west of the village (largely National Trust, leased to the Countryside Council for Wales) embraces the *Gower Coast Nature Reserve* (NT Visitor Centre. Roughly March–Dec but with varying days and times. Tel. 01792-390707) with a Limestone Trail and Worms Head. The *Limestone Trail* (in part dangerous cliff; booklet from Visitor Centre), a three-miles-long anticlockwise circuit starting from and returning to Rhossili car park, passes seven points of interest, the first being a spot from which the remains of a ship, the 'Helvetia', may be seen on the beach where she was wrecked in 1887. 2. Old Castle, on the seaward side of the track, represents the earthwork traces of an Iron Age defended settlement. 3. Rhossili Vile is an open field system of narrow strips dating from Saxon times and largely still in use today. 4. Kitchen Corner, where limestone was quarried in the 18 and 19C and then loaded into boats at the foot of the cliff. 5. Coastguard Lookout, where the southerly slope acts as a suntrap which, with the limestone below, enriches this spot with plant life. 6. Tears Point is a flat-topped headland of bared limestone, the surface of deposits several thousands of feet deep. 7. Fall Bay, with a raised beach of conglomerate shells. *Worms Head*, deriving its name from the Norse for serpent, consists of two rocky islets connected with the mainland by a natural causeway for about two and a half hours either side of low tide and with each other by a narrow neck of rock. The outer head rises abruptly to a height of 200ft, and ancient animal bones have been found in the cave at its foot, which must in those remote times have been a lot more accessible. The water thrown up by the blowhole near the west extremity can be seen from Rhossili.

Rhossili Down, a National Trust property of over 500 acres and a launch-pad for hang-gliders, stretches for nearly two miles northward from Rhossili village. The *Beacon* (633ft), near the south end, is the highest point in Gower. Farther north, on the east slope, there are two burial chambers known as *Sweyne's Howes*, 'howes' being the ancient word for 'mound' and one tradition being that this is the burial place of Sweyne Forkbeard, said to have given his name to Swansea.

As noted earlier, walkers can cross Rhossili Down to Llangennith, but motorists must return some *6m* to Llanddewi, from where small roads north and then west in rather under *4m* reach **Llangennith** where the church is of interest, if only as an example of continuity. The largest church on Gower, it is a 12C rebuilding of the church of a small priory founded here in the 6C by St. Cenydd and destroyed by Viking raiders in 986. The tower, curiously placed north of the nave, has a saddle-back roof and is a good example of the Gower fortified type, and an ancient graveslab inside the church may be that of St. Cenydd.

Burry Holms, two miles northwest (one mile walk), an islet marking the north arm of Rhossili Bay, may be accessible for about two hours each side of low water. On the islet there are traces of Iron Age earthworks and the ruins of a medieval monastic chapel, while at low water the remains may be seen of the 'City of Bristol' which ran ashore in Rhossili Bay in 1840; and in this area, too, have been found doubloons and other coins from a Spanish galleon wrecked in the 17C.

2m (backtracking east, then north) **Cheriton**, where the 13C church is one of the most pleasing in Gower, noteworthy features being the south door-way, the good Early English arches and the tower with its saddle-back roof. The church at *Llanmadoc*, half a mile west of Cheriton, is said to have been founded by St. Madog, a follower of St. Cenydd; however his simple church has long disappeared and rebuilding of 1865 left little of its 13C successor. The *Bulwark*, belonging to the National Trust, is a large hillfort to the south of the Cheriton to Llanmadoc road.

   Whiteford Burrows, the peninsula reaching north into Burry Inlet, is a nature reserve of dunes and saltmarsh. Cars must be left at Llanmadoc (Cwm Ivy, just north) and visitors are asked to keep to the paths, one of which (four miles) starts from the Warden's house and heads out towards Whiteford Point. Visitors are warned that swimming is dangerous and that unexploded shells may be found away from the paths.

   Approaching (*1m* from Cheriton) *Landimore* there are fragments of a castle. *1m*. **Weobley Castle** (Cadw; see p. 11), with an exhibition on the history of Gower, is the ruin of a large 13–14C fortified manor well illustrat-ing the era in which comfort was becoming almost as important as security. Owned by the De la Bere family until the 15C and damaged during Owen Glendower's uprising, the property later passed to the Herberts and the Mansels. Beyond the 14C gatehouse there is a single ward with the mid 13C keep, the oldest part of the castle, to the right. The remaining ruins, mostly later 13C, include the chapel, completing the south side, and the kitchens and hall on respectively the east and north. From a more remote era, there is a standing stone in a field behind Windmill Farm, south of the road and roughly opposite the castle approach. At (*1m*) *Llanrhidian* a stone on the green, possibly the remains of the village cross, seems later to have been used as a pillory, and in the village church porch there is a carved stone bearing human and animal figures and thought to date from the 9C. Note also, on the exterior south wall, the intriguing rhymed epitaph of Robert Hary (died 1646).

   B4271 is now followed east for (*5m*) *Fairwood Common* (Swansea airport), whence A4118 reaches central **Swansea** (see Rte 38) in a further *5m*.

40

Carmarthen

CARMARTHEN, in Welsh Caerfyrddin, rises from the west bank of the Towy some eight miles above the river's mouth.

Tourist Information. Lammas Street. Tel. 01267-231557.

History. Carmarthen is the site of the Roman Caer Maridunum, the ruined walls of which were still standing in the time of Giraldus (12–13C) and something of the amphitheatre of which survives today. Later, in popular Dark Ages mythology, Merlin, or Myrddin or Fyrddin to give him his native name (hence the town's Welsh name), was born here, son of a king's daughter and, so she claimed, of a spirit. In c 1096 the

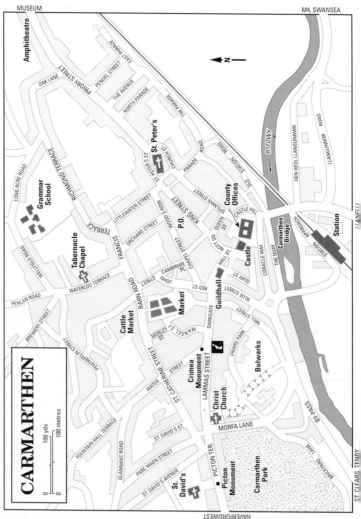

CARMARTHEN

Normans established a castle and walled borough here, the former being restored by
Edward I c 1313, in which year the town was granted its first charter, soon becoming
an important port and centre of the wool trade, exporting to Flanders and elsewhere
and in 1353 being declared the staple (monopoly) wool centre of Wales. Prosperity was
interrupted in the early 15C, when the town was taken by Owen Glendower in 1403
and 1405, but by 1450 the first festival officially using the name 'eisteddfod' could be
held here; metrical rules codified for this occasion are still applied to the Chair Poem
of the National Eisteddfod. In 1555 Robert Ferrar, Bishop of St. David's, was burnt at
the stake in what is now Nott Square as soon as the heresy laws were reintroduced by
Mary I. During the Civil War the castle was held for the King, but soon capitulated
(1646) to General Laugharne and was later slighted. Carmarthen continued to prosper
as both port and administrative and trading centre; iron smelting and tinplate works

were established in the 18C and trade was boosted by the arrival of the railway in 1856. Change and some decline followed the port developments farther east along the coast (the tinplate works closed in 1900), Carmarthen gradually becoming of administrative rather than industrial importance.

Sir William Nott (1782–1845), victor of the First Afghan War; Brindley Richards (1819–65), composer of 'God Bless the Prince of Wales'; Sir Lewis Morris (1833–1907), the poet, and E.W. Tristam (1882–1952), best known for his work in preserving medieval wallpaintings, were natives of the town. Sir Richard Steele, the Irish man of letters, died of a stroke in King Street in 1729.

The **Guildhall**, at the hub of several pedestrian streets, may, with Nott Square, be regarded as the town centre; rebuilt in 1767, it is successor to one of 1583. Nott Square is named for the victor of the First Afghan War (1841–42), while in an earlier context a monument recalls the martyrdom in 1555 of Bishop Ferrar. To the southeast, on a bluff above the river, County Hall occupies the site of the *Castle*, the only surviving features of which are a length of curtain wall and a 14C gatehouse.

King Street, leading out of Nott Square, in some 300 yards reaches 12–14C **St. Peter's Church**, with a fortified tower. In the south chapel is the altar-tomb, with effigies, of Sir Rhys ap Thomas (died 1525), supporter of Henry Tudor, and of his wife, and here too are memorials to Bishop Ferrar, Sir Richard Steele and General Knott, while Carmarthen's Roman ancestry is represented by a Roman altar in the west porch. Priory Street, leading northeast beyond St. Peter's Church, is a name recalling that an Augustinian priory once stood between here and the river; founded in about 1130, and burnt in 1435, this priory was the place at which the 'Black Book of Carmarthen', the oldest manuscript extant in Welsh, was written in the late 12C (now in the National Library, Aberystwyth).

At the junction of Priory Street and Oak Lane (300 yards from the church) stood, until recently, Merlin's Oak, probably planted by a local school-teacher in 1660 to honour the Restoration of Charles II. Later, however, this oak assumed Merlin mythology (that Merlin had prophesied that should the oak fall, so also would the town), but by the 1980s it had become no more than a dry and withered stump, now removed to the entrance to the Civic Hall (Knott Square) while a short length has found a home in the Carmarthen County Museum. The remains of the *Roman Amphitheatre* are beside the main road about a quarter of a mile farther east.

ENVIRONS OF CARMARTHEN. The **Carmarthen County Museum** (Mon–Sat 10.00–16.30. Tel. 01267-231691) is at Abergwili on A40 a mile east of Carmarthen. In a former palace of the bishops of St. David's, the museum illustrates regional archaeology (with some Ogham/Latin stones), history, natural history and daily life. It was at this palace that Bishop Davies and William Salesbury worked together to produce their Welsh Book of Common Prayer and New Testament (1567). *Bryn Myrddin*, or *Merlin's Hill*, just north of A40 a mile east of Abergwili, claims, as of course do many other places thoughout Britain, to be where Merlin sleeps.

At **Llansteffan** (or Llanstephan), seven miles south of Carmarthen on the west bank of the Towy approaching its mouth, a large ruined *Castle* overlooks the estuary. Built during the 11–13C, but successor to earlier defensive earthworks on this site, the castle's main feature is a fine gate-house of 1280 which seems to have been converted to a keep and living quarters. *St. Anthony's Well*, a quarter of a mile southwest of the castle, a wishing well said to have had medicinal properties, has a niche in which the figure of a saint perhaps once stood.

For Carmarthen to *Swansea*, *Cardiff* and the *Severn Bridge*, see Rte 35; to *Aberystwyth* via *Aberaeron*, see Rte 41A and via *Lampeter* and *Strata Florida*, see Rte 41B; to *Cardigan*, *Fishguard* and *St. David's*, see Rte 42; to *Haverfordwest* and *St. David's* or *Fishguard*, see Rte 43; to *Tenby*, *Pembroke* and *Milford Haven*, see Rte 44.

41

Carmarthen to Aberystwyth

A. Via Aberaeron

A484 and A486 to Synod Inn. A487 to Aberystwyth. Total distance 47m.—
7m. Cynwyl Elfed.—*8m.* **Llandysul**.—*10m.* Synod Inn.—*6m.*
Aberaeron.—*13m.* **Llanfarian**.—*3m.* **Aberystwyth**.

The first part is scenically pleasant, ascending narrow, winding and wooded valleys and passing a number of wool mills. Later, this Route crosses duller country. For the first 12 miles, Rte 42 coincides with this one.

Carmarthen, see Rte 40. *3m.* Bronwydd Arms for the *Gwili Railway*, a private venture (of 1975) aimed at preserving a stretch of the old Great Western Line and offering a short ride by steam or diesel (late July and Aug: daily 11.00–16.30. Other occasions as locally advertised. Tel. 01267-230666). A484 ascends the twisting wooded valley of the Gwili, in *4m* reaching *Cynwyl Elfed*, just before which B4333 bears northwest as an upland shortcut to Newcastle Emlyn on Rte 42. This Route continues north with the Duad in *5m.* reaching a fork at which Rte 42 bears away northwest for, in under two miles, the Museum of the Welsh Woollen Industry. The Teifi is crossed before (*3m.*) **Llandysul**, birthplace of Christmas Evans (1766–1838), orphan son of a cobbler who became a Baptist minister because his first choice, the Presbyterians, demanded an academic standard he did not have. Mainly active in Anglesey, he attracted huge crowds to his oratorical and fiery sermons. The church here is of interest for its Norman tower and, in the Lady Chapel, a Celtic altar brought here from a nearby hillfort. Llandysul is a wool centre, in the district being several mills (with shops) which welcome visitors. One such is *Rock Mill* (Mon–Fri 09.00–17.00. Tel. 01559-362356) at Capel Dewi, some two miles northeast, a rare example of a working woollen mill still powered by water. *10m.* Synod Inn, where Rte 46 comes in from the southwest and from where the small resort of *Newquay* is just four miles north.

6m **Aberaeron** (*Inf.*) is a small place of some character with a number of Georgian-style houses, notably in Alban Square to the east of the main through road. The small harbour can be crossed by cable car (1988; successor to the Aeron Express of 1885–1932), and on the Quay there is a popular *Sea Aquarium and Animal Kingdom Centre* (April or Easter, whichever earlier—Oct: daily 10.30–20.30 in late July and Aug; 11.00–17.00 in other months. Tel. 01545-570142). For Aberaeron to *Dolaucothi* and *Brecon*, see Rte 27.

1m. At the church at *Llanddewi Aberarth* there are two incised stones, one a 9C cross and the other hog-backed. *12m.* **Llanfarian**, where Rte 41B joins from the east just before the river Ystwyth is crossed. About a mile and a half beyond the river a crossroads is reached whence Rte 23B heads east along A4120 for Devil's Bridge and beyond. This Route here turns northwest, passing on the left *Pen Dinas* (415ft), a ridge between the rivers Ystwyth and Rheidol marked by a monument to the Duke of Wellington and a hillfort, the latter interesting in that there seem originally to have been two separate enclosures, joined into one during the 1C BC. *3m.* (from Llanfarian) **Aberystwyth**, see Rte 22.

B.   Via Lampeter and Strata Florida Abbey

A485 to Lampeter. B4343 to Pontrhydfendigaid. B4340, B4275 and A485 to Llanfarian. A487 to Aberystwyth. Total distance 52m.—*5m. Pont-ar-Sais* (for **Llanpumpsaint**).—*11m.* **Llanybydder**.—*5m.* **Lampeter**.—*4m. Llanfair Clydogau.*—*4m.* **Llandewi Brefi**.—*3m.* **Tregaron**.—*6m. Pontrhydfendigaid* (for **Strata Florida Abbey**).—*11m.* **Llanfarian**.—*3m.* **Aberystwyth**.

Carmarthen, see Rte 40. A485 heads north, on the outskirts of Carmarthen leaving *Abergwili*, with the Carmarthen County Museum (see Rte 40) a mile to the east along A40. *5m. Pont-ar-Sais*, a mile and a half west of which is **Llanpumpsaint**, the Church of the Five Saints. These were Ceitho, Celynen, Gwyn, Gwyno and Grynnaro, brothers (during the 6C) and members of the Cunedda family which, being semi-royal, presumably had little problem in arranging this mass sanctification. In the church the medieval altar-slab bears nine consecration crosses. Beyond Pont-ar-Sais the road crosses hilly wooded country, in *12m.*, beyond **Llanbydder**, reaching *Pencarreg* where the church is worth a visit for its curious ancient font bearing human heads.

4m. **Lampeter**, or Llanbedr Pont Steffan, lying below wooded hills on the west side of the Teifi at the crossing of several roads and at one time known for its river ford, has long been the chief centre for the upper Teifi valley. *St. David's College*, the oldest Welsh degree-granting institution, was founded in 1822 by Bishop Burgess of St. David's and in 1971 became a constituent college of the University of Wales. The original buildings, by C.B. Cockerell (1827), are grouped around a quadrangle and lie within pleasant grounds which, contrastingly, contain both an ancient motte and modern university buildings. For Lampeter to (W) *Aberaeron* and (E) *Brecon*, see Rte 27.

A485 provides the fast and direct approach to Tregaron, but this Route chooses the quieter and more interesting B4343 along the east bank of the Teifi, across the river being a succession of hillforts—Castells Olwen, Allt-Goch and Goetre—all, however, minor. *4m. Llanfair Clydogau*, once the site of Roman silver mines, was on the Roman Sarn Helen. Southward from here this military highway (now minor roads) reached the Dolaucothi gold mines; northwards, Sarn Helen crossed the river and in about four miles reached the fort of Bremia (see below).

4m. **Llanddewi Brefi**, where St. David (Dewi) attended a synod in 519, possibly convened to refute the Pelagian heresy but more probably for the enactment of local rules of discipline. The *Church of St. David* stands on a holy mound which, tradition insists, rose under the saint as he preached here; with, it is said, the voice of a trumpet, inspired by the Holy Spirit perched on his shoulder in the form of a dove. Today's church, however, although some 700 years old, is considerably more recent than this theatrical occasion, having been built in around 1287 in association with a college established here by Bishop Beck of St. David's for a precentor and 12 prebendaries. Nevertheless, in keeping with its dramatic past, the church's transepts suddenly collapsed during the 19C. Inside the church there are some venerable stones, one, the tallest, being known as St. David's Staff and another bearing an Ogham inscription. This latter has been sadly mutilated, one suggestion being that it commemorated a heretic of the persuasion which David came here to denounce. But perhaps the most interesting corner of this church is the northwest exterior angle of the nave, where, forming part of the fabric of the upper wall, two stones (one of them upside down) bear some fragmentary Latin inscription. Once, certainly in the late 17C, these two stones were a part of a single free-standing memorial in the churchyard and Llandewi Brefi indeed owes much to a scholar of 1698 who, realising that this memorial dated back to long-lost centuries, recorded the full inscription. It read then: 'hic jacet idnert filivs jacobi qui occisvus fvit propter predam sancti david', or 'Here lies Idnert son of Jacobus who was slain because of the plunder of the Sanctuary of David'. Idnert is generally accepted to have been a murdered Bishop of Llanbadarn Fawr (see Rte 22), but what is important here is not so much Idnert's identity as that this is the earliest known inscription referring to David, one carved moreover within a century or so of when he was here. The sad thing is that during the 18 or 19C the nave needed repair and the mason responsible—presumably illiterate, certainly no antiquarian, but quick to spot a useful stone—broke it up and incorporated its pieces in the wall. Today only two separated fifths of the original can be seen, the remainder probably embedded elsewhere in the wall with the inscription tantalisingly buried inwards.

From Llandewi Brefi Roman enthusiasts may cross the river to meet A485, then turn left to pass the junction with B4578, the arrow-straight modern form of Sarn Helen. Just south of this junction a lane to the left crosses a small humped bridge over a disused railway and arrives at a farm where permission can be asked to visit what remains of the fort of *Bremia*, today no more than seemingly haphazard banks and ditches and a few sorry stones which may represent the baths.

3m. **Tregaron** (*Inf.*), a small town and centre for the surrounding hill sheep farms, owes its name to Caron, a local chieftain and self-declared bishop of the 2–3C. Twm Shon Catti (Rte 24) was born here (1530), as was also Henry Richard (1812–88), advocate of international arbitration and founder of the Peace Union, to whom there is a memorial. At *Llangeitho*, four miles west, a centre of Methodism, there is a statue to the Rev. Daniel Rowlands (1713–90), a revivalist, who was born there. For the drover hillroad, across to (18m) *Llanwrtyd Wells*, see Rte 24. *Brimstone Wildlife Centre* (Easter–roughly Oct: daily 10.00–18.00 or 11.00–15.30 in Oct. Tel. 01974-821439), some five miles northwest of Tregaron by A485 and B4577, is particularly popular with children who can enjoy a variety of features such as tropical butterflies, a collection of horses and ponies (parades twice daily), pony trekking, many small animals, a wildflower meadow and a lake and wetland walk. Also here are a shop, picture gallery, restaurant and tearoom.

Continuing north from Tregaron along B4343, **Cors Caron Nature Reserve** for some four miles fringes the west of the road. The reserve, an area of some three square miles either side of the meandering Teifi and of particular interest to botanists and ornithologists, includes three raised peat bogs, the largest being on the west side and the other two on the east. The bogs are 'raised' in that they appear as domes with the centre up to 20ft higher than the edge. This feature has developed over millennia through several stages: briefly, the dropping of glacial moraine forming a dam; the growth of a lake; the silting of the lake, the arrival of vegetation, and the formation of a fen; the vegetation rots, becoming waterlogged, sinking, and under pressure turning to peat; and the shaping of a dome because the peat has formed more easily above the waterlogged centre than above the edges from where the rainfall can seep away. The natural state of the bogs has been damaged by peat cutting (which however ended in 1960), the west bog being the least affected but the other two having only the centres of their domes undisturbed. The reserve can be well viewed from the disused railway embankment below which there are parking areas.

6m (from Tregaron) *Pontrhydfendigaid* means 'Bridge near the ford of the Blessed Virgin'.

*Strata Florida Abbey (Cadw; see p. 11), a mile or so southeast, was once one of the most celebrated abbeys in Wales.

History. The name is a Latinised form of 'Ystrad Fflur' meaning 'Vale of Flowers'. Although this abbey, a Cistercian house, is known to have been founded in 1164, tradition suggests that there may have been a predecessor, perhaps Cluniac, near Old Abbey Farm, a mile and a half south of Pontrhydfendigaid, where in the 19C foundations were excavated and removed. The founder of 1164 was probably Robert FitStephan, a vassal of the Clares. Two years later his lands were overrun by Rhys ap Gruffydd. Grandson of the founder of the earlier house, and perhaps finding Cistercian ideals of simplicity and poverty akin to local monastic tradition, Rhys refounded the abbey in 1184 and began the existing church, although he died before its dedication in 1201. The greater part of the ruins date from this time, or a few years later (the east extension of the presbytery). The chapter house and the monks' choir are of the 14C, while the cloister is 15C and early 16C. The abbey, wholly Welsh in character, was the political, religious, and educational centre of the country in the 12C and 13C, in 1238 witnessing an assembly of Welsh princes summoned by Llewelyn the Great to swear allegiance to his son Dafydd. Economically the abbey flourished largely from wool, provided by the sheep which grazed on its lands which extended as far as Rhayader. During the Owen Glendower troubles the abbey was abandoned as such, being used as military stables. The building of the stone cloister dates from some time after the return of the monks. After the Dissolution the estates passed through various hands, the Crown assuming responsibility for the ruins in 1931.

Apart from remains of the cloister and the chapter house, the ruins seen today are those of the church.

The CHURCH, in Transitional Norman style, is on the usual Cistercian plan, having an aisled nave of seven bays, transepts (each with three chapels), and an aisleless presbytery. At the west end of the *Nave* the doorway (not quite in its original medieval form) is richly ornamented, with a framing cluster of rolls, continuous from the ground, tied together at intervals by bands ending in crosier-like ornaments. Inside, the arcades were of unique local character, the clustered piers being raised on plain screen walls about 5ft high, an arrangement not known elsewhere in England or Wales though occasionally found in Ireland. The *Crossing* was filled by a monks' choir, with screen walls largely blocking all directions except east. On the east of the choir narrow openings gave access to the

Transepts, each with three east side chapels, originally vaulted. Remains of altars can be seen, and many of the medieval tiles have been relaid (not *in situ*). The designs on the tiles merit study. In the north transept there is a memorial (1951) to Dafydd ap Gwilym (c 1320–80), described by Borrow as 'the greatest of his country's songsters'. Born near Aberystwyth, he may be buried either here at Strata Florida or at Talley. The *Presbytery* belongs to two periods, the two west bays being the earlier part and the east bay an addition of c 1250. Later came two more alterations. In the 14C the floor was raised, two steps being placed under the east arch of the crossing; and in the 15C the altar was raised and moved west, leaving space behind for two chapels. Some of the tiles laid during the 15C alteration have been reset. Beyond the south end of the south transept is the *Sacristy*, with doors from both the cloister and the transept.

Strata Florida Abbey. Door at the west end of the nave

The CHAPTER HOUSE, immediately south of the sacristy, is in two parts and of two periods (13C and 14C), the oldest masonry being the southeast and east wall remains. It seems that the older east part of the building was abandoned, becoming part of the cemetery (note the two graves through the walls). Rhys ap Gruffydd belonged to the princely house of Dinefwr, many members of which were buried here. It is thought that the line of tombs outside the angle of the south transept and presbytery represents earlier burials (two of the headstones bear pre-Norman ornamentation). Later burials were in the chapter house, where one slab has been exposed. The CLOISTER, with two doors to the south aisle, had five bays on its north side, each with a window, some of the sills of which survive. The alcove at the centre of the north side was for a lectern. After the Dissolution the west walk was divided into rooms which, with the now ruined west building, formed part of a house.

Teifi Pools, a cluster of small lakes in wild country two and a half miles northeast of the abbey and accessible by a lane and paths, are the source of the Teifi.

B4343, leading north from Pontrhydfendigaid, in eight miles reaches *Devil's Bridge* on Rte 23B.

B4340 is now followed northwest through *Ystrad Meurig*, where there are traces of a castle of the Clares. Beyond, reaching Ystwyth Forest, the Ystwyth is crossed; there is a FE picnic site a quarter of a mile east of the bridge. *6m* (from Pontrhydfendigaid) *Black Covert, Trawscoed*, near the junction of B4340 and B4575, is another FE picnic site and the start of a forest walk which includes a hillfort and a butterfly reserve. *5m* (by B4575) *Llanfarian*, where Rte 41A is joined. For Llanfarian to (*3m*) **Aberystwyth**, see Rte 41A.

42

Carmarthen to Cardigan, Fishguard and St. David's

A484 to Cardigan. A487 and B4582 to Nevern. A487 to St. David's. Total distance 60m.—*15m* Henllan—*3m*. **Newcastle Emlyn.**—*3m*. **Cenarth.**—*7m*. **Cardigan.**—*7m*. **Nevern.**—*2m*. **Newport.**—*7m*. **Fishguard.**—*16m*. **St. David's**.

Over the latter part of this Route diversions should be made down side roads in order to enjoy the coastal scenery.

For **Carmarthen** (see Rte 40) to (*12m*) road junction A484/A486, see Rte 41A. *3m. Henllan*, for the Teifi Valley Railway (Easter–Oct: daily. Trains hourly from 11.00. Tel. 01559-371077) offering a narrow gauge steam or diesel ride above the river (forty minutes; also waterfall visit, woodland walks, picnic and play areas etc.). **Drefach Felindre**, a mile south, was, with many surrounding villages, between 1870 and 1930 the leading woollen manufacturing district of Wales (at the beginning of the century there were 43 mills), an era recalled today by the *Museum of the Welsh Woollen Industry* (Mon–Sat, or Fri in Oct–March, 10.00–17.00. Tel. 01559-370929), a branch of the National Museum of Wales. Opened in 1976 and occupying parts of a working mill (Cambrian Mill, built 1902), the museum tells the story of the industry from medieval times onwards; shows a comprehensive collection of machinery and tools; includes an exhibition tracing the progress of wool from sheep to fabric; and offers a variety of demonstrations.

The road now descends the Teifi, as known today for its salmon as it was in the 12C when Giraldus praised it for abounding with finer salmon than any other river in Wales. However, the beavers, also mentioned by Giraldus, have long disappeared. *3m.* **Newcastle Emlyn** is a small centre serving the surrounding farming community. Of the original Norman castle, thought to have been on the river's north bank, there is no trace. The 'new' castle was a 16C rebuilding by Sir Rhys ap Thomas of an earlier structure; designed as a fortified manor, it was later held for the King during the Civil War but afterwards slighted, little now remaining above ground other than the gateway to an inner ward. It was in *Adpar*, across the river, that the first printing press in Wales was set up in 1719. *Felin Geri Mill* (Easter–Oct: daily 10.00, or 10.30 on Sun, to 18.00. Tel. 01239-710810), at Cwm Cou just over a mile northwest by B4331, is a 16C working water-mill producing stone-ground flour. Other attractions here include some rare breed animals, walks, a picnic area, a fishing museum and falconry demonstrations.

3m. **Cenarth**, a most attractive, almost hidden riverside village with rapids (salmon leaping; best in October) and the *National Coracle Centre* (Easter–Oct: daily 10.30–17.30. Also by appointment. Tel. 01239-710980). Here—with a workshop, and examples from Wales, Iraq, Vietnam, India and America—the story of coracles worldwide is attractively told (in summer coracles are when possible afloat), while, adjacent, visitors may also wander round a 17C flour-mill, successor to one mentioned by Giraldus in 1188.

7m. **Cardigan** (*Inf.*) is a pleasant small town on the Teifi some three miles above the river's mouth; hence Cardigan's Welsh name of Aberteifi.

History. A port and the site of primitive fortification in pre-Norman times, the first stone castle here was built in the late 11C or early 12C by Gruffydd ap Rhys. Later, in c 1170, this became a residence of Rhys ap Gruffyd who strengthened the fortifications and in 1176 organised here the first recorded eisteddfod, although this word is not actually used in contemporary chronicles. Town and castle later passed to the Earl of Pembroke who in 1240 rebuilt the latter. Town privileges were granted by Edward I but not confirmed by charter until 1542. In 1645 the castle fell to Parliament, Jeremy Taylor being among the captured garrison. During the 19C the town's prosperity declined with the silting of the estuary.

Cardigan was the home of Mrs Katherine Philips (1631–64), the 'matchless Orinda' who inspired Jeremy Taylor's 'Discourse of Friendship' (1657).

Cardigan's perhaps most attractive feature is the Teifi bridge, of ancient origin and rebuilt in 1726. Immediately to the north is the *Castle*, in fact little more than bits of the keep and two ruined towers surviving from the Earl of Pembroke's rebuilding of 1240. From just northwest of here High Street and Pendre curve northwards passing the old covered market and, roughly opposite, Priory Street, a name recalling a medieval Benedictine house that once stood here.

Gwbert-on-Sea, three miles north of Cardigan on the east side of the Teifi estuary, is a small resort known for its little bays and cliff walks. Just offshore is the cliffbound *Cardigan Island*, home of seals, birds and half-wild Soay sheep. *Mwnt*, a mile and a half east of Cardigan Island, is a coastal National Trust property of nearly 100 acres (beach, parking, facilities).

For Cardigan to (N) *Aberaeron* and (S) *Tenby*, see Rte 46. For *Cilgerran Castle* also see Rte 46.

This Route crosses Cardigan Bridge, immediately bearing north along B4546 for, in under a mile, **St. Dogmael's Abbey**, in origin an early Welsh house, sacked by the Vikings and then refounded in 1115 by Robert Martyn, Lord of this district of Cemaes, for monks of the reformed Benedictine Order brought over from Tiron in France. The modest ruins comprise fragments of the refectory and the north and west walls of the nave of the church, the most notable feature being the ball-flower ornament on the moulding of the north door. The site includes a collection of inscribed stones, effigies and suchlike, and also the *Parish Church* (1850) which houses the Sagranus Stone, inscribed in Latin and Ogham and thus (in 1848) providing the key for the interpretation of the Ogham alphabet.

Returning to Cardigan Bridge, this Route heads south, almost immediately forking right along A487 for (*2m*) *Croft*, from where B4582 in *5m* reaches **Nevern**, with, on a hill to the northwest, the remains of its *Castle*. Originally a fortress of the local Welsh chieftains of Cemaes, the site was rebuilt as a motte-and-bailey in c 1100 by the Norman Robert Martyn, Marcher Lord of Cemaes. His grandson William, however, moved to Newport before the end of the century, Nevern then being taken over by Rhys ap Gruffyd (his father-in-law) who built a stone castle on the east angle of the ward. The ruins are overgrown, but the motte can be seen together with some fragments of the stone castle.

But the most interesting feature of Nevern is its *Church of St. Brynach* (15–16C, but with a Norman tower), dedicated to a 5C Irish holy man whose cell was on Carn Ingli (the Hill of the Angels, three miles southwest) and famous for its carved stones. The two inside the church, now forming window sills in the south transept, were found in 1906 embedded in the wall of the passage to the chamber over the chapel. The Maglocunus Stone (?5C) bears both Latin and Ogham inscriptions commemorating Maglocunus (Welsh Maelgwn), son of Clutor. It is of interest that the chieftain who granted land to St. Brynach for his church was called Clether or Clutor and was related to Brynach's wife, but there is no evidence that this Clutor and the one on the stone are the same. The other sill, the Cross Stone (10C), bears a cross of entwined Viking pattern. There are two more stones in the churchyard. The Vitalianus Stone, immediately east of the porch, is inscribed in both Latin and Ogham. The *Great Cross, farther east, is one of the most perfect Celtic crosses in Wales. Dating from the 10C the cross is 13ft high and bears elaborate patterning. Note, on the east and west sides, the examples of the abbreviated writing of the period, that on the west standing for 'dominus', and that on the east possibly for 'Halleluiah!'. There are several other items of interest around the churchyard. To the east of the Great Cross the tombstone epitaph to the infant children of the Rev. D. Griffiths is as amusing as it is touching. Just beyond, a memorial stands to the Rev. John Jones (vicar here 1842–52), who helped Lady Charlotte Guest in translating the 'Mabinogion' into English. A faintly inscribed stone will be found on the north wall of the church (west corner of the sill of the second chancel window); this has been cut to fit its present position and is thought to bear part of a vertical Latin inscription of c 400. On the northeast corner of the north transept there is a consecration cross, and by the churchyard entrance there is an 18 or 19C mounting block. A short way west of the church, beyond a stile, the Pilgrim's Cross, cut into the rock, was probably a shrine along the road from Holywell to St. David's.

Pentre Ifan. A typical communal burial chamber dating from perhaps 2500 BC. It would have been covered by a long mound

ENVIRONS OF NEVERN. The burial chamber of *Pentre Ifan, two miles south beyond A487, is remotely sited (but accessible by car) on an open hillside, with rocky moorland above and the tumbled summit of Carn Ingli with its Iron Age fort and settlement, once the home of St. Brynach, filling the west. A communal burial place dating from earlier than 2000 BC, the still remarkably intact main structure consists of a long capstone supported by massive uprights.

Castell Henllys (Easter–Oct: daily 10.00–17.00. Tel. 01239-79319), two miles southeast of Nevern and to the north of A487, is an Iron Age and Romano-British hillfort, part under excavation and part reconstructed to show huts, crafts, crops and suchlike.

2m. **Newport**, once capital of the Marcher lordship of Cemaes, the only such lordship not to have been abolished by Henry VIII, and said to have had a brisk wool trade until in Tudor times the plague diverted the market to Fishguard, is now primarily a holiday place popular for its beaches and sea fishing. The *Castle* (no adm.), dating from the 13C and, for the lords of Cemaes, successor to Nevern, is now incorporated into a modern mansion. For the *Presely Hills*, to the south of Newport, see Rte 46. 3m (from Newport) *Dinas* is a village at the base of *Dinas Island*, a 400 acre promontory ending as Dinas Head (463ft). At Cwm-yr-Eglwys, at the promontory's southeast base, only the belfry and a wall survive of a church said to have been founded in the 6C and destroyed by a storm in 1839.

4m. **Fishguard** (Abergwaun. *Inf.*) is a pleasant small town perched high above its *Old Harbour*, an inlet at the head of which, at the mouth of the Gwaun, is the quite picturesque Lower Town, the setting for Dylan Thomas's 'Under Milk Wood' filmed here in 1971. Fishguard is associated with the last invasion of Britain, a farcical affair in which on 22 February 1797 three French frigates arrived off Carreg Wastad Point (see Pen Caer below) and landed 1400 convicts under the command of the Irish-American

General Tate. Local people and militia gathered under the energetic Earl of Cawdor and on 24 February Tate, appreciating that his situation was hopeless (both militarily—tradition insists that he mistook red-cloaked Welsh women for British soldiers—and also because his drunken rabble was threatening to shoot him if he did not sue for peace) signed unconditional surrender at the 'Royal Oak' where relics of the occasion are preserved. At nearby *St. Mary's Church* can be seen the headstone of Jemima Nicholas, 'The Welsh Heroine who boldy marched to meet the French invaders', personally capturing no fewer than 14 Frenchmen. Aged 47, a cobbler by profession and, it is reported, of brawny build and fearsome mien, she was awarded a pension which she enjoyed until her death at the age of eighty-two.

The main road drops sharply to *Goodwick*, once a fishing village but now effectively the base for *Fishguard Harbour*, known for its sea services with Rosslare in Ireland. The harbour (as also that at Rosslare) was built in 1894–1906 by the specially formed Fishguard and Rosslare Railways and Harbours Company, and it was on 30 August 1906 that services, previously running from Neyland (Milford Haven) to Waterford, were transferred to Fishguard and Rosslare.

PEN CAER DIVERSION. The direct road to St. David's is A487, but a diversion can be made through the broad promontory of **Pen Caer** with prehistoric remains, cliff scenery and places associated with the invasion of 1797. From the village of St. Nicholas, the last place visited on Pen Caer, a choice of roads lead back to A487.

The principal hamlet is *Llanwnda*, best approached by motorists from the southwest end of Goodwick. Reaching the high ground, this road turns right and then left at a cemetery for Llanwnda, near this second turn being a small incised stone set in a bank (along the lane dropping down from here are traces of at least two burial chambers). Giraldus was for a while rector at Llanwnda and, centuries later during the 1797 invasion, the church was attacked by the drunken French-Irish rabble and looted of its plate. There is a cross cut into the east end of the exterior nave wall, and just south of the church there is a burial chamber, interesting for the labour-saving way in which one end of the capstone rests on the ground and the other on an upright standing in a pit. *Carreg Wastad* (path from Llanwnda; about half a mile, northwest) was the landing place of the invaders, eight of whom were drowned (memorial stone). The road westward from Llanwnda in a mile reaches *Tre-Howel Farm* at which General Tate set up his headquarters; stocked ready for a wedding, it well suited the soldiery who speedily drank themselves incapable. A mile west beyond Tre-Howel there is a road junction, the northward choice in another mile reaching *Strumble Head*, with parking, a lighthouse and fine coastal scenery. The southward road, running below the height of *Carn Fawr* with a hillfort, continues to *St. Nicholas* where the church has an inscribed stone built into its wall and, in the choir, two Ogham stones. There is a burial chamber half a mile south of the village and a standing stone and tumulus about three quarters of a mile to the east.

Along the direct road (A487) for St. David's, in 5m. from Fishguard, a small crossroads is reached at which signs direct to two typically Welsh experiences, to the north a woollen mill, to the south a cheese centre. The former is *Melin Tregwynt* (Mon–Fri 09.00–17.00. Shop also open Sat 09.00–17.30. Tel. 01348-891225) where the weaving of pure new wool textile can be watched (also restaurant and picnic area). The latter is *Llangloffan Farm-house Cheese Centre* (tel. 01348-891241), winner of several awards. The farm is run chiefly on organic principles and cheese-making can be seen Mon–Sat 10.00–12.30 in May–August, and Mon, Wed, Thur, Sat in April and October (also tearoom, farm shop and play area).

11m. **St. David's** (Tyddewi. *Inf.*), because of its cathedral officially a city (although the smallest such in Britain), is in practice little more than a village straggling across an almost treeless and often either misty or wind-swept plateau above the little river Alun down beside which in Glyn Rhosyn (valley of the little bog) are the Cathedral and Bishop's Palace. The village offers two marine life attractions—the *Oceanarium* (daily. Summer 10.00 to late evening. Winter 10.30–16.00. Tel. 01437-720453) and the *Marine Life Centre* (daily. 10.00–17.00, or 18.00 in July and Aug. Tel. 01437-721665), both with play and picnic areas—while also in the upper village is the partly ruined *Tower Gate*, the main entrance to the cathedral close, a large enclosure, some three quarters of a mile in circumference and still in large part surrounded by a wall which though frequently restored is in origin of c 1300. This gate is the last survivor of four, and it and the precinct wall are in the main attributable to Bishop Gower (1328–47) although it has been suggested that the octagonal flanking tower on the north, which is 50 years older than the rest, was originally a detached bell-tower.

The foot approach to the cathedral is by a flight of steps known as the Thirty-nine Articles. Motorists should follow signs to parking in the valley.

If its city is the smallest such in Britain, ****St. David's Cathedral** is the largest, finest and perhaps most interesting church in Wales.

History. The see was traditionally founded by St. David, patron saint of Wales, in c 550 when he transferred his monastery from Whitesands Bay (a mile and a half northwest) to Glyn Rhosyn, but both the church and the monastery he is supposed to have built here have long disappeared. William the Conqueror is known to have paid homage at the saint's shrine, but soon afterwards, in 1088, the Vikings sacked and burnt both the cathedral and its associated settlement. Despite this, St. David's flourished, kings continuing to make their pilgrimage to a place so remote and sanctified that two pilgrimages here equated with one to Rome.

The present building was begun in 1180 during the episcopate of *Peter de Leia* (1176–98), the third Norman bishop (the first was Bernard, who succeeded the Welshman Wilfred). His nave still stands. Giraldus gives a gossiping account of the see in 1188; he was himself afterwards nominated to the bishopric, but failed to secure it (in spite of three appeals to Rome), partly because of his connection with the Welsh royal line, and partly, no doubt, because he argued for the independence of the Church in Wales. In 1220 the central tower fell, demolishing the choir and transepts; but these, with the lower stage of the tower, were rebuilt practically in the original style by 1250. The successive addition of the chapel of St. Thomas, the ambulatory, and the Lady Chapel (by *Bishop Martyn*, 1296–1328) completed in broad outline the ground plan of the church. *Bishop Gower* (1328–47) raised the height of the nave and chancel, inserting the Decorated windows, and added the middle stage of the central tower. *Bishop Houghton* (1361–88), Lord Chancellor to Edward III, achieved fame by being excommunicated and then himself excommunicating the Pope from the cathedral steps; *Bishop Vaughan* (1508–22) completed the top stage of the tower, and also vaulted the Lady Chapel. Other bishops during the 16C were *Bishop Ferrar* (1548–55), the Marian martyr burnt at Carmarthen, and *Bishop Davies* (1561–68), who procured the first Welsh translation of the Bible.

Archbishop Laud (1621–26) was appointed bishop on relinquishing the president-ship of St. John's College, Oxford, but he never came to St. David's. During the Civil War much of the lead was stripped from the roofs, and the east parts of the cathedral became dilapidated. *Bishop Bull* (1705–10) was known for his strong anti-Catholic

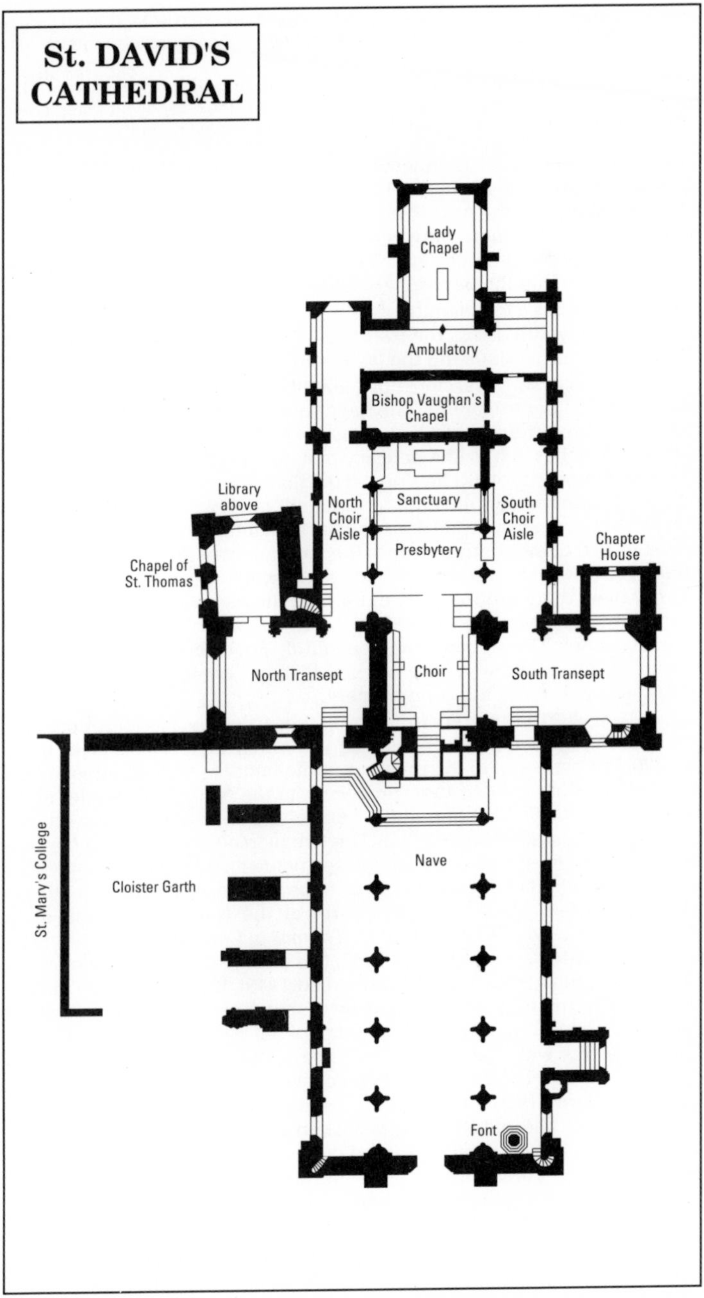

St. DAVID'S CATHEDRAL

Lady Chapel

Ambulatory

Bishop Vaughan's Chapel

Library above

North Choir Aisle

Sanctuary

South Choir Aisle

Chapter House

Chapel of St. Thomas

Presbytery

North Transept

Choir

South Transept

St. Mary's College

Cloister Garth

Nave

Font

preaching during the reign of James II, and *Bishop Thirlwall* (1840–74) as a classical historian and for his addresses relating the attitude of the Church to contemporary political issues.

The west front was rebuilt by John Nash at the end of the 18C. The modern work of restoration, begun in 1846, was afterwards carried on (1862–78) by Sir Gilbert Scott who rebuilt the west front to what is thought to be its original design.

The exterior is plain but dignified. Points to note are the lack of high-pitched roofs to the nave and choir; the 125ft high tower; and the huge buttresses on the north side of the nave. The 13–14C building (Chapel of St. Thomas, and library) in the angle between the north transept and the presbytery was originally of three storeys. The south porch is the work of Bishop Gower, except that the parvise was added in c 1515.

The interior has a total length of 298ft; a width across the nave and aisles of 68ft; and a width across the transepts of 131ft. General features are the softly tinted purple slate and the lavish late-Norman ornament.

The NAVE is of six bays, clerestory, and triforium, with a varied wealth of chevron and other ornament. The flat * *Roof* of Irish oak, probably erected during the treasurership of Owen Pole (1472–1509), is unique in having a number of arches of fret-like delicacy that apparently carry the ceiling but are in fact pendants of it. The slope of the floor, due to its original construction on ill-drained and ill-prepared ground, is very noticeable; there is a rise of 14ft between the west door and the high altar. Under the second arch from the east of the south arcade is the monument of Bishop John Morgan (1496–1504), with his recumbent effigy and sculptures round the base. On nearby piers there are traces of murals. At the east end of the south aisle there is a beautiful 13C tomb-niche of a vested priest with a curiously shaped canopy. The elaborate and beautiful * *Rood Screen*, one of the chief glories of the cathedral, is the work of Bishop Gower, whose tomb, with effigy, occupies the south compartment.

The TRANSEPTS, entered from the nave aisles by Norman doorways instead of by the usual arches, were largely rebuilt after the fall of the tower in 1220; but here, and in the presbytery, the builders, though adopting the Pointed arch, assimilated their new work to the Norman character of the nave. In the *North Transept*, at the back of the choir stalls, is the reputed Shrine of St. Caradoc (died 1124). The two pierced quatrefoils in the base (like those in the shrine of St. David, see below) may have been intended for the insertion of a diseased limb in hope of cure, or for the reception of alms. The great window on the north of the transept was put in by Butterfield in 1846. The *Chapel of St. Thomas of Canterbury*, off the east of the north transept, a vestry until 1952, has been restored as a memorial to Bishop Prosser (Archbishop of Wales; died 1949); it contains a 13C double piscina. The room above, reached by a stair from the north aisle of the presbytery, was originally the chapter house but is now the *Chapter Library*. Originally this was divided into two floors, of which the upper was the Treasury, but this latter has now been converted to a gallery in memory of Bishop Havard (1956). The library cases were restored in 1955 by the Pilgrim Trust. The oldest book is Bishop Lyndewode's 'Provinciale sue Constitutiones Angli' (1505), still today quoted as an authority on Church law. Also in the library are some beautiful fragments of the former organ case (?by Grinling Gibbons), broken up during restoration work.

East of the nave there follow in succession the Choir, the Presbytery, the Sanctuary, Bishop Vaughan's Chapel, the Ambulatory, and the Lady Chapel.

The CHOIR takes the place of the crossing below the tower, which rests on four fine arches. The circular-headed arch on the west is part of the original wall of Peter de Leia, while the other three are Pointed and date from the rebuilding after 1220. The *Lantern* exhibits the beautiful Decorated work of Bishop Gower. The 28 Choir Stalls date from c 1470, and their design, without the usual tabernacled canopies, is unusual if not unique. Most of the misericords are original and, as always, interesting. The Bishop's Throne, nearly 30ft high and one of the few medieval examples left in Britain, is perhaps from the time of Bishop Morgan, though surrounded by earlier work by Gower. On either side there is a seat for a chaplain. Another rarity (though found in some parish churches) is the Parclose Screen between the choir and presbytery. The Choir Aisles are either side of the presbytery and sanctuary. In the *North Choir Aisle* is the tomb of Rhys Gryg (died 1233), fourth son of Rhys ap Gruffydd; the effigy is, however, of the 14C. The *South Choir Aisle* contains the tomb of Bishop Gervase (Iorwerth; 1215–29) alongside that of Bishop Anselm de la Grace (1231–47), and the recumbent effigy of a knight who may be Rhys ap Gruffydd (died 1197). Another effigy has been suggested as being that of Giraldus, and a slab bears an interesting inscription to Silvester the Physician (?13C).

To the east of the choir is the PRESBYTERY, comprising bays with chevron and other ornament and originally lighted on the east by two tiers of lancets. The lower row, which formerly looked into the open space now occupied by Bishop Vaughan's Chapel, is now blocked, and enriched with glass mosaics. The upper tier was reconstructed by Gilbert Scott, from surviving fragments, in place of a poor but genuine window of the 15C. The roof, of 1461, was likewise restored by Scott. On the north of the presbytery is the late 13C *Shrine of St. David* once a magnet for crowds of pilgrims. In the middle is the large altar-tomb (with a handsome modern brass) of Edmund Tudor (died 1456), father of Henry VII, brought here at the Dissolution from the church of the Grey Friars at Carmarthen. On the south, as noted above, is the beautiful recumbent effigy of Bishop Anselm de la Grace (1231–47),

Misericord in St. David's Cathedral

alongside that of Bishop Gervase (1215–29). On the south side of the SANCTUARY is a rare series of wooden sedilia (1460–81), and here the floor is paved with encaustic tiles, many of which are old.

BISHOP VAUGHAN'S CHAPEL, entered from the aisles, is a fine example of late Perpendicular work, with a fan-tracery *Roof (1508–22). Originally this was an open space, bounded by the presbytery and by the three walks of the ambulatory; it was also apparently neglected and dirty, being described as 'vilissimussive sordidissimus locus in tota ecclesia' and the sum of fourpence paid for its cleaning in 1492. The arrangement, unique among British cathedrals, may have been due to the 13C builders' reluctance to block up the three lower lancet windows on the east of the presbytery. An unexplained feature is the recess on the west side, with an opening at the back that looks into the presbytery. This is 12C work of De Leia's time; but of the four crosses (brought from elsewhere) immured around the opening, the one below it, hidden by a coffer, may possibly be a relic of a pre-Norman church. This recess, found walled up by Gilbert Scott, concealed a quantity of bones—possibly those of St. David or St. Justinian, or both—embedded in mortar and probably hidden here at the Reformation; they are now in the coffer just referred to. On the east side of the chapel stands the Altar of the Holy Trinity, made up of old fragments, with a niche and window on either side, an unusual and curious arrangement.

The AMBULATORY, with a vaulted east walk, contains several 13–14C recumbent effigies. The LADY CHAPEL was the last part of the cathedral to be restored, with a replacement for Bishop Gower's vault which fell in 1775. In addition to fine sedilia, the chapel contains two tomb-niches, probably the work of Gower. The one on the south (restored; no effigy) is thought to be that of Bishop Martyn (1296–1328), the original builder of the chapel. The other, on the north, perhaps originally the tomb of Bishop Beck (1280–96; builder of the Bishop's Palace), has been restored as a tomb for Bishop Owen (1897–1926).

On the north side of the nave, and once connected with it by a cloister, are the ruins of ST. MARY'S COLLEGE, founded for secular priests in 1377 by Bishop Houghton and John of Gaunt, fourth son of Edward III. The chief feature is the *Chapel*, above a barrel vault, with a plain tower attached to its southwest corner. This originally formed the south range of the quadrangle. During work on the conversion of the buildings into a cathedral hall (1965), a tomb, believed to be that of Bishop Houghton, was discovered.

The remains of the *Bishop's Palace (Cadw; see p. 11) are on the farther side of the Alun rivulet. Started by Bishop Beck and continued by Gower, the palace was mostly built between 1280–1350 and may have had the additional purpose of serving as reception centre for pilgrims to the shrine of St. David. The decay of the palace dates from the time of Bishop Barlow (1536–48), who stripped the lead from the great hall, though perhaps not, as local tradition asserts, to portion his five daughters all of whom he married off to bishops.

The palace consists of a single large quadrangle, the open arcade and parapet that run round the top of the whole building on the outer side being typical of Gower's work. The entrance to the quadrangle is by a plain gateway at the east end of the north face. Immediately to the left of this is what is supposed to have been the *Private Chapel* (c 1350), raised, like the rest of the palace, on a series of vaults which provided basement rooms and storage. The *Bishop's Hall* (late 13C), on the east side of the quadrangle, has a later entrance porch with a curious doorway exhibiting the semioctagonal head characteristic of Gower's work. To the south of this hall is the *Kitchen*; to the north, the *Solar*. The *Great Hall* (1327–47), on the south side, is noticeably larger than the Bishop's Hall and was doubtless used for public purposes. It is approached by a fine porch at its northeast corner, with an ogee doorway enriched by canopied niches with now mutilated figures, and has a beautiful rose window at the east end. At its northwest corner is the *Chapel* with a piscina and a west bell-turret. The west side of the quadrangle seems to have been occupied by domestic buildings, stables etc.

ENVIRONS OF ST. DAVID'S. The promontory, in the south part of which St. David's lies, is a district known for its cliff scenery, its many bays and its associations with David and other saints. It was described by Giraldus as a remote and infertile corner, but, though the latter term still applies, the district can be crowded in summer. Much of the coastal land is owned or protected by the National Trust, largely as the result of an appeal in 1939 and substantial help from the Pilgrim Trust. Small roads or lanes fan out from St. David's to many of the bays, and the Pembrokeshire Coast National Park's coastal path follows the coast.

Traditionally **St. Non's Bay**, half a mile south of St. David's, is where St. David was born, probably early in the 6C. His mother, it seems, was Non (or Nonnita), possibly a nun and daughter of a local chieftain called Brechan, and his father, Sandde, a member of the noble house of Cunedda, though whether Non was seduced, coerced or perhaps married by Sandde is not recorded. Further tradition says that Non later crossed to Brittany, only then becoming a nun; in any event what is claimed to be her tomb is in a chapel at Dirinon in France, not far from Brest. St. David's birthplace is marked by a small ruined chapel of indeterminate age but in origin probably pre-Norman (it lies north to south, and this, together with the primitive masonry at the southwest angle, suggests a possibly rare survival of early British church building). However, again according to tradition, it was not at the adjacent holy well that David was baptised but at a spring beside the Alun at *Porth Clais* (half a mile west; road from St. David's), an inlet later said to have served as harbour for St. David's monastery beside Whitesands Bay and which today is the pretty home of small pleasure craft which cluster below the rough remains of a harbour wall that recalls the prosperous 19C days of coal and limestone.

St. Justinian, two miles west of St. David's, owes its name to St. David's confessor and friend who was associated with *Ramsey Island*, a mile offshore and since 1992 owned by RSPB. The home of Red Deer, the largest breeding colony of Atlantic Grey Seals on the Welsh coast and of countless birds, the island may be visited by a limited daily number of people by application to St. Justinian Lifeboat Station or by tel. 01437-720285.

St. Devynog is said to have founded a monastery on the island as early as the 2C, and in the 5C Justinian, a Breton nobleman, became a hermit here. He became also St. David's confessor and friend, a relationship which led him into one particularly black adventure. Told by some sailors that his friend was sick, Justinian accepted their offer to row him across the sound. When halfway, however, Justinian began to have doubts, deciding that the sailors were in fact devils. So he recited Psalm 79, whereupon, doubtless on hearing the words 'Pour out thy wrath upon the heathen', the sailors turned into crows and flew away. Sadly, Justinian's victory was short-lived for the thwarted sailor-devils later returned to the island and took possession of his servants who, on his return from the mainland, attacked and beheaded him. David later transferred his friend's remains to a shrine in his new church.

It is sad that apart from the place's name the only physical reminder at St. Justinian of its doughty saint is a neglected roofless chapel, a charmless relic of the 16C which may or may not be successor to an earlier dedication. For the rest, St. Justinian is a picturesque corner where low green cliffs enclose an intimate bay in which the dominant feature is the lifeboat house perched high above its long slide down to the water. The rocks to the west of Ramsey Island are known as the *Bishops and Clerks*.

Whitesands Bay (or Porth Mawr), some two miles northwest of St. David's and reached by a good road (B4583), is a popular sandy beach. In prehistoric times it was from here that traders sailed to Wicklow in Ireland for copper and gold, and the *Burrows*, the dunes behind the bay, are traditionally the site of the perhaps legendary Roman settlement of Menevia and later of St. David's first monastery. **St. David's Head** (no road), a bold promontory with cliffs 100ft high, forms the northern projection of Whitesands Bay.

Off the approach to Whitesands Bay are a farm park and a farm museum. *St. David's Farm Park* (April–Oct: daily 10.00–18.00. Tel. 01437-721601), half a mile out of St. David's, is home to a comprehensive display of rare breeds of farm animals—these including various pigs, four-horned Manx Loghtan and small Soay sheep, Bagot goats, and white and Highland cattle—while other attractions include picnic area, café, shop and antique farm wagon rides. A short distance farther on towards Whitesands Bay is *Lleithyr Farm Museum* (May–Oct: Tues–Sun but open Mon in school holidays, 10.00–17.00. Limited opening Easter and April. Tel. 01437-720245) with a collection, all under cover, of bygone farm equipment; also tearoom and shop.

For St. David's to *Haverfordwest* and *Carmarthen*, see Rte 43.

43

Carmarthen to Haverfordwest and St. David's or Fishguard

A40 to Haverfordwest. Either A487 to St. David's or A40 to Fishguard. Total distance 44m.—*9m*. **St. Clears**.—*5m*. **Whitland**.—*8m*. **Canaston Bridge** (for **Llawhaden Castle**).—*3m*. **Picton Castle**.—*4m*. **Haverfordwest**—*15m*. **St. David's** or **Fishguard**.

From **Carmarthen** (see Rte 40) the road skirts the alluvial plain between the mouths of the Towy and Taf to reach (*9m*) **St. Clears** (where Rtes 44A and 44B break away). In 1406 Owen Glendower was defeated here by the men of Pembroke, and in 1843–44 the village was a focus of the Rebecca Riots. The *Church* has a tower that batters to the top, and preserves also the carved Norman chancel arch of a small Cluniac priory which was attached in 1291 to St. Martin-des-Champs in Paris, while, just south, the remains of a motte recall those Norman days. *5m*. **Whitland** (*Inf.* Canolfan Hywel Dda, see below), is historically important as the meeting place of the assembly convened by Hywel Dda in 930 to codify Welsh tribal customs into a single legal system, one so successful that the code lasted until the conquest by Edward I, and indeed in some respects until the Act of Union of 1536. Today Whitland honours this past with a *Memorial* complex comprising a Visitor Centre (Canolfan Hywel Dda. Easter–Sept: Mon–Sat 10.00–17.00. Tel. 01994-240867); a paved area with brickwork representations of the arrival of the delegates to Hywel Dda's assembly; and six small gardens, one for each of the main legal themes, namely Society and Status, Crime and Tort, Women, Contract, the King, and Property. *Whitland Abbey*, today sad and insignificant fragments beside a farm complex a mile to the northeast, was once a great Cistercian house, the 'Alba Domos' of Giraldus, founded by Bernard, the first Norman bishop of St. David's, in 1143. The abbey became mother-house to Cwmhir in the same year and to Strata Florida in 1164.

Beyond Whitland A40 leaves the Taf valley, in *5m* crossing A478 (Rte 46, with *Narberth* immediately to the south) and in another *3m* reaching **Canaston Bridge**, close to three places of interest. To the south, both within under two miles, are an early 19C mill and a theme park. The former, *Blackpool Mill* (Easter–Oct: daily 11.00–18.00. Tel. 01437-541233), beside the Eastern Cleddau river, dates from 1813 and is considered to be one of the finest examples in Britain of a water-powered mill. Other attractions at Blackpool include caverns showing replicas of animals—hyenas, wolves, bears—all once hunted here; a shop and tearoom; and riverside and forest walks, one of these in under two miles reaching the remains of a church of a commandery of the Knights of St. John. *Oakwood* theme park (Easter–Sept: daily 10.00–17.00 or later. Tel. 01834-891373) is a short way farther south along A4075.

Llawhaden Castle (Cadw; see p. 11), a mile north of Canaston Bridge, though now ruined, was once an important residence of the bishops of St. David's.

History The land around Llawhaden was long a rich possession of the see of St. David's, and in 1115 Bernard, the first Norman bishop, built a circular motte fortification here. However, in 1192 Rhys ap Gruffyd razed this castle (of which all that remains today is the moat) and it was not until the early 13C, by when the bishops had recovered the place, that a stone castle was built. Later, in the early 14C and probably under the direction of Bishop Martyn, Llawhaden was rebuilt and extended as a large fortified mansion. Bishop Barlow is generally supposed to have stripped the roof of its lead and to have left the castle to decay.

Within its circular moat, the castle comprises a single irregular ward round which lie the domestic buildings. The *Gatehouse*, at the southwest corner, is largely a late 14C addition. To its west are the *Garrison's Quarters*, today a ruined two-storey building which would probably have been a hall above an undercroft, with, at an angle, the kitchen beyond. Adjoining and immediately northwest of the garrison's hall are the foundations of a circular tower, a survival of the early 13C stone castle's curtain wall, which can be traced along the exterior of the garrison's hall. In the *North Range* of buildings, too, the main rooms were on the first floor above vaulted storerooms, but of this upper floor little remains. In the centre the hall extended northwest to southeast, with on its left the Bakehouse and Kitchen, and to its right the Bishop's Private Chamber. The *South Range*, to the east of the gatehouse, comprised two storeys of rooms above undervaults, with beyond, at the castle's southeast corner, the Chapel, originally joined to the bishop's chamber. The southeast tower contained the chaplain's living quarters. *Llawhaden Church* dates mainly from the 14C, but has a north tower which is somewhat older.

Continuing west from Canaston Bridge, A40 skirts the northern boundary of Slebech Park and in about 3m reaches the approach to Picton Castle, with gardens and the Graham Sutherland Gallery. Originally a Norman motte guarding the meeting of the eastern and western Cleddau, the stone castle dates from c 1302 when it was built by Sir John Wogan; a Welshman married to a Norman lady, he was Justiciary of Ireland from 1295–1313. The castle was taken by Owen Glendower in 1405, by the Royalists in 1643 and by Parliament in 1645; a west wing was added in 1800, and in 1954 the castle became the home of the Hon. Hanning Philipps, a descendant of the medieval owners. The main visitor interest at Picton is the Graham Sutherland Gallery, in the castle courtyard and showing a large collection of works presented by the artist and his wife as a token of the inspiration he drew from Pembrokeshire over many years. Videos on the artist are shown and during the summer there are temporary exhibitions, including work by other artists. The gallery is a branch of the National Museum of Wales and is open April–Oct: Tues–Sun and Bank Hol. 10.30–12.30, 13.30–17.00. Nov–March by arrangement. Tel. 01437-751296. The Castle, externally little changed apart from the addition of the west wing, has limited opening (tel. 01437-751326), but the Gardens, which include plants and shrubs from Scotland's famous Lochinch Gardens, are open April to October.

Wiston, two miles north of A40 roughly opposite the turn to Picton Castle, takes its name from Wizo, one of the Flemish colonists planted in this district by Henry I. Something survives of the motte and bean-shaped ward of his castle of c 1120; it was destroyed in 1220 by Llewelyn the Great, and the keep on the motte is probably later 13C rebuilding.

4m. **Haverfordwest** (Hwlffordd. *Inf.*), spread below and around its 13C castle, is a busy centre on the Western Cleddau. With some steep streets and several Georgian houses, much of the town has been designated a conservation area.

History. Although the name is a legacy of the days of Viking raids, it was around the Norman castle built here in c 1120 by Gilbert de Clare that the town grew, helped no doubt by Henry I's Flemish settlers. Gruffydd ap Rhys took the town and castle soon afterwards, in 1135, but both were back in Norman hands by 1153 when Henry II visited here. Other kings who came here were John in 1210, Edward I in 1284, Richard II in 1394 and Henry Tudor (before Bosworth, 1485). In 1220 Llewelyn the Great burnt the town, and in 1407 Owen Glendower's French mercenaries did the same, though they failed to take the castle. During the Civil War Haverfordwest changed hands several times. In 1642 it was held for Parliament; in 1643 for the King; in 1644 it was occupied by Parliament's General Laugharne, and in 1645 by the Royalist Sir Charles Gerard; later in 1645 Laugharne returned, and finally the castle was slighted.

During the 18 and 19C Haverfordwest became a prosperous port, trading largely with Bristol and Ireland; and recent years have seen effective conservation measures, such as a wide listing of scheduled buildings and the diversion of traffic away from the centre.

The *Castle*, much of the fabric of which has received major conservation treatment, represents the shell of the essentially 13C inner ward and today houses, largely in the gaol built here in 1820, the town's *Museum and Art Gallery* (Mon–Sat 10.00–16.30. Tel. 01437-763708), mainly concerned with the local story. In the Art Gallery the permanent collection, the flavour of which is also mainly local, alternates with temporary exhibitions.

High Street, to the south of the castle and with some Georgian façades, climbs to *St. Mary's Church*, dating originally from c 1250–70 although the north aisle and the clerestories were added during the 15C. Features worth noting are the 15C roofs of the nave and north aisle; at the raised west end of the nave the mutilated effigy of a pilgrim with scallops on his satchel, almost certainly indicating that he visited the shrine of St. James of Compostella in Spain; and the fine 13C work of the arches of the chancel and north arcade, their capitals of stiff figures enlivened with masks and small animals—Barn Street, to the west of St. Mary's, is worth a visit, among the buildings here being the *Tabernacle* of 1774 and a house showing elaborate ironwork.

Quay Street, leading south with the river, becomes Old Quay which, in about a quarter of a mile from Castle Square, passes, beside the river, some remains of a *Priory Church* founded for Augustinian Canons in about 1207 but largely demolished at the Dissolution.

A DIVERSION NORTH EAST can visit a farm museum, a manor museum in a country park, and a reservoir country park. B4329 out of Haverfordwest in just over a mile (Crundale) reaches a fork, along the righthand prong smaller road being, in another three miles, *Selvedge Farm Museum* (Easter–Sept: daily 10.00–18.00. Tel. 01437-731264) showing farm equipment in use over the last century; here also are a nature trail and picnic area, a tearoom and shop, and, for the children, a pets corner and two play areas. The lefthand fork (B4329) is taken for, in three miles, **Scolton Manor** (May–Sept: Tues–Sun 10.00–16.30. Tel. 01437-731328), dating from c 1840 and today, with splendid period rooms on three floors, housing a museum devoted to Pembrokeshire life from prehistory to the present. The associated Country Park (All year Tues–Sun 10.00–16.30 but to 19.00 Easter–Oct. Tel. 01437-731457) offers an environmental centre, nature trails, arboretum, cafeteria and play and picnic areas. *Llys-y-Fran Reservoir and Country Park* (daily 08.00 to half an hour before sunset in March–Oct or to 16.00 in Nov–March. Tel. 01437-532694), reached in another four miles, is a lake (dam at the south end) providing picnic sites, restaurant, shop, and facilities for water sports.

TO ST. DAVID'S. A487. *6m. Roch Castle* (no adm.), to the east off the main road, takes its name from the outcrop on which it stands, a site said to have been chosen by the Norman Adam de la Roche because of his fear of snakes (the story goes that despite this protection he was killed by the bite of a snake brought in with some firewood). What is seen today is one surviving 13C D-shaped tower with projecting chambers; a block of flats has now been added. *2m.* The coast is briefly touched at *Newgale*, a scattered, straggling holiday village with a pebble bank and a long sandy beach. Here, at exceptionally low tide, may be seen the stumps of a submerged forest, known to Giraldus and described by him as a 'grove of ebony'. From here on much of the coast is either owned or protected by the National Trust. The road, though, keeps inland, in *3m* reaching *Solva*, until the 19C a modestly important port but today a picturesque small haven at the head of its narrow, winding creek. From Solva a small road runs upstream for a mile beside the little river to find *Middle Mill* (Mon–Fri 09.30–17.30. Also, Easter–Sept Sat 09.30–17.30 and Sun 14.00–17.30. Tel. 01437-721597). Attractively sited in its valley, Middle Mill (weaving may normally be watched) specialises in carpets and rugs although its shop tempts with much else. *4m.* **St. David's**, see Rte 42.

TO FISHGUARD. A40. *3m. Poyston*, a mile to the east, was the birthplace of Sir Thomas Picton (1758–1815), Governor of Trinidad and distinguished commander during the Peninsular War, who was killed at Waterloo. In about *2m*, approaching Treffgarne, A40 crosses the Western Cleddau and runs, with the river and the railway, through the wooded **Treffgarne Gorge**, lined with hillforts on either side. Brunel brought his railway as far as here by 1845, only to be defeated by the ancient hard rock, and it was only after another 60 years that the line was completed. *Nant-y-Coy Mill* (July and Aug: Mon–Sat 10.00–18.00; Sun 14.30–17.30. Other months: Tues–Sat 10.00–17.30. Tel. 01437-741671), in origin of 1332 or earlier, was rebuilt in 1844 and today offers a variety of attractions such as a cottage showing bygones, many of local provenance, craft workshops, shop and tearoom and nature walks. Owen Glendower is said to have been born at Little Treffgarne on the east side of the river. *10m.* **Fishguard**, see Rte 42.

44

Carmarthen to Pembroke and Milford Haven

Two choices are offered; the direct, inland main road, or generally minor roads close to the coast. The two come within a little over a mile of one another at King's Moor Common, and meet at Pembroke. The coastal choice, longer by some ten miles, is the more scenic and interesting.

A. Direct

A40 to St. Clears. A477 to Neyland. B4325 to Milford Haven. Total distance 39m.—*9m.* **St. Clears.**—*12m.* **King's Moor Common (Kilgetty).**—*6m.* **Carew Cheriton** (for **Carew Castle**).—*4m.* **Pembroke.**—*8m.* **Milford Haven**.

Carmarthen, see Rte 40. For Carmarthen to (9m) **St. Clears**, see Rte 43.

2m. **Llanddowror** was at the heart of the 18C drive for education for all. The vicar here, Griffith Jones, working with Sir John Philipps of Picton, one of the founders of the Society for Promoting Christian Knowledge, and with Mrs Bridget Bevan of Laugharne, was the leader of a trio who organised travelling schools, so successful that by the date of Griffith Jones's death in 1781 nearly a third of the population of Wales could read the bible. *10m.* **King's Moor** crossroads, for, a short way north, **King's Moor Common (Kilgetty) Information Area** with WTB and Pembrokeshire Coast National Park information offices, AA and RAC telephones, and *Avondale Glass* where glass making and blowing can be watched and the products bought. The enterprise is open Easter–Oct with, normally, glass making Mon–Fri 08.00–14.30 or 13.00 on Wed. The shop is open Mon–Fri 08.00–17.00; Sat 08.00–13.00. Tel. 01834-813345. Nearby, a short distance north along A478, are, first, a pottery and then a farm. *Begelly Pottery* (March–Oct: daily 09.30–17.30 or 12.00 on Sat. Telephone for winter opening. Tel. 01834-811204) provides demonstrations and a well-stocked showroom. *Folly Farm* (mid April–Sept: daily 10.00–17.30. October: daily 12.00–17.00. Tel. 01834-

812731), a short way farther, gives the opportunity to experience and even play an active part in various aspects of a Welsh dairy farm. The bottle-feeding area (under cover) is particularly popular with children, for whom there are also a pets' corner, tractor and trailer rides, an adventure playground and a rally kart track, while there is also a museum showing how this farm was worked in the past.

6m. **Carew Cheriton** where the large early 14–15C church, with a mounting block at the entrance, shows various features of interest including tombs of the Carew family, one of these being that of Sir Nicolas (died 1311) who built the earliest stone part of Carew Castle. On the north of the chancel there is an effigy of a vested priest of c 1325, while on the south, and dating from about 1300, rests a very small female figure, either a child or perhaps indicating a heart-burial. The tiles of c 1500 on the chancel floor may at some time have come from Carew Castle, and the detached 14C chantry, or perhaps mortuary chapel, used in 1846 as a school, is a rare survival of an in any case unusual feature.

Just to the north along A4075, in the hamlet of Carew, beside the road and near the castle entrance, stands *Carew Cross*, a magnificent monument nearly 14ft high and with elaborate geometric and intertwined patterns showing both Celtic and Scandianvian influence. Erected in c 1035 to honour Maredudd (killed in battle that year), with his brother co-prince of Deheubarth, the cross was made in two parts, the wheel at the top fitted into position by a tenon.

For Carew Castle and Carew Tidal Mill use one of the two free car parks (one with picnic area) in the village, from where a round walk of about a mile takes in both sites. Car access to the mill only for disabled.

Carew Castle (Easter–Oct: daily 10.00–17.00. Tel. 01646-651782) is an imposing ruin on a low ridge above a tidal creek of the Carew river.

History. The earliest castle, of which nothing survives, is said to have been built by Gerald de Windsor, an Anglo-Norman chieftain, at the close of the 11C. Another tradition is that the estates came to him as the dowry of his wife Nest, daughter of Rhys ap Tewdwr, sister of Gruffydd ap Rhys, and mistress of Henry I. Their son assumed the name of Carew, and their daughter was the mother of Giraldus. The earliest authentic stone structure was the fortified mansion of the Carews, built c 1270–1320. In 1480 Carew was sold to Sir Rhys ap Thomas, who remodelled the place and added the Great Hall. Sir Rhys entertained Henry Tudor after his landing on Milford Haven in 1485, and in 1507 here held a great tournament to celebrate the Garter bestowed on him by Henry, now Henry VII. In 1558 the castle was granted to Sir John Perrot, who rebuilt the whole of the north side in a purely domestic Tudor style. In the Civil War Carew was held for the King in two sieges (1644 and 45), but the damage was apparently such that it was not lived in after 1686.

Architecturally Carew spans the period between the military structures of the 13C (west) to the fortified manors of Tudor times (north). The plan is roughly rectangular with a three-quarter drum-tower at each corner, the two on the west being strengthened externally by curious semi-pyramidal spurs. The entrance on the east, the weakest side, was specially protected, the whole front being covered by an outer ward and the actual gateway by a narrow barbican which compelled approach at right angles; it was also flanked on the south by the drum at the southeast angle, and on the north by a special tower protruding from the curtain. The original *Carew Manor House* was built inside this east curtain and included a chapel in the special tower just referred to; it is representative of the period when defence was moving outwards to a curtain and away from a keep. The late 15C *Great*

Hall built by Sir Rhys ap Thomas, with its fine entrance tower, is on the west of the ward (upper storey), while on the north is *Sir John Perrot's Manor* with its large windows and oriels. **Carew Tidal Mill** (opening as for castle), just west of the castle and a rare example of a restored mill of this kind, dates back to 1558 although the four-storey main building is largely restoration of the early 19C. There is an introductory film, and the milling process is explained at automatic 'talking points'.

4m (from Carew Cheriton) **Pembroke** (*Inf.*) is a historic town with a single Main Street which runs for over half a mile along a narrow ridge above the Pembroke river. Considerable lengths of the town's 13C walls survive, particularly on the south, the walls originally being integral with the castle and served by three gates, West and East gates being at either end of the Main Street while the North Gate guarded what is now the bridge across the river. Today there is a lengthy one-way traffic system, above and below the walls, but with convenient parking below on the south and opposite the *Pembroke Visitor Centre* (April–Oct: Mon–Sat 10.00–17.30. Nov–March: Some weekend opening. Tel. 01646-622388) serving both as Tourist Information and as a visitor centre in which imaginative features bring Pembroke's past to life.

Adjacent to the Visitor Centre, paths connect to the upper town where of course the main site is the massive and imposing ruin of * * *Pembroke Castle* (April–Sept: daily 09.30–18.00. March and Oct: daily 10.00–17.00. Nov–Feb: Mon–Sat 10.00–16.00. Tel. 01646-681510), occupying the west end of the ridge and sprawling over a promontory above the river and the inlet known as Monkton Pill.

History. Roman coins have been found on this site, and it may later have been a Viking stronghold, but the first castle here was built c 1095 by Arnulf de Montgomery. Described as a 'slender fortress of stakes and turf', it was left in the hands of Arnulf's steward, Gerald de Windsor (probably builder of Carew), who withstood a siege by the Welsh in the following year and in 1102, when Montgomery fell from favour, was granted the castle by Henry I. Three years later Gerald rebuilt the place. The earldom of Pembroke (see below) was created in 1138, the title later passing to the Marshals, who were largely responsible for the castle the remains of which are seen today. The oldest part is the keep, thought to have been built by William Marshal in c 1210, and the whole castle seems to have been completed, initially by his five sons in succession, by the end of the century. In 1452 Henry VI granted Pembroke to Jasper Tudor, and in 1457 his nephew Henry Tudor, later Henry VII, was born here. Throughout the Civil War the castle was held for Parliament, but in 1648 the town's military governor John Poyer surprisingly declared for the King. Cromwell then besieged Pembroke for 48 days, subjecting it to continual artillery battering until, after capturing the water supply, he was able to compel surrender. The castle was then slighted and Poyer was shot in London early the following year. Neglected and used as a quarry for over 200 years, the castle was restored in 1880, 1928, and later.

The *Earldom of Pembroke* was created in 1138, Gilbert de Clare, popularly known as 'Strongbow', being the first holder of the title and first of a long line of powerful and rapacious Lords Marcher. Later, families enjoying the title included the Marshals, De ValEnces, Hastings and Tudors, one of these last being Jasper, uncle to Henry VII. On the creation of the earldom the Pembroke lands, mainly south of Milford Haven, became a county palatine (independent of the national administration), the earls retaining their local sovereignty until the palatinate was abolished in 1536.

The ground-plan is an outer ward to the east, and beyond, above the curve of the promontory, the smaller and rather older inner ward. The entrance to the OUTER WARD is across the ditch, now filled in, which separated the castle from the town, and then by the Gatehouse, noteworthy for its external barbican (restored 1880–85), compelling oblique approach, and for its internal semicircular angle-towers connected by an arch, possibly intended to carry a wooden platform manned by defenders. Within the gatehouse (with an exhibition) there is a maze of rooms and passages. The walls of the ward are strengthened by five circular drum-towers, connected by passages. On the south and west sides the first tower is the Henry VII Tower, confidently stated by Leland (official antiquary to Henry VIII) to be Henry's birthplace. Note the very individual privy in the adjacent wall. Westgate Tower (destroyed 1648, restored 1931) stands at the point where the southern town wall, with the West Gate, joined the castle. The Monkton Tower is different from the others in having separate entrances to its floors. It stands to the south of the Inner Gatehouse, surviving only as foundations, on the inner curtain. This, approached from below by a twisting path, was the original and only entrance to the castle during the period when it consisted of the inner ward only; when, not long afterwards, the outer ward was built, the path was built over and a new and higher Water Gate opened beside Monkton Tower. On the east side of the ward Northgate Tower marks the point where the north town wall joined the castle curtain. Much of the tower's outer wall, destroyed in 1648, is a rebuilding of 1934. To the north the Mill Gate marked the exit to the tidal mill below, the dam of which, with a drawbridge, was the entrance to the town through the North Gate. Mill Gate and the mill were protected by the rectangular St Ann's Bastion (restored 1929).

Just within the INNER WARD stands the circular Great Keep, 75ft high and 24ft in diameter internally at the bottom, with walls 19ft thick at the base. It was possibly built by Gilbert de Clare, but more probably by William Marshal in c 1210. Originally four storeys, it is now open from ground level to the domed stone roof. The chief entrance was on the first floor, up wide steps, the foundations of which were discovered in 1932; the basement entrance was apparently added at an early date. The staircase is a restoration of 1928. At the top, square holes in the outer parapet were probably for the attachment of an archers' platform. The domestic apartments, largely crowded into cramped space northeast of the keep, are not on the scale of the rest of the castle. From south to north, beside the inner curtain, are the Dungeon Tower; the Oriel, probably a Tudor adaptation of an earlier antechamber; and the Norman Hall, the hall being above a basement and access through either the Oriel or the Northern Hall, again a main floor above a basement. A stairway (dark and often slippery) leads from the Northern Hall down to the Wogan, a large natural cavern probably used as a store; the cavern can also be reached by the path around the base of the castle. The Chancery, to the west of the Norman Hall, seems to have been a Tudor addition. In the southwest of the inner ward are the scanty remains of the Chapel, alongside the gloomy Western Hall.

Just outside the castle, on Westgate Hill, are a *Museum of the Home* (Easter–Oct: daily, but closed some Thur and Sat, 10.30–17.30. Tel. 01646-681200), an eclectic collection of bygones spanning the last three centuries, and a *Sea Historic Gallery* (Easter–Oct: Tues–Sat, but open Bank Hol. 10.30–17.00. Tel. 01646-682919) with also a sea aquarium. *Monkton Priory*, half a mile west of the castle across Monkton Pill, was founded by Arnulf de Montgomery in 1098 for Benedictine monks as a cell of Sées in Normandy; the priory was given to St. Albans, in 1473. The church has a long, narrow barrel-vaulted nave, and the monastic chancel, though part of the original structure, was re-arranged during the 14C. After lying in ruins for many years, the church was restored in 1878–87, and, from traces of two small half-blocked windows on the north exterior of the nave, it has been suggested that the masonry here incorporated the south wall of a pre-Norman church.

For *Castlemartin Peninsula*, extending south and west from Pembroke, see Rte 45.

A4139 crosses the river to reach **Pembroke Dock**, a town which, already building wooden warships during the 18C, began to boom after 1814 when the Admiralty Dockyard moved here from Milford Haven; the first ships, 'Valorous' and 'Ariadne', were launched two years later in 1816. Much expanded during the First World War, the government dockyard was in 1930 handed over to the Royal Air Force and Pembroke Dock became well known as a flying boat base playing an important part in the Second World War's Battle of the Atlantic. Today Pembroke Dock is concerned with the oil-related activities of Milford Haven and the ferry service to Rosslare in Ireland, and for the visitor the place to aim for is *Hobb's Point* which not only gives a view across the water but is also of some historic interest. The point owes its name to Nicholas Hobbs, the owner of this land until it was bought by the government in about 1753, and today an information board outlines the activities that later took place here, helping the visitor to picture such scenes as the fitting out of warships and Queen Victoria's Crimea soldiers assembling here in 1854–56 awaiting their turn to be ferried out to the transports. Later, in modern and contrasting context, cars waited here for the ferries which preceded the opening of the bridge in 1975. Hobbs Point is also today the embarkation point for summer cruises in Milford Haven and up Daugleddau (Two Swords), the common estuary of the Western and Eastern Cleddau rivers (tel. 01646-685627).

A477 crosses upper Milford Haven by a toll bridge to *Neyland*, the main trading port to southern Ireland until superseded by Fishguard in 1906 and now a recreational area with a large marina.

MILFORD HAVEN is the name both of the huge natural harbour and of the town (see below) on its north shore. The magnificent natural harbour, described by Nelson as the best in the world and with sheltered roadsteads for the largest ships, is some ten miles long by up to two miles broad, and at its head breaks into several tidal inlets reaching far inland, the longest being the estuaries of the Western and the Eastern Cleddau. Until c 1800, however, the haven served only as temporary refuge. The Norsemen came here (in King Alfred's time one expedition wintered with 23 ships), and both Henry II and John, each with 4–500 ships, set sail from here to conquer Ireland. In 1407, 12,000 French mercenaries landed here to fight for Owen Glendower against Henry IV, and in 1485 Henry Tudor, Earl of Richmond, came ashore at Mill Bay with a small retinue from Brittany to begin the campaign that would end with victory at Bosworth Field and his crowning as Henry VII. In the late 18C Sir William Hamilton (husband of Nelson's Lady Emma) inherited from his first wife the local manors of Pill and Hubberston. He appreciated the potential of the haven but, far away as Envoy Extraordinary to the Court of Naples (a post he held from 1764–1800), there was nothing he could personally do, so he appointed his nephew, the Hon. R. F. Greville, as his agent. In 1790 an Act of Parliament sanctioned the establishment of a town, and at about the same time a naval dockyard was opened, which, however, in 1814 moved to Pembroke Dock. The railway came in 1863, but, although there was some optimistic investment (Milford Haven docks were completed by 1888), large ships failed to use the place. However, the Neyland trawler fleet moved to Milford Haven which by the opening years of the present century had become one of

Britain's leading fishing ports. During both wars the Haven was busy with Atlantic convoys, but after 1945 there was a general decline and trawling also began to disappear, although many varieties of fish, including sewin, a sea trout found only in Welsh waters, are still landed at Milford Haven.

New life came with the 1960s as the Haven began to develop into a major oil port, and today it is used by the leading oil companies whose activities have brought huge tankers and a growing spread of oil-related installations.

In summer the best way to see the Haven is by cruise boat from Hobbs Point, Pembroke Dock. For the north shore, see Marloes and Dale Peninsula below. For the south shore (Castlemartin Peninsula), see Rte 45.

8m (from Pembroke) **Milford Haven** town (*Inf.*) was, as noted above, the creation of R. F. Greville who, empowered by the Act of Parliament of 1790, imported a group of Quaker whalers who had been unsettled by the American War of Independence and contracted a refugee Frenchman, J.-L. Barrallier, to lay out the town and dockyard in the squared pattern which survives today. Most visitors will head for the Marina area (well signed; near the station), with parking below Victoria Bridge and the focus of a variety of family attractions, such as go-karts, a lightship, a wooden 3-master, fishing quay, dry dock, boat excursions, and a choice of restaurants. Here too are the contrasting Kaleidoscope and nearby Milford Haven Museum. *Kaleidoscope Discovery Centre* (10.00–17.00. March–Oct: daily. Nov–Feb: Tues–Sun, but open Bank Hol. Tel. 01646-695374) is a spacious hall filled with electronic and computer gadgetry offering experiences, puzzles and illusions. From here a short walk reaches *Milford Haven Museum* (Easter–Oct: Tues–Sun 11.00–17.00. Tel. 01646-694496) in a former whale oil warehouse of 1797. Here the visitor first meets R.F. Greville telling how he founded the town, then moves on through a succession of themes—fishing, the market, war, whaling—to reach the oil age.

St. Katherine's Church, half a mile east of the museum at the end of Hamilton Terrace, has Nelson-Hamilton associations including, in the churchyard, the grave of Sir William Hamilton and, in the church, a bible and prayer book presented by Nelson. Also here, in the porch, are an Egyptian porphyry bowl and a replica of the truck (mast-top disc) of the French battleship 'L'Orient' which blew up at the Battle of the Nile (1798). The bowl had been acquired by Greville, the genuine truck had been presented by Lady Hamilton in honour of Nelson, and Greville had the happy thought to combine the two into a font. However the bishop objected on the grounds that the bowl was pagan and that the truck had been 'polluted ... by blood and carnage'. So the font idea was dropped, the bowl remaining however in the church while the truck is now in the National Maritime Museum at Greenwich.

The small remains of *Pill Priory*, built in 1200 by Adam de la Roche, are on the town's north edge, while to the northeast, beyond the head of the Pill Inlet, there are slight remains of the medieval *Castle*. *Gellyswick Bay*, to the west of the town, is popular for bathing and sailing.

The indented MARLOES AND DALE peninsula, forming the north shore of Milford Haven and ending as two promontories, extends nearly ten miles westward from Milford Haven town, from which an unclassified road (passing Pill Priory mentioned above) runs into the peninsula. But the main road is B4327 from Haverfordwest. The three principal villages are Marloes, St. Ishmael's and Dale; to the west there are several islands; and the

Pembrokeshire Coast National Park footpath, crossing some National Trust land, follows the coast with its cliff scenery and sandy bays (information centre at Broad Haven at the northeast base of the peninsula (tel. 01437-781412).

Marloes is an inland village, with Marloes Sands around the bay a mile to the southwest. The west extremity of the bay is defined by *Gateholm Island* (from the Norse for Goat Island), which is an island only at high tide and on which there are traces of a settlement, possibly early monastic. *Martin's Haven* (boats to the islands, see below) is at the road's end west of Marloes.

St. Ishmael's, a village in the south central part of the peninsula, is named after a 6C colleague of St. Teilo. On the north outskirts of the village a motte recalls Norman if not earlier times, while the Long Stone, half a mile northwest, is the tallest standing stone in the Pembrokeshire Coast National Park. A story attaches to *Mullock Bridge*, on B4327 roughly halfway between St. Ishmael's and Marloes. Sir Rhys ap Thomas of Carew Castle is said to have given his word to Richard III that if Henry Tudor tried to pass through Pembroke it would only be by riding over his body. So when Henry landed at Mill Bay Sir Rhys both satisfied his conscience and ensured his own future by lying under the bridge while Henry rode across; he then hastened to Carew where he welcomed the invader.

Dale, to the south, is a small holiday village and sailing centre (boats to the islands, see below). *Dale Castle* (no adm.), a modern residence, stands on or near the site of a medieval manor first mentioned in 1293 as belonging to one, Robertus de Vale. Around the promontory to the south are Iron Age earthworks across the base of Dale Point; *Dale Fort*, a Victorian fort now a Field Studies Centre; *West Blockhouse Point*, site of coastal defences first erected in about 1580, rebuilt in 1852–57 and in occupation until 1950; and, just beyond, *Mill Bay*, where Henry Tudor landed on 7 August 1485. At *St. Ann's Head*, accessible by road, there are a coastguard station and lighthouse.

Islands. All three main islands are nature and wildlife reserves. *Skomer* (Dyfed Wildlife Trust) is ruggedly scenic and known for seabird colonies (best April–mid Aug), flowers (best May–June and July) and seals (all year). Nature trail and information centre. *Skokholm* (Dyfed Wildlife Trust). Generally of turf and red sandstone, and the site of Britain's first bird observatory. Famous for Manx shearwaters and migrants. The Trust offers catered accommodation and a choice of courses. *Grassholm* (RSPB). Small island ten miles offshore with a huge gannetry of some 30,000 pairs; also seals and Manx shearwaters.

There is limited access, with or without landing, to the islands. For information, apply Dale Sailing company, Brunel Quay, Neyland. Tel. 01646-601636. Or Dyfed Wildlife Trust, 7 Market Street, Haverfordwest, SA61 1NF. Tel. 01437-765462. Or any Pembrokeshire Coast National Park information centre (nearest, Broad Haven. Tel. 01437-781412).

B. Via the Coast and Tenby

A40 to St. Clears. A4066 to Pendine. Unclassified to Saundersfoot. B4316
and A478 to Tenby. A4139 to Pembroke. A477, B4325 to Milford Haven.
Total distance 49m.—*9m*. **St. Clears.**—*4m*. **Laugharne**—*5m*. **Pendine.**—
8m. **Saundersfoot.**—*3m*. **Tenby.**—*6m*. **Manorbier Castle.**—*4m*. **Lamphey
Bishop's Palace.**—*2m*. **Pembroke.**—*8m*. **Milford Haven.**

Carmarthen, see Rte 40. For Carmarthen to (*9m*) **St. Clears** (for Rtes 43 and
44A), see Rte 43.

4m. **Laugharne** is a quiet rural town, with Georgian houses, on the west
bank of the estuary of the Taf, here over half a mile wide and about to
broaden further as it meets that of the Towy.

History. For long the history of the town was that of its castle. Founded during the 12C
and for a while held by Rhys ap Gruffyd, it was destroyed by Llewelyn the Great in
1215, then rebuilt by the De Brian family. It was Sir Guy de Brian who in 1307 granted
a charter by which the town was administered by a portreeve (chief officer) elected
every six months by the citizens, a system which in some respects is still honoured
today. In Tudor times the castle came to Sir John Perrot who, as he did at Carew,
converted the place into a mansion. At the time of the Civil War Laugharne was the
home of the general of the same name who held the castle for Parliament in 1647 but
later sided with the King. In the 18C Mrs Bridget Bevan (died 1779), associate of Griffith
Jones of Llanddowror (see beginning of Rte 44A), lived here, and in more recent years
Laugharne was the home of the poet Dylan Thomas (died 1953) who is buried in the
churchyard.

The *Castle* (Cadw; see p. 11), of which little survives, comprises two 12–13C
towers and traces of Sir John Perrot's mansion. In the town, the name King
Street is an ancient one, commemorating a visit by Henry II, and here it is
worth glancing into the tower of the *Town Hall* which contains a curious
small prison furnished with a wooden bench with a pillow end. *St. Martin's
Church* (14C, modernised 19C) also repays a visit, here being the remains
of a Bronze Age man, found during the construction of a local housing
estate; a 10C Celtic cross (restored); and a wood carving of St. Martin of
Tours, brought from Oberammergau in 1866 and the work of a member of
the Lang family, long actively associated with the Passion Play. The poet
Dylan Thomas spent the last years of his life in Laugharne (he is buried in
the churchyard of St. Martin's), doing much of his writing at what is now
known as *Dylan Thomas's Boathouse* (Easter–Oct: daily 10.00–17.15. Other
months: daily except Sat 10.30–15.00. Tel. 01994-427420), some 15 minutes
walk from King Street by Victoria Street and narrow Dylan's Walk (no cars),
the walk repaid by interpretations, memorabilia, tearoom, art gallery and
estuary views.

Llandawke, a mile and a half west by narrow but motorable lanes, is a lost little hamlet
with a very primitive 13C church as simple and evocative as any in Wales. It shelters
an ancient stone, inscribed in Ogham and Latin perhaps seven centuries before this
church was built, and also the 14C effigy of a lady, perhaps Margaret, sister or daughter
of Sir Guido de Brian, the local lord. The honorific of Saint which she sometimes enjoys
seems to be a purely local canonisation, and if today the lady looks somewhat worn,
this is because she spent centuries out in the churchyard before being brought under
cover.

5m. **Pendine** is a straggling small resort, today a place of cafés, souvenir
shops and caravans but with sands which have an honoured place in
motoring and aviation history. Between 1924–27 the world's land speed

record was five times attempted here, three times by Malcolm Campbell (1885–1948) and twice by J.G. Parry-Thomas, the latter being killed here in 1927; his car was buried near the beach until dug up in 1969 for restoration. The final speed achieved by Malcolm Campbell was 174.88 mph in 1927, though by 1935 (at Bonneville, Utah) he raised this to over 300. In 1933 Jim and Amy Mollison (Amy Johnson) took off for a non-stop flight to New York, but lack of fuel forced them down only 60 miles short of their objective. For a fee, modern motorists can drive, but not speed, on the beach. The *Burrows*, stretching east to the Taf estuary, are a Ministry of Defence area (danger zone).

The road climbs inland to (*2m*) Marros, with a quaint 'neolithic' war memorial, before dropping to (*3m*) *Amroth*, an inland and seaside village at the southeast extremity of the Pembrokeshire Coast National Park and where the stumps of a now submerged forest may be seen at low tide. *Colby Woodland Garden* (NT. April–Oct: daily 10.00–17.00. Tel. 01834-811885), for woodland walks, including one to Amroth, and also a walled garden, is a mile to the north. *2m*. *Wiseman's Bridge*, where in 1944 Winston Churchill watched a D-Day rehearsal. *1m*. **Saundersfoot**, today a holiday resort with a harbour crowded with small craft, dates from 1829 when the harbour was built for the export of the anthracite mined a short way inland and brought here by tramway.

3m. **Tenby** (Dynbych-y-Pysgod. *Inf.*), an ancient and picturesque walled town and lively resort, sprawls along and spills down an abrupt promontory, narrowing to only a few yards at its southeast end. The promontory, separating North Beach and the harbour from South Beach and Castle Beach, ends as the detached spur of St. Catherine's Island.

History. From the evidence of coins found on St. Catherine's Island during the construction of the fort there in the 19C, Tenby may have existed in some form in Roman times, but the first mention of the place is in a poem of c 875 which names the fortress on the promontory as Dynbych-y-Pysgod (Fortlet of the Fishes), the modern word Tenby being a development of Dynbych. This poem praises the court here of the prince, Bleiddudd ap Erbin, a patron of bards. Around 1111 the town, growing to the west of the castle, was settled by Flemish clothworkers, but soon afterwards suffered the usual violence of the times. The castle was taken in 1153 by Rhys ap Gruffydd, in 1187 his son sacked the town, and in 1260 it was taken by Llewelyn the Last. During a part of this time (1172–75) Giraldus was rector here. Although by 1386 the castle was close to ruins, the town, granted a charter by Henry IV, became a flourishing port (importing wines and salt and exporting coal and cloth), a status which lasted until well into the 16C. In 1457 the town walls were strengthened by Jasper Tudor, and in 1471, after the Battle of Tewkesbury, Henry Tudor found refuge here before escaping to Brittany. The defences were again strengthened under the threat of the Armada. Although garrisoned for the King during the Civil War, Tenby surrendered in 1644 after a siege of only three days. After decline during the 17C and 18C, the town was rescued in the 19C by Sir William Paxton and others who, helped by the opening of the railway, were able to develop the resort to which Tenby largely owes its present day character.

Robert Recorde, author of 'Ground of Artes', the earliest important mathematical treatise, and inventor of the = sign, was born here in 1510. Augustus John, the artist, was born in 1878 at Belgrave House.

From the north entrance to the town the street succession The Norton, Crackwell Street and Bridge Street curves generally southeast down to Castle Hill, the streets immediately to the right being the main shopping area. Along South Parade, the west edge of this shopping area, runs the surviving length of the *Town Wall*, which, lined roughly across the base of the promontory and with a short return section on the north (now mostly destroyed), was the town's inland defence. First built perhaps in the 13C, strengthened by Jasper Tudor in 1457 and again in 1588 when the Spanish Armada threatened, the wall is some 20ft high with external bastions all of which bar one are cylindrical. South Gate, about halfway along the length of the wall, is protected externally by a semicircular barbican (*Five Arches*), which retains its sole original entrance on the north side, with (a favourite medieval trap for attackers) a right-angled turn. From Five Arches St. George's Street leads east, passing on the left, below St. Mary's church, an old archway once giving access to the churchyard and prison.

St. Mary's Church is of several periods, the oldest being a 13C rebuilding of an earlier church. But much of today's structure dates from the 15C, with extensive modification during the 19C, these two periods representing Tenby's peaks of prosperity. Features of the exterior are the large South Porch of c 1500, with, above the inner door (refashioned in the 18C), a small window of a 13C chapel; the late 13C Tower, unusual for being to one side of the chancel, with a 15C spire; the 15C West Door, inserted into an older wall and ornamented with moulding and a double-ogee head, all that survives of a large west porch built in 1496 and demolished in 1831; and, to the west, the slight remains of a building erected in conjunction with this porch, probably as a chantry and school. Inside the church, the Nave, basically of the 13C, was much altered in the 15C when the north arcade and a row of arches on the south side were added. The roof was restored in 1966, as was also the pulpit of 1634 with ample ladies around the top. The north aisle is an early 15C addition, while the south aisle results from a throwing together in the late 15C of a number of chapels, its fine roof dating from the same time. The Chancel (13C) was enlarged in about 1470 by the addition on the east of steps and a raised Sanctuary, with a crypt below. The panelled ceiling (restored 1962) has elaborately carved bosses, 75 of which are original. The Chapel of St. Nicholas (north), with the tomb of Bishop Tully of St. David's (1460–82), is an addition of 1480, and St. Thomas's Chapel (south) is also a 15C addition, among the monuments here being two with effigies of Thomas White (died 1482) and his son John (died 1490), both mayors of Tenby, the former at the time of Henry Tudor's escape in 1471.

The *•Tudor Merchant's House* (NT. April–Oct: Mon–Fri 11.00–18.00; Sun 14.00–18.00. Tel. 01834-842279), on Quay Hill a short way east of St. Mary's, though with furnishing of different periods, survives architecturally as a rare example of a prosperous merchant's home of the later 15C. Among notable features are a fine contemporary local-style (Flemish) chimney, contemporary murals, and original fireplaces and chimneys on each of the three storeys.

Bridge Street descends to the *Harbour* (note that several bollards are made from cannons) from where there is a choice of boat trips, the most popular being to Caldey Island. South of the harbour, beyond the narrow neck of the promontory, *St. Catherines Island*, a detached rock not accessible at high tide, still shows the remains of a small fort built in 1869 but now dismantled. On Castle Hill, the small green extension promontory to the east of the harbour, are a statue to Prince Albert (J.E. Thomas, 1865) and the minor remains of the *Castle. Tenby Museum* (Easter–Oct: daily 10.00–18.00. Other months: Mon–Fri 10.00–12.00, 14.00–16.00. Tel. 01834-842809), set up here as long ago as 1878, is both museum and art gallery. The former shows archaeological and historical material relating to Pembroke, and to Tenby in particular, this including a maritime section, while in the art gallery, with a permanent collection and temporary exhibitions, the emphasis is on local interests and local artists, which include Augustus and Gwen John. In the north of the town, off Mayfield Drive, not far from North Beach car park and in the unusual setting of a 19C chapel, *Silent World* (April–Sept: daily 10.00–17.00 or 18.00. Tel. 01834-844498) includes an aquarium of regional marine life, a small wildlife art gallery and shop.

CALDEY ISLAND (boats normally June–Sept: Mon–Fri 10.00–16.00, frequent. Crossing 20min. Calm weather only). Lying rather over two miles south of Tenby and owned by Cistercians, Caldey measures under two miles from west to east but less than a mile from north to south at the widest point. The landing jetty is about halfway along the north coast and close to the abbey. Features of the island are the abbey (the monks of which farm), the flowers (from which the monks distil scent), an Ogham stone and the seabirds. The island's Welsh name of Ynys Pyr probably stems from the name of the Celtic first abbot.

History. Excavations have revealed evidence of early occupation in the form of Stone Age human remains, flint tools and Roman pottery of the 1C. The first monastery seems to have been a Celtic foundation of the late 5C, probably a colony from St. Illtyd's house at Llantwit Major, though some authorities suggest that Caldey may have been the earlier foundation. The most famous abbot of those days was St. Samson of Dol, the patron saint of Caldey, some of whose relics are still preserved. How long this Celtic monastery lasted is not known, but it was presumably still in existence when the Caldey Ogham stone was given its Latin inscription added in the early 9C. Nothing more is heard of the island, except that it became a nest of pirates and fell prey to Norse raids, until 1127 when it was given to the Benedictines of St. Dogmaels who built the priory church and associated monastic quarters. These Benedictines held peaceful possession for over 400 years, until 1534 when their monastery was dissolved and the island given by Henry VIII to secular owners.

Caldey passed through several hands, until 1897 when it was bought by the Rev. W. Done Bushell who did much restoration work. In 1906 it was sold to Aelred Carlyle and became the home of the Anglican community which he founded and which in 1913 was received into the Church of Rome as Benedictine. In 1928 the Benedictines moved to Prinknash Park in Gloucestershire, their place being taken by Cistercians from Chimay in Belgium and their monastery raised to the status of abbey in 1958.

On the cliffs, facing Tenby, there is a round Norman tower, now converted to a chapel. The principal building on the island is the *Abbey*, built in 1907–11 (tours for male visitors), the church of which, seriously damaged by fire in 1940, was restored by 1951 and is now typically Cistercian in its austerity. *St. David's Church*, near the abbey, in plan closely resembles the Irish churches of the 8C and 9C and in origin is probably as old if not older. However it was largely rebuilt by the St. Dogmaels Benedictines (note the Norman west door) so that it could serve as the island's parish church, and it was restored at the turn of the current century by W. Done Bushell. To the south is the *Old Priory*, probably on or close to the site of the early Celtic house. Originally built by the St. Dogmaels Benedictines, the structure seen today dates from the 13–14C, with 15C additions, and is of interestingly defensive character. The restored *Church of St. Illtyd*, with a leaning spire, houses the Caldey Ogham Stone, a slab of sandstone with a cross and a double inscription, one in Ogham (5–6C) and the other in Latin added in the early 9C; the inscription bids those who pass to pray for the soul of Catuoconus (Cadogan).

Beyond the Old Priory the track continues to the lighthouse of 1828. *St. Margaret's Island*, off the northwest tip of Caldey, is a nature reserve and bird sanctuary.

From Tenby, scenic walks can be taken along the cliffs, the walk northwards to
Saundersfoot via Monkstone Point being particularly popular. Southwards, the
National Park coastal path leads to *Penally* and *Lydstep*, for both of which see below.

At *Gumfreston*, just over a mile west of Tenby on B4318, there is a small and primitive
12C church (14C tower) with a unique semicircular recess (perhaps a baptistery) on
the north of the nave; traces of murals (martyrdom of St. Lawrence); a bronze Sanctus
bell; and, in the churchyard, medicinal springs. *Manor House Wildlife and Leisure
Park* (Easter–Sept: daily 10.00–18.00. Tel. 01646-651201), a short way farther along
B4318, offers exotic birds and animals, an adventure playground, a model railway, a
tropical plant house and falcon displays.

For Tenby to *Cardigan* and *Aberaeron*, see Rte 46.

Tenby is left by A4139. Just outside the town there is a road to the right
signed Penally, off which, almost immediately, a small road, again to the
right, in a few yards reaches a path up to *Hoyle's Mouth*, a cavern sometimes identified with the Cave of Belarious in Shakespeare's 'Cymbeline'.
Excavations during the 19C produced palaeolithic flint tools, a human jaw
and teeth, and bones of extinct animals, some of these finds being in Tenby's
museum. This small road continues for two miles to *St. Florence*, a village
which in medieval times was a harbour (today's Ritec stream was a sea inlet)
and a centre of Flemish influence. The primitive 13C church of local type
has a curious little dark chapel off the south transept.

2m (from Tenby) **Penally**, a village by one tradition both the birth and the
burial place of St. Teilo. The 13C church houses a fine wheel-cross of the
10 or 11C and also a fragment of a 9C cross-shaft; and here too is the
graveslab of William and Isemay de Raynoore (1260–90), in dark slate with
the alabaster faces let into it in low relief. *2m. Lydstep Head* (footpath from
village), a headland of 54 acres with precipitous limestone cliffs, was in 1936
given to the National Trust by the Pilgrim Trust.

2m. ***Manorbier Castle** (Easter–Sept: daily 10.30–17.30. Tel. 01834-
871394), a commanding pile above the bay of the same name, was in origin
a manor house which however soon became fortified, although in fact the
castle was never attacked. Historically Manorbier is best known as the
birthplace of Giraldus.

History. The name may derive from Maenor Pyr (Manor of Pyr), the man believed to
have been the first Celtic (5C) abbot of Caldey. Odo de Barri, the Norman to whom
these lands were granted in about 1095, built a wooden hall within earthwork
defences, but it was his son William who in the early 12C began the stone castle,
Giraldus being born here soon afterwards in about 1146; forty years later, in 1188, he
visited here during his journey with Archbishop Baldwin, describing Manorbier as the
pleasantest place in Wales.

The De Barri family ownership continued into the 14C, after which, and continuing
into modern times, Manorbier had several owners, these including lengthy periods
under the Crown.

The castle is entered by the 13C Gatehouse, on the right being the Old
Tower, in part of the 12C and thus dating back to William de Barri. Beyond,
walls and ruins (peopled here and there by lifesize figures, including of
course Giraldus) enclose a large court, today notable for a colourful garden
which makes good use of the ancient wall behind. The principal ruins are
the Gatehouse, inside still showing something of the workings of the
drawbridge and portcullis; the Round Tower (c 1230), beside the shop; and,
at the far end of the court, the 13C chapel and 12C hall.

In *Manorbier Church*, across the valley and with a convenient car park
offering a good view of the castle, is the effigy of Walter de Barri, half-

brother of Giraldus. *King's Quoit*, a burial chamber, will be found above the east arm of Manorbier Bay.

4m. The ruins of •**Lamphey Bishop's Palace** (Cadw; see p. 11), dating from the early 13C to the late 16C and one of the several manors of the medieval bishops of St. David's, lie just northeast of Lamphey village. Despite the troubled early medieval period, and in contrast to the palace at St. David's itself, Lamphey has virtually no defensive features and survived as a prelates' country retreat of some elegance and comfort.

History. It is known that Wilfred, the last Welsh bishop before the appointment of the Norman Bernard, was here in 1096. The earliest surviving stonework (early 13C) is parts of the walls of the old hall, to the west end of which the camera (private apartments) was added later in the century. Bishop Gower (1328–47) much extended the palace, adding a new hall (Great Hall), angled away from the southeast corner of the earlier one, a battlemented wall enclosing the courtyard, and the gatehouse. In the 15–16C, largely under the influence of Bishop Vaughan (1509–22), the camera was remodelled and a chapel was added beyond the north side of the old hall. Finally, with the Reformation, Lamphey passed to the Crown, being granted in 1546 to the Devereux, earls of Essex; Robert, the favourite of Elizabeth I, lived here as a boy.

Approaching the palace by road a stream is reached, the marshy hollows on either side of which mark the site of the fishponds, first mentioned in a survey of 1326. At the palace the most notable architectural features are Bishop Gower's typical high battlemented parapets carried on arcades which rise above the roofs, and the circular chimneys above the camera and great hall marking the period of Devereux ownership.

The main range of the palace extends roughly west to east to the south of the *Gatehouse* with its arcades. The *Camera* (c 1250, and 15–16C), at the west end, was a two-storeyed building, the attendants occupying the ground floor and the bishop having his private apartments above, these comprising a main room and, projecting to the south, bedroom and garderobe. Access for the bishop was by either of two stairs at the northeast and southeast corners. The bedroom and garderobe area was extended in the 15C. Of the fireplace in the centre of the north wall, the lower part is original, but the circular chimney above, as also that at the northwest angle of the building, are Devereux insertions. The *Old Hall* (early 13C), extending east from the camera, is a much ruined two-storeyed building in which the actual hall occupied the upper floor. A garderobe juts out to the southwest, and it has been suggested that this and the bishop's garderobe were drained by a channel from the stream, though no trace of this has been found. The *Chapel* (early 16C), on the north side of this hall, must have replaced a chapel elsewhere. Also on the upper floor, it has a traceried window of five lights in its east wall, and two other windows, each of three lights, in the north wall. The small projection to the northeast was the Sacristy. Bishop Gower's *Great Hall* (1328–47, and 16C), forming the east end of the palace range, is a two-storeyed building with a huge, long vaulted ground floor lit by slits. The hall above was over 70ft long, and from the camera the bishop reached it by crossing the old hall and then using a short passage. The fireplace in the northeast corner and the southward projecting garderobe are the main Devereux features. The Gower arcaded parapet is best seen from the north side.

For (*2m*) **Pembroke** and Pembroke to (*8m*) **Milford Haven**, see Rte 44A.

45

Castlemartin Peninsula

Measuring some nine miles from east to west and six miles from north to south, the Castlemartin peninsula extends west and southwest from Pembroke, its shores being those of Milford Haven and the outer Bristol Channel. The peninsula is known for its sandy bays and rugged cliff scenery along the south and west coasts (much of it National Trust property), but some restrictions may be placed on visitors by the Ministry of Defence ranges which spread across much of the southern part of the peninsula (red flags and roadside warnings). The northern part of the peninsula, fringing Milford Haven, is spoilt by oil installations and a large power station. Castlemartin Black Cattle were one of the two breeds which early in this century were crossed to produce today's Welsh Black. Castlemartin is also associated with the Castlemartin Yeomanry, the force which in 1797 so efficiently dealt with the French landing near Fishguard, thus earning the distinction of the only Battle Honour awarded for action on British soil (Lord Cawdor, commander of the Yeomanry, owned the Stackpole estate; now National Trust, see below).

The clockwise round described below starts from Pembroke and, excluding diversions, covers some 29 miles.

Pembroke is left by B4319 which, after about two miles, reaches a minor road east to *Stackpole* (or *Cheriton*) *Elidor* where the church, with a Norman tower, contains several effigies, these including Richard de Stackpole and his wife (14C) and the coloured kneeling figure of Roger Lort, with his wife and 12 children (17C). The adjacent National Trust Stackpole property of some 2000 acres includes woodland, eight miles of cliffs, two beaches and a hillfort on Greenala Point (parking at Stackpole Quay and Broadhaven).

After rather over another mile along B4319 another minor road bears south for **Bosherston** with a church (1250–70) interesting for a passage-squint which projects externally in the angle between the south transeptal chapel and the chancel. In the churchyard, what is probably a Preaching Cross (?14C) may have been adapted from an older Crucifixion, the evidence being the differing stone of the shaft and the cross and the relief Christ at the intersection; possibly dismantled at the Reformation, the original shaft seems to have been lost and later replaced by a new stumpy one. From a National Park car park by the church a path (two mile round) visits the *Lily Ponds* (or *Fish Ponds*), partially the result of silting and partly artificial creation during the 18C and at their best in June. The walk passes below an Iron Age or earlier fort, tactically sited between the westernmost two inlets. A standing stone (the Harold Stone), about half a mile north of the ponds, shows two cup marks.

Ministry of Defence ranges stretch west from Bosherston and a notice board beside the road states whether or not the approach is clear to **˙St. Govan's Chapel** (a mile south), fascinating for its primitiveness, its age (at least 13C and possibly as early as 6C), its legends and for its extraordinary position blocking a narrow cleft in the cliff.

History and Legend. St. Govan, a 6C Irishman from Wexford, was a follower of St. Ailbe (died 527), a native of Solva, near St. David's, who founded the monastery at

Dairinis near Wexford. After a visit to Rome, St. Govan entered Dairinis, of which he eventually became abbot. It was in his old age that he came to Pembroke (presumably because of the link with St. Ailbe), intending to live out his closing years as a contemplative hermit, and it is at this point that legend takes over. Walking along these cliffs, he was attacked by ruffians, whereupon, in response to his prayer for help, the cliff opened, folded gently around him and then opened again as soon as the terrified attackers had fled—a rescue which left any worthy Celtic 'sanctus' with little choice but to build his cell here. St. Govan died here in 586 when, tradition continues, he was buried beneath his chapel's altar.

Descending to the chapel the visitor enters a world of primitive piety and charming legend. As to the structural age of this place, much if not all the stonework is probably medieval replacement of some much earlier original, but there can surely be little doubt that the rock cell and well are very early Christian. In the tiny chapel there is a stone altar, to the side of which steps lead to a small cell cut in the rock; here there is a fissure, said to be the one which miraculously sheltered St. Govan and which today grants the wishes of anyone able to turn round within it without touching the sides. On the south wall of the chapel are a piscina, an aperture and a window, and in the upper plastering of the west wall there is a circle containing an inscription of unknown age or meaning. Apparently there was once a well in the floor near the door, known for its ability to cure eye and skin complaints, and the well now seen outside the chapel, though now dry, was also effective both for granting wishes and curing. And, to complete the chapel's story, the boulder outside is known as Bell Rock because it hides a silver bell, once in the little bell-tower, stolen by pirates but retrieved by angels and secured within the rock.

When the range is clear, walkers can follow the path west above precipitous cliffs 100 to 160ft high, soon reaching *Huntsman's Leap,* a narrow fissure over which a horseman is said to have leapt—successfully, though soon afterwards dying of fright. Beyond, soon after Huntsman's Leap, and again at the east and west ends of Bullslaughter and Flimston bays, there are remains of clifftop fortifications, the last fort being above the isolated *Elegug Stacks* (roughly three miles from St. Govan's Chapel), massive limestone pillars alive with breeding birds between April and early August ('elegug' is Welsh for guillemot). From here a small road connects to B4319 at *Warren.*

From St. Govan's Chapel, motorists must retrace through Bosherston to rejoin B4319, now followed west and in under two miles reaching *Warren,* with the small road south to Elegug Stacks (see above). In *Castlemartin,* a short way farther west, the church contains a Norman font and an organ of 1842 said once to have been owned by Mendelssohn. From here B4319 returns to the coast at *Freshwater West,* with a beach notoriously dangerous for bathing. Just beyond, in the southeast angle where B4319 meets B4320, is the *Devil's Quoit,* a burial chamber with a 12ft capstone. The village of *Angle,* to the west at the end of B4320, stands at the west of Angle Bay which opens into Milford Haven.

B4320 is now followed east through somewhat desolate surroundings with oil installations and the Pembroke Power Station to the north. However, the church at *Rhoscrowther,* on the south edge of the oil installations, recalls through its dedication those very different 7C days when St. Decuman was born here, later, it is said, paddling a coracle across to Dunster in Somerset where he was martyred in 706 while at prayer. The church, though basically Norman, was considerably rebuilt in both the 19 and early

20C. B4320 in another five miles reaches *Monkton* and **Pembroke**, for both of which see Rte 44.

46

Tenby to Cardigan and Aberaeron

A478 to Cardigan. A487 to Aberaeron. Total distance 56m.—*10m.*
Narberth.—*14m.* **Crymych (Presely Hills).**—*7m.* **Cilgerran Castle**.—*2m.*
Cardigan.—*23m.* **Aberaeron**.

The first half crosses the Presely Hills, with many prehistoric sites and a choice of walks and minor roads. Between Cardigan and Aberaeron diversions can be made to the coast with its cliff scenery.

Tenby, see Rte 44B. *5m.* **King's Moor Common Information Area** (for *Avondale Glass, Begelly Pottery* and *Folly Farm*), see Rte 44A which is crossed here. *3m. Templeton* owes its name to the fact that it once belonged to the Knights Templar of Slebech who may have had a hospice here. Traditionally it was near here that a battle was fought in 1081 which established Gruffydd ap Cynan and Rhys ap Tewdwr as princes of northern and southern Wales. *Sentence Castle*, a motte immediately west of Templeton, is, with nearby Narberth Castle, traditionally the site of the 'Mabinogion's' legendary court of Pwyll, Prince of Dyfed. Perhaps Narberth was the site of the court, and perhaps Sentence was the nearby mound of Gorsedd Arberth to which Pwyll was wont to withdraw, for the mound had the magical property that if anyone high-born sat here he could only leave after either receiving a wound or seeing a wonder. Pwyll was lucky, and met the beautiful Rhiannon.

2m. **Narberth** (*Inf.*), originally Castell yn Arberth and, as noted above, traditionally associated with the 'Mabinogion', is today a small town sprawled over a steep hill. The town's origins may reach back to an early Dark Ages castle, perhaps that of Pwyll, and it is known that Narberth was burnt by the Norsemen in 994. The *Castle*, in the south part of the town, though successor to others, including an early Norman fortress destroyed by the Welsh in 1115, is now no more than fragments of the castle built in about 1246 by Sir Andrew Perrot; later given by Henry VII to Sir Rhys ap Thomas of Carew, it was dismantled after the Civil War. The town's 'Mabinogion' association is well brought to life at the *Landsker Visitor Centre* (April–mid Oct: daily 10.00–17.00. Mid Oct–March: limited weekend opening. Tel. 01834-860061), in the town centre, here also being tourist information facilities as also a local craft shop. Nearby is the small *Wilson Museum* (Easter–last Sat in Sept: Mon–Sat 10.30–17.00. Tel. 01834-861266), illustrating many aspects of local life, mainly in Victorian and Edwardian times. *Heronsbrook*, just southwest, is a country park and waterfowl centre, with several ponds, walks, picnic areas and some rare farm breeds (Easter–Sept: daily 10.00–18.00. Tel. 01834-860723).

A40 (Rte 43) is crossed just north of Narberth. Beyond (*5m.*) *Llandissilio* the road climbs the ridge that separates the Eastern Cleddau valley from that of the Taf. *Penrhos Cottage* (Easter, and mid May–Sept: daily except

Mon, and also Sun morning, 10.00–13.00, 14.00–17.00. Tel. 01437-731328), three miles northwest from Llandissilio, is an example of what was known as an overnight house (if, with the help of friends, a man could build a cottage between sunset and sunrise, then he was entitled to claim all the land within a stone's throw of the door). Dating from the early 19C, the cottage is preserved with its original furnishings. *9m.* (from Llandissilio) **Crymych**, for the Presley Hills.

The PRESELY HILLS (or Mynydd Preseli, or various other spellings), contained within a fat pouch of the Pembrokeshire Coast National Park hanging southward between Cardigan and Fishguard, may be said to be the last southern outriders of the Cambrian Mountains, that rather vague range running much of the length of Wales which, though named on many maps, is better known for its parts than for its whole. An open, wide-shouldered brown moorland picked out with patches of afforestation and with rocky outcrops similar to the tors of Dartmoor, the hills lift, in places surprisingly steeply, to 1760ft above the surrounding pastoral landscape. Flocks of Welsh mountain sheep graze their home areas and mountain ponies are also to be found. But it is the wealth of prehistoric archaeology that is the main interest here. Not only are the hills dotted with cairns, burial chambers, standing stones, stone circles and suchlike, but they also provided, between about 2000–1500 BC, the 'blue stones' for Stonehenge, these (weighing up to four tons) being dragged some 140 miles, part of the way along the ancient trade route from Ireland; a route which, incidentally, explains Geoffrey of Monmouth's belief that the stones in fact came from Ireland. Walkers are warned of the dangers of bogs and mists.

The hills are crossed by A478 (this Route), by B4313 running southeast from Fishguard, and by B4329 running southwest from Cardigan, these latter two crossing at Greenway (Rosebush). Several minor roads and lanes link these, but not across the main mass of the hills which lies between A478 and B4329, between Crymych on the former and Greenway. Most of this part is accessible only to walkers. Two choices are described below, one for walkers (a basic six miles from A478 near Crymych to B4329 near Greenway) and a motorists' circuit of some 20 miles.

Walkers. What is sometimes called the Bronze Age Track grew out of the movement between the main centre of the Beaker People on Salisbury Plain and Whitesands Bay near St. David's, and thence by boat to Ireland's Wicklow Hills with their copper and gold. From the east the starting-point is *Croesfihangel Tumulus* (a mile southwest of Crymych and just off A478), an eroded burial mound which has produced urns and cremated remains dated to 1000 BC. On *Foeldrygarn*, a height a short way northwest, there is an Iron Age hillfort with ramparts defending the east gate while the others rely on the steep slopes. Hut sites were excavated here in 1899, finds (some in Tenby's museum) including beads, pottery and a stone lamp. The cairns on top may be Bronze Age burials, and this hill provided five volcanic dolerite stones for Stonehenge.

Beside the track, a short mile from Croesfihangel, there is a small Bronze Age burial mound (*Carn Ferched*). To the south of the track after another short mile *Carnmenyn* (Cairn of the Boulders) was the main source of Stonehenge's dolerite stones, while *Carnalw*, a mile north of Carnmenyn, provided four blue rhyolite stones. Next (in half a mile) the track reaches *Bedd Arthur* (Arthur's Grave), an oval of stones, probably Bronze Age and erected perhaps 2000 years before Arthur's time. Continuing west (and passing a branch track for *Cerrig Meibion Arthur*, see Motor Circuit) the track in two miles reaches a point just north of *Foel Cwmcerwyn* or *Presely Top* (1760ft), the highest point of the hills and with several burial cairns. In legend it was here that Arthur and his men had one of their running fights with the giant boar Twrch Trwyth, once a king but punished for his evil ways. Two of Arthur's sons were among the many warriors killed by the boar and are commemorated by Cerrig Meibion Arthur (see Motor Circuit). In another one and a half miles the track reaches B4329 at *Bwlch Gwynt* (Windy Pass), here joining the Motor Circuit.

A **Motor Circuit** may start along the minor road which heads west off A478 immediately south of Crymych, within the first mile passing the tumulus which marks the start of the Bronze Age Track. Beyond, this very minor road—part through fields, part across moorland, part unfenced—hugs the southern slopes of the hills to reach, in rather over three miles from Crymych, a fork near the junction of several streams. Here the righthand road should be followed, this almost immediately reaching another fork, *Gors-Fawr Stone Circle*, half a mile down the lefthand road here, being of the early Bronze Age with 16 stones and two outliers. It has been suggested that it may have been of some ritual significance that the line of sight between these outliers aims directly at Carnmenyn (see above). The righthand small road in a mile and a half crosses the little Afon Wern at a lonely unfenced spot on the border of the National Park. Here, just north, are the *Cerrig Meibion Arthur*, the Stones of the Sons of Arthur, killed on Foel Cwmcerwyn by the savage boar Twrch Trwyth (see Walkers, above). This road now briefly heads south, almost immediately passing *Maen-y-Parc*, a probably Early Bronze Age standing stone which may have been deliberately shaped. Beyond, in another two miles, B4313 is reached, a mile to the west being two more prehistoric sites; *Dyffryn Circle* is an early Bronze Age burial mound surrounded by stones, and, just to its east, stands the *Budloy Stone*.

B4329 is now followed northeast, in rather over a mile north of *Greenway* reaching *Bwlch Gwynt*, or Windy Pass, at the end of the walkers' Bronze Age Track. Here, to the west, rises *Foel Eryr* (Eagle Mountain. 1535ft) with a Bronze Age cairn. The name *Tafarn-y-Bwlch* (Tavern of the Pass), a mile north of Bwlch Gwynt and now a farm, recalls that this was once a coaching and drovers' inn. *Brynberian* is another mile and a half farther north along B4329, half a mile to the south being *Bedd-yr-Afanc* (Monster's Grave), thought to be a Neolithic long cairn, or gallery grave, of perhaps 2500 BC and of its kind unique in Wales.

Motorists may now either continue to Cardigan by B4329 and A487, or, at *Crosswell* (a mile beyond Brynberian), navigate minor roads back to Crymych.

Leaving Crymych, A478 continues north, in *7m* reaching the ruins of **Cilgerran Castle** (Cadw; see p. 11) which, though small compared to some, are theatrically and romantically sprawled across a steep promontory above the Teifi. The ruins have inspired artists such as Richard Wilson and J.M.W. Turner and in the 18C and 19C the boat excursion up from Cardigan was a principal local attraction.

History. An early castle may have been built by Roger de Montgomery c 1093, but it is known that this site was developed by Gerald de Windsor, to whom it was granted by Henry I. It was taken and at least partly destroyed by Rhys ap Gruffydd in 1164; taken by William Marshal, Earl of Pembroke, in 1204; recovered by Llewelyn the Great in 1213; and finally retaken by William Marshal's son, William, in 1233. This last rebuilt the castle, and it is to this period that most of the surviving structure belongs. But

Cilgerran was soon neglected, and is recorded as being in ruins by 1326. There were frequent changes of ownership during the Wars of the Roses, and, with the abolition of the Marcher Lordships in 1536, Cilgerran passed to the Vaughans who seem to have lived here until the early 17C. Thereafter the place became no more than romantic ruins. Cilgerran was acquired by the National Trust in 1938, and has since been placed under the guardianship of the Crown.

Occupying a steep promontory above the Teifi and a tributary stream, the castle required little defence on the west and north, but was vulnerable from other directions. The main castle is the inner ward, protected on the east and south by two large round towers and a gatehouse, joined by curtain wall. This inner ward is separated by a ditch from a much larger outer ward to the south, itself defended by a wall and ditch.

The modern entrance is at the southwest corner of the OUTER WARD, which represents the bailey of the early Norman motte-and-bailey castle. On the west little defence was necessary. On the south there was a ditch and wall, but though the former can be made out, very little survives of the wall. On the east there was a wall, but this collapsed during slate quarrying in the 19C, and, apart from a short section at the northeast corner, the wall seen today is 19C replacement. The most interesting feature of the outer ward is the rock-cut ditch which separates it from the inner ward.

The INNER WARD is entered at its southwest corner by the *Gatehouse* (early 13C), which stood beyond a drawbridge over the ditch and was defended by two portcullises. The two round towers and associated curtain wall all date from the early 13C. The *East Tower*, probably the first to be built, was of four storeys and projects outwardly well clear of the curtain wall, this enabling the wall to be covered by fire from the tower. The ground floor is entered directly from the ward. The room on the top floor had a fireplace, and the tower's only outward-facing window. The *West Tower* is generally similar, though one difference was that the entrance was at the first floor, probably by wooden steps, the ground floor being reached by a trap-door from the first (the present doorway into the ground floor is a 14C modification). Other work included the wall dividing the ground floor into two, and the stair on the east side of the new ground floor entrance. The very ruined *Northwest Tower* was a rectangular 14C addition. Of the buildings that would have filled the ward only traces survive. The *Kitchens* would have been against the curtain to the south of the Northwest Tower, and in the southwest corner of the ward something of a 13 or 14C limekiln can be seen. The oldest parts of the castle (12C) are two short sections of wall; one between the kiln and the gatehouse, and the other some remains on the edge of the cliff halfway along the ward's north side.

2m. **Cardigan**, see Rte 42, crossed here. A487, heading northeast, runs at some distance from the sea, but several roads lead to the coast with its cliff scenery. *17m. Synod Inn.* For **New Quay**, on the coast, and (*6m*) **Aberaeron**, see Rte 41A.

INDEX

Topographical names are in **bold** print; names of persons in *italics*; other entries in roman print. Where there are several references, the more important are in appropriate cases printed bold.